D1195648

Difference troubles examines the implications for social theory and sexual politics of taking difference seriously. It explores the trouble difference can make not only for the social sciences, but also for the very people – feminists, queer theorists, postmodernists – who champion difference. Seidman asks how social thinkers should conceptualize differences such as gender, race, and sexuality, without falling into the trap of reducing them to an inferior status. He looks to the new social knowledges for innovative approaches to difference, while pointing out the conceptual, ethical and political difficulties which can characterize them. This is a wide-ranging and sophisticated discussion of contemporary social theory and sexual politics, focusing on questions of difference, knowledge and power. It culminates in a persuasive case for a pragmatic approach to difference troubles in theory and politics.

Difference troubles

Cambridge Cultural Social Studies

Series editors: JEFFREY C. ALEXANDER, *Department of Sociology, University of California, Los Angeles,* and STEVEN SEIDMAN, *Department of Sociology, University at Albany, State University of New York*

Difference troubles

Queering social theory and sexual politics

Steven Seidman

University at Albany, State University of New York

CAMBRIDGE
UNIVERSITY PRESS

PUBLISHED BY THE PRESS SYNDICATE OF THE UNIVERSITY OF CAMBRIDGE
The Pitt Building, Trumpington Street, Cambridge CB2 1RP, United Kingdom

CAMBRIDGE UNIVERSITY PRESS
The Edinburgh Building, Cambridge CB2 2RU, United Kingdom
40 West 20th Street, New York, NY 10011-4211, USA
10 Stamford Road, Oakleigh, Melbourne 3166, Australia

First published 1997

Printed in the United Kingdom at the University Press, Cambridge

Typeset in Times 10/12½ pt   [SE]

A catalogue record for this book is available from the British Library

Library of Congress cataloguing in publication data

Seidman, Steven.
    Difference troubles: queering social theory and sexual politics /
Steven Seidman.
        p.   cm.
    Includes bibliographical references and index.
    ISBN 0 521 59043 4. – ISBN 0 521 59970 9 (pbk.)
    1. Pluralism (Social Sciences)   2. Difference (Psychology) – Social
aspects.   3. Feminist theory.   4. Gay and lesbian studies.
    5. Postmodernism – Social aspects.   I. Title.
    HM276.S445   1997
    301′.01–dc21   97-8908   CIP

ISBN 0 521 59043 4 hardback
ISBN 0 521 59970 9 paperback

Contents

Preface

In a sense, it is coincidental that the title of this volume evokes Judith Butler's *Gender Trouble*. Coincidental in that the essays are not intended as a response to or elaboration of Butler's seminal text. Coincidental too in that the essays in this volume do in fact explore the difference that difference makes for social theory and politics. At the same time, Butler's book, in a sense, makes possible my own, as the texts of Lacan, Derrida, Foucault, Kristeva, Irigaray, Said, Memmi, Adrienne Rich, Dennis Altman, the Combahee River Collective, and so on make possible the texts of Butler – and indeed those of many contemporary social thinkers who have made the theme of difference central to social analysis and politics.

The aim of *Difference troubles* is to expose the way social theory, in particular sociological and lesbian/gay theory, has resisted conceptualizing difference as a central axis of subjectivity and social life. Recognizing difference as a key social structuring principle disturbs foundational notions of the subject, knowledge, history, and politics that give coherence to much current social thinking. Difference troubles means then the troubles theory and politics have with bringing differences of (say) nationality, race, ableness, gender, and sexuality into social analysis and political practices without defining them as inferior, subordinate, retrograde, or primitive.

Difference causes trouble not only for types of theorizing that rely heavily on Enlightenment assumptions about a unitary subject, narrative of progress, and transcendent notions of knowledge. Difference also makes trouble for types of theorizing – and politics – which have sought to affirm difference, indeed which have asserted their own foundation in social difference. In this regard, I focus on sexual theorizing and politics, in particular, efforts to ground lesbian and gay theory and politics in the assertion of a common "minority" sexual identity. The troubles difference present to at least certain identity-based theories and politics are twofold. First, to the extent that identity-based knowledges and politics cohere around a unitary notion of identity (e.g., the assertion of a common lesbian or gay identity), it is difficult to consider differences within identity-based communities. In part, queer theory emerged to expose the normalizing and disciplinary role of sexual identity politics. And yet, queer theory is not without its own difference troubles. These are not so much the difficulties of suppressing differences as those of accommodating a strong assertion of difference with a commitment to a critical social theory and left politics. Although I do not believe, as some do, that a difference-based theorizing subverts the possibility of critique, it does create problems – for example, with respect to the grounds of critique, normative or ethical standards and justifications, conceptualizing oppositional subjects, and proposing constructive political projects.

Difference troubles is then primarily deconstructive in its impulse. I aim to criticize certain currents of theorizing and politics to the extent that they have been structured by assumptions or endorse practices that suppress or devalue important social differences. Of course, it is impossible to fashion concepts without ignoring some differences or positioning some of them as peripheral. For example, if, in order to avoid a concept of women in general we speak of white, middle-class, American women of the 1990s, we are still suppressing differences that pertain to sexuality, ableness, religion, ethnic-national heritage, physical attractiveness, and so on. Social theories and politics cannot be fashioned that will be inclusive of all differences. Acknowledging this excess of difference does not mean that we should ignore difference or that diverse conceptual strategies are equally defensible with regard to the way they handle differences. Rather, it means that social analysts must think hard about which differences matter in social theory and politics, why, and the potential impact of particular theoretical and political strategies upon a range of social differences. As I see it, this line of thinking points to a "pragmatic" approach to theory or conceptual strategies and politics, a position I sketch throughout the volume but clarify programmatically in the epilogue. Accordingly, the critical aim of this book is connected to a positive proposal both for making the theme of difference central to social theory and politics and for defending a pragmatic approach to questions of knowledge and power.

A word is in order regarding the concept of "queering" which figures prominently in this volume. I view queering as deconstructive – that is, as a discursive strategy involving the displacement or the placing into doubt of foundational assumptions (e.g., about the subject, knowledge, society, and history) for the purpose of opening up new possibilities for critical social analysis and political practice. I call this deconstructive move "queering" because I intend to make strange or "queer" what is considered known, familiar, and commonplace, what is assumed to be the order of things, the natural way, the normal, the healthy, and so on. In the spirit of deconstruction, queering does not mean improving upon or substituting one set of foundational assumptions and narratives for another, but leaving permanently open and contestable the assumptions and narratives that guide social analysis and assessing them in terms of multidimensional, pragmatic considerations. Moreover, queering suggests, for me, making sexual theory and politics central to social theory – for example, showing the entanglement of social theory in the making of sexual selves and orders, analyzing the way sexual meanings structure nonsexual social theoretical discourses, and taking the formation of regimes of sexuality as central to social analysis. How would social theory and politics be different if it were queer – that is, if it understood its own standpoint as local, as one among many, and if it took sexual differences and meanings as both structuring its knowledge and as a constitutive part of social organization and change?

A perspective that aims to "queer" social discourse does not of course assume any immunity from its own decentering spirit. Queering occurs from a situated, particular standpoint. Its own deconstructive project must be turned upon itself, exposing its own investments in certain subjectivities, social orders, and social ideals. Thus, the queering of theory must ultimately turn against its own implicit foundational assumptions and metanarratives. This does not entail the paralysis of theory or politics, but rather bringing a heightened critical reflexivity to its own practices and a willingness to clarify the ethical-political or socially productive implications of its own positions. In an important sense, the queering of theory and politics is a cultural project – a desire to shape a discursive culture that assumes unstable foundations, that aims to speak across communities, that deploys a pragmatic type of social reason, and fashions narratives that avoid unidimensional stories of progress or regress.

Acknowledgements

There are many individuals who have read through various chapters or responded to them, sometimes in print. Many thanks to Jeff Alexander, Dennis Altman, Bob Antonio, Bill Bogard, Patricia Clough, Norman Denzin, Jan Willem Duyvendak, Rosemary Hennessy, Chrys Ingraham, Richard Lachmann, Charles Lemert, Linda Nicholson, Laurel Richardson, Mary Rogers, Michael Schudson, Marion Smiley, Bernie Yack, and Iris Young, and members of the Great Barrington Theory and Culture Group. Many of these chapters were first presented at conferences or at the invitation of various universities and colleges. I have learned much from these discussions and wish to thank, in particular, the organizers of the "Organizing Sexuality" conference in Amsterdam (1993), the people associated with the Dutch journal *Krisis* for their discussions on multiculturalism and democracy, and the Departments of Sociology at Wellesley, Queens College, the University of Massachusetts at Amherst, Washington State University, UCLA, and especially Colorado State College for their critical but generous response to some of my ideas, the political theory colloquium series at the University of Wisconsin, and Neil Smelser at the Center for Advanced Studies in the Behavioral Sciences at Stanford for organizing an engaging conference on social diversity and cultural conflict. At times, when I had doubts about what and why I was writing, my students made me think it mattered after all. I wish to thank Melinda Mecilli, Kathy Dixon, Nancy Fischer, Joseph Sullivan, Debbie Donovan, Chet Meeks, and Xun Xu, who have taught me much about the theory and politics of difference.

Over the last few years Jeff Alexander and Linda Nicholson have been special friends and colleagues. They have responded to my work with consistent intelligence and much needed critical acumen. Linda especially has been a constant intellectual presence in all my work. Patricia Clough and

Charles Lemert have occupied a special place in my life and in my work. I share with them a deep ambivalence towards sociology and a relentless commitment to analyzing the world, including the world of sociology, with an attentiveness to the unconscious in its friendly and sometimes malicious voice.

Many of the essays have been published previously, although I have edited and sometimes considerably revised them. Chapter 1 was initially published in *The Sociological Quarterly*, 37 (Fall 1996); chapter 2 appeared in *Cultural Studies*, 1 (1996); chapter 4 is based on an article that appeared in *Sociological Theory*, 12 (July 1994); chapter 6 appeared in *Fear of a Queer Planet*, ed. Michael Warner (Minneapolis: University of Minnesota Press, 1993), chapter 7 was published in *Social Postmodernism*, ed. Linda Nicholson and Steven Seidman (Cambridge: Cambridge University Press, 1995); chapter 8 initially appeared in *Social Text*, 19/20 (Fall 1988); and chapter 10 appeared in *Sociological Theory*, 9 (Fall 1991). I am grateful to the publishers for permission to draw on this previously published material.

The Cambridge Cultural Society Studies Series has flourished under the steady, intelligent guidance of Catherine Max. It is a pleasure to once again personally express my appreciation for her commitment to publish innovative and critical work in the area of cultural studies and social theory.

I dedicate this book to my son Andy. I never cease to be astonished at his openness to difference, if not an equal enthusiasm for social theory. It is to him and his generation that I place my hopes for a world that sits easier with difference.

Introduction

The contemporary reconfiguring of social theory

In academic and public life in the United States, in many European nations, and elsewhere, major social conflicts now pivot upon how to think about social differences. Do cultural differences (ethnic, racial, national, gender, sexual, or religious) override human or social commonalities? Should public policy, law, and institutional norms take account of social differences? If differences structure moral and epistemic values, how does this affect the shape of knowledge? And how should political organizations and movements organize themselves around social differences? Diversity management practices in corporations, multicultural curricula in schools, the discursive politics of deconstruction – in these and numerous other areas the "problem of difference" is a key issue today for policy makers, educators, corporate leaders, unions, social activists and, most importantly for this book, intellectuals.

For intellectuals, this reconfiguring of the field of public debate and conflict has been marked by the emergence of a new division between "modernists" and "postmodernists." The former are said to defend cultural universalism and the idea of Western social progress; the latter criticize the former as holding an increasingly anachronistic world view based on narratives of reason and progress which conceal the dynamics of domination and social control. At the core of this debate is the meaning of social differences for concepts of reason, morality, and democracy. Modernists tend to defend universalism or the idea of a transcendent truth and morality that ultimately appeals to some notion of the unity of reason or humanity. Postmodernists aim to expose universalism as illusory and as erasing, submerging, or marginalizing sociocultural diversity; they champion the values of individuality, locality, diversity, and ambiguity as the conditions of a democratic society (for efforts to stake out a third, alternative position, see, on the side of modernism Benhabib 1992 and Taylor 1994 and, on the side of postmodernism Fraser 1995 and I. Young 1990). Similarly, the current debate over democracy often pivots on the problem of how to conceive and handle issues of social and cultural difference. Conservatives and many liberals champion social differences but only within a tight cohesive framework of consensus and sociocultural unity. In contrast, "radical democrats" often press for a notion of a strong democracy as resting on a robust concept of social difference while assuming only a weak, shifting, at best temporary, transient notion of consensus. At issue is the question of whether today it is still credible and desirable to invoke an ideal of a unified humanity, of a transcendent truth, a strong notion of cultural consensus, and the very idea of social progress.

In many Western societies, intellectuals, especially academics, have posed the question of difference not only in terms of the social dynamics of class, race, nationality, or gender but in relation to the *question of knowledge*. Indeed, the problem of difference has become so important today in part because social differences are, according to some thinkers, important influences upon moral values and knowledges. A major issue of contention is less whether or not to acknowledge or seriously consider difference but whether differences of, say, ethnicity, race, or religion, penetrate "deeply" into cultural life. If gender or race are differences that shape moral outlook and epistemic values in profound ways, this suggests a world, and a world of thought, fractured and fragmented in ways unimagined and perhaps unimaginable within Enlightenment cultural traditions. Furthermore, if the way we comprehend the world is influenced by our particular social statuses and interests as, say, white, middle class, or American, our knowledges will be neither value neutral nor politically inconsequential. I will suggest in this volume that taking difference seriously compels us to rethink questions of ethics and truth from the vantage point of assuming that knowledge and power are closely intertwined.

In schools and universities, in corporations and the mass media, in politics and the law, *the problem of difference* has become inescapable. This issue revolves around determining how social differences, for example, differences of religion, age, race, ethnicity, ableness, sexuality, gender, class, and nationality are to be understood. On the one hand, such differences may be viewed as simply creating social variations of a common humanity or producing diversity within a unified social system. On the other hand, social differences may at times be said to run deep and override social similarities, thereby troubling notions of human commonality and social unity.

The awareness of the problem of difference and the efforts to engage it theoretically and politically are hardly recent developments. The question of how to theorize social difference was present at the very beginning of the modern Western era. Western modernity was inaugurated with the age of global exploration and commerce between the twelfth and sixteenth centuries, which involved the theoretical and political encounter with different or strange cultures and civilizations. Modern social thought in part originated and took the form that it did from the effort to understand these social differences (Hodgen 1964; Seidman 1983). One mode of understanding is perhaps especially telling. Beginning in the eighteenth century European thinkers developed a stage theory of social evolution and progress (Bury 1955; Meek 1976; Nisbet 1970). All societies, past and present, were arranged in a temporal, hierarchical evolutionary pattern. Past or "simple" societies represented a "primitive" state of humankind, while the new industrializing societies represented the most "advanced" condition of humanity (for arguments regarding the "racialization" of this evolutionary narrative, see Stocking 1982; Young 1995). Predictably, those societies of "primitive" social development were non-European, in contrast to Western societies whose industrializing dynamic was thought both a sign of social advancement and the future of *all* humanity.

The idea of social progress which occupied Western thought from around the late seventeenth century through to the twentieth incorporated social differences but only as they were understood as non-threatening – for example, as suggesting the inferiority or transience of "otherness." Societies or civilizations whose social institutions, values, and knowledges were nonWestern or premodern were not a challenge to the superiority and inevitable globalization of modern Western institutions and culture. Social differences were denied in the sense that so-called nonmodern and nonWestern societies were not viewed as alternative social formations to Western industrializing societies, with their own complex and integral sociocultural values and forms of life.

The theoretical denial of difference by means of figuring nonWestern societies as "the past" ("primitive," "ancient," or "traditional"), as "nonrational" or as inherently despotic or "child-like" and therefore as inferior and as destined either to extinction or "modernization" can be interpreted as part of Western colonialism and empire-building (Fabian 1983; Said 1979; Young 1990, 1995). Modern social theory was formed as part of the formation of nation-states, the shift from absolutism to the modern bureaucratic state, the emergence of a world capitalist system, and as part of the age of Western colonialism and imperialism (on the link between empire and social science, see Asad 1975; Fabian 1983; Said 1985, 1994). Few modern social theorists, not Marx, not Durkheim and not Weber, doubted that Western modernity pointed to the future of *all* humanity and that the globalization of the West was the necessary and desirable vehicle for driving humanity forward towards its destined endpoint – one world prefigured in the universalistic aspects of contemporary Western nations. This was the vision of Marx who, we might recall, in *The Communist Manifesto* reveled in the imagery of modernity steamrolling over non-Western and non-modern societies as history spiralled towards the communist millennium. Who can forget Marx's rapture as he considered British colonization and the "Western modernization" of India (cf. Said 1979; Turner 1978; Young 1990 and Ahmad 1992 for a dissenting view). The globalization of the West was no less the fated outcome of history for Max Weber. The "Author's Introduction" (1958) to his comparative study of society and religion (*Gesammelte Aufsatze zur Religionssoziologie*) grandly pronounced the universality and anticipated globalization of Western social developments such as bureaucratization, capitalism, science, and formal-rational law. If social thinkers such as Condorcet, Comte, Saint-Simon, Marx, Spencer, or Durkheim embraced the Westernization of the globe as social progress, Weber was more apocalyptic but no less certain that the world was becoming the image of Western modernity. Whether social thinkers shared the millenarianism of Marx or gravitated towards Weber's mournful perspective (e.g. Simmel and Spengler), their contemporaries and successors, from Comte to Parsons and Habermas, hardly wavered in their presumption of global Westernization. From this perspective, nonWestern and pre-modern social institutions, values, and knowledges which diverged from "modernity" would likely face social extinction or at best survive as cultural objects destined for the museum or the guided tour.

Modern Western social thought – and Western histories – are neither homogeneous nor uniform. Despite the emancipatory impulse of the Enlightenment, the social knowledge developed around narratives of progress, identitarian logic, scientism, and the assertion of a transcendent reason and humanity (see Adorno and Horkheimer 1972; Baudrillard 1983; Bauman 1991; Jardine 1985; Lyotard 1979), often had the effect of sacrificing or suppressing individuality or social difference. By contrast, counter-Enlightenment discourses often defended the integrity and value of social differences – of local, regional, and national cultures and traditions. Some critics of the Enlightenment sought to avoid, though not always successfully, perspectives that framed social differences in terms of the tropes of the "past," "transition," "inferiority," or "cultural survival."

In nineteenth-century European and American romanticism (e.g. in the social ideas of Herder, von Humboldt, and Walt Whitman), in strains of German historicism (e.g., Ranke, Dilthey, and Meinecke), and in the "philosophical conservatism" of Edmund Burke, de Bonald, and de

Maistre, there was a defense of social difference. Folk cultures, religious communities, ethnicities, and local and national traditions were imagined as simply "other," without being stigmatized as "the past," "transitory," or "inferior." Indeed, some of these discourses (e.g., Herder) celebrated the proliferation of human and social differences as a sign of the glory of humankind and God's creation (see Berlin 1980; Taylor 1989). However, at least certain prominent strains in these counter-Enlightenment discourses promoted difference in the interests of defending tradition and social hierarchy against modernity and movements of democratization. Moreover, neither romantics nor philosophical conservatives in the end avoided an appeal to a notion of human or social unity (e.g., the *Volk*) or to a divine or transcendent reason, nature or "tradition," which functioned to restrict or mute social differences. For example, German historicism posited a view in which history was composed of a multiplicity of distinct national societies, each of which needed to be understood according to its own unique cultural traditions. Nevertheless, from Ranke to Troeltsch and Weber, historicists defended a notion of a unified national identity, often conceived in ethnic terms, which effectively suppressed social differences *within* the nation (e.g., Popper 1957; Loader 1976).

Enlightenment and counter-Enlightenment themes and viewpoints have often coexisted uneasily in the same thinker or school of thought. An example is the Chicago School of American Sociology which flourished in the early decades of this century. Abandoning the goal of fashioning grand evolutionary theories in the style of Comte, Spencer, and their American disciples (e.g., Lester Ward), the Chicago sociologists preferred descriptively rich, local ethnographic types of research which focused on individuals or groups (the negro, immigrant, the "marginal" individual, the prostitute, and delinquent) often forgotten or overlooked in the optimistic evolutionary theories of their colleagues. The aim was, in part, to show the costs of progress and to give voice to those who were marginalized or left powerless in the march of history. Nevertheless, while the Chicago sociologists wished to recover the lives of marginalized individuals, they viewed these "others" as instances either of individual pathology or of social maladjustment, and thus the inevitable casualties of social progress.

Even allowing for its complex and contradictory character, a good deal of modern social theory has misconceived the nature of social differences. There has been a persistent failure to preserve the tension that is located when "otherness" is understood – as neither past nor future, as neither inferior nor superior. This tension arises, in part, from the way social differences challenge the ethnocentric presumption of the superiority of one's own form of collective life and defamiliarize "the natural" or "the order of things."

In the main, Western social thinkers have not doubted the veracity of Enlightenment narratives of progress or the belief that Western modernity marked a definite advance of human reason and freedom. Differences of race, ethnicity, gender, religion, and nationality that sometimes divided humanity into antagonistic communities have been understood as a product of irrational prejudice or cultural traditions based upon custom and myth. In other words, social differences between individuals and collectivities, including entire civilizations, have often been interpreted as indicators of irrational human or social forces and, accordingly, perceived as impediments to social progress. Most defenders of the Enlightenment believe, moreover, that, with the advance of modern rationality through the sociohistorical agencies of science, formal-rational law, bureaucracy, and capitalism, differences of, say, ethnicity or religion, are destined, if not to disappear, then to become merely superficial variations of a human commonality, adding nuance to social life but not threatening harmony or progress. Within the West, this social vision has been widely assumed to be both necessary and desirable. For at the root of Enlightenment thought is a utopian ideal of a "world society" made up of abstract citizens equal before the law and governed by a common social reason. Whatever social good has been done in the name of this emancipatory social vision (and I think its social benefit to be considerable), it has also, and quite unintentionally for the most part, legitimated the destruction of particular social identities and multiple local communities and traditions that have given coherence and purpose to the lives of many peoples. It is perhaps an odd paradox that the deeply moral vision of a rational society associated with the Enlightenment has unleashed a fiercely nonrational colonizing social force that makes the power of tradition or religion almost pale by comparison (cf. Adorno and Horkheimer 1972; Bauman 1991).

Much of the debate in modern social theory has occurred within an Enlightenment framework. Whatever the differences between, say, Marx and Weber, Durkheim and Spencer, Small and Park, or Parsons, Dahrendorf, and Habermas, they have not seriously questioned an Enlightenment perspective that assumes a narrative of progress, a universalistic concept of reason, and a homogenizing, linear view of history. In truth, there have been very few dissenters from this tradition. Even so, some social thinkers did stretch, even challenge, certain aspects of the Enlightenment tradition. Marx, as we know, criticized the notion that bourgeois capitalism represented the "end of history," but only to historicize this epoch as the necessary precursor, and unconscious vehicle, of historical progress. Weber criticized the narrative of progress but never questioned the inevitability of the globalization of the West nor did he doubt the superiority, at some level, of developments such as modern science, formal legal systems, or "monocratic" bureaucracy. In the American context, the pragmatic philosophical movement of the early decades of this century revealed a hospitality to difference that also found compelling sociological articulations. For example, against "Americanizers" who defended an aggressive program of assimilation through detaching immigrants from their ethnic traditions, Robert Park and W. I. Thomas, at least in some of their writings, defended the importance of maintaining particular ethnic communities and identities (Wacker 1983). However, where cultural pluralists such as Horace Kallen and Randolph Bourne argued that social pluralism sustains a robust, dynamic society, Park and Thomas justified ethnic particularism as a *temporary* measure to ease the way towards assimilation while avoiding pathological social consequences (Persons 1987). Broad philosophical movements such as romanticism, historicism, and pragmatism contained important openings to imagining a vital social pluralism. In truth, however, there were few social thinkers who actually crafted such a social theory and politics, at least in the first half of this century.

This intellectual culture began to change after World War II. To be sure, the transformation was neither abrupt nor sweeping. Both within and outside the disciplines, Enlightenment modernizing perspectives remained dominant. And yet a sea-change in social knowledges was unmistakable. A number of more recent theoretical perspectives – varieties of feminism, gay liberationism, queer theory, anti-racist social theory, postcolonial discourse, poststructuralism, cultural studies, and postmodernism – recenter social thought and politics around the theme of difference (cf. West 1994). The shape of intellectual culture in the 1990s is decidedly different from the pre-World War II period. Today, at least in many European nations, and very definitely in England, the United States and Australia, the Enlightenment heritage, one that has been institutionally elaborated in medical, therapeutic, criminological, and penal practices and knowledges, and not least in the human science and humanistic disciplines, is being challenged in a way that puts into doubt some of the key ideas and social hopes of this tradition. Whether it is feminist critiques of particularistic masculinist knowledges parading as universal, queer theorists exposing the role of medical and scientific knowledges in producing a sexual social regime organized around normative heterosexuality, the poststructural deconstruction of a unified, stable "subject" of knowledge and history, or the postcolonial critique of Western constructions of the "colonial other," these new social knowledges have compelled many of us to rethink the heritage of the Enlightenment.

Why this shift in public intellectual culture? Why this effort to recenter social knowledges and politics around the problem of difference? What social hope, with what ethical and political import, does this cultural shift entail? In this book I will suggest ways of explaining this shift, though this is not my principal aim. Others have outlined broad sociohistorical explanations that I have at times referenced but have not critically engaged with (for an overview, see Kumar 1994). My own account of this shift has emphasized the importance of the so-called "new social movements" (see chapters 6 and 9). The critical perspectives generated by these movements expose the ways differences of gender, race, sexuality, and ethnicity are naturalized and normalized in the dominant culture, thereby contributing to the making of social hierarchies. For example, feminists have criticized the discourses and social practices that figure women as the inferior, subordinate "other" to men. Similarly, anti-racist social critics have contested the constructions of the "nonwhite other" as the inferior or subordinate counterpart to the privileged, superior "white." In short, these critical social analysts aim to reveal the ways in which social practices and representations conceive of social differences as markers of social inferiority and position the "other" (e.g., women or African-Americans) as subordinate. Moreover, new social movement theorists have emphasized the role of expert knowledges in this process. Finally, while the intent of some of these new social movement theorists has been to assert the equality between "the subordinated other" and "the dominant group" by claiming a human equivalence or identity between them ("homosexuals are like heterosexuals" or "women are like men" or "blacks are no different than whites"), others have sought to defend the value of preserving social difference. In these latter discourses, difference is said to penetrate "deeply" into the self and group life but is not understood in terms of inferiority or deviance. In certain currents of the discourses and practices of the new social movements we can observe a rethinking of social knowledge which proposes a robust social theory, politics and ethics of difference.

Of course, the development of the new social movements, and especially the postmodern turn in some of their social knowledges, has to be situated in relation to broader social events. Perhaps it is impossible to imagine these movements without grasping the global turmoil and events associated with movements of decolonization (Grimal 1978; Holland 1985; Said 1994). The American civil rights movement, and subsequently the black power movement, which arguably served as the model for many of the protest movements of the period, were prefigured by nationalist revolts against

European colonial powers. Is Huey Newton or Eldridge Cleaver imaginable without Frantz Fanon and Pan-African thinking as it evolved in Africa and the Carribean? Similarly, the student movements and the New Left were, in part, sparked off across Europe and the US by the colonial struggles in Vietnam and the popular revolts in Cuba and the Chinese Cultural Revolution. These international developments must, in turn, be grasped in relation to broad changes in the social structure and political economy of Western societies. Current discussions of post-Fordism, globalization, deindustrialization and telematic (information-based) societies, point to a social structural context for the new social movements. For example, shifts to regimes of decentralized and customized production, flexible labor specialization, economies of scope, and the rise of a distinctive service class of workers, impacts on the social and political organization of the body, desire, identity, and dynamics of domination and resistance (Haraway 1985; Lash and Urry 1987, 1994; Offe 1985). The writings of Harvey (1990), Jameson (1991), Lash and Urry (1987), Offe (1985), Portoghesi (1992), among others, have sought to identify these changes, and chart their significance for the politics of identity and difference. This is important work, though I detect at times a reductionist current in their heavy reliance on an overdetermined marxist political economy. My own sympathies are with efforts to frame the broader social context of identity-based social movements by rethinking the concept of civil society (Alexander 1993; Cohen and Arato 1992; Seligman 1992), by offering original analyses of telematic societies inspired often by Baudrillard and Lyotard (e.g., Bogard 1995; Haraway 1985; Lyon 1994; Poster 1990), and by developing the post-marxism of Foucault's theorization of a disciplinary society. Wherever one comes out on these discussions, the larger point is that for many intellectuals in the West there is a perception that the present is a period of major social change, shown in one aspect by a new alignment of the politics of culture and in new configurations of identity, political economy, and social structure. This has prompted attempts to craft original social perspectives – new narratives of social change and new vocabularies of the self and the social to grasp the present and its possible futures.

If we can describe the current changes in the West as a shift from "modernity" to "postmodernity," it might be instructive to imagine a parallel with what many nineteenth-century theorists characterized as the great transformation from a "traditional" to a "modern" type of society (on the dangers of this dichotomous thinking, see Yack forthcoming). My purpose in raising this parallel is not to argue that the depth and breadth of change is identical but that there is a similarity which helps place the theorization of social change. For Comte, Marx, Durkheim, and Weber, the conceptual dichotomy between tradition and modernity that framed their social narratives was experientially based. The notion of "tradition" described the milieu in which they came of age. These men grew up in households and locales that were often village-like, agrarian, organized around revered or traditionally legitimated conventions and customs, and still very much religiously robust cultures. For example, Durkheim "grew up within the confines of a close-knit, orthodox and traditional Jewish family" (Lukes 1973: 41). Is it mere coincidence that his concept of "mechanical solidarity" (referring to traditional social formations) was defined as a type of social bond based on strong affective ties and religiously based common beliefs? At the same time that these social thinkers were firmly rooted in a traditional-like society, their coming of age was in one sense a personal encounter with modernity, as they were progressively exposed to secular reason, industrialization, urbanization, science, and democratization. Durkheim's anguished break with Judaism occurred after he had moved from the small town of Epinal to Paris, and after being exposed to the cosmopolitan ideas of Jean Jaures and Henri Bergson, among others, at the École Normale Supérieur. Durkheim's defense of role-specialization, his substitution of society for God, and his defense of individualism despite its anomic and egoistic dangers was a way of positioning himself as a modern. Similarly, Weber can be said to have experienced the tradition/modernity divide in the two women who were most central to his life. With her religious piety and conventional feminine identity, Weber's mother exemplified tradition. As a feminist and writer, Marianne Weber's intellectual independence signaled her positioning as a modern. The narratives of modernization and its costs by Durkheim and Weber were, in part, expressions of their own personal struggles, in which the tensions between tradition and modernity often remained unresolved.

Is it any different for some of us today who have come of age in a society exhibiting the contradictory, conflicting currents of modernity and postmodernity? If these two terms refer less to two distinct, polar-opposite social epochs than to conflicting but co-present sociocultural currents touching on core personal and social values and hopes, are our struggles any different from those of Marx or Weber or Spengler or Spencer?

My own intellectual trajectory often feels parallel to the sociological classics in the limited sense of trying to articulate conflicting personal experiences through the language of social theory. Like many people of my generation (b. 1948), I reached adulthood even as I absorbed modernity, with its emphasis on individualism, autonomy, the privatization and eventual abandonment of religion, scientism or the belief in science as universal reason, and an unwavering faith that Western development marked human progress. Of course there were events in childhood that led to doubts, for example, forced individuation as a result of my mother's early death was frightening and painful. While idiosyncratic personal events may have left me wondering at times about what I took to be "the order of things," it was public events that disturbed my life to a point of compelling me to question what was, after all, a faith in at least a certain idea of the culture of the Enlightenment.

I was too young to grasp the significance of the initial wave of movements of decolonization. However, the protests of the civil rights and liberation movements, the counterculture and the Vietnam antiwar protests, the student rebellions and the New Left, were formative events in my coming of age. Having grown up in all all-white, middle-class, suburban neighborhood, the images and ideas of black power, women's liberation, and their ferocious critique of liberal middle America, were profoundly troubling. Criticisms of the US disturbed my naive belief that social equality was the essential telos of this nation. Moreover, such rebellions began to challenge the dogma that we are all, despite our differences, the same and shared a common way of life. To be sure, these movements have articulated their social and ethical ideas in a way that emphasizes humankind's commonality and unity. However, the powerful images of black pride which pivoted on a positive idea of racial difference, and radical feminist constructions that stressed women's difference, made it difficult to imagine that my own experience or values were or should be identical with at least many Blacks and many women. Similarly, regular television coverage of villages in Vietnam torn apart by American bombs in the name of countering what appeared to me a phantom communist threat seemed oddly surreal and most assuredly at odds with a narrative of progress. The vast social destruction of Vietnamese culture wrought by Western advanced science and technology mocked the dominant assumption within my culture of the superiority of the Occident and the inferiority of the Orient.

The movements of sexual liberation were perhaps the most formative events in my emerging adulthood. As a young person I struggled with what eventually I came to identify (through reading the standard popular medical and advice literature) as my homosexuality. This difference scared me and I exercised enormous willpower to deny and conceal this shameful side of myself. Sexual difference was, in other words, associated with inferiority and a horrid sense of strangeness. I wanted to be "just human" and to be like everyone else – to be the abstract citizen or the equally abstract "normal" individual. While the sexual and countercultural movements lessened the guilt that I internalized as a child about my body and desires as a potential medium of pleasure and identity, the gay movement – and not a few years in therapy – eventually allowed me to affirm this difference and not simply as a variation of a common humanity but as one that was basic to my personal and social identity. While many individuals would come to embrace their homosexuality as marking out an expanded common space of humanity, many others, including myself, eventually came to value the ways a lesbian or gay social identity suggested specific and varied ways of being different. None of these experiences in my emerging adulthood turned me against the Enlightenment but they created some critical distance from a culture which I had unquestionably absorbed at home, at school, and in the media. These doubts were mostly expressed in a sort of folk language of romanticism and a populist politics.

My intellectual coming of age as an academic (1970s and 1980s) occurred as I was struggling to understand many of these personal and social conflicts. Like many Americans born in the late forties and early fifties, I experienced academe as the heartland of the culture of the Enlightenment. However, after the Sturm and Drang of the 1960s and 1970s, I welcomed the academy, despite my ambivalence towards its one-dimensional intellectualistic and bureaucratic culture. A kind of second coming of age as an academic intellectual meant reacquiring the heritage of the Enlightenment but this time as an intellectual culture or as a set of beliefs about reason, Western modernity, and the individual as the subject of knowledge and history. Becoming a sociologist meant absorbing this Enlightenment culture, though often in its critical version and with all the ambivalence shown in Weber, the Frankfurt School and the romantic popularism of Mead, Goffman, and C. W. Mills. Still, I initially shared what has come to be called the project of the Enlightenment – a view of modernization as an emancipatory, if unfinished, historical movement. For some years the critical social perspectives of the Enlightenment, as articulated in the traditions of marxism and classical sociological theory, served as a cultural medium for my own critical social hopes.

And yet, in the past decade I have felt compelled to reconsider the Enlightenment social theoretical tradition – to entertain the possibility that the very rationalism and universalism that promises emancipation may be entangled in domination, that its scientistic culture is one that suppresses a dense, elaborated social reason that would extend to a sense of ethical and political responsibility towards its own practices, that its progressivist hopes and narratives are a part of a dynamic of colonization, and that its language of rights, constitutionalism, and legality in part, conceals disciplinary forms of social control. This reconsideration is less a wholesale abandonment of this tradition than an effort to absorb into a postmodern or pragmatic social reason some of the social values associated with the Enlightenment. This is what I understand as the aim of much current critical social studies, from postmodern feminism, queer theory, and postcolonial studies to the defense of radical democracy and critical multiculturalism. A dramatic shift in the culture of social reason is today understood by at least some intellectuals as a condition of preserving the critical intent and social hopes that have been identified with the Enlightenment. And at the heart of this cultural and political ferment is a rethinking of the problem of difference and the interrelation of knowledge, power, and society.

Difference troubles traces the failure of much modern social thinking to conceive of social differences, whether figured as nation, race, gender, sexuality, religion, or civilization, without defining such differences as historically transient, a cultural survival, irrational, or inferior. I am not, let me emphasise, advocating the abandonment of "modern" theoretical traditions, a position I consider to be frivolous. Bodies of social thought as heterogeneous, multileveled, and thick with social significance as modern or classical social thinking cannot and should not be evaluated along only one dimension or in terms of one thematic concern such as the problem of difference. There is much in modern social thought that should be defended and elaborated upon such as its elegant critical narratives of social change and crisis, its aspiration towards epistemological clarity and reflexivity, its complex language of the social institutions and culture, its exposure of the natural as social, and so on. Its not my task in this volume to sort out what should be preserved and what should be discarded in modern traditions of social theory (for such efforts, see Alexander 1995; Calhoun 1995; Clough 1994; Lemert 1995; Seidman 1994a). I only intend to comment on the limits of modern social thought as it bears on conceptualizing social difference. Moreover, to avoid a critique which might wrongly be tied to an ethos of lament or nostalgia, I try to imagine what social knowledge might look like if it were to structure differences in ways that I recommend and if we were to assume that knowledge is part of the making of the world.

With regard to my critical intent, I argue that the limits of modern social knowledges in dealing with the problem of difference are at least twofold. First, there is a failure to imagine social differences beyond figuring them as "the past," "transitional," "nonrational," "despotic," "child-like," and "inferior," and therefore positioning them as socially subordinate. It is as if modern social thinking could only frame difference in an oedipal or narcissistic way – as something to be erased by being positioned as inferior or as something to be refused by conflating all difference into a global sameness. But social differences can also be approached as having their own complexity and sociocultural integrity. The second failure involves a resistance to considering how differences of, say, nationality, cultural status, gender, race, class, or physical and mental ableness shape the practices of social knowledge, including its core categories and thematic content. Social differences are not only an object of social knowledge, but shape the practice of knowing. Differences not only structure social life but because social knowledge, including the knowledges produced by experts, is itself part of society, they are structured by social differences. Social knowledges are therefore always situated ways of knowing not only in the limited sense of yielding partial perspectives but in that they are made possible by, and give expression to, the particular social standpoint of their producers. Hence, social knowledges are not only perspectives on the world but are part of their making. The question of knowledge is then inseparable from questions of power – from questions about the kind of society we as knowledge producers are fashioning. In short, the question of social knowledge is inescapably also a question of ethics and politics.

The focus of these chapters is on social knowledge. I wish to trace the ways difference has unconsciously (for the most part) structured social thinking and how much modern theorizing has resisted acknowledging this social structuring. Moreover, this volume is about power, about the social role of mostly expert knowledge producers in the making of the world, about how knowledge as a social fact is productive of the self and society, and about the failure of much modern social thinking to acknowledge its own social productivity. I wish to expose this resistance to address the ethical and political significance of its own practices. Why does this resistance occur? What are its consequences? And what alternatives are available?

I urge a rethinking of social knowledge that places ethical and political reflexivity at the center of disciplinary practices. Such an endeavour does not deny or diminish the importance of empirical-analytical social understandings and explanations. Quite the contrary, I aim to extend theoretical reflexivity to an awareness of the ways in which the production of knowledge, as with other social practices, is sociohistorically situated and interested – an activity which, like other social forces, is part of the making of the world. It is not the abandonment of "rationality" that is implied here but the thickening and deepening reflexivity of social reason.

Part I deals with the human sciences and especially sociology. The focus on sociology reflects, in part, my own disciplinary affiliation but it is also necessary to the extent that sociology has been a chief vehicle for articulating and transmitting major traditions of social theory – from Comtean positivism, marxism, and the classical theory of Weber and Durkheim, to the neglected sociology of Du Bois and Charlotte Perkins Gilman and the contemporary theorizing of Parsons and Bourdieu. In other words, sociology has been and still is at the center of social theory in many Western nations. The structure and dilemmas of sociological theory are pertinent to many of the key contemporary debates about social knowledge.

Chapter 1 outlines a historical, institutional, and theoretical framework for thinking about problems of knowledge, difference, and power. Combining Fredric Jameson's notion of the political unconscious with Foucault's perspective on power/knowledge, I analyze the largely unconscious entanglement of the human sciences in the "making" of social worlds. Over the next chapters, I focus more directly on sociology's repressive approach to difference and its refusal to reflect upon its own ethical and political purposefulness. Chapter 2 is a postmodern critique of the unconscious resistance that blocks sociology's self awareness of its own ethical and political character. I would no longer defend some of the propositions advanced in this essay yet its combative spirit, aimed at opening sociology to new ways of approaching social difference and to rethinking its own practices of knowledge production, remains important to the extent that sociology is a viable disciplinary tradition of critical social knowledges. Chapter 3 contrasts British cultural studies with American sociology in order to make the point that the latter may be viewed as a cultural tradition to be assessed pragmatically by what it allows us to say and do about social life. My aim is to prompt sociologists to distance themselves critically from their disciplinary culture of scientism and objectivism. Chapter 4 underscores the resistance of sociology to the new theorizing and research on sexuality that sometimes appears in the guise of queer theory. Moreover, I emphasize sociology's participation in the making of a sexual social system that marks all desires and bodies as either homosexual or heterosexual while making the latter normative. In chapter 5 I explore the challenges which feminism, queer theory, and postcolonial studies offer to sociology. I argue that even sociologists who want to frame difference in a non-reductive, non-diminished way are often unable to escape either denying social differences or positioning them in an ordinate/subordinate structure. These chapters propose rethinking social knowledge in ways that take a less repressive view of difference and in ways that imagine a power/knowledge link that cannot be grasped in an objectivist or scientistic perspective. In this regard, these chapters begin to consider the implications of pragmatism for the human science disciplines.

Part II shifts the focus from the human sciences to recent gay and lesbian studies, especially queer theory. Although much of this body of work began

– and continues – outside the academy, it has migrated, and recently with a vengeance, into the university. It is rapidly becoming part of many disciplines and part of the public culture of many societies.

The question of difference, and the question of power/knowledge, have been at the center of lesbian and gay studies and queer theory. Indeed, these knowledges emerged in response to the defining of homosexual sexual difference as inferior. Moreover, the knowledge/power theme is central to the current debate over homosexuality in that the idea of "the homosexual" is a product of largely medical-scientific knowledges in this century which constructed a polluted homosexual identity in contrast to the purity of heterosexuality. The recent appearance of social knowledges produced from a gay-affirmative standpoint aim to rethink in a positive way the social and moral status of homosexuality. At stake in these discussions is precisely the question of what an affirmative rethinking of sexual difference entails.

Chapter 6 assesses a range of discourses of homosexuality that emerged in close connection with the shifts in the lesbian and gay movement. The focus of this chapter is the shift from a gay liberationist and lesbian-feminist perspectives to an "ethnic model" which views the difference of same-sex gender preference as the cornerstone of a positive identity and community. I criticize this ethnic model as either assimilating a lesbian/gay to a straight identity or reducing the differences between gay and straight to a minimum. Moreover, the ethnic model has suppressed differences among lesbian-and-gay-identified individuals, thereby reproducing a repressive politics of identity. Queer theory is in part a response to these theoretical and ethical-political problems of the ethnic model. Queer theorists aim to rethink difference and the relation between knowledge and power in a way that avoids such a narrowing of identity politics. In chapter 7, I argue that many queer theorists approach difference as the basis of subjectivity and social life. I interpret queer theory as an effort to substantially rethink the fundamentals of a theory of sexuality and homosexuality. This effort involves a view of agency as something rooted in language and discourse rather than in modern substantialist notions of a subject; it also approaches knowledge itself as a key social force in the making of sexual identities and a system of social control organized around a norm of heterosexuality. I criticize queer theory to the extent that its social perspectives slide into a textual or discursive idealism and have not seriously considered the ethical-political implications of making difference so fundamental to theory and politics.

In part III I focus a bit more on the political aspects of the debates about knowledge, identity, and social difference. I chart the ways social knowledge becomes part of the world. Additionally, I consider some of the ways theorizing difference from, broadly speaking, a "postmodern" perspective affects how we approach the politics of knowledge and democratic politics in general.

The AIDS epidemic may be interpreted as illustrating the politics of knowledge. First, the very question of who gets to define the etiology and epidemiology of AIDS, and which – or whose – practices govern knowledge production and application (treatment), have been at the heart of AIDS activism, most impressively with regard to ACT Up (Elbaz 1993; Epstein 1995). Secondly, the association of AIDS and homosexuality in the United States inevitably has meant that the response to AIDS would be implicated in discursive struggles over homosexuality. AIDS has indeed incited a nationwide discussion about the meaning and social role of homosexuality. Chapter 8 analyzes various discursive responses to AIDS in terms of the ways they have understood homosexuality in moral and political terms in American culture. While the AIDS crisis helped fuel an antigay backlash, it also stimulated a renewed radicalism. Chapter 9 sketches the emergence of this radical impulse in American gay politics. I consider various currents of gay radicalism but focus on the political meaning of a queer movement.

In Chapter 10, I return to the academy as a site of the politics of knowledge. My aim, though, is less to criticize dominant social knowledges than to consider the implications of thinking difference positively for the practice of knowledge production and justification. I try to imagine what an academic culture might look like if difference were approached in a postmodern way and knowledge justified in the language of a critical pragmatism. In this chapter, and in the epilogue, I sketch the outlines of a pragmatic approach to knowledge production and justification.

Many social analysts have argued that if social differences are assumed to strongly influence knowledge, the conditions of a democratic culture and polity are undermined. Thus, critics of a postmodern turn have insisted that its assumption that knowledge and power are closely interconnected makes a rational consensus and therefore a democratic political culture impossible. Politics is effectively turned into *Realpolitik*. The defense of a strong politics of difference suggests to many critics a dogmatic, illiberal kind of identity politics in which social differences are linked to a separatist and nationalist agenda. Such an identity politics may indeed be inconsistent with a democratic culture and polity.

However, an affirmative politics of difference does not have to take this form. It is possible to imagine a robust notion of difference coinciding with a strong notion of democracy. In chapters 11 and 12, I aim to make a plausible case for this position. Chapter 11 engages with debates in the US over sexual diversity. I argue that the core sexual conflicts are less around sexual rights and representation than issues of sexual meaning and ethics. Moreover, in the struggles over moral boundaries and rules, in the formation of public sexual cultures (e.g., gay, lesbian, bisexual, S/M cultural communities), and in the appearance of movements such as the queer and transgendered movements, we can detect a clash between "modern" and "postmodern" principles of sociocultural organization. The latter represents, I suggest, an advance of social democratization. In chapter 12, I continue to explore the possibilities and shape of democracy in the US and elsewhere today. I sketch a sociological defense of a group-based model of democracy which pivots upon a concept of multiple, democratic and socially open public cultures.

I am convinced that it is a terribly important task today for anyone who wishes to defend a strong notion of democracy that avoids a narrow identity politics to begin to outline how difference and democracy might coexist, how knowledge might be thought of as closely linked to power yet capable of establishing critical perspectives and standards of assessment to mediate disputes and what social institutions and conventions might look like in a democratic society. This book is one effort in imagining such a democratic political and intellectual culture.

PART I

Resisting difference: the malaise of the human sciences

1

The political unconscious of the human sciences

The human sciences or what we sometimes call the behavorial and social sciences have not been especially friendly towards the idea of the unconscious. Even in psychology, at least in the United States, the unconscious has not fared well. As in the broader culture of the United States, the individual who is made into an object of psychological knowledge is typically an ego-centered, present-centered self. The idea of a self driven by unconscious wishes and desires is troubling to an American culture which celebrates the self-made individual and whose political culture relies heavily on a code of self-reliance and individual responsibility. Not surprisingly, the unconscious as psychological force has not played much of a role in sociology. Sociological paradigms such as conflict theory, exchange theory, rational choice theory, marxism, and (American styled) structural sociology construct a self which is egocentric. And yet, this self-interested, rational calculating, present-centered self is, according to sociological conventional wisdom, a self which is formed and moved by forces unseen by the individual. Sociology is unthinkable without a notion of a sociological unconscious. However, in contrast to the Freudian unconscious with its illogic of perverse desire relentlessly transgressive and decentering, the sociological unconscious is productive of social order.

Two quick examples. In *The Division of Labor in Society*, Durkheim argues that in traditional societies the lack of structural heterogeneity and interdependence makes possible cultural uniformity which, in turn, produces societal cohesion. Recall that Durkheim insisted that traditional type societies are intolerant of individualism and social difference. Deviation from common belief and practice threatens social solidarity. If it is only cultural unity which provides social coherence, difference is socially subversive. Accordingly, a repressive system of law and social custom governs social life. Repressive practices aimed at restoring cultural uniformity may appear to be acts of rationally calculating, egocentric individuals but are driven by an unconscious social logic. In the face of trangressions, the collective conscience experiences the threat of social chaos; it cannot act directly but induces a pervasive distress in individuals driving them to punish deviation and restore social unity. Individuals function as the unconscious instruments of a social logic. In a similar manner, Marx's *Capital* can be read as exposing an unconscious "material" or "structural" compulsion. Is not *Capital* the ironic story of the logic of capital, a logic which operates behind the backs of individuals to produce and reproduce the capital/wage-labor class relation but ultimately scripts its own supersession? The critique of political economy intends to make laborers conscious of a social unconsciousness that rules their lives. *Capital* reads the suffering of laborers as the logic of capital. It simultaneously reads the logic of capital as marking a grand historical finale: the end of capitalism, which is the hidden telos of capital, inaugurates humankind's deliberate fashioning of its destiny.

I wish to make the argument that there is a political unconscious to the human sciences. This refers to ways disciplinary conventions operate, often without the explicit intentions of social scientists, to suppress, if not erase, epistemological and social difference. This is a political willfulness which has been alternatively denied or celebrated as the progress of reason and humankind. However, this assault on difference has never been fully successful, for at least some epistemic and social "others" have flourished in non-academic social spaces – sometimes on the periphery, other times in the social center. Indeed, and somewhat ironically, submerged knowledges and communities of discourse have never ceased actively to shape the formation of the humans sciences. They do so in part through their inevitable production and subjugation – as "other" by the human sciences and in part through their equally inevitable mobilization, from time to time, against their marginalized status in relation to the human sciences. This is a history and political willfulness which should be exposed not to nourish an ethos of anti-science but to make "us" aware of the self-limiting aspects of Western culture and to release "us" from the cultural fixations which unknowingly inflict social harm and occasion human suffering.

This dark side to the progress of science has been veiled in the dominant Enlightenment culture, a case perhaps of the victors writing their own story of triumph. We in the West, particularly in the United States, have absorbed a master Enlightenment narrative relating a tale of science superseding myth, truth overpowering fiction, freedom triumphing over bondage, and progress installed in place of a tireless cycle of social advancement and decline. The Enlightenment signifies more than a master narrative; its core beliefs and values are woven into Western institutional practices and legitimations. Of course, this culture has been contested. As the figures of Burke, Wordsworth, Hegel, and Nietzsche indicate, there has been a history of counter- and anti-Enlightenment criticism. Moreover, some social analysts have interpreted the dominant view of Western Enlightenment (that modernity marks a breakthrough to a rational and superior epoch) as another example of a civilization naturalizing and universalizing its own cultural premises (e.g., Becker 1932; Baudrillard 1975; Sahlins 1976). Enlightenment cultural beliefs revolving around science, progress, and rationality are read as the myths of the modern – no different in principle from the mythic symbolic ritualized cultures of "the primitive." This reenchantment of Enlightenment culture is important as a strategy of contesting Western ethnocentrism. It is even more compelling if linked to a critique of the ideological role of Enlightenment narratives in legitimating and concealing a history of repression of epistemological and social differences (cf. Jardine 1985; Said 1979). These narratives of the progress of science and the West have simultaneously unleashed a relentless will to suppress the traditions of multiple communities and concealed this cultural colonization. It is the compulsion to erase epistemological and social difference – a compulsion concealed behind the sacred canopy of enlightenment and progress but also exposed by the very "otherness" it calls forth – that is the political unconscious of the human sciences.[1] I wish to contribute to severing the tie between knowledge and a repressive politics of identity.

This is the theme I will explore tentatively, even as I state it in a vigorous way. A cautionary word is in order. This is not intended as a brief against science, much less against the West or the Enlightenment. It is not science that I am criticizing but a certain culture of science to the extent, and I underscore this, *to the extent* that this culture, with good intentions perhaps, has been built upon the suppression of epistemological and social difference. It is not the end of science that is anticipated but the end of its privileged epistemic and social status and its entanglement in a history of subjugation. It is, moreover, in the name of the Enlightenment values of autonomy, individuality, and pluralism that I criticize this culture of science.

This chapter is divided into four sections. In the first section, I recommend a Foucauldian conceptual strategy to analyze knowledge as a social and political force. The next section elaborates this strategy in the context of a counter-Enlightenment narrative of the development of the human sciences in Western societies. Central to this narrative is the view that the science/nonscience binary operates as a boundary marker and a social power. In the third section, I propose that this binary relies on a "foundational" discourse that is logically incoherent and unstable. In the concluding section, I tentatively consider some implications for the human sciences of abandoning both the science/nonscience binary and secure epistemological foundations. I propose the concept of postdisciplinarity as a counterpart to the "postmodernizing" of social knowledge.

Knowledge, society, and power: some preliminary conceptual remarks

The Enlightenment tradition has held contradictory positions regarding the relationship of knowledge, society, and power. On the one hand the *philosophes* and their successors have insisted on the socially embedded and interested character of knowledge. In this regard, they have sought to discredit opponents (e.g., the church, humanists, psuedoscientists, metaphysicians) by exposing the social interests or ideological structure of their knowledges. Thus, the *philosophes* criticized the clerical hierarchy by revealing the role of religion in legitimating their secular power and material privilege. Similarly, Marx and Weber criticized beliefs about capitalism as "natural," for they obscured its social and political history. On the other hand, despite the social role they defend for their own discourses, "Enlighteners" maintain that their ideas somehow rise above their social interests and historical situatedness to represent a realm of the general and the true.

To maintain both that the link between social interests and knowledge exposes its "local" and ideological meaning and that some knowledges can be a social force for emancipation and yet be "nonlocal" and nonideological, assumes that certain types of knowledge can escape a *particularizing* social causality by virtue of the unique *social or intellectual conditions* of their production. What conditions make possible the production of nonlocal, nonideological knowledge? Two positions or strategic "models" of knowledge, society, and power prominently frame this discussion.

The first model – which I will call the "scientistic" model – emphasizes the unique theoretical or sociological "logic" of scientific knowledge. The former assumes that the empirical-analytical or conceptual logic of science (e.g., the emphasis on observation, experiments, replication, and falsification) is different from that of nonscientific ideas. Moreover, this distinctive logic is said to make it possible for science to produce nonlocal, nonideological knowledge – that is, representations which reflect the structure of reality not the particular structure of human interests. The claim that science alone can yield objective knowledge by virtue of its unique empirical-logical structure unites the empiricism of Condorcet or Montesquieu with Comte's positivism, Kant's transcendentalism, logical positivism, Popper's objectivism, and the axiomatic theory of Hempel.

To the extent that this position separates conceptual from social practices it is vulnerable to the charge of "idealism." A sociological version of the scientistic model aims to articulate the uniqueness – and transcendent character – of science via a social logic. In this regard, Merton's theory of science, which emphasizes the institutionalization of a historically unique normative culture (e.g., norms such as skepticism and universalism) and disciplinary practice (e.g., competition, rewarding originality, criticism, empirical replication), is indicative of a sociological version of a scientistic model. Merton argued both that social forces shape science and that science reveals nonlocal truths. This was possible because social forces were said to impact only on the disciplinary matrix of science, not on its contents. Indeed, Merton reasoned that the very normative conditions that made Western science possible created the intellectual and institutional space for the empirical, experimental logic of science to operate independently of social interests, at least as it bears on the contents of science.

In the 1960s and 1970s, critics assailed the scientistic model in both its "idealist" and "materialist" versions. With regard to the former, the new philosophy of science figured science, including its basic concepts and explanations, as thoroughly social. Critics of the scientistic model such as Thomas Kuhn, Paul Feyerabend, and Mary Hesse contested the concept of a logic of science that would demarcate a boundary between knowledge and belief. Against the scientistic model, they underscored the theoretical context of observations, the linguistically mediated character of reality, the underdetermination of theory by facts, and so on. While Kuhn might ultimately have retreated from the implications of his critique, the new sociology of science pressed forward challenging the separation of society and knowledge. Through detailed ethnographic studies, these sociologists documented the influence of social factors not only on the disciplinary matrix of science but on its core concepts, explanations, and observations. Although some of these sociologists were agnostic with regard to the epistemological status of science, others concluded that these studies implied the collapse of the science/nonscience division as the basis of a knowledge/belief binary. While some interpreted the logic of science as disclosing a social logic, other critics (feminists perhaps foremost) elaborated powerful criticisms of the social role of science. These theoretical and social criticisms gave rise to a "political" paradigm of science. Science was approached as a site of social conflict and understood as entangled in social relations of domination and subordination.

A second model of knowledge, society, and power is linked closely with marxism and the sociology of knowledge. Its emphasis is on the social logic of knowledge, but the focus is not the institutional aspects of knowledge production (e.g., the normative culture of science or its reward system) but the broader sociohistorical positioning and social interests of intellectuals. I will call this model "historicist," as it emphasizes that knowledge develops from a situated historical standpoint. For example, Marx argued, as is well known, that social-class position impedes or makes possible a true social perception. Thus, he proposed that only the proletariat, because of their unique sociohistorical location, could grasp the whole truth of capitalism as driven by class exploitation and the irrational logic of capital. Mannheim broadened Marx's thesis by insisting on the general principle of the socially situated, perspectival character of all social knowledge – including marxism. Yet Mannheim excluded natural science and mathematics from this sociohistorical logic. Moreover, despite the social logic of his position he maintained that objective social knowledge is possible through the extraordinary efforts of free-floating intellectuals. Their marginality allows them, Mannhein thought, to forge general, synthetic truths from the plurality of local, partial perceptions.

The historicist model evolved in at least two conspicuous directions. On the marxist side, knowledge, including science, was approached as an "ideology" or a social and political force – though marxism itself was exempted from such ideological exposure. Within the tradition of Western marxism, Habermas (1971) developed the historicist model to its logical limits. He posited an intrinsic link between knowledge and power through the concept of human interests, but avoided the particularizing implications of this move by framing human interests as quasi-transcendental and figuring its related knowledges as quasi-objective. From the perspective of the sociology of knowledge, the historicist model culminated in the work of Berger and Luckmann (1967). They elaborated the sociology of knowledge into a general social theory of the knowledge-based, social construction of reality. However, their own theorizing was exempted from the particularizing logic of constructing "the social." To the extent that the historicist model could not explain its own thesis of the social construction of reality in the terms of its own theoretical logic, it surrendered to a contradictory position.

Both the scientistic and historicist models grant that society shapes knowledge and that knowledge can be linked to power. However, the connections are viewed as more contingent than necessary and more extrinsic than intrinsic. Knowledge is viewed as capable of achieving a relative "autonomy" from society, and to that extent the relationship of knowledge and power is ultimately contingent and extrinsic. The contrast term to "knowledge" is "belief," by which is meant virtually all ideas that are imagined to be so thoroughly penetrated by social interests that their authority derives less from representing or mirroring reality than from their subjective, social or political role.

Both models have been driven by contradictory strains toward a position that asserts an intrinsic knowlege/power nexus. Thus, the scientistic model of (say) logical positivism evolved via the critiques of Wittgenstein, Quine, and others into a "political" paradigm of science in Kuhn and Feyerabend. The Mertonian sociology of science, which approached science as both social and transcendent, has, in one line of development, given way to Latour's (1986) thoroughly Foucauldian framing of science as power. The historicist model has fared no better. Whereas marxism exposes the particularism of class interest in the universalistic knowledges of the bourgeois, anti- and post-marxists have uncovered the decidely local conceptual and interest structure of marxism. Similarly, the sociology of knowledge has never escaped the incoherence of being unable to explain its own claims to knowledge. Both the scientistic and historicist models have moved toward a position that concedes that knowledge, including science, is necessarily situated, perspectival, structured by human interests, and intrinsically involved in the making of the world (i.e. is a mode of power).

Paralleling shifts within the disciplines that involve reexamining the relation between society, knowledge and power, new "postdisciplinary" discourses such as feminism, queer theory, cultural studies, deconstruction, and so-called postmodernism have made the relationship of knowledge and power a central theoretical and political concern. These discourses have analyzed the ways science, especially the human sciences, have participated in the making of social worlds and social hierarchies. Knowledge is analyzed as an independent social and political force – productive of forms of subjective and social life and, contrary to dominant Enlightenment traditions, not always beneficient. In short, discourses within and outside the disciplines have converged around the notion that knowledge cannot be imagined apart from power. Linking knowledge and power in a tight way implies a notion of the political unconscious – of a politics of knowledge that pivots around struggles between dominant and subjugated knowledges.

But how should we view the knowledge/power nexus? Broadly speaking, my own recommendation is Foucauldian. From this perspective, societies are said to be structured, in part, by dominant regimes of truth. These regimes are characterized by the following: (1) specific rules are authorized for generating and validating knowledge, (2) specific practices of knowledge production are institutionalized, (3) specific agents with socially validated "expertise" are given institutional authority, and (4) specific social practices are accorded public legitimacy by virtue of their connection to dominant knowledges, for example, the link of science and medicine or psychiatry and therapeutic practice. Every regime of truth, moreover, produces "subjugated," or subordinate, marginalized knowledges. These knowledges – and practices of knowledge production – are devalued and suppressed but remain historically effective. Hence, knowledge is always implicated in power both in its role of suppressing some knowledges, their producers, and the lifeworlds from which they issue, and in its role of being socially productive – for example, producing identities, shaping institutional practices, and generating norms and normalizing standards.

Foucault's comments on knowledge/power in "Two Lectures" (1980) are especially relevant. Critical of the Enlightenment story that couples the progress of reason with the scientization of knowledge, Foucault asserts that scientization is connected to the making of a disciplinary system of social control. This disciplinary order operates by creating and managing subjugated populations and their knowledges. However, the very process of producing social hierarchies makes possible the formation of new types of social identities and modes of political mobilization. In the postwar world, Foucault says, subjugated peoples and knowledges across the globe are in revolt. This dynamic of subjugation and revolt might be read as a Foucauldian view of the political unconscious. The reassertion of subjugated knowledges, which Foucault observes in the surfacing of new voices connected to the revolt from below (e.g., prisoners, psychiatric subjects, homosexuals, women, immigrants, de-colonized peoples), exposes the "progress" of reason and science as a political process.[2] In a sense, this chapter aims to draw out some of the implications of a Foucauldian politics of knowledge for the human sciences.

The cultural politics of science

Modern social theory has not been, and still is not, uniformly framed as scientific theory. One thinks, say, of Rousseau, de Bonald, Hegel, Gramsci, Marcuse, Arendt, de Beauvoir, Lewis Mumford, Barbara Ehrenreich, Michael Harrington, Foucault, Cornel West, Audre Lorde, Adrienne Rich, and so on. Nevertheless, what is striking is that much modern social theory is framed as science: Hobbes's *Leviathan*, Montesquieu's *Spirit of the Laws*, Smith's *Wealth of Nations* – Comte, Marx, and Malinowski, Parsons, Dahrendorf, and Bourdieu. This is particularly true of the discourse that has evolved under the name "sociology." Sociologists, from Comte to Coleman, envision sociological theory as scientific. It is the claim to science that is said to separate sociological from social theory and sociology from all other talk of the social.

Why the compulsion for talk of the social to claim science? I propose that the sign "science" functions as a boundary marker. It signifies what talk of the social counts as knowledge and therefore deserving of public authority and national resources. All nonscientific social talk is positioned in a subordinate epistemic and social status. Subjugated or inferiorized discourses of the social circulate under the signs of ideology, opinion, tradition, myth, religion, philosophy, literature, and rhetoric. Science confers legitimacy and authority on a discourse, its producers, and the social values and ideals of the discourse. In a word, *science is power* – the power not only to silence or marginalize *all* nonscientific talk but also to contribute to the making of selves and social worlds, as Foucault has argued in his genealogies, and feminists in their political critiques of science. I assume therefore that when sociologists claim the status of science, whatever else may be entailed in this assertion, it is a political act, for it necessarily enacts a hierarchical science/nonscience binary that has power effects – that is, scientific talk, its authors, and its corresponding institutional practices are authorized as credible or valid by virtue of its register as truth while nonscientific talk, its authors, and discursive practices are devalued and marginalized.

Science has circulated in Western cultures as a marker of truth/falsity, of legitimate/illegitimate ideas, and of credible/discredited knowledges. In the early modern period, the struggle around science was understood as a conflict over what counts as knowledge, who has the power to speak, and what kind of society will prevail. For example, in certain European nations (and in the United States somewhat later and with less antagonism), church figures were keenly aware that the claim of science to knowledge carried a potential threat to their social authority.[3] If truth was grounded in fact and reason alone, the epistemological foundation of the church – revelation and the biblical tradition – and its secular power were illegitimate. As one historian has written, "As the seventeenth century closed . . . philosophers turned to science for . . . criteria of truth, and they used science as a weapon to mount the first serious attack that Christianity itself had sustained since European civilization appeared. From that time on, Christianity has become ever more tangential to the living concerns of European civilization, and science ever more central as it has assumed the mantle Christianity once wore" (Westfall 1986: 218). The church was not alone in its suspicion of science; local folk traditions, humanistic and literary traditions, and diverse naturalistic and metaphysical philosophies struggled against their own delegitimation as credible knowledges the claim of science to be the exclusive medium of truth (on the struggle between literature and the social sciences, see Lepenies 1988; Shumway 1994: 28).

Contrary to the Whiggish Enlightenment tale of an epoch of darkness succeeded by the Age of Reason, a scientific culture did not abruptly achieve dominance in the eighteenth and nineteenth centuries. Despite the intervention of the state and secular authorities, the scientization of knowledge has been resisted and has achieved only partial institutional success. From the seventeenth century through at least the middle of this century, there has been a plurality of traditions of legitimate knowledges, knowledge producers, and sites of knowledge production. In part, this has reflected the decentralized structure of Western societies through the nineteenth century, especially the United States, despite the centralizing, unifying forces of nationalism and capitalism. In part, the continued social credibility of religious, humanistic, and folk traditions in Western societies impeded the scientization of knowledge. I do not think I would be terribly mistaken in saying that it was not until the post-World War II period, at least in the United States, that science began to achieve institutional dominance among competing knowledges.

The scientization of the human studies was inseparable from the consolidation of the university as the major site for the production of knowledge. We must be mindful, however, that it was relatively recently that human studies has found its chief social location in the university. The founding figures of the modern tradition of the human studies were not university professors (e.g., Montesquieu, Saint-Simon, Condorcet, Comte, Marx, Herbert Spencer, and Lester Ward). The university did not become an important place for the creation of social knowledges until the mid twentieth century. For example, in the United States the university was *not* the principal site for the production of social knowledges through the early decades of this century. Churches, labor unions, bohemian and feminist countercultures, and a public culture of learned societies, libraries, newspapers, magazines, and books served as key social sources for the making of social knowledges.[4] Many of the social discourses created in these nonacademic settings resisted scientization without surrendering a commitment to an elaborated, analytically driven empirical social analysis (e.g., the feminist social thought of Charlotte Perkins Gilman and Emma Goldman, the Christian socialist economics of Richard Ely, the Black nationalism of W. E. B. Du Bois, the radical cultural criticism of Max Eastman or Randolph Bourne, the critical social theory of Thorstein Veblen or Lewis Mumford or the public social thought of Walter Lippmann and John Dewey). Whereas the fate of nonscientific discourses of nature, for example, Native American traditions, folk philosophies, and romantic and idealist views of nature, was to experience virtual erasure in the face of the colonizing power of the natural sciences, the same has not been true of the human studies. In the course of this century, the champions of strong programs of social science have not, even today, managed effectively to silence and discredit their nonscientific rivals. In part this reflects the continued vigor of nonacademic social bases for the production of social knowledges. Contrary to what Russell Jacoby has argued in *The Last Intellectuals*, a vital, diversified culture of public intellectuals remains an integral part of American life – from neoconservatives and liberal public intellectuals organized around think tanks, policy institutes, magazines, newspapers, radio, and television, to new public cultures created by feminists, lesbians and gay men, people of color, and evangelical Christians.[5]

Indeed, the social sciences have been considerably less successful than the natural sciences in discrediting nonscientific rivals. The result is that diverse traditions of nonscientific human studies flourish in American and European public cultures and contest the monopolistic designs of science. One example of a tradition of public social discourse that has circulated inside and outside academia is marxism. Of course, we are familiar with scientific versions of marxism, but it is the nonscientific statements of marxism that have dominated European intellectual culture in this century (e.g., Lukacs, Gramsci, Korsch, the Frankfurt School, the Praxis School, Sartre's existential marxism, and phenomenological marxism). Many marxist intellectuals were either nonacademics or if professors their ideas were interdisciplinary and addressed to a nonacademic public of party ideologues, cultural elites, activists, and public intellectuals. Feminism is perhaps an even more compelling case than marxism in the United States, of a public social discourse critical of a scientific human studies that occupies a space both within and outside the academy. One thinks, for example, of public feminist intellectuals such as Catherine Mackinnon, Mary Daly, Adrienne Rich, Barbara Ehrenreich, bell hooks, Audre Lorde, Gloria Anzaldua, and Gloria Steinem. The same can be said of recent lesbian and gay studies and in much of what is called cultural studies. These varied social discourses, many of which resist scientization, have a social basis and audience both inside and outside the university.

It is my impression that movements of critique have paralleled the progressive scientization of the disciplines in the postwar period in the United States. In particular, the social rebellions and new social movements in the sixties and seventies were often critical of the scientization of disciplinary knowledges. For example, New Left theorists and some feminists often disputed the claim of the disciplines to scientific status and protested the assumed equivalence of science and knowledge. Some offered political critiques asserting the entanglement of the human sciences in the making of social hierarchies. By the mid-1970s, these critical social knowledges were making their presence felt in academia. A parallel dynamic of resistance to scientization issued from the New Right and conservative critics who contested scientization on the grounds that it promoted a secular, liberal politic.

I believe that these political critiques of the human sciences and a growing public perception of the entanglement of the disciplines in power dynamics have provoked legitimation problems for the human sciences. This has been especially true for sociology. Unlike economics, which could claim to deliver expert knowledges essential to state management, or psychology, whose value might be redeemed by its ties to a culture of self-redemption, sociology lacks a clear social use value in the public mind. In the face of a public suspicious of the entanglement of science and power, a vocal academic-based critique of scientization, and a prolonged economic downturn since the late 1970s – all of which present serious legitimation problems for the human sciences – many sociologists have redoubled their efforts to secure a scientific status. I perceive a link between these efforts to restore disciplinary prestige and the retreat of sociologists from public life into a discipline-centered, scientistic ideology. For example, much sociological theory since the mid-1970s has been produced exclusively by and for sociologists. Interestingly, I would contrast the retreat of sociological theory from public engagement with some recent anthropological theory. Anthropologists such as James Clifford, Renato Rosaldo, George Marcus, Talal Asad, and Peggy Sanday are nonscientific in their epistemological self-identification and are read across disciplines and by a broad intellectual public. Perhaps these social thinkers are indicative of a countermovement now occurring in disciplinary cultures, moving toward a deliberate bridging of the human sciences with literature, rhetoric, and ethics.

Permit me one further observation regarding the current reorganization of Western knowledges. If it is not already painstakingly clear to all of us (except those who can't or won't look beyond their narrow disciplinary horizon), the human sciences are being challenged by new languages of the social. Many of these languages have emerged outside the human sciences, in literary or film theory, cultural studies, feminism, queer theory, and postcolonial studies. These discourses draw less from Durkheim, Weber, Parsons, and Mead than from psychoanalysis, poststructuralism, semiotics, and linguistic theory, and they have developed their own vocabularies of the social. In their focus on the body, sexuality, and the interlocking of gender, race, and class, in their textualized images of the social and in their emphasis on power/knowledge regimes and processes of normalization and discipline, they are forging alternative traditions of social inquiry (cf. Clough 1994; Lemert 1995). Thus, I anticipate some rather unpleasant boundary skirmishes and cultural wars against the monopolization of legitimate social discourse by science.

Instead of pursuing this topic, I want to return to thinking about science as a boundary creator and to linking the scientization of social knowledge with the suppression of nonscientific knowledges. Central to the conceptual and political boundary work involved in differentiating science and nonscience has been the role of foundational discourses.

Foundationalism, epistemic privilege and social power

Foundationalism refers to efforts to provide a warrant for the claim to knowledge of a specific tradition of thinking or type of inquiry. Foundational thinking amounts to arguments that authorize particular standards and types of discourse as knowledge (Harding 1986; Rorty 1979). In the context of modern Western cultures, the claim of a discourse to representational truth or the correspondence of word and world has been *the* standard in assessing the validity of discourses. Moreover, to the extent that science has been assumed to be the paradigm of knowledge, much foundational theorizing takes the form of providing accounts of how science is possible and stipulating the line of demarcation between science and nonscience.

In the human sciences, foundationalism refers to efforts to stipulate and justify the most basic premises, concepts, and explanatory models that should guide social analysis. Justification involves specifying general standards and types of argumentation that can allow a disciplinary community to decide between competing conceptual strategies. In the human sciences, social discourses are judged by their representational truth as best we can indicate by empirical markers. For example, important statements of foundational theory in sociology would include Marx and Engels's *The German Ideology*, Durkheim's *Rules of Sociological Method*, Parsons's *Structure of Social Action*, Coleman's *Foundations of Social Theory*, Alexander's *Theoretical Logic in Sociology*, and Collins's *Conflict Sociology*.

As an example of foundationalist theorizing, consider *The German Ideology*, Marx and Engels's critique of an idealist tradition of thinking about the social. They recommend an alternative set of premises and categories that at times they characterize as materialism. If idealism's foundational language revolved around the categories of mind, reason, culture, and critical reflection, materialism's include physicality, labor, mode of production, and class conflict. These categories are foundational because it is by means of these that we are said to know society and history. What justifications are offered for materialism? To take one example, Marx and Engels argue that individuals must first reproduce their material existence before they can produce culture; hence labor, as that material practice through which we actively engage with external nature, has an epistemo-logical – because ontological – primacy over the categories of mind and consciousness. All of Marx's justificatory rationales are of this type – pre-sumed rational arguments, logically compelling – but are they? Marx claims the epistemological priority for materialism by appealing to the ontological primacy of physical reproduction through the medium of labor. But bodily need is always implicated in symbolic processes; and labor is unthinkable without assuming it to be a culturally embedded practice (i.e., normatively guided and value directed). Leaving aside Marx and Engels's fateful reduc-tion of labor to economic production, which ignores that sexual and gender dynamics are attached to reproductive and household labor, their framing of labor as the foundational category of a materialist social theory is, even on cursory review, hardly compelling.[6]

Foundational arguments then aim to stipulate a particular set of premises and categories and justify them on the grounds that they are true. Such metatheoretical argumentative strategies have been pivotal in the making of a culture of science. They have provided a warrant for the exclu-sive claims of science to truth and therefore for the formation of a scien-tific culture that not only excludes or marginalizes all nonscientific social discourses but that discredits all standards besides "truth" in assessing social ideas. This move involves the exclusion of moral and political considerations in developing and assessing disciplinary knowledges.

Foundational arguments are deployed in the struggle over which knowl-edges and knowledge-producing practices are entitled to public authority. In the late eighteenth and nineteenth centuries, there was a multiplicity of social knowledges. Knowledge was a contested political sphere; the asser-tion of science as the exclusive standard of knowledge was resisted. The early advocates of the human sciences (e.g., Condorcet, Smith, Saint-Simon, Comte, and Spencer) deployed foundational arguments to author-ize their own discourses as science while delegitimating rival social knowledges by claiming that only their ideas were valid because they were based on fact and reason, not tradition, revelation, or "pure" reason.

Foundational arguments have not disappeared even as science has put together a string of victories in the twentieth century. One reason is that struggles over what counts as knowledge, who has the right to produce it, and which social practices and conventions in the production of knowledge are legitimate have not disappeared. In the face of ongoing struggles over social knowledges, including resistance to the scientization of knowledge, foundational arguments continue to serve as one site of cultural conflict.

Rivalry *among* scientific paradigms of social knowledge has provided an additional impetus for foundational discourses. Foundational arguments aim to adjudicate internal disciplinary conflicts. This intent is central to understanding the decidedly metatheoretical turn of much disciplinary theory. For example, much current sociological theory is foundational in that it addresses core premises and categories with the aim of articulating epistemic standards. Let me elaborate a bit to clarify this.

Sociology is a discipline rife with empirical and interpretive disputes. Such endemic conflict not only threatens the coherence of the discipline but endangers its legitimacy and therewith its warrant for public authority and resources. Disciplines such as sociology, whose social role is at best ambivalently received by the public, aim to minimize disciplinary conflicts. Accordingly, sociologists place a premium on strategies that promise disciplinary unity. One response to disciplinary disorder has been to appeal to method and fact to stipulate order. When this fails, as it most assuredly has in sociology, theory steps in. The promise of theory is that it can provide unity or at least a credible defense of its possibility. The strategy of "theorists" is to identify a limited set of core presuppositions and problems that are assumed to structure empirical interpretive analyses and that can account for a range of disciplinary discord. Theory aims to provide a general theoretical logic or casuistry which can guide sociologists in their decisionmaking. The hope is that agreement on core premises and categories will translate into higher levels of empirical and interpretive consensus or render such disputes increasingly more local or less discipline-wide and thus more circumscribed empirical disputes. This is the project that inspires many of the most impressive current theoretical statements in sociology, for example, Giddens's *Central Problems in Social Theory*, Alexander's *Theoretical Logic in Sociology*, Turner's *Structure of Social Interaction*, and Coleman's *Theoretical Foundations of Social Theory*.

The foundational turn of current sociological theory has promoted a preoccupation with metatheoretical debates, for example, the problem of social order, the nature of social action, the relation between agency and structure, or the interrelation between the micro/macrolevels of society, explanation versus understanding as modes of knowledge, and conflict versus order models of society. Underlying this foundational theorizing is the hope to deliver on the promise of providing conceptual grounds for disciplinary unity or at least guidelines for conceptual and empirical decisionmaking to lessen disciplinary discord.[7]

Foundational arguments have not, however, succeeded in achieving such theoretical consensus in sociology. There is virtually no standardization of language, no agreement on central problems, and no consensus on standards to evaluate our conceptual and empirical choices. For example, with regard to standards governing empirical statements, should the chief standard be predictability, explanatory comprehensiveness, quantitative precision, conceptual economy, descriptive richness, aesthetic appeal, or practical utility? And what, after all, counts as "the empirical" and who is to decide this and according to what standards? In the face of such foundational disarray, theorists have often appealed to the "classics" to serve as exemplars and therefore as standards of social knowledge. Such appeals are compelling only if we can agree on which figures and texts are classic and why. But who is the "we" who decides classic status, by what or whose standards, without being ethnocentric and exclusionary? Parsons canonized Weber and Durkheim as the core of the classic tradition, a move that entailed the displacement of Comte and Spencer – the two major classic figures for much of pre-Parsonian American sociology. Giddens, among others, added Marx to the canon but left out Du Bois and Charlotte Perkins Gilman. Appealing to the classics to resolve foundational disputes merely shifts the site of contestation; it narrows disciplinary disputes only by canonizing certain texts and authorizing certain voices while silencing others.

I do not wish to press further the empirical case against foundationalism since what is taken as foundational and what is taken as empirical indicators of foundational success in the human sciences can reasonably be contested. The empirical, I am afraid, does not provide a safe ground on which to adjudicate interpretive disputes, since it can never escape its own conventional or, if you will, socially constructed status and normalizing role. In other words, to the extent that the appeal to "the empirical" as the final arbiter of interpretive disputes serves to regulate whose statements – and what kinds of statements – pass as valid, to that extent it remains a site of contestation. So let me shift my attention from the issue of the empirical success to the logic of foundationalism.

I intend to introduce a series of provocations that are troubling to the foundationalist project and hence to the science/nonscience binary and so perhaps to key aspects of Western cultures of science. My first provocation: foundationalism in the human sciences seems trapped in an inescapable instability or an immense vulnerability to reversal. To the extent that foundational arguments are implicated in the science/nonscience binary, they relentlessly provoke their own subversion. Every effort to assert a universal language of the social elicits a reading as an ideological particular. Thus, Marx disputes the claim to science by the classical economists on the grounds that their silence around class is symptomatic of a bourgeois-class ideology. Non-marxist sociologists turn the ideology critique against Marx by interpreting his global collapse of the social into class war as itself symptomatic of a working-class ideology; feminists critique both marxism and sociology on the grounds that their core concepts of the social naturalize and universalize a masculine standpoint. Nonfeminist social theory conflates the social with the public sphere and a naturalized male dominant gender order. Feminists have themselves often been criticized for their ideological silences around race, class, and sexuality. This is a standard critical trope in the human sciences. We discredit a theory by revealing its ideological meanings. This move carries epistemic force only because of the authority of the science/ideology binary. But this binary makes this move equally inevitable, another case perhaps of an unconscious compulsion driving the disciplines.

A second provocation: foundationalist arguments are inspired by a utopian hope of theoretical closure. This hope is almost never stated or justified and thus all foundational efforts are vulnerable to the charge of incompleteness. Foundational arguments stipulate and justify what premises and categories should guide social analysis. But how do we know what should be included in a vocabulary of the social? In the absence of such a stipulated, agreed upon understanding, any foundational proposal can be criticized for its omissions (cf. Turner 1992). Thus, marxism is taken to task for its silence on gender; Durkheim neglects power; Blau's structuralism does not permit agency; Mead lacks a macrosocial theory, and so on.

Even if we could agree on which foundational issues to address, what standards would guide our conceptual decisions? For example, in the 1970s and 1980s the question of the relation between idealism and materialism was debated as a key foundational issue in sociology. Sociologists proposed different models: marxist, parsonian, and phenomenological. The yield of this dispute was an immense proliferation of conceptual strategies with, needless to say, little consensus. In the end, theorists lined up behind one or another framing of the idealist/materialist great divide – invoked the classics, appealed to ethnocentric values or ideals, and constructed allegories of freedom and progress to authorize their position. Today, a main site of "theory" contention is the so-called micro/macro debate, but the configuration of this "theory" dispute rehearses the idealist/materialist debates. My own view is that such disputes are probably irresolvable; there is no right way to frame the micro-macro issue, if by right we mean corresponding to the real. There may be useful ways to frame this issue in light of specific empirical, interpretive, or practical aims. This, however, figures such disputes in a pragmatic register that hardly requires a foundational justification.

A third – and final – provocation: I have repeatedly invoked a "we" who stipulates foundations. Who is this "we?" In the Enlightenment tradition, the "we" who know the world are often assumed to be ahistorical or transcendent producers of knowledge. It is not you or I as a particular racial, gendered, sexual, national, or cultural self who produces knowledge, but you and I as instances of a universal agency – reason or mind. Science is imagined along the lines of Goffman's total institution. Its austere regime transforms civilian minds, which are saturated with particularistic values and interests, into scientific minds inspired by the quest for truth. But if asylums and the military fail to remake the self, so too does science.

The human sciences cannot assume both that the self is socially produced and that the mind is autonomous. As individuals are shaped by their nationality, cultural tradition, class, and race, so too are the knowledges they produce. The human sciences are unthinkable without this assumption but are perhaps unthinkable, as we currently imagine them, with this assumption. How can we both assert that humans act and think the way they do because of our particular sociohistorical circumstances and in the same breath declare that we can escape such social causality when we enter the scientific domain? For example, how can sociologists, whose business is to analyze institutional and group ideologies, naively accept the self-understanding of scientists as nonideological? Just as Goffman discovered that civilians retain much of their civilian identities in the military or asylums, the "we" who stipulate foundations and know the world cannot abstract from the "we" who are say American, middle class, gay, white, and late twentieth century.[8]

Toward a postdisciplinary culture of human studies

If there is little consensus about which foundational problems are central and what standards should guide judgments of validity, perhaps theoretical consensus is not the aim of foundational proposals. Perhaps, as I have suggested, foundationalism accrues purpose and moral force through its unconscious willfullness and productivity – to wit, foundationalism marks boundaries of inside/outside and knowledge/nonknowledge. Foundational discourses contribute to the making of hierarchies of knowledge and power. Such discursive interventions aim to authorize and privilege some voices while discrediting and silencing others. This is what is meant by the political unconscious of the human sciences; perhaps this lies behind the compulsive drive to establish foundations.[9]

I remind you that I did not intend to compose a brief against science. Indeed, it is in part the critical reflexivity of a scientific culture that makes possible the exposure of science's political unconscious. My message is not anti-science. Rather, this "deconstruction" aims to press beyond the science/nonscience binary in order to imagine, if you will, a postmodern and postdisciplinary culture of knowledge and human studies. But what would such a culture look like and what are the implications of this deconstruction for sociology?

A guiding impulse of this chapter is to defend, on both logical and empirical grounds, a warrant for a culture organized around epistemological pluralism. With respect to the logical force of this proposal, I have argued that the contradictory, unstable logic of foundationalism in the human sciences, and its entanglement in a repressive politic, gives intellectual and moral credibility to abandoning foundationalism and disavowing the science/nonscience binary. I have alluded, moreover, to the empirical reconfiguring of social knowledges in a direction suggesting an altered and perhaps postdisciplinary culture, for example, the formation of new domains of social knowledge such as cultural studies, communications, gender studies, comparative literature, queer theory, and postcolonial studies. These fields of knowledge point to the institutional consolidation of hybrid knowledges that underscores the blurring of the lines between the human sciences, literature, rhetoric, ethics, and philosophy and obscure the boundaries between scholarship and partisanship. I take such developments as suggesting a postdisciplinary culture of knowledge – one not organized around the science/nonscience binary, not structured along current disciplinary lines, but one that acknowledges multiple knowledges and is based less on a strong notion of truth as the arbiter of belief than on pragmatics.[10]

What are some of the implications of such a postdisciplinary culture of knowledge for sociology and the human science disciplines in general? Refusing justifications of sociology that rely on the claim that its warrant derives from mirroring the actual structure of the social world means that we would approach sociology, in the short term, as an evolving, heterogeneous tradition. Its value would pivot on what its discursive practices allow us to say and do – for example, the kinds of dangers or social stress points it can alert us to; the ways its social descriptions provide coherence and purpose to our collective lives; its accounts of the social sources of discontent and its proposed social remedies; the usefulness of its social knowledges for social groups (e.g., policy makers, public officials, citizens, social activists, and bureaucracies) oriented to (say) social legislation, institutional rationalization, moral critique, or political mobilization. In short, judgments about the value of sociological knowledges would depend less on whether they are true in the sense of a correspondence between word and world than on their social purpose and consequences. A shift from a truth-driven, foundational scientific culture to a pragmatic culture would mean that sociological knowledges would be formed less by specialty area or disciplinary problems than by an engagement with public life. The "post-modernizing" of sociology would permit, and indeed encourage, the integration of ethical and, where appropriate, political reflection into its discursive practices.

While some of the conventions and practices of sociology would prove valuable and be sustained, in the long term, a postdisciplinary academic culture anticipates the end of sociology as a distinct discipline. With its emphasis on the pragmatics of knowledge and the abandonment of the science/nonscience binary, a postmodern culture would trouble the disciplinary boundaries between sociology and the humanities and the institutional boundaries between "scholar" and "citizen." A new human studies would freely mix the empirical conventions of the social sciences with (say) philosophical, literary, and rhetorical strategies of argumentation (e.g., in sociology, see Agger 1992; Bellah 1986; Brown 1992; Denzin 1991; Lemert 1995; Richardson 1991). I am not suggesting a new orthodoxy for the human studies. Quite the contrary, I imagine an academic culture that would value multiple strategies of talking about "the social," varying with tradition and social purpose. There would be "positivistic" research addressed to the ongoing need for information to rationalize (instrumentally) social processes, interpretive studies oriented to enhancing intercultural communication, social narratives intent on changing public perceptions, and ethically and politically engaged studies aimed at shaping the outcome of social conflicts.

From the vantage point of the political unconscious of the human sciences, a postmodern and postdisciplinary culture has much to recommend it. There is no illusion of bringing to an end the historical effectiveness of a political unconsciousness in the human studies. To the extent that some kinds of boundaries of inside/outside are marked out or conventions of argumentation and justification are established, a political unconscious will operate in the form of historically effective subjugated knowledges and communities of inquiry. However, a culture that substitutes multidimensional for unidimensional standards of justification and favors local, *ad hoc*, temporarily negotiated, *pragmatic* discursive strategies that acknowledge the play of interests and values in knowledges would encourage a fluid movement between subjugated invisibility and public visibility and an open play of discursive and social differences. The political unconscious would perhaps lose some of its historical efficacy and be more easily and frequently exposed to critique; dominant knowledges would be continuously pressured to justify themselves, while subjugated knowledges would be less effectively marginalized. In short, the defense of a postmodern and post-disciplinary culture pivots on the claim that a vital, democratic intellectual culture should include, at its core, the recognition of epistemic and social differences. I do not think that this is possible without having initially considered the operation of the political unconscious in the making of social knowledges.

But, you might ask, would there be no basis to assess social vocabularies? Would all talk be equally valid, thereby leaving us without a rational basis to criticize or settle disputes peaceably? Of course, criticism and mediating social disputes would occur. Abandoning foundationalism does not mean the disavowal of criticism or standards of moral and political judgment. The question is whether epistemological pluralism permits a reasoned defense of standards of criticism. Of course, a lot hinges on what is meant by a "reasoned" defense of critique.

I do not believe that appeals to the "empirical" can today serve as compelling grounds to resolve disputes between knowledge claims, at least to the extent that such disputes go beyond specific statements to broader interpretive disagreements or involve conflicts between different knowledge regimes.[11] Let me quickly add that abandoning the empirical as a privileged site for adjudicating interpretive disputes does *not* mean that we reject empirical arguments, only that such arguments are recognized as conventional and therefore assessed by what specific empirical-analytical conceptual strategies allow us to say and do. Empirical arguments are always open to contestation by interpretive communities that may either disagree over particular interpretive accounts while sharing broad empirical conventions or hold to different conventions of the empirical (Davidson 1973; Derrida 1976; Feyerabend 1975; Rorty 1982). Moreover, if we can no longer invoke the empirical to warrant statements exclusively by their truth value, reason-driven standards (e.g., coherence, logical consistency, or comprehensiveness) are no more a guarantee of success in securing agreement in disputes that move across interpretive communities. Reasoned standards are equally conventional. They may permit local agreements but are less helpful on global disagreements across communities and thus remain sites of contention (Davidson 1990; Rorty 1982; Winch 1963; Wittgenstein 1958).

Is our only choice in settling epistemic or social disputes either rational universalism or power? I do not think so. There is a third way: the pragmatic option. Standards of critique or assessment are framed pragmatically or by asking after the purposes or consequences, the aims and intellectual, social, and moral implications of a discourse or social practice. Critical judgments and social negotations would be situational, provisional, or temporary and involve *ad hoc* discursive strategies. Many of "us" (i.e. Anglo-Americans and Europeans) already implicitly use such justifications. While we may invoke the universal by appealing to (say) natural law, Judeo-Christian truths, or Kantian or utilitarian reason, have we not relativized these cultural universals into particular cultural traditions? And if we have, does not our moral discourse – critical, judgmental, mediating – quickly shift from a discourse of grounds and universal reason to one of pragmatics, that is, situational factors, consequential considerations, identifying shared elements from traditions, improvising *ad hoc* strategies, and so on.[12]

2

The end of sociological theory

Sociological theory has gone astray. It has lost most of its social and intellectual importance; it is increasingly disengaged from the conflicts and public debates that have nourished it in the past; it has turned inward and is largely self-referential. Sociological theory is today produced and consumed almost exclusively by sociological theorists (cf. Geertz 1983; Sica 1989; Skocpol 1986; Turner and Wardell 1986). Its social and intellectual insularity accounts for the almost permanent sense of crisis and malaise that surrounds contemporary sociological theory. This distressing condition originates, in part, from its central project: the quest for foundations and for a totalizing concept of society.

The renewal of sociological theory as a critical public discourse requires that we disavow scientism, i.e. the increasingly absurd claim to be an epistemically privileged discourse. We should relinquish our quest for foundations or the search for the one correct or grounded set of premises, conceptual strategy, and explanatory model. Sociological theory will be reinvigorated if and when it becomes "social theory." My critique of sociological theory and advocacy of social theory as a social narrative with a moral intent will be advanced from the standpoint of a "postmodern" perspective (regarding postmodernism, see Bauman 1988; Brown 1990; Kellner 1988; Kroker and Cook 1986; Lemert 1991; Nichoson 1990; Seidman and Wagner 1991).

Anticipating the end of sociological theory entails renouncing the millenarian social hopes that have been at the center of modernist sociological theory (cf. Baudrillard 1975, 1981; Foucault 1978, 1980; Lyotard 1984). "Postmodernism," or at least the version I will defend, carries no promise of liberation – of a society free of domination. Postmodernists give up the "modernist" idol of complete human emancipation in favor of deconstructing false closure, prying open present and future social possibilities, detecting fluidity and porousness in forms of life where hegemonic discourses posit closure and a frozen, natural social order. The hope of a great transformation is replaced by the more modest aspiration of a relentless defense of choice, democratization, and struggles for social justice. A postmodern perspective offers the possibility of a social analysis that takes seriously the history of cruelty and constraint in Western modernity without succumbing to the backward-looking criticism of conservatives or the liberal retreat from social criticism.

Sociological theory/social theory: a difference that matters

I would like to posit a distinction between social theory and sociological theory. Social theories typically take the form of broad social narratives. They relate stories of origin and development, tales of crisis, decline, or progress. Social theories are typically closely connected to contemporary social conflicts and public debates. These narratives aim not only to clarify an event or social configuration but to shape its outcome – perhaps by legitimating one outcome or imbuing certain actors, actions, and institutions with historical importance while attributing malicious or demonic qualities to other social forces. Social theory relates moral tales which have practical significance; they embody a will to shape history. Marx wrote *The Communist Manifesto* and the successive drafts of the critique of political economy in response to current social conflicts, as a practical intervention for the purpose of effecting change – to wit, contributing to the transformation of wage-labor into the proletariat (i.e., into self-identified members of the working class antagonistic to capitalism). Weber wrote *The Protestant Ethic and the Spirit of Capitalism* in part to stimulate the building of a politicized German middle class motivated to seize power. Durkheim intended *The Division of Labor in Society* to legitimate and shape the Third Republic against attacks from the right and left. Social theories aim to accurately represent social life, but they arise from ongoing contemporary conflicts and aim to affect them. Their moral intent is never far from the surface. Their success is evaluated by their moral, social and political significance, not simply by their empirical or explanatory correctness.

Sociological theory, by contrast, intends to uncover a logic of society; it aims to discover the one true vocabulary that mirrors the social universe. Sociological theorists typically claim that their ideas arise out of humanity's self-reflection as social beings. They approach theory as part of humanity's continuous dialogue on "the social." Sociological theorists aim to abstract from current social conflicts to reflect on the conditions of society everywhere, to articulate the language of social action, conflict, and change in general. They seek to find a universal language, a conceptual casuistry that can assess the truth of all social languages. Sociological theory aims to denude itself of its contextual embeddedness; to articulate humanity's universal condition. Insofar as sociological theory speaks the language of particularity, it is said to have failed. It aspires to elevate itself to the universal, to the level of theoretical logics or central problems or to the study of social laws or the structure of social action. The intent of sociological theorists is to add to the stock of human knowledge in the hope that this will bring enlightenment and social progress.

The story I wish to tell is not that of a movement from social theory to sociological theory. Social theory and sociological theory have, at least since the eighteenth century, lived side by side and frequently have been intertwined. Marx wrote social theory but also sociological theory; Weber may have penned the *Protestant Ethic* but he also wrote methodological essays that attempted to offer secure epistemological foundations for his conceptual strategies. Durkheim wrote the *Division of Labor* but also the *Rules of Sociological Method*, which set out a logic of sociology; Parsons wrote the *Structure of Social Action* but also *The American University.* Although sociological and social theory intermingle in the history of social thought, I want to suggest that within the discipline of sociology, especially since the post-World War II period, the emphasis has been on sociological theory. Indeed, social theory is often devalued; it is described as ideological. Sociological theorists are encouraged to do sociological theory, not social theory. In the discipline of sociology, sociological theorists stake their claim to prestige and privilege on their ability to produce new analytic approaches or explanatory models to presumed universal problems. I want to claim further that the hegemony of sociological theory within sociology has contributed to rendering sociological theorists insular and their products – theories – socially and intellectually obscure and irrelevant to virtually everyone except other sociological theorists. As sociological theorists have moved away from social theory, they have contributed to the weakening of public moral and political debate.

A critique of sociological theory as a foundationalist discourse

Many sociological theorists have accepted a concept of theory as a foundational discourse (cf. Seidman 1989; 1990; 1991a, 1991b). We have come to define our principal task as providing foundations for sociology. This entails giving ultimate reasons for why sociology should adopt a specific conceptual strategy. We have assigned ourselves the task of defining and defending the basic premises, concepts, and explanatory models of sociology. We have assumed the role of resolving disciplinary disputes and conceptual conflicts by presuming to be able to discover a universal epistemic rationale that provides objective, value-neutral standards of conflict resolution. Sociological theorists have stepped forward as the virtual police of the sociological mind. In the guise of upholding reason and safeguarding intellectual and social progress, we have proposed to legislate codes of disciplinary order by fashioning a kind of epistemological casuistry that can serve as a general guide to conceptual decision-making.

The quest for foundations has pressured sociological theory into becoming a metatheoretical discourse. Its disputes are increasingly self-referential and epistemological. Theory discussions have little bearing on major social conflicts and political struggles or on important public debates over current social affairs. Sociological theory has diminished impact on crucial public texts of social commentary, criticism, and analysis. And if I am not mistaken, sociological theory functions as little more than a legitimating rhetoric for on-going research programs and empirical analyses. Theory texts and conferences are preoccupied with foundational disputes regarding the logic of the social sciences, the respective merits of a conflict versus order paradigm, the nature of social action and order, the conceptual link between agency and structure or a micro and macro level of analysis, the problem of integrating structural and cultural analysis, and so on. These discussions are rehearsed endlessly using a short list of rhetorical tropes, such as the appeal to classic texts or the higher values of humanism or scientism to legitimate a favored vocabulary or conceptual strategy.

Has this discursive proliferation produced a centered, evolving vital theoretical tradition? No. Instead of a concentrated, productive discourse focused on a limited set of problems that exhibits sustained elaboration, we find a dispersed discursive clamoring covering a wide assortment of ever-changing issues in a dazzling diversity of languages. These vocabularies of social discourse typically imply divergent (if not incommensurable) philosophical, moral, and ideological standpoints. In this discursive clamor, there is virtually no standardization of language, no agreement on what are central problems or standards of evaluation. There is a virtual babble of different vocabularies addressing a heterogeneous cluster of changing disputes. Indeed, a good deal of this discourse involves struggles to authorize a particular dispute, conceptual vocabulary or justificatory rationale (e.g., empirical adequacy or explanatory comprehensiveness). Typically, a text backed by a social network briefly captures the attention of some of the principal players in the field. A discussion ensues; local skirmishes break out in journals, books, and conferences; a particular vocabulary may acquire salience among sociological theorists. Such coherence, however, is typically short-lived as the field is always divided and rival theorists with their own agenda and networks clamor for recognition and reward. This metatheoretical proliferation has yielded little, if any, conceptual order or progress.

Foundational disputes have, to date, admitted of little, if any, consensus. Why? Because the criteria that guide conceptual decisions seem, in the end, local, heterogeneous, and perhaps ultimately incommensurable. How do "we" judge or prioritize epistemic standards that include empirical adequacy, explanatory comprehensiveness, quantitative precision, empirical predictability, logical coherence, conceptual economy, aesthetic appeal, practical efficacy, and moral acceptability? And how do "we" agree on what theoretical foundations might look like? What would need to be included (or excluded, for that matter)? What would closure or comprehensiveness look like (Turner 1991)? And what, after all, should serve as a standard of validity here? Finally, who is to make these decisions? Who, in other words, are the "we" that legislates justificatory strategies?

If one conclusion to date seems painstakingly clear, even if resisted equally painstakingly, it is that metatheoretical disputes do not appear to be resolvable by appeals to abstract or formal reason. Rival ontological and epistemological claims seem meaningful only insofar as they are tied to practical interests or specific forms of life. Yet, if this is true – and I am only claiming that from my historical and social vantage point this point seems compelling – then foundational discourses can hardly escape being local and ethnocentric. This point suggests that the search for foundations for our conceptual strategies should be abandoned in favor of pragmatic types of justification.

The notion that foundational discourses cannot avoid being local and ethnocentric is pivotal to what has come to be called "postmodernism" (e.g., Rorty 1979, 1982, 1991). Generally speaking, a postmodern perspective exposes the ways the products of the human studies – concepts, explanations, theories – bear the imprint of the particular interests and standpoint of their creators. This suspicion may be posed as follows: how can a knowing subject, who has particular interests and values by virtue of living in a specific society at a particular historical juncture and occupying a specific social position defined by his or her class, gender, race, sexual orientation, ethnic and religious status, produce concepts, explanations and standards of validity that are universally valid? How can we both assert that humans are constituted by their particular sociohistorical circumstances and also claim that they can escape their embeddedness by creating nonlocal, universally valid concepts and standards? How can we escape the suspicion that every move by culturally bounded agents to generalize their conceptual strategy is not simply an effort to impose particular, local interests on others?

A postmodern perspective elicits the suspicion that science is tied to particular social projects of Western modernization and to a multiplicity of more local, more specific struggles around class, status, gender, sexuality, race, nationality, and so on. Thus, feminists have not only documented the androcentric structure of sociology but have analyzed critically the politics of science in its normative constructions of femininity and womanhood (e.g., Andersen 1983; Harding 1986; Harding and Hintikka 1983; Jagger and Bordo 1989; Keller 1985; Millman and Kanter 1975; Smith 1979 and 1989). Because this relentless epistemological suspicion is turned against disciplinary discourses by, say, feminists, and because the same trope is rehearsed among African-Americans, gay men and lesbians, Latinos and Asians, the disabled and so on, no social discourse can escape the doubt that its claims to truth are tied to and yet mask an on-going social interest to shape the course of history. Once the veil of epistemic privilege is torn away, science appears as a social force enmeshed in particular cultural and institutional power struggles. The claim to truth, as Foucault has proposed, is inextricably an act of power.

This epistemic suspicion is at the core of what we can loosely call "postmodernism." This perspective challenges the definition of theory as a foundational discourse. A postmodern critique does not deny the possibility of success in the quest for foundations, it urges only that from the standpoint of the history of such foundational efforts, and from the vantage point of "modern Western" consciousness which has itself generated this relentless epistemic doubt, this project does not seem compelling or credible.

Aside from this epistemic doubt, there are practical and moral reasons to consider in assessing the value of a foundational project. The latter is said to exhibit a bad faith: concealed in the will to truth is a will to power. To claim that there are universal and objective reasons to warrant a social discourse, to claim that a discourse speaks the language of truth is to privilege that discourse, its carriers, and its social agenda. Insofar as we believe that social discourses are social practices which, like other social forces, shape social life and history, privileging a discourse as true authorizes its social values and agenda (Brown 1990).

Social discourses, especially the broad social narratives of development produced by sociological theorists, but also the specialized discourses produced by demographers, criminologists, or organizational sociologists, shape the social world by creating normative frameworks of racial, gender, sexual, national and other types of identity, social order, and institutional functioning that carry the intellectual and social authority of science. A discourse that bears the stamp of scientific knowledge gives its normative concepts of identity and order an authority, while discrediting the social agendas produced by other discourses defined as nonscientific. To claim to have discovered the true language of society delegitimates rival paradigms – now described as merely ideological or, at best, as precursors to the age of science – and their social agendas. This claim to science entails a demand to marginalize or withdraw privilege and its rewards from discursive rivals. Indeed, to claim epistemic privilege for a social discourse is to demand social authority not only for its social agenda but for its producers and supporters. In a word, the politics of epistemology is bound up with social struggles to shape history.

When one appeals solely to the truth of a discourse to authorize it intellectually and socially, one represses reflection on its practical-moral meaning and its social consequences. A discourse that justifies itself solely by appeals to truth will not be compelled to defend its conceptual decisions on moral and political grounds. The practical and moral significance of the discourse will not be examined or considered in a cursory way. On the other hand, if theorists were to assume that all appeals to universal standards or justificatory strategies are not ultimately compelling, they would be forced to offer, in addition to empirical or analytical arguments, "local" moral, social and political reasons for their conceptual decisions. Disputes between rival theories or conceptual strategies would not be over epistemic first principles – e.g., individualism versus holism, materialism versus idealism, micro versus macro level analysis, instrumental versus normative concepts of action and order. Instead, theorists would argue over the empirical-analytical, social, moral and political consequences of choosing one or another conceptual strategy.

A pragmatic turn has distinct advantages. It expands the parties who may participate as more or less equals in a debate about the present and future organization of social life. Where a discourse is redeemed ultimately by metatheoretical appeals, experts step forward as the authorities. This contributes to the enfeeblement of a public realm of moral and political debate because social questions are deemed the domain of experts. By contrast, when a discourse is judged by its conceptual and practical consequences, more citizens are qualified to participate in this discursive sphere. A pragmatic move, in principle, implies an active, politically engaged citizenry participating in a democratic public realm.

A postmodern perspective contests a representational concept of science whose legitimacy hinges on an increasingly cynical belief in science's enlightening and empowering role. This Enlightenment legitimation obscures the social entanglement of the disciplines and permits them to abandon moral responsibility for their own social efficacy. This approach emphasizes the practical and moral character of science. It views the disciplines as implicated in heterogeneous struggles around gender, race, sexuality, the body and the mind, to shape humanity.

Sociology as social narrative with a moral intent

Foundational theorizing is by no means a product of the social scientific disciplines. The attempt to resolve conceptual disputes or to authorize a particular conceptual strategy by appealing to some presumably universal or objective justification has accompanied – and preceded – modern social thought. Yet the institutionalization of social science and the phenomenal growth of the disciplines in the twentieth century has greatly contributed to the rise of theory specialists whose expertise revolves around metatheoretical or foundational concerns. Although foundational discourses may play a beneficial role at certain sociohistorical junctures (e.g., during periods of epochal transition, such as the eighteenth century), my view is that today they contribute to the social and intellectual insularity and irrelevance of much sociological theory, at least in many Western societies. Moreover, I have registered an epistemological doubt about the likely success of the foundational project. This suspicion has been a systematic feature of modern Western social consciousness at least since Marx.

From a postmodern perspective, justifications of conceptual strategies appear to be unable to avoid a local ethnocentric character. This is not an argument denying the possibility of foundations; I offer no proof of the impossibility of achieving such a grounded social discourse. My epistemic doubt is local, if you will. It stems from my understanding of the historical failure of foundational efforts; it reflects a sympathy for the relentless epistemic doubt generated by "modern" Western social science itself.

I propose that we give up the effort to secure foundations in favor of local, pragmatic rationales for our conceptual strategies. Instead of appealing to absolutist justifications, instead of constructing theoretical logics and epistemic casuistries to justify a conceptual strategy, to lift them out of contextual embeddedness and elevate them to the realm of universal truths, I would favor local, pragmatic rationales for our conceptual approaches. Instead of asking what is the nature of reality or knowledge in the face of conflicting conceptual strategies – and therefore going metatheoretical – I suggest that it might often be more productive to assess conflicting perspectives by evaluating their intellectual, social, moral, and political consequences. Does a conceptual strategy or approach promote precision or conceptual economy? Does it enhance empirical predictability? What social values or forms of life does it promote? Does it lead to relevant policy-related information or perspectives that might be useful for activists? Pragmatic justifications shift the debate from that of the foundations of knowledge to that of social and intellectual consequences.

The quest for foundations has been connected closely to the project of creating a general theory (Seidman and Wagner 1991). Many modern social theorists have sought to elaborate an overarching conceptual framework that would be true for all times and places. The search for the one right language that would mirror the social world, that would uncover the essential structures and dynamics or laws of society, has been integral to sociological theory. In *The German Ideology*, Marx and Engels believed that they had uncovered a universally valid language of history and society. In their view, the categories of labor, mode of production, class, and class conflict, amounted to what they considered to be a general theory that captured the essential structure and dynamics of history. In *The Division of Labor in Society* and in *The Rules of the Sociological Method*, Durkheim proposed the dual categories of collective representations and social morphology as the conceptual basis for a universal theory of society; Parsons imagined that the *Structure of Social Action* and *The Social System* established a universal set of premises and concepts that would unify and guide all social inquiry. This quest to discover the one true language of the social world, to uncover its laws, general structure, and universal logic, has been an abiding aim of sociological theory.

The quest for a totalizing general theory, in my view, is misguided. My arguments parallel my reservations about foundationalism. General theories have not succeeded; their basic premises, concepts, and explanatory models, along with their metatheoretical rationales, consistently have been shown to be local, ethnocentric projections (e.g., Turner and Wardell 1986). The project of general theory has pushed theorists into the realm of meta-theory as theorists look to articulate a general standpoint from which to resolve conceptual or paradigm disputes; this project has isolated theorists from sociologists engaged in on-going research programs and empirical analyses. The quest for foundations and a totalizing theory has marginalized theorists from the major public debates of the times. Moreover, when concepts get stretched to cover all times and places or to be socially inclusive, they become so contentless as to lose whatever explanatory value they have. These flat, contentless general categories seem to inevitably ignore or repress social differences (Nicholson 1991). For example, the categories of labor, mode of production, or class conflict may be useful to explain nineteenth century England but perhaps much less so to explain late nineteenth

century Germany or the United States and surely less relevant as we move
to societies that are more kinship or state centered (e.g. Balbus 1982;
Baudrillard 1975; Habermas 1977, 1984, 1987; Nicholson 1986; Rubin 1975).

If social theorists surrender or marginalize the project of foundationalism and the quest for general theories, what's left for "theory"?
Undoubtedly, some theorists will argue that a more modest version of the
project of general theory is still feasible, such as Merton's middle-range theories or some variant, say, in the mold of Skocpol's *States and Social
Revolution*. I won't dispute the value of these alternatives, though I believe
that they remain too closely tied to scientism and a "modernist" ideology
of enlightenment and progress that have been suspect for decades. Instead,
I wish to propose that when theorists abandon the foundationalist project
in the broad sense – elaborating general theories and principles of justification – what they have left is social theory as social narrative. When we strip
away the foundationalist aspects of Marx's texts, what remains are stories
of social development and crisis; when we purge Durkheim's *Division of
Labor in Society* of its foundationalist claims, we have a tale of the development of Western modernity. The same applies to Parsons, Luhmann, or
Habermas. I am not recommending that we simply return to the grand
stories of social evolution from Condorcet to Habermas. If social theory is
to pivot around its role as a critical social narrative, I believe it must be a
narrative of a different sort than those of the great modernists. In the
remainder of this section, I will outline one version of such a social narrative.

I imagine one verson of a postmodern social narrative that would be
"event-based" and therefore careful about its temporal and spatial boundaries. By event-based, I mean that the primary reference point of such narratives would be major social conflicts or developments analyzed in their
specific national or international sociohistorical context. Event-based
social narratives would gravitate towards densely contexual analyses.

The grand narratives of the great modernist social theorists responded
to the big events of the day but typically disregarded their temporal and
spatial settings. Instead of locating events in their specific sociohistorical
setting, the grand narratives of the "classics" typically framed events as
world historical and crafted stories of the course of Western, if not human,
history. Instead of telling the story of capitalism or secularization in, say,
England or Italy, they analyzed these events as part of a sketch of
"Western" or human development. Thus, instead of analyzing the unique
industrial development of England or Germany, which had "capitalistic"
aspects, by being attentive to their dramatic differences and singular histo
ries, Marx proposed a theory of capitalism that purported to uncover

essential, uniform processes in all "capitalist" social formations. His "theory of capitalism" outlined a history of Western and ultimately human development that disregarded the specificity of particular "Western" and non-Western societies. To be sure, Marx counseled that the uniform operation of capitalism would vary in different societies, even if the essential dynamics and direction of history were set by the "laws of capitalism." Marx assumed that the fact that different societies have divergent national traditions, geopolitical positions, political, cultural, familial-kinship, gender, race and ethnic structures would not seriously challenge the claim that his model of capitalism set out the essential dynamics and direction of human history.

In my view, this was a serious mistake. Even if one takes Marx's model of capitalism to be useful for analyzing nineteenth-century dynamics of socioeconomic change, I believe that the immense sociohistorical differences among European and Anglo-American societies and between them and non-Western societies would affect seriously the form and functioning of industrializing dynamics. If we assume that individual societies evolve their own unique configurations and historical trajectories, social analysis would be well advised, both as a matter of empirical-analytical adequacy and practical-moral and political advantage, to proceed in a more event-based, historical manner rather than from the heights of general theory.

The Eurocentrism of these grand narratives has been exposed (e.g. Baudrillard 1975; Said 1979; R. Young 1990). Human history in these modernist tales really meant Western history. NonWestern societies were relegated to a marginal position in past, present, and future history; their fate was presumed to be tied to that of Europe and the United States. The West, in these stories, was the principal agent of history; it showed the future to all of humanity. Behind this conceit was the arrogance of the western theorists, with their claim that the Western breakthrough to "modernity" carried world historical significance. The great modernists claimed not only that Western modernity unleashed processes that would have world impact, but also that modernization contained universally valid forms of life (e.g., science, bureaucracy, socialism, organic solidarity, secularism). Not much effort is required to grasp that behind the aggrandizing intellectualism of the modernists were the expansionist politics of the age of colonialism (e.g., Said 1979; Young 1990).

These grand narratives seem to bear the mark of their own national origin. They contain an element of national chauvinism. These modern theorists projected their own nations' unique development and conflicts onto the globe as if their particular national pattern were of world historical importance. These totalizing conceptual strategies that attempted to sketch a world historical story seem today naive and misguided. The grand narratives of industrialization, modernization, secularization, democratization, these sweeping stories that presume to uncover a uniform social process in a multitude of different societies, these stories with their simplistic binary schemes (e.g. Tonnies's *Gemeinshaft* to *Gesellschaft*, Durkheim's mechanical to organic solidarity) which purport to relate a story of change over hundreds of years, should be abandoned. They repress important differences between societies; they perpetuate Western-world hegemonic aspirations and national chauvinistic wishes.

Although I believe we should abandon the great modernist narratives, general stories are still needed. This is so because in all societies there occur certain events and developments that prompt highly charged social, moral, and political conflicts. The various parties to these conflicts frequently place them in broad narrative frameworks. In order to imbue an event with national moral and political significance or to legitimate a specific social agenda, social narratives may be fashioned that link the event to the larger history and fate of their society or humanity. This process is clear, for example, in the case of the AIDS epidemic: the spread of HIV in the United States occasioned social discourses that relate a fairly broad story of the failure of the "sexual revolution" or, indeed, the failure of a liberal, permissive society (see chapter 8, this volume; Sontag 1988; Watney 1987). The construction of broad social narratives by theorists still has an important role.

These narratives can offer critical views of the past, present, and future; they can present critical alternatives to current dominant perspectives; they can provide symbolic cultural resources on which groups can draw in order to redefine themselves, their social situation, and their possible future. I consider exemplary of the kinds of critical social narratives I recommend, texts such as Linda Gordan's *Woman's Body, Woman's Right* (1977), which offered a critical feminist interpretation of the conflict over birth control; Jeffrey Weeks' *Coming Out: Homosexual Politics in Great Britain* (1977), which proposed a redescription of the social and historical making of the "modern homosexual"; or Barbara Ehrenreich's and Deidre English's *For Her Own Good* (1979) and Robert Bellah's *The Broken Covenant* (1975), which propose redescriptions of the present opening up new practical-moral and political standpoints. Broad social narratives that cover large chunks of time and space are quite clearly still very important.

The kind of social narratives I am recommending will depart from those of the great modernists in an additional way: such narratives abandon the centrality of the ideas of progress or decadence which have served as the unifying themes of much modern Western social thought. From *philosophes* like Condorcet or Turgot to Comte, Marx, Durkheim, and Parsons, their stories of social development are variations on the motif of human advancement. They amount to salvationist tales. In reaction to the stories of the *philosophes* and their successors, there were fashioned the great tales of lament or decadence by Rousseau, Bonald, Schiller, Weber, Simmel, Spengler, Adorno and Horkheimer. Both the modernist narratives of progress and the counter-Enlightenment motif of decadence are decidedly Eurocentric. In all cases the site of the fateful struggles of humanity is the West. Indeed national histories are important in these narratives only in so far as they exhibit a pattern of progress or decadence. These stories typically disregard the enormous social complexities and heterogeneous struggles and strains within a specific society at a specific time. They have one story to tell, which is rehearsed relentlessly on a national and world historical scale. In the end, they blend easily into powerful rhetorics of national and Eurocentric chauvinism or rhetorics of world rejection.

The great modernist stories of progress or decadence almost always operate with one-dimensional notions of domination and liberation. Ignoring actual complex conflicts and power dynamics with their ambiguous calculus of gains and losses, benefits and costs, pleasure and pain, these grand narratives frame history and social conflicts in stereotypical millenasian or apocalyptic images. For these modernists, the dynamics of domination are merely a matter of freedom lost or gained; whole strata, indeed whole epochs, are described as unfree, alienated, or repressed; large chunks of time are regarded as periods of darkness or light, freedom or tyranny. History is thought to play out a unidimensional human drama revolving around the human quest for liberation against the forces of domination.

These images of liberation and domination are often tied to essentialist concepts of the human subject (see Butler 1990; Foucault 1978; Spelman 1989; I. Young 1991). Many modernists presuppose an abstract notion of the individual whose identity or nature is fixed. This unified human subject is thought to be in a constant struggle for freedom. The forces of oppression, in this tale, aim to deny humanity's quest for liberation. Human freedom is identified with the realization of human nature. Most modernist social narratives are underpinned by these notions of progress, liberation, domination, and the idea of a human subject who is oppressed and striving for emancipation. As an obvious example, in the *1844 Manuscripts* Marx relates a story of the struggle of humanity to actualize its full nature by overcoming an alienated human condition. Although this tale of humanity's struggle for self-realization is later transfigured into the struggle of the working class to overcome capitalist oppression, there is no change in the focus on a world historical drama in which "humanity" – now in the guise of the working class – resists oppression to achieve a state of freedom. This same symbolic configuration reappears in the contemporary identity politics of the black liberationist, women's, and gay movements. In all these movements, a world historical drama is depicted involving human-ity's struggle to overcome a state of domination to achieve liberation.

The problem with this narrative relates not only to the shortcomings of the categories of progress, to the flattened out concepts of domination and liberation, as I have already stated, but also to the concept of the human subject that is assumed. Although Marxists, feminists, or gay liberationists may have abandoned the essentialist strategy of speaking of humanity as if this referred to a fixed unchanging essence across all times and places, many of them continue to appeal to the agency of women, blacks, homosexuals or the working class. Yet these categories are no more fixed and unchang-ing or uniform in their meaning than the concept of humanity. Without rehearsing an argument that is now being played out with a vengeance among people of color, feminists, and gay and lesbian intellectuals, I believe that the language of agency, whether it be that of womanhood or the working class, is viewed by many parties to these debates as normative (e.g. Spelman 1988).

For example, some feminists have criticized an essentialist discourse – both androcentric and gynocentric – of gender that posits a bipolar gender order composed of a fixed universal "man" and "woman." Such agentic concepts are understood as social constructions in which the discourse of gender, including the feminist discourse, is itself a part of the will to shape a gendered human order. The discourse of gender is tied to ongoing strug-gles to assign gender identities and social roles to human bodies. Womanhood and manhood are seen as neither a natural fact – nor a settled social fact but part of a ceaseless, contested struggle among various groups to establish a gender ordering of human affairs (see the essays collected in Nicholson 1990). Therefore those who appeal to the agency of women or homosexuals or African-Americans intend to become part of the clash of interests struggling to shape a system of identity, normative order, and power. Discourses that use categories such as woman, man, gay, black American, and white American need to be seen as social forces embodying the will to shape a gender, racial, and sexual order; they seek to inscribe in our bodies, specific kinds of desires, expectations, and social identities.

My point is not that such categories of identity should not be used but that we need, first of all, to recognize their socially efficacious character. Although they are attached to a discourse of truth, they are inextricably entangled in the very constitution of identities, normative orders, and power relations. Secondly, we must be aware that just as there is no "humanity" that acts as an agent (because humans exist always as particular national or tribal, gendered or aged, religious or ethnic beings), the same is true with respect to "women" or "blacks" or "homosexuals." These categories do not have a uniform meaning and social import across different societies or even within any given society. For example, same-sex intimacies do not carry an essentially fixed and common meaning across different histories. As many historians have argued compellingly, the concept of homosexuality and "the homosexual" exhibit historically and culturally specific meanings that cannot be applied to all experiences of same-sex intimacies (e.g. Foucault 1978; Halperin 1989; Katz 1983; Weeks 1977; Williams 1986). Moreover, even within a given society at a specific historical juncture, these categories of identity and agency (woman, man, homosexual, black American) acquire diverse meanings but do so, in part, because such identity categories always combine in highly idiosyncratic and diverse ways. Just as individuals are not simply instances of the abstraction "humanity," we are not embodiments of the abstractions of woman or man. Even within the contemporary United States, "woman" does not have a uniform meaning. It varies by ethnic, racial, religious, or class status as well as by factors relating to sexual orientation, age, or regional characteristics. There is no reason to believe that a middle-class southern heterosexual Methodist woman is going to share a common experience or even common gender interests with a northern working-class Jewish lesbian. It is equally naive to assume that whatever gender commonalities they do share will override other divergent interests and values.

This argument suggests, of course, that the experience of oppression and liberation is not flat or unidimensional. Just as an individual's identity is varied in innumerable ways, his or her experience of self as empowered or dis-empowered will be similarly multidimensional. This can best be articulated by shifting from an essentialist language of self and agency to conceiving of the self as having multiple and contradictory identities, community affiliations, and social interests. Our social narratives should be attentive to this concept of multiple identities; our stories should replace the flat, unidimensional language of domination and liberation with a multivocal notion of multiple, heterogeneous struggles and a many-sided experience of empowerment and disempowerment.

Insofar as "postmodern" social narratives are seen as narratives with all the rhetorical, aesthetic, moral, ideological, and philosophical aspects characteristic of all storytelling, their social role would have to be acknowledged explicitly. "Postmodern" social analyses amount to stories about society that carry moral, social, and ideological significance.

The kind of social narratives I am arguing for would do more than acknowledge their moral and social character; they would take this moral dimension as a site for a more elaborated analysis. I believe that there are fruitful possibilities here for sociological theorists to shift their reflexive analytical focus from metatheoretical foundational concerns to practical-moral ones (cf. Bellah et al. 1985; Rosaldo 1989). In other words, I am urging that the effort theorists have invested in foundational, general theorizing, an effort which has yielded so little and has cost us so dearly, be shifted in part to moral or ethical analysis.

Needless to say, I am not counseling a shift to foundational moral theory or to the search for universal values or standards of justification. I wish to endorse a pragmatic, socially informed moral analysis. From such a standpoint, it would not be sufficient simply to invoke general values (e.g., freedom, democracy, solidarity, order, material comfort, pleasure) or moral imperatives (e.g., individuals should be treated with respect or dignity or should be treated as ends in themselves) either to justify or to criticize current social arrangements or to recommend changes. Social criticism should go beyond pointing to the deficiencies of current social realities from some general moral standpoint. We should be compelled to argue out a standpoint through an analysis that is socially informed and pragmatic. The social critic has a responsibility, it seems to me, to not only say what is wrong with current realities in some general way but to make his/her critique as specific as possible so as to make it socially relevant. Similarly, the critic should outline the social changes desired and what consequences follow for the individual and society. Again, this forces social criticism to be potentially socially useful to (say) policy makers, activists, legislators. It also makes theorists more accountable for their criticisms.

Finally, insofar as the social critic cannot appeal to transcendent or universal moral standards to justify his or her moral standpoint, critique must be justified by an appeal to "local" values or traditions. Lacking a transcendental move, the "postmodern" critic must be satisfied with local justifications of those social forms of life he/she advocates. The justification will perhaps take the form of endorsing a specific social arrangement because it promotes particular social values that are valued by certain specific communities. This kind of pragmatic moral argumentation must be informed by a sociological understanding that allows one to analyze the impact of proposed changes on individuals and society. For example, a postmodern feminist critique of gender arrangements should do more than document and criticize gender inequalities and discrimination against women from a moral standpoint that values freedom and equality. It also would show what a gender order of equality in specific social domains would be like and what social impact such changes towards gender equality would have. In addition, feminist critique in a postmodern mode would appeal to specific traditions, practices, and values to justify these change.

Recognizing that social narratives have a socially effective or productive character, we would not try to purge them of this character but would try to acknowledge it and, indeed, to seize it as a fruitful source of an elaborated social reason. How so? Not, as I have said, by simply offering a general criticism or defense of social forms from the high ground of some abstract moral values or standpoint. And certainly not by trying to ground one's moral standpoint by appeal to some objective universal element (e.g., nature, God, natural law). Rather, I would recommend a pragmatic, socially informed moral analysis in which the critic defends social arrangements by analyzing their individual and social consequences in light of specific traditions, values, and practices.

Theorists would become advocates. We would be advocates, however, of a slightly different sort from (say) public officials or social activists. Unlike the advocacy of these partisans, which typically might take the form of moral or national appeals, or the presentation of documents or data, or appeals to particular social interests, the advocacy of theorists would take the form of elaborated social and moral argumentation over consequences and social values. Like other partisans, we would be advocates for a way of life, but unlike them, we would be compelled to produce elaborated social and moral discourses. As theorists would be in a role of encouraging moral public discussion; we would be catalysts for public moral and social debate. We would be advocates, but not narrow partisans or politicos. Our value would be both in providing socially informed analyses that would be useful to partisans and in promoting an uncoerced public moral discussion in the face of various partisans who repeatedly act to restrict such elaborated discourse. We would become defenders of an elaborated reason against the partisans of closure and orthodoxy, and of all those who try to circumvent open public moral debate by partisan or foundational appeals.

Conclusion

Sociological theory, in my view, has become insular and irrelevant to all but theory specialists. At least in part, this insularity is connected to a foundationalist project that has been at the center of much modern Western social thought. Ironically, the institutional successes of sociology have been accompanied by the gradual obtuseness of sociological theory. Today, sociological theorists are largely entangled in metatheoretical disputes revolving around the search for a general, universal grounded science of society.

I have suggested some reasons for why there is little likelihood of navigating out of this morass. Moreover, although the foundationist project may have had beneficial practical significance from the eighteenth century through the latter part of the nineteenth century in Europe and the United States, which was linked to legitimating "modernity" against its critics, it has lost most of its social benefits, at least in the contemporary United States and perhaps in many western European nations. The argument that the foundational project is important for the defense of certain desirable social arrangements can hardly be seriously entertained given the social and intellectual insularity of disciplinary theory. I do not doubt that the foundational, totalizing theoretical project might still be valuable for promoting a reflexive, critical reason. Yet the same intellectual and social values can be cultivated just as easily in a "postmodern" culture.

Under the banner of postmodernism, I have pressed for a major reorientation of sociological theory. To be revitalized, theory must be reconnected in integral ways to ongoing national public moral and political debates and social conflicts. This vital tie between theorizing and public life accounts for the continuing attractiveness of classical social theory, but that connection has been broken. To reestablish that tie I have urged that sociological theory reaffirm a core concept of itself as a social narrative with a moral intent. I have proposed, however, that a postmodern social narrative should depart in certain important ways from those of the great modernists. I recommend an event-based, nation and international-based narrative. Postmodern narratives would discard or seriously reexamine the core modernist concepts such as progress, liberation and humanity. The basic postmodern concepts will revolve around the notion of a self with multiple identities and group affiliations, which is entangled in heterogeneous struggles with multisided possibilities for empowerment.

Finally, postmodern narratives would acknowledge their practical-moral significance. Moral analysis would become a part of an elaborated social reason. Theorists would become advocates, abandoning the increasingly cynical, unbelievable guise of objective, value-neutral scientists. We would become advocates but not narrow partisans or activists. Our broader social significance would lie in encouraging unencumbered open public moral and social debate and in deepening the notion of public discourse. We would be a catalyst for the public to think seriously of moral and social concerns.

3

Relativizing sociology: the challenge of cultural studies

The relationship between sociology and cultural studies resists a simple or global description, whether it be one of antagonism or kinship. Nevertheless, I wish to emphasize the ways the latter challenges the former. I intend to do this for the purpose of relativizing sociology as a discourse of "the social." Approaching sociology as a local practice, viewing its conceptual strategies and thematic perspectives as indicative of a particular tradition rather than as a universal language of the social, is, I am wagering, useful in that it allows us to become aware of the singular discursive organization of sociology, for example, to have its disciplinary silences and conventions exposed. I am to induce a certain critical disengagement from the culture of sociology in order to imagine new disciplinary possibilities for social knowledge. Perhaps such a "therapeutic" exercise might permit us to project other ways we might wish to frame "the self" and "the social." If the therapeutic model is to be believed, it is only by making us aware of unconscious compulsions and unnecessary constraints that change is possible.

I intend then to play off "cultural studies" against "sociology" not to suggest that the former is better in the sense of right or true. I do not believe this. I do believe though that in figuring sociology as a local, not a universal practice, in reading its discursive conventions as a tradition (or multiple traditions) not the very language of the social universe, we gain a critical attitude towards this discipline. I am of the opinion that critique and change is especially pressing at this juncture in sociology's disciplinary history. Much sociology seems to be drifting into a deadening insularity, often unseen and without protest, as many sociologists still march under the triumphant banner of expertise or hold to an indubitable faith in the Enlightenment. Perhaps an engagement with alternative social knowledges such as cultural studies might allow sociology to have its theoretical and

political unconscious exposed in ways troubling enough to risk a disciplinary self-examination and reformation.

Admittedly, I have framed this discussion in a suspiciously essentializing
way. Such suspicions can perhaps be lessened if I insist that terms such as
sociology or cultural studies have no right or correct way of being referenced. Their heterogeneity, their instability, and the surplus of meanings
they accrue is, I think, inescapable. As I now see such matters, conceptual
moves gain whatever legitimacy they manage by virtue of what they allow
us to do or say assuming a purpose at hand in a particular conversation at
a precise time and place. There is no right or wrong, true or false way of
fixing conceptual meaning, only different ways, the value or credibility of
any specific way being related to the purpose at hand in a particular
conversation governed by particular conventions regarding the authorization of knowledge. So, to turn to the conversation at hand, I merely wish
to recommend, with no legitimacy claimed beyond this conversation and
its purpose, that it might be useful at least to those of us who care about
the kinds of issues this conversation raises, to think of cultural studies as
different in some important ways from at least much of what passes for the
central traditions and practices of at least "American sociology."

A word is surely in order regarding my usage of the terms "cultural
studies" and "sociology." Is it not foolish or at least contradictory to speak
of such a binary? After all, are not many cultural studies practitioners sociologists and do not many sociologists claim to be doing cultural studies?
True enough. And yet I still wish to figure an opposition or at least highlight stress points. How is this possible? Would such a positioning gain
plausibility if by cultural studies I intend the work of the Birmingham
Centre for Contemporary Cultural Studies and by sociology I mean the
research and discourses produced by American sociologists, work which is
largely organized around disciplinary area specialties and which has largely
been untouched by a British or European tradition of cultural studies?
Additionally, if I note that cultural studies in the past decade has become
increasingly uncoupled from sociology, especially in Australia (where academic knowledges are less organized around sharply demarcated disciplines) and in the United States (where cultural studies is housed primarily
in the humanities or in new interdisciplinary programs such as
"communications"), does the figuring of a critical tension between cultural
studies and sociology accrue credibility? Let's continue.

To repeat, I will be using the term cultural studies in a very specific and
narrow way. It will refer to the work of the Birmingham Centre for
Contemporary Cultural Studies (est. 1964) and to work inspired by the
Centre. Initially, I propose to describe certain general features of this tradi-

tion of cultural studies. I then turn to the American context since this is where, I think it is fair to say, cultural studies in the restricted sense I am using this term is being elaborated in ways that make for intriguing clashes with dominant disciplinary knowledges.

If we follow what is by now a conventional narrative, British cultural studies "originated" in the writings of Raymond Williams (1958, 1961, 1962) and Richard Hoggart (1957). Their work challenged a dominant tradition in the humanities in postwar England. Culture had been approached as literary and artistic texts and practices to be analyzed in terms of general aesthetic standards. Judged by presumed universal aesthetic values or ideals, popular cultures were viewed as inferior, often interpreted as a sign of the degrading effects of mass communication and commercialization.

Hoggart and Williams made two critical moves. First, they argued that literary-aesthetic culture the realm of what was considered serious literature, art, and music – is simply one expression of culture.[1] The latter refers to a wide range of meanings and practices that make up social life. "Culture" was said to comprehend the lived experiences of all individuals and groups as manifested in language, everyday mores and behaviors, ideologies, and the spectrum of texts and representations described by the terms literature, art, knowledge, and religion. Thus, in *The Uses of Literacy* Hoggart proposed to trace the changing culture of the English working class. Combining memoir and historical sociology, Hoggart analyzed not only the music or the popular literature of the working class but everyday linguistic styles, family and neighborhood dynamics, and cognitive frameworks that define "private" and "public" and local and cosmopolitan. Similarly in *Culture and Society* (1958) Williams not only traced images of "culture and society" in the literary history of modern England; he related aesthetic culture to a broader pattern of cultural meanings. This turn away from a literary-textual approach to a nonreductionist social analysis of culture is developed by Williams in *The Long Revolution* (1961). This text traces the rise of the novel and the theatre in modern England as part of the formation of a text-based, literate public sphere. Stuart Hall comments on the significance of this text. "It shifted the whole ground of debate from a literary-moral to an anthropological definition of culture. But it defined the latter now as the 'whole process' by means of which meanings and definitions are socially constructed and historically transformed, with literature and art as only one . . . kind of social communication" (Hall 1980a: 19).

Enlarging the concept of culture to include the practices and meanings of everyday life was coupled to a second important move by Hoggart and

Williams: All cultural expressions were to be analyzed in relation to a social context of institutions, power relations, and history. Thus, in an important programmatic statement on cultural analysis, Williams insisted that "the analysis of culture . . . is the clarification of the meanings and values implicit and explicit in a particular way of life . . . Such analysis will include . . . the organization of production, the structure of the family, [and] the structure of institutions" (1961: 42). Thus, in *The Long Revolution*, Williams analyzed English literary culture in relation to a "materialist" understanding of broad social changes in education and the mass media. Similarly, in *The Uses of Literacy*, Hoggart situated working class cultural practices in class-structured social settings, for example, in pubs, clubs, households and neighborhoods. Hoggart's judgement of the changes in working class culture was decidedly mixed, and evidenced a nostalgic strain, but he insisted on situating cultural meanings in their actual social setting – a lesson exquisitely made by another major inspirational figure of cultural studies, E. P. Thompson (1963).

The first generation of British cultural studies made everyday life an object of cultural analysis. Cultural studies could aspire to go beyond aesthetic-literary criticism to become a critical social theory. Nevertheless, Williams and Hoggart were primarily literary critics and their analysis of culture, however brilliant, only pointed towards the articulation of culture and society.

I take it as quite important that the second generation who shaped British cultural studies were not literary critics but chiefly sociologists (e.g., Stuart Hall, David Morley, Dorothy Hobson, Paul Willis, Phil Cohen, Dick Hebdige, Ian Chambers, Angela McRobbie; see the comments by Hall 1980a: 20-26). They took over the project of the former generation, what Stuart Hall (1980a: 25) once called a "complex marxism" – marxist less by any commitment to economism or the reign of class analysis than by a certain aspiration to grasp the formation of contemporary societies, by an insistence that cultural meanings are not free floating but must be contextualized in relations of power, and by a critical intent to intervene into contemporary public life. Yet the second generation were critical of the humanistic, anti-theoretical marxism of Williams and Thompson. On the one hand, Stuart Hall and his colleagues drew heavily from French structuralism insisting on a non-intentionalist, semiotic framing of cultural meanings. On the other hand, culture was not to be reduced to texts and representations but to include social practices and institutional structures anchored in history and analyzed in relation to class, gender, racial, or national dynamics. The work of Althusser (1971) and Gramsci (1971), and to a lesser extent Foucault, was in this regard pivotal in broadening the concept of culture while avoiding either an idealist (via structuralism) or materialist (via marxism) reductionism. Similarly, in the spirit of Althusser and Gramsci, the second generation of cultural social critics aimed to pre- serve a concept of a social whole while disavowing Hegelian notions of an expressive totality. They advanced the idea of "the social" as a conjunctural articulated order. Culture was seen as part of the daily reproduction of social life, to be analyzed at the level of meaning, social structure, power rela- tions, and history. Much like the Frankfurt School, the second generation of cultural studies sought a theoretical standpoint, roughly marxist, which transcended the idealism/materialism, agency/structure, and base/super- structure dualisms. This was to be a social perspective which imagined society as articulated in various practices and structures – none of which, in principle, was assumed to be casually determining in the last instance.

Crossing the Atlantic, it is perhaps noteworthy that what we might call a British-inspired movement of American cultural studies has been housed primarily in the humanities. Literary theorists have decisively shaped the transplantation of British cultural studies in the United States. The result is that American cultural studies has been characterized by a strong move towards textualizing the social (e.g., Byars 1991; Hall 1992; Murdock 1989; O'Connor 1989). However, this textualizing strain has been checked, to some extent, by an on-going commitment to marxism. We might situate cultural studies in the United States as the creation of an academic left responding in part to the problematization of marxism engendered by the end of communism and the disenchantment with Eurosocialism and to the critique of marxism by the discourses of the new social movements, e.g., feminism, lesbian and gay studies, lesbian-feminism, and anti-racist theor- izing. Yet while certain prominent currents of poststructural and post- modern theorizing, which have lately been associated with these new social movements have effectively abandoned marxism, most versions of cultural studies have not – though it must be said that the defense of marxism is often little more than a vague appeal to the importance of the economy or class rather than the deployment of marxism as a theoretical standpoint (Hall 1990). The articulation of marxism and semiotic analysis, as David Morley (1992: 4–5) laments, has been decidedly feeble, often hardly more than a rhetorical gesture. What most versions of British and British inspired American cultural studies seem to share is an ideal of rethinking marxism in light of new critical social knowledges such as feminism or poststructuralism.

Let me suggest one final way of positioning cultural studies. In the States – perhaps less so in Britain or Australia – cultural studies (again, in the narrow way I am using this term) is, in part, a response to the fracturing of the left in the 1970s and 1980s into quasi-ethnic oppositional communities of feminists, queers, African-Americans, and so on. Cultural studies perhaps formed (in the late 1980s) with the hope that it might serve as something of a common critical approach uniting into a progressive block a fractured left and a left divided between defenders of a neo-marxist socialist politics and advocates of a post-marxist identity based politics. Claiming a more friendly relation to marxism than many feminists or queers or those marching under the banner of postmodernism – while intending to absorb aspects of these left critiques of marxism – cultural studies seems at times to imagine itself as the heir to the tradition of Western marxism.

Cultural studies resists – or so its practitioners claim – any definitive description because its form and character is self-consciously conjectural or context-specific. Nevertheless, for those who would benefit from a definition that resonates broadly with my general description, I offer the one provided by the editors of *Cultural Studies*:

Cultural studies is an interdisciplinary, transdisciplinary, and sometimes counter-disciplinary field that operates in the tensions between its tendencies to embrace both a broad anthropological and a more narrowly humanistic conception of culture . . . It is typically interpretive and evaluative in its methodologies, but unlike traditional humanism it rejects the exclusive equation of culture with high culture and argues that all forms of cultural production need to be studied in relation to other cultural practices and to social and historical structures. Cultural studies is thus committed to the study of the entire range of a society's arts, beliefs, institutions, and communicative practices. (Grossberg et al. 1992: 4)

Having sketched at least a rough working language in which to speak of cultural studies, I want to briefly and pointedly comment on three ways cultural studies challenges American sociology.

Imagining the social

To begin, I intend to say something about cultural studies as a way of framing the social that departs in important ways from at least certain prominent conventions in American sociology. I should like, however, to have an initial point at least registered. Sociology has, I think, assumed a monopoly on so called systematic analyses of society. Sociologists claim to offer the only systematically empirical, analytical, and wholistic discourse of "the social." No other discipline can make this claim – not economics, political science, anthropology, or philosophy; nor can the social discourses which conventionally might be thought of as "political ideology," public commentary, or folk belief seriously contest sociology's monopolistic claim to furnishing systematic, wholistic social understandings. The challenge of cultural studies to sociology, at one level, is that it makes a credible claim of having provided systematic analyses of the social that are empirical and analytical and that offer perspectives on whole societies. Moreover, cultural studies, like American sociology, has its own journals, professional networks, conferences, associations, and at times institutional departments or academic affiliations. Finally, although cultural studies draws from European and American sociological traditions, it figures the social differently in some key ways from American sociology. How so?

In contrast to the dominant intellectual strains in American sociology, cultural studies has made, so to speak, the textual or, better yet, the semiotic turn (cf. Hall 1980a; Turner 1992). Social realities are approached as a field of signs, meanings, or, if you will, texts. Whether the object of analysis is television programs, films, romance novels, fashion, or subcultural practices, the social is likened to a text. This suggests a view of the social as deeply cultural or as organized by signs and meanings patterned in relations of identity and difference. Objects and behaviors are viewed as saturated with meanings that are organized by codes whose coherence is to be uncovered through disciphering their symbolic units and operation (e.g., Hall 1980b; Fiske 1982; Hartley 1982).

Textualizing society does not necessarily entail abandoning concerns of power, oppression, resistance or agency. Texts are said to have multiple and contradictory meanings. They may articulate dominant ideologies that naturalize and normalize inequalities but the contradictory meanings of texts allow for readers – audiences, spectators, producers and consumers of texts – to resist dominant ideologies or to refashion textual meanings in empowering ways. And, as many cultural analysts have reiterated, readers or interpreters of texts occupy multiple social locations and identities which engender varied, sometimes subversive, ironic readings. Moreover, texts are not approached as universes unto themselves but are conceptualized as positioned both in relation to other texts – the principle of intertextuality – and in relation to social practices and conflicts – gender-based, class-based, and so on – that produce texts and are affected by them (Dyer 1982; Hall 1992; Morley 1992; Turner 1992; Williamson 1980).

Cultural studies makes a strong semiotic turn but retains, if you will, the materialistic and agentic aspects of marxism. Texts are produced by social practices in particular institutional contexts which have histories and none of these aspects – texts, social practices, institutions, and histories – can or should be abandoned in favor of a false totalization. This is the mistake of structuralism – which totalizes the symbolic code – or of humanism – which totalizes individual choice or will – or of marxism which totalizes social structure.

American sociology, even today, has not made a semiotic turn. The dominant models of "the social" in speciality areas from demography, criminology, to the sociology of organizations or race, are either variations of humanism in which agents are imagined to willfully construct society or versions of "structuralism" which installs "social structure" as the organizing social principle or key variable, for example, social class, the market, population, structural location, or network positioning. Even the recent emergence of cultural sociology in American sociology often figures culture as discrete, isolated values, beliefs, attitudes, identities, or ideologies. If American sociologists manage, which is still exceptional, to avoid reducing culture to motivation, intentional action, ideology, or social structure, they rarely articulate a notion of a semiotic order of signs, meanings and symbolic codes (cf. Lamont and Wuthnow 1990: 287, 294). There are of course exceptions to this disavowal of culture as a symbolic or semiotic order in American sociology (e.g., Alexander 1989a, 1989b; Berger and Luckmann 1966; Gottdiener 1985; Gusfield 1981; Zerubavel 1981). Interestingly, sociologists who have made a case for a strong version of cultural sociology have often been situated in a Durkheimian and functionalist tradition which has largely been marginalized in American sociology since the late sixties (e.g., Lloyd Warner, Talcott Parsons, Edward Shils, Robert Bellah, Jeffrey Alexander). Of course, the Durkheimian and functionalist traditions were a principal source of semiotics and structuralism as well as the pioneering symbolic anthropology of Victor Turner (1967) and Mary Douglas (1966), both of whom have had little influence in American sociology.

The difference between cultural studies which has made the semiotic turn and American sociology which has not is evident in research in the area of the media and mass communication. Whereas many American sociologists have focused on content analysis aimed at identifying and quantifying discrete values and beliefs and with tracing media effects on its audiences, British cultural studies has approached television or film as an internal order of signs and meanings organized by codes and conventions. It analyzes the process of encoding or the making of meanings, the rules and conventions governing the production of media texts, their ideological role in naturalizing and normalizing the dominant meaning systems and institutions, the multiple ways individuals are positioned and defined in these texts, the multiple audiences and the varied ways media texts are decoded or interpreted and used (e.g. Fiske 1987; Hall 1980a: 117–118; Hartley 1982; Hobson 1980; Morley 1980). For example, in an early essay which engaged both the sociological literature in "deviance" and the media, Stuart Hall (1974) analyzed the social production of "political deviance."

Specifically, he sketched a perspective emphasizing the role of the media in classifying certain types of behavior, which might very well be viewed as legitimate political dissent or social protest, as deviant or "pathological." Instead of simply analyzing the manifest content of media communications, for example, identifying the frequency of word usage or manifest social values, Hall proposed a "semiological analysis" which approaches media representation as a system of discourse internally organized by "codes" and "logics-in-use" (pp. 74-75). He identifies the "majority/minority" symbolic opposition, a figure which is inflected by binaries such as normal/abnormal, moral/decadent, mature/immature, or healthy/mentally disturbed, as a chief structuring principle in British media representations at the time. Semiotic analysis, however, is not sufficient. "In the end, these different aspects of the process by which abnormal political events [political deviance] are signified must be returned to the level of the social formation, via the critical concepts of power, ideology, and conflict." (1974: 86) While deploying the Althusserian and Gramscian ideas of the ideological production of hegemonic consensus or legitimation, Hall insists on the "autonomy" of cultural analysis. The relations between semiotic orders of meanings and structural dynamics of class and state formation are never simply linear, reflective, or superstructural. While structured by power and relations of domination, cultural meanings have their own internal order; signs are always polysemic or exhibit contradictory and surplus meanings; their relations to social structure and power relations is always a matter of empirical conjuctural analysis.[2] "These issues can only be clarified only by the study of a specific [empirical] conjuncture between the different levels of practice and institution in a historical moment" (1974: 86). The point to be underlined is that the semiotic turn of cultural studies opened up new fields of social analysis, new ways of analyzing media, audiences, subcultures, dynamics of ideology, consensus making, domination, resistance, and power which have largely been absent from American sociology.

It is just a conjecture but I suspect a connection between the semiotic turn in cultural studies and its thematic shift from the more conventional social structural concerns of marxism and American sociology to a perspective featuring the centrality of symbolic production, knowledges, and cultural conflict in contemporary Western societies. I note something of a parallel with French social theory, especially the early work of Baudrillard (1975, 1981), Lyotard (1984), and Foucault (1979), each of whom broke away from the dominant traditions of marxism and sociology because, in part, they imagined postwar Europe to be undergoing major changes that rendered less compelling the standard languages and thematic perspectives of social analysis, for example, the language of class or conflict or bureaucratization.[3] In this regard, cultural studies seems to parallel French "postmodern" theory in viewing the new role of the mass media, the saturation of daily life by commerce and commodification, the new technologies of information, and the foregrounding of cultural politics as signaling perhaps a second "great transformation" in post-Renaissance Western societies.

In its re-centering of social analysis on symbolic production and politics, cultural studies is effecting a dramatic shift away from American sociology and from the marxism of the academy which has continued to look to social structure – to social class, economic dynamics, bureaucracy, occupations, status groups, market exchanges, population dynamics, and network structures, as the core categories for understanding Western societies. For example, the Foucauldian turn in British and especially American and Australian cultural studies is virtually absent in American sociology. Like Marx or Durkheim in the last century, Foucault has proposed a new way of thinking about the self, the social, and history (Seidman 1994). He has elaborated original perspectives on power, knowledge, modernization, politics, and so on. A Foucauldian perspective shifts the ground of social analysis to a focus on the making of bodies, desires, and identities, to power/knowledge regimes and to dynamics of normalization, discipline, and surveillance. A Foucauldian paradigm urges a shift from orthodox Enlightenment models of science and theory to the critical strategies of geneaology and archaeology. Foucauldian inspired social analysis has proven remarkably productive but almost all of this work has been done outside sociology e.g., Mark Poster (1990), Donna Haraway (1991), Gane and Johnson (1993), Caputo and Yount (1993), Ball (1990), Messer-Davidow et al. (1993).

I leave this section with a question: why have American sociologists resisted making the semiotic, Foucauldian turn, especially at the very moment when European theorists look to America as the key site for a potentially second great transformation of Western societies? Why have sociologists resisted the symbolic, refused the notion of a semiotic order of signs and meanings? Such questions potentially expose the epistemological and political unconscious of sociology, i.e. its boundaries and the defensive reactions that maintain such borders.

Imagining the self

A second site of difference between cultural studies and American sociology relates to the theorization of the "self" or individual agency. My interest is less the question of whether agency is addressed or whether, for example, action is approached in "instrumental" or "normative" terms or how agency can be articulated at a "micro" and "macro" level, then core assumptions about the individual as a subject of knowledge, society, and history.

Put simply and in a very general way, a good deal of American sociology assumes the individual as a foundation of social life and figures the self as an internally coherent, rationally calculating agent. Cultural studies departs from these assumptions by imagining the individual as socially produced; as occupying multiple, contradictory psychic and social positions or identities; and by figuring the self as influenced by unconscious processes.

Classical sociology assumed its shape in part as a critique of the methodological individualism and essentialism of classical political economy and much of early modern liberalism and rationalism. We might recall Marx's critique of the presocially constituted subject in *The German Ideology* and more relentlessly in the *Grundrisse*. Similarly, I remind you of Durkheim's critique of Spencer, the English liberal economists and French humanists for anchoring their theories of knowledge and society in a presocial essential self. Durkheim argued that the individual was a social and historical event and seemed to function more as a symbolic or religious idea in Western modernity than a concrete experiential reality.

As we survey contemporary American sociology, many of its major paradigms such as exchange theory, conflict sociology, rational choice, symbolic interactionism, or network analysis, posit a subject of knowledge and agent of action that is presocially formed – for example, assumed to be a self oriented to maximize pleasure and minimize pain; assumed to be a rationally calculating subject; and assumed to be a subject that is naturally sexed as male or female and naturally sexual, indeed naturally and normatively heterosexual. This is a self who is figured as ego-and-present-centered and programmed (seemingly by nature) to be goal-directed, strategically rational, and social, i.e. compelled to interact or engage in social exchange. Propelled by external forces (e.g., class position, market position, the division of labor, or social role), or driven by conscious ego needs or by discrete interests, values and beliefs, this is a self that dwells and navigates on the social surface. American sociology appears to have forgotten or to have abandoned its original impulse as a critique of the notion of a presocial self and a critique of the idea of "society" as a creation of a conscious rational subject.

In this regard, cultural studies signals a return to the European classical social theorists who aimed to furnish a sociohistorical account of the making-of-the-subject and to expose a social and political unconsciousness in the movement of individuals, societies and histories. Cultural studies is less a literal return to the European classics than an effort to re-articulate the classical critique by drawing on the contemporary work of Althusser, Gramsci, Barthes, Foucault, feminists and psychoanalysts, especially Lacan.

In both British and American cultural studies, social accounts of the self or subject lean heavily, though by no means exclusively, on either discursive or psychoanalytic narratives. For example, drawing on Althusser's argument that ideology interpellates selves, British media studies have empirically analyzed the ways television, film, advertisements or fashion, define and position a self. Mass media discourses do not simply influence the attitudes, values or behaviors of audiences but construct the self in a normative and normalizing way, for example, as a masculine gendered self or a British national self. The encoding/decoding paradigm of media studies, still perhaps a dominant paradigm despite revisions, is premised on the Althusserian concept of ideology as a social practice and discourse whose force depends on a process of interpellation (Hall 1980a; Hartley 1982; Morley 1992; Williamson 1980). The self, for example, the consumer or audience, is viewed as a social production, as a subject formed, in part, through the ways he is inscribed in discourses and practices. However, because the self is always interpellated in many discourses and practices, she is said to occupy contradictory psychic and social positions and identities – in principle, making possible opposition to dominant ideologies. Whether the focus is encoding processes in the media, reception studies or subcultural analyses, the self is assumed to be socially and historically produced and positioned in contradictory ways to structures of dominance and hierarchy.

A striking feature of cultural studies, especially in strains of American cultural studies influenced by feminism and film theory, is its turn to psychoanalytic theory to explain the formation of subjectivity (e.g., Penley 1992; Radway 1984; Bhabha 1992; Curti 1992). The psychoanalytic turn is particularly impressive if the boundaries between cultural studies and poststructural analysis are blurred (e.g., Butler 1990; De Lauretis 1987; Cornell 1992). I can do no more than briefly remark on this turn to psychoanalysis and perhaps suggest what recommends it for sociology.

Why psychoanalytic theory as a key resource for feminism and cultural studies? At least one answer is that psychoanalytic theory has provided one of the few vocabularies describing the *social formation* of subjectivity. Accordingly, psychoanalytical theory makes possible an explanation of gender identity, male domination, and sexuality which focuses on the interplay between psyche and society and on intrapsychic dynamics. Psychoanalytic theory is a social theory in that at least both object relations (see Chodorow 1978; Greenberg and Mitchell 1983) and Lacanian theory (See Grosz 1990) that hold the key events in the making of subjectivity and selves are social. Whereas object relations theory revolves around a notion of introjected social relations, Lacanian theory speaks of the introduction of the human infant into the realm of language and the symbolic – a process that elicits the mirror phase, castration fears, and the appropriation or not of the phallus which, for Lacan, are the primary moments in self formation. The power of psychoanalytic theory pivots on the presumption of the unconscious, a concept that in its broadest sense refers not only to repressed wishes and forbidden desires but to primary processes such as identification, introjection, projection, transference, or oedipal conflicts. Indeed, psychoanalysis is largely a theory which intends to expose the logic of the unconscious, to trace its voices as they surface in disguised form in the conscious life of the individual and the group. It is the appeal to an unconscious logic which is its singular contribution, a logic that explains the formation of a subject yet decenters it. Psychoanalytic theory views the self as formed in the matrix of language and communication; it frames a subject who is internally fractured and divided; this is a self driven by unconscious desires, wishes and fears. Social analysts have drawn on psychoanalytic theory to explain the formation of gender binary concepts and heteronormativity (e.g., Butler 1990; Chodorow 1978; De Lauretis 1994; Coward and Ellis 1977; Mitchell 1974; Rose 1986); to grasp the power of mass culture by interpreting the relation between the self and mass culture as reiterating primary psychological processes relating for example to preoedipal and oedipal dynamics (e.g., Radway 1992). Finally, Lacanian psychoanalysis has contested key Western humanistic assumptions regarding a natural, internally unified, ego-and-present centered subject who rationally produces knowledge, social life, and history (Grosz 1990).

Psychoanalysis no less than marxism or classical sociology proposes a depth social theoretical logic for explaining the formation of selves and social life. If Marx can be said to have exposed the unconscious social logic of capital through the labor theory of value, price theory, the theory of surplus value, capital accumulation, the law or profit and its decline – a social logic which proceeds behind the backs of agents – psychoanalysis can be said to have furnished an analogous social logic explaining the inter-subjective formation of subjectivity. Instead of the unconscious workings of capital, psychoanalysis exposes the operation of primary processes such as oedipal conflicts and castration complexes, shifts from the Real to the Symbolic, the mirror phase, dynamics of multiple identification, regression, narcissism, and so on to make sense of the formation of subjectivity, gender, sexuality, and some of the unconscious psychological and intersubjective aspects of group life. Psychoanalysis offers a language of an intricate, dense, psychic and intersubjective life, a life of fantasies, wishes, fears, shames, desires, idealizations, identifications, that cannot be comprehended by a vocabulary of interests, means-ends rationality, cost-benefit calculations, need dispositions, or values or by the surface psychologies of behaviorism, cognitivism, or symbolic interactionism. Only psychoanalytic theory posits an unconscious life that shapes and impels the willfulness of an ego-present-centered self, connecting selves to objects, roles, identities, people, relations, groups, and institutions in ways that we are often unaware of yet mighty powerful in their operation and effect.

Psychoanalytic theory has shown its productiveness as a theory of subjectivity, as a theory of gender and sexuality, as an account via primary processes of the relation between the mass media and the individual, as a way of imagining multiple identities and as a challenge to western humanism. Why have sociologists refused any serious engagement with psychoanalytic theory? Why have American sociologists who purport to aspire to social accounts of the self assume a presocial subject or have recourse to minimal, surface concepts of the self as ego-and-present centered, as driven by discrete needs and interests, and as navigating the world by deploying a strategic means/ends rationality? What is it about sociology that operates to refuse the unconscious? What disciplinary resistances or what defensive reaction formations structure sociological practices?

Imagining social knowledge

A third and final point of difference that I wish to emphasize between cultural studies and American sociology pertains to general approaches to knowledge and conceptions of the role of the academic intellectual. As these issues have been a topic of much dispute within American sociology in this century, and as we could describe a range of positions cultural studies holds on this issue, my comments will aim to draw out differences by contrasting particular, though prominent, strains within both cultural studies and American sociology.

Cultural studies aims to speak about the social in a language that is no less empirical and explanatory than sociology. Indeed, in the case of British cultural studies, as I previously mentioned, many of its chief figures have been sociologists who have deliberately and positively drawn on both the European and American traditions of sociology (see Hall 1980a). Even where cultural studies departs from dominant American sociological conventions of the empirical, for example in their turn to semiotic and symbolic analysis, such studies are no less empirical in that they are argued through appeals to documentary evidence or, in the case of ethnographies, lived experience (Willis 1980). There are, moreover, genres of cultural studies, especially in the United States where such work is often housed in departments of English, film, or communication, which are not empirical in the sense of relying on ethnography, interviews, observation, archival research, statistical analysis or standard historiography. I am thinking of studies which analyze literary texts or films such as Spike Lee's *Malcolm X* or advertisements for the purpose of uncovering cultural codes, for example, knowledges or symbolic logics that frame bodies in relation to a binary gender order or that construct racialized identities (e.g. Dyson 1995) or code identity in a civilizational binary of Orient/Occident (e.g., Said 1978). These studies proceed on the assumption that the discovery of such "textual" codes renders them sites for "empirical" social analysis as well as exposes them as social forces in their own right.[4] Such cultural/textual studies are no less empirical than the media studies of British cultural sociologists or the quantitative studies of social structure by American sociologists. They are *differently* empirical but that does not make textual analysis any less able to speak "empirically" about gender, sexuality, race, the state, nationalism, and so on.[5]

Cultural studies departs from American sociology not in being non-empirical or nonanalytical. In fact, both discursive formations, especially as practitioners of cultural studies have been trained as, or seriously influenced by, sociologists or historians, share many of the same conventions of the empirical as markers of the real and the true. Perhaps an argument could be made that cultural studies gravitates towards historical, contextualizing, and interpretive styles of empirical social analysis whereas much of American sociology is structural and quantitative. Even if this claim is credible, these are minor differences in comparison to what I take to be a major difference: Cultural studies, or at least a prominent strain in it, views social knowledge as having value in so far as it contributes to shaping the outcome of public conflicts. Cultural studies abandons the standpoint of value neutrality to legitimate its knowledges; it acknowledges and announces that its concepts and perspectives are deliberately angled to moral and political concerns and gain their warrant less from claims about the progress of science and social enlightenment than by its practical-moral and political aims. A dominant strain of cultural studies defines the social knowledges it produces as political, as having value by virtue of its intellectual interventions into everyday struggles for social justice.

To the extent that cultural studies aspires to craft academic knowledges in relation to social movements and public conflicts, the positioning of the academic intellectual is somewhat at odds with those sociologists who frame the academic intellectual as an objective, morally and politically detached scientist. We might say, risking a somewhat over used term, that cultural studies imagines the academic as a public intellectual. Recall that two of the key figures in the founding of British cultural studies, Richard Hoggart and Raymond Williams, taught for most of their careers as adult education tutors for a mostly working-class student body. Unlike some of their successors, they never abandoned a belief that the working class and indeed the Labour Party were the driving force for any progressive change in Britain. Their successors may have had more conventional academic careers, and their faith in the working class is surely less certain, but their work is no less intended to engage current public conflicts. From the numerous studies of popular subcultural and gender resistance inspired by E. P. Thompson's (1963) monumental effort to recover an indigenous and autonomous working class culture (Chambers 1985, 1986; Cohen 1980; Hebdige 1979; McRobbie and Garber 1976), to studies which expose the class, race, and gender structuring and ideological role of the media (e.g., Morley 1992; Hobson 1980), to sociologically informed political critique such as Hall's critical rethinking of Thatcherism as a mode of right wing politics (1988), to the establishment of the Institute for Social Policy in 1987 at Griffith University in Australia inspired by the CCCS, cultural studies has aspired to be a politically engaged academic practice.

Stuart Hall (1992) has at times evoked Gramsci's concept of the "organic intellectual" to describe an ideal (p. 281). Such "organic intellectuals," though academic and often lodged in a particular discipline, intend to draw on disciplinary knowledges as a resource to speak to the key public conflicts of the day. Parallelling Foucault's notion of the local intellectual, the organic intellectual aims less to propose grand theories and make weighty pronouncements about the evolution of humanity than is a type of intellectual who is connected to specific groups, movements or struggles and fashions her work as public interventions. The organic intellectual speaks less from the general standpoint of humanity and human justice than from a specific social location addressing events or developments at a particular historical conjuncture. The organic intellectual is always socially and politically situated and it is precisely this embeddedness that motivates public engagement and makes possible an effective public intervention.

American sociology has never spoken with one voice on the matter of knowledge and the role of the academic intellectual. This is a discipline that claims not only Weber and Durkheim and the rhetoric of value neutrality but Marx and W. E. B. Du Bois, Charlotte Perkins Gilman, Robert Lynd, C. Wright Mills, Alvin Gouldner, Robert Bellah, and Dorothy Smith who advocate a critical-moral role for sociology. Nevertheless, in contemporary

American sociology the friends of scientism continue to speak with authority. To be sure, moral justifications of knowledge have never been far from the surface. Sociologists, from Blau to Collins, have insisted that the value of their work lie in its contribution to public enlightenment or social problems. Sociology is assumed to have a moral, even a political role. Its role is to make available to the public a body of scientific knowledge which might allow citizens to assess the real state of social affairs and make social policy beyond partisan politics and the clash of interests. This moral framing of sociology has not included an acknowledgement of the moral and political meaning of its own conceptual categories and strategies. The politics of knowledge is said to pertain to the uses citizens make of science, not to science itself. Ideally, ideology is to be extrinsic to sociological knowledge. This position however has been subject to escalating suspicions – from feminists to poststructuralists and postmodernists who have exposed the gendered, raced, sexed, eurocentric, classed-based character of the human sciences and its entanglement in power relations – from legitimating groups to constructing normative identities and enforcing processes of normalization and surveillance (e.g., Harding 1986; Foucault 1980; Said 1978; Seidman 1994).

In this regard, cultural studies reissues the challenge to the project of a scientific sociology. Why have American sociologists refused their own practical-moral intentionality even as the entanglement of sociology and the human sciences in the politics of the everyday have been repeatedly exposed? Why do many sociologists cling to an objectivism that contradicts the guiding premise of sociology, i.e. that the human is the social and the social is organized by the principle of difference.

Afterword

This essay is not intended to be a brief *for* cultural studies and *against* American sociology. This binary is unstable and perhaps collapses into incoherence if pressed more intently than I did. Moreover, cultural studies, at least its British version and the American rearticulation have their own problems – for example, a lingering neomarxism that is in tension with its strong culturalism, an abandonment of literary-aesthetic critique, a tendency to lapse into scientism in British cultural studies, a textualist reductionism in some American cultural studies, and a resistance to address in a serious manner its own normative commitments and rationales. More to the point, I believe it is naive and arrogant to judge elaborate, multi-faceted traditions of social inquiry such as "cultural studies" or "American sociology" in a global manner – as if it is possible to somehow rank them as better or worse or inferior or superior. By what possible standards or, better yet, by whose standards do "we" make such judgements and how do "we" decide whose standards and who is the "we" who decides? In the face of a relentless deconstruction of all such "foundational" efforts, no matter how sincere or inspired by humanitarian goals, to articulate a nonlocal theoretical standpoint, nonlocal standards of judgement, or a noncontextual vocabulary of "the Real," it would seem that the dream of reason to anchor itself in a nonarbitrary, nonlocal, disinterested discursive space ought to remain under permanent suspicion, if not abandoned outright. To be specific, cultural studies does not recommend itself because its language of cultural codes or its models of a layered self are warranted by their mirroring of the social universe. Nor are the quantitatively oriented empirical approaches to the social in American sociology to be recommended because they are closer to the world "as it actually is." There is, as I see such matters, no nonlocal, nonparticular, decontextualized way of deciding between what are simply different ways of mapping the social world, if the pivot of assessment is which language is closer to the real. This does not mean, though, a paralysis of critical will. We can understand traditions of social inquiry in terms of their embedded problematics and social will; we can, moreover, assess them in light of pragmatic considerations. In short, my intent has definitely not been to praise cultural studies or damn American sociology.

My aim has been twofold. First, to relativize sociology, thereby hoping to induce a certain critical reflexibility in a discipline which sometimes fantastically imagines its conventions and languages of the social as providing a privileged access to the social universe. And in the name of this scientism denies its own ethical and political willfulness. Secondly, to suggest that American sociologists might favorably consider certain conceptual moves in cultural studies not because they get us closer to the truth; rather, because they open up new and perhaps productive (in terms of the aims and conventions of American sociology) ways of framing the social and make possible important political interventions.

Why press for relativizing sociology? One reason is that its perhaps the only way to get sociologists, at least American sociologists, to approach what they do as itself a social construction and political practice. To the extent that sociologists imagine that their conceptual strategies and vocabularies give them privileged access to social reality, they surrender a certain reflexivity about the sociohistorical situatedness and practical-moral aspects of their own social knowledges. Problematizing the scientistic project does not mean abandoning sociology; rather it suggests approaching sociology as just one tradition of interpreting the social which is itself implicated in the making of the social world. This perspective does not devalue sociology but assesses its value pragmatically or in terms of what sociology allows us to say or do about the social and the ways it is entangled in its making. By sketching "cultural studies" as an alternative discourse of the self and the social, I merely wish to pressure American sociologists to consider the local and practical-moral willfulness of their own practices. To say it differently, relativizing sociology allows us to frame it as a social practice and to reflect upon the social interests that shapes its formation and, in turn, shapes the formation of the social. Relativizing sociology makes possible a genealogy of this discipline, an inquiry aimed at exposing its social and political unconsciousness. I take this to be a valuable project to the extent that the scientistic self-understanding of sociologists and its supposedly innocent will to truth continues to mask its own social productivity.

As we in the United States and perhaps in Europe increasingly occupy a "postmodern" sociopolitical terrain, we may not be forced to abandon all judgements or normative standpoints but we may well be pressured to abandon what now appears as a naive, and no longer innocent, hope of warranting social ideas by appeals to the very nature of the social world. Let us put this hope and project, noble as it is, and humanitarian as its motivations have been, to rest. As we can perhaps see clearer today, difference extends deep into the culture – into our ways of knowing and judging.

Does such an acknowledgement of epistemological difference and plurality entail a surrendering of critique? No. I imagine a "pragmatics of knowledge" in place of a "logic of knowledge." Here I can emphasize my second point: If I recommend certain aspects of "cultural studies" to American sociologists, it is not because I think that they will get us closer to social reality but because of possible conceptual and social practical gains. Regarding the former, I merely note that perhaps an argument could be made (though I won't make it here) that at least certain conceptual moves in cultural studies suggest productive ways of handling problems or concerns which are considered important by some American sociologists, e.g., relating social structure and culture, meaning and power, agency and constraint, or articulating a stronger notion of culture. There are, in addition, potential practical-moral or social advantages to cultural studies. For example, to the extent that cultural studies assigns to cultural codes the status of social facts of the first order, "culture" is positioned as a primary site of social structuration and therefore of the politics of domination, resistance and justice. Cultural studies places struggles over meanings, identities, knowledges, and the control of discursive production and authorization on an equal footing with struggles over the distribution of material resources. Similarly, the psychoanalytical turn in some versions of cultural studies, especially in feminist social theory, suggests similar sorts of disciplinary and practical-moral "gains." A psychoanalytic perspective troubles the rather surface, ego-centered, rationalistic models of self and action that still dominate American sociology. Psychoanalysis opens up new ways of talking about self-formation and the dynamics of group life. From a practical-moral point of view, psychoanalysis contests the extreme voluntarism of much American society and sociology, a world view which undoubtedly expresses a position of social privilege. Psychoanalysis points to a layered concept of the self and therefore makes possible new ways not only of imagining self and the social but a much more layered, complex model of the interpenetration of self and society, and therefore of the dynamics of domination and resistance.

As I said in the beginning, these ideas are part of a larger project of thinking about what social knowledge might look like if we abandon or seriously rethink a modern Enlightenment framework. What happens to sociology if we no longer fetishize the Real as the primary warrant for our knowledges? What happens to the human sciences when our knowledges are viewed as saturated with a social and political willfulness, when their investment in the myth of the Enlightenment, in the grand narrative that Truth can redeem humanity, is exposed as itself complicit with a social will which has surely, whatever good its realized, has left its mark in a trail of blood and ruined lives. Awakening from this grand stupor may not mean the end of the human sciences but surely, at least we can hope, the end of their defensive denial of their own social productivity. Relativizing sociology means living with the moral and political responsibility of the productivity – both the good and the bad – of our own will to truth.

4

The refusal of sexual difference: queering sociology

If we follow the recent history and theory of sexuality, we are asked to assume that sexuality is a social fact. What is imagined as sexuality, its personal and social meaning and form, varies historically and between social groups. Indeed, if we are to take seriously Foucault's *The History of Sexuality* (1980), the very idea of sexuality as a unity composed of discrete desires, acts, developmental patterns, and sexual and psychological types, is itself a recent and uniquely "modern" Western event. For example, the ancient Greeks imagined a sphere of pleasures (*aphrodisia*) which included eating, athletics, man/boy love, and marriage, not a realm of sexuality (Foucault 1985). This new theorizing figures sex as thoroughly social: bodies, sensations, pleasures, acts, and interactions are made into "sex" or accrue sexual meanings by individuals, groups, discourses, and institutional practices. Framing "sex" as social unavoidably makes it a political fact. Which sensations or acts are defined as sexual and what moral boundaries demarcate legitimate and illegitimate sex and who stipulates this is political. Paralleling class or gender politics, sexual politics involves struggles around the formation of, and resistance to, a sexual social hierarchy (Rubin 1982).

The current theorization of sex as a social and political fact prompts a rereading of the history of modern societies and social knowledges. In this chapter, I offer a sketch of a critical reinterpretation of classical and current sociology from the vantage point of recent Western queer studies. In an admittedly preliminary way, I argue that, until the 1980s, classical and contemporary sociology has either assumed the naturalness of the domain of the body and sexuality or the universality of "modern" western categories of sexuality. The rise of an affirmative lesbian and gay or queer studies exposes the participation of sociology in the making of a sexual social system organized around a hetero/homosexual binary and the normative status of heterosexuality. This critical field of social knowledge (i.e. queer studies) challenges sociology to re-examine both its implicit politic of sexual identity and its conceptual foundations which lack an analysis of the social formation of "bodies" and "sexualities."

We are familiar with the standard accounts of the rise of sociology. For example, sociology is described as born in the great transformation from a traditional, agrarian, and corporatist hierarchical order to a modern industrial, class based but formally democratic system. The so-called classic sociologists are "classics" precisely because they are said to have provided the core perspectives and themes in terms of which contemporary social scientists analyze and debate the great problems of modernity. These perspectives include Marx's theorization of capitalism as a class-divided system, Weber's thesis of the bureaucratization of the world, and Durkheim's theory of social evolution as a process of social differentiation. The classics posed the question of the meaning of modernity in terms of the debates over capitalism, secularization, social differentiation, bureaucratization, class stratification, and social solidarity. If our view of modernity derived exclusively from the sociological classics, we would not know that a central part of the great transformation were efforts to create a sphere of sexuality, to organize bodies, pleasures, desires, and acts as they relate to personal and public life, and that this entailed constructing sexual identities (often interrelated with racial, gender, class, and national identities), producing discourses and cultural representations, enacting state policies and laws, that made personal life the site of religious and familial intervention. In short, the making of embodied sexual selves and codes has been interlaced with the making of the cultural and institutional life of western societies.

The standard histories link the rise of the modern social sciences to social modernization (e.g., industrialism, class conflict, and bureaucracy), but are silent about sexual conflicts. At the very time in which the social sciences materialized announcing a social understanding of the human condition, they never questioned a natural order linking sex, gender, and sexuality. Such silences cannot be excused on the grounds that sexuality had not become a site of public organization, conflict, and knowledges. From the eighteenth through the nineteenth centuries, there were public struggles focused on the sphere of the body, desire, pleasure, intimate acts and their public expression – struggles in the family, church, law, and in the realm of knowledges and the state. The women's movement flourished in Europe between the 1780s-1790s, the 1840-1860s and between the 1880s and 1920, the key junctures in the development of modern sociology. Struggles over the "women's question" were connected to public conflicts around sexuality. Sexual conflicts escalated in intensity and gained public attention between the 1880s and World War I – the "breakthrough" period of classical sociology. In Europe and the United States, the body and sexuality were sites of moral and political struggle through such issues as divorce, free love, abortion, masturbation, homosexuality, prostitution, obscentity, and sex education. This period experienced the rise of sexology, psychoanalysis, and psychiatry (Irvine 1990; Birken 1988; Weeks 1985). Magnus Hirshfeld created the Scientific Humanitarian Committee and Institute for Sex Research in Germany. Homosexuality became an object of knowledge. For example, Karl Heinrich Ulrichs published twelve volumes on homosexuality between 1864 and 1879. One historian estimates that over 1,000 publications on homosexuality appeared in Europe between 1898 and 1908 (Weeks 1985, p. 67).

What is striking is the silence in classical sociological texts regarding these sexual conflicts and knowledges. Despite their aim to view the human condition as socially constructed, and to sketch the contours of modernity, the classical sociologists offered no accounts of the making of modern bodies and sexualities. Marx analyzed the social reproduction and organization of labor but not the process by which laborers are physically or sexually reproduced. Weber sketched what he assumed to be the historical uniqueness of the modern west. He traced the rise of modern capitalism, the modern state, formal law, modern cities, a culture of risk-taking individualism, but had little to say about the making of the modern regime of sexuality. The core premises and conceptual strategies of classical sociology defined the real and important social facts as the economy, church, military, formal organizations, social classes, and collective representations.

Although the classical sociologists did not make the social formation of sexuality a thematic concern or integrate it into their core sociological analytic framework, this does not mean that they completely ignored this topic. For example, Georg Simmel (1984) wrote several essays on human sexuality (see Bologh 1990 on Weber). Simmel's ideas about sexuality were inseparable from his views of gender. To simplify and state his ideas in contemporary terms, Simmel argued that men and women are different in basic ways. He speaks of the "trans-historical basis of sexual difference" (1984: 106). Men's essential nature is to "objectify" their selves through creating a public world of culture, organizations, and institutions. Male sexuality is viewed as an extension of this instrumental, objectifying principle – that is, it is "penetrative" and reproductive in its core, defining impulse. Moreover, because men's essential character is to be social and cultural producers, sex is an important but only partial aspect of their selves. By contrast, women are defined thoroughly by their feminine nature which is said to be self contained, organic, personalistic, and emotionally spontaneous. Women's femininity leads to a life organized around the private, domestic sphere – as wives, mothers, and caretakers of the household. Simmel assumes that women's femininity is thoroughly sexualized and hence sexuality is said to infuse their entire being. Somewhat paradoxically though precisely because a woman's sexuality is more fundamental she experiences her sexuality as both needing men more than they need her (since men's primary life is in the public realm while women's life is in the domestic sphere) and as somewhat independent of men, to the extent that women's femininity sexualizes aspects of her life (e.g., pregnancy and mothering) that men do not share. The relative autonomy of women's sexuality does not mean however that women can define their sexuality apart from men or that their desires or pleasures are different from men's. Women never escape their (hetero)sexuality since their lives are organized around men, for example, around pregnancy, children, motherhood, and the feeding and caring of men. If Simmel had inquired into the social formation of this gender and sexual configuration or if he had examined the social factors producing this historically distinctive gender and sexual order, he would have proposed a powerful sociology of sexuality. However, Simmel assumed the naturalness of bipolar gender identities, with sexuality a mere extension of this gender order, and the naturalness and normative status of heterosexuality.

Perhaps the failure of the classical sociologists to make sexuality into a primary topic of social analysis is related to their privileged gender and sexual social position. They took for granted the naturalness and validity of their own gender and sexual status in just the way, as we sociologists believe, any individual unconsciously assumes as natural and good (i.e. normal, healthy, and right) those aspects of one's life that confer privilege and power. Thus, just as the bourgeoisie had asserted the naturalness of class inequality and their rule, individuals whose social identity is that of male and heterosexual have not in the main questioned the naturalness of a male dominated, normatively heterosexual social order. It is then hardly surprising that the classics never examined the social formation of modern regimes of bodies and sexualities. Moreover, their own science of society contributed to the making of this regime whose center is the hetero/homo binary and the heterosexualization of selves and society.

Sociology's silence on sexuality was broken as the volume level of public sexual conflicts and discourses was turned up so high that even sociologists' trained incapacity to hear such sounds was pierced. Confining my remarks to early American sociology, isolated and still-faint voices speaking to the issue of sexuality can be heard through the first half of the twentieth century. Indeed, sociologists could not entirely avoid addressing this theme in the first few decades of this century.

Issues such as municipal reform, unionization, economic concentration, the commercialization of everyday life, race relations, and colonialism were important topics of public debate. At the same time, Americans were gripped by conflicts that placed the body at the center of contention. The women's movement, which in the first two decades of this century was closely aligned to a socialist and cultural radical politics, emerged as a national movement. Although the struggle for the right to vote was pivotal, no less important were feminist struggles to eliminate the double standard that permitted men sexual expression and pleasure while pressuring women to conform to Victorian purity norms or suffer degradation if erotic desires were claimed. As women were demanding erotic equality with men, there were public struggles to liberalize divorce, abortion, and pornography; battles over obscenity, prostitution, and marriage were in the public eye (e.g., Peiss 1986; D'Emilio and Freedman 1988; Seidman 1991; Smith-Rosenberg 1990). Sex was being discussed everywhere – in magazines, newspapers, journals, books, the theatre, and in the courts. For example, in the millions of volumes of sex advice literature published in the early decades of this century, there is manifested a process of the sexualization of love and marriage (Seidman 1991). Books such as Theodore Van de Velde's *Ideal Marriage* ([1930] 1950), which constructed an eroticized body and intimacy, sold in the hundreds of thousands. Americans were in the first stages of a romance with Freud and psychoanalysis; social radicals such as Max Eastman, Emma Goldman, Edward Bourne, and Margaret Sanger, connected institutional change to an agenda of sexual and gender change (Marriner 1972; Simmons 1982; Trimberger 1983). Despite the vigorous efforts of vice squads and purity movements, pornography flourished and obscenity laws were gradually liberalized.

In the first half of this century, sex was put into the public culture of American society in a manner that sociology could not ignore. And yet sociologists managed to do just that to a considerable degree. Through the mid-century, sociologists had surprisingly little to say about sexuality. For example, the Chicago School of Sociology studied cab drivers, immigrants, factory workers, and "troubled" youth but had little to say about the domain of sexuality. Sociologists such as Park, Cooley, Thomas, Parsons, and Ogburn had much to say on urban patterns, the development of the self, political organization, the structure of social action, and technological development – all worthwhile topics – but little or nothing to say on the making of sexualized selves and institutions. Finally, while sociologists were surveying every conceivable topic, and while a proliferation of sex surveys were stirring public debate (e.g., Dickinson and Beam 1932; Davis 1929; Kinsey 1948 and 1953), sociologists did not deploy their empirical techniques to study human sexualities.

Indicative of this neglect by sociologists, the index of the *American Journal of Sociology* reveals that between 1895 and 1965 there was one article printed on homosexuality and thirteen articles listed under the heading of "Sex," most of which concerned issues of gender and marriage. Similarly, the index of the *American Sociological Review* indicates that between 1936 and 1960 there were fourteen articles published under the heading of "Sexual Behavior," most of which were focused on gender or the family. The absence of a sociology of sexuality was noted by a contemporary sociologist:

The sociology of sex is quite undeveloped, although sex is a social force of the first magnitude. Sociologists have investigated the changing roles of men and women . . . [and] the sexual aspects of marriage . . . Occasionally a good study on illegitimacy or prostitution appears [e.g., Davis 1937, 1939]. However, when it is stated that a sociology of sex does not exist, I mean that our discipline has not investigated, in any substantial manner, the social causes, conditions and consequences of heterosexual and homosexual activities of all types. (Bowman 1949)[1]

It took the changes of the 1950's and the public turmoil of the sixties for sociologists to begin to take sex seriously. The immediate postwar years are sometimes perceived as conservative. However, the war and patterns of mobility, prosperity, and social liberalization relaxed social constraints. Indicative of changes in the American culture of the body and sexuality, the fifties witnessed rock music, the beginnings of the women's movement, the appearance of homophile organizations, and the figures of the beatnik and the rebel for whom social and sexual transgression went hand in hand. The sixties made sexual rebellion into a national public drama. The women's movement, gay liberation, lesbian-feminism, the counterculture, magazines such as *Playboy* and sex manuals such as *The Joy of Sex*, cultural radicals like Herbert Marcuse and Norman O. Brown, made sexual rebellion central to social change.

A sociology of sexuality emerged in postwar America (e.g., Henslin 1971; Reiss 1967). Sociologists approached sex as a specialty area like organizations, crime, or demography. Sex was imagined as a property of the individual whose personal expression was shaped by social norms and attitudes. Sex and society were viewed as antithetical; society took on importance as either an obstacle or tolerant space for sexual release. The idea of a "sexual regime," of a field of sexual meanings, discourses, and practices that are interlaced with social institutions and movements, was absent from sociological perspectives. Moreover, although sociologists studied patterns of conventional sexuality, most conspicuously, premarital, marital, and extramarital sex, much of this literature was preoccupied with "deviant" sexualities, for example, prostitution, pornography, and most impressively, homosexuality.

A sociology of homosexuality emerged as part of the sociology of sex (e.g., Reiss, Jr. 1964; Gagnon and Simon 1967a, 1967b; Sagarin 1969). Sociologists turned to homosexuality as an object of knowledge in the context of the heightened public visibility and politicization of homosexuality. The social context of the rise of a sociology of homosexuality needs to be at least sketched.

Between the early decades of this century and the mid-1970s, homoerotic desire was defined by scientific-medical knowledges as indicative of a distinctive sexual and sometimes gender human type: the homosexual. In other words, individuals for whom homosexual desire was important in their emotional and sexual desires now saw themselves as a unique type of person. Ironically, the framing of homosexuality as a social identity proved to be productive of homosexual subcultures. To simplify a very complicated story, homosexual subcultures evolved from the marginal, clandestine homophile organizations of the fifties to the public cultures and movements of confrontation and affirmation of lesbian-feminism and gay liberation in the seventies (Adam 1987; D'Emilio 1983; Faderman 1981). Integral to the transformation of homoerotic desire into a lesbian and gay identity was the framing of this desire in scientific-medical knowledges. From the early 1900s through the 1950s, a psychiatric discourse that figured the homosexual as a perverse, abnormal human type dominated public discussion. Kinsey (1948, 1953) challenged this psychiatric model by viewing sexuality as a continuum. Instead of assuming that individuals are either exclusively heterosexual or homosexual, he proposed (with the support of thousands of interviews) that human sexuality is ambiguous with respect to sexual orientation or that most individuals experience both heterosexual and homosexual feelings and behaviors. Kinsey's critique of the psychiatric model was met with a hard-line defense of this medical-scientific model (e.g., Bergler 1956; Bieber 1962; Socarides 1968). At the same time, new social models of homosexuality appeared which suggested an alternative to both the biological and psychological models of psychiatry and Kinsey. These social approaches viewed the homosexual as an oppressed minority and a victim of unwarranted prejudice and social discrimination (e.g., Cory 1951; Hoffman 1968; Hooker 1965; Martin and Lyon 1972). By the early 1970s, the women's and gay liberation movements had fashioned sophisticated social understandings of homosexuality which viewed homosexuality as normal and natural. Moreover, they criticized the institutions of heterosexuality, marriage and the family, and conventional gender roles for oppressing homosexuals and women (e.g., Altman 1971; Atkinson 1974; Bunch 1975; Rich 1976).

The growing national public awareness of homosexuality and the rise of new social concepts of homosexuality prompted sociologists to study homosexuality. Through the early 1970s, sociologists viewed homosexuality as a social stigma to be managed; they analyzed the ways homosexuals adapted to a hostile society. Sociologists studied the homosexual (mostly the male homosexual) as part of a deviant sexual underworld of hustlers, prostitutes, prisons, tearooms, baths, and bars (e.g., Reiss 1961; Humphreys 1970; Weinberg and Williams 1975; Kirkham 1971). Much of this sociology was inspired by a humanitarian impulse: to show the homosexual as a victim of unjust social discrimination. Nevertheless, sociologists contributed to the public perception of the homosexual as a strange, exotic other in contrast to the normal, respectable heterosexual.

Sociological perspectives on sexuality in the sixties and early seventies proved influential in shaping knowledges of sexuality and homosexuality, e.g., the labeling theory of Howard Becker (1963), Goffman (1963), and Schur (1963) and the "sexual script" concept of John Gagnon and William Simon (1973). However, in the late seventies and early eighties a new sociology of homosexuality was fashioned primarily by lesbian-and gay-identified and often feminist sociologists. This new cadre of sociologists took over the conceptual tools of sociology, as well as drawing heavily upon feminism and critical social approaches circulating in the lesbian and gay movements to study gay life (e.g., Plummer 1975, 1981; Troiden 1988; Warren 1974; Levine 1979a, 1979b; Murray 1979; Harry and Devall 1979). This work underscored the social meaning of homosexuality. It contributed to recent gay theory, which has largely neglected sociological research as a distinctive social tradition of sex studies (Epstein 1996). The sociology of homosexuality from the early 1970s through the 1980s has not played a major role in recent lesbian and gay theory debates, in part, because sociologists did not critically investigate the categories of sexuality, heterosexuality, and homosexuality. They did not question the social functioning of the hetero/homosexual binary as the master category of a modern regime of sexuality (Stein and Plummer 1996; Namaste 1996). Moreover, sociologists lacked an historical perspective while perpetuating an approach that isolated the question of homosexuality from dynamics of modernization and politics.

As sociologists were beginning to approach sex as a social fact, there were, as I alluded to previously, social perspectives on sexuality that were developed by the women's and gay movements. With the formation of homophile groups in the 1950s (e.g., the Mattachine Society and the Daughters of Bilitis), homosexuality was either theorized as a property of all individuals or as a property of a segment of the human population. Viewing homosexuality as natural was intended to legitimate it. Moreover, despite the radicalization of gay theory in lesbian feminism and gay liberation in the 1970s, few challenged the view of homosexuality as a basis of individual and social identity. A good deal of lesbian feminist and gay liberationist theory aimed to reverse the dominant sexual views by asserting the naturalness and normality of homosexuality. The notion of homosexuality as a universal category of the self and sexual identity was hardly, if at all, questioned in the homophile, lesbian feminist and gay liberationist discourses (exceptions include Altman 1971; McIntosh 1968).

As the initial wave of an anti-homophobic, gay affirmative politics (roughly from 1968 to 1973) passed into a period of community building, personal empowerment, and local struggles, we can speak of a new period in lesbian and gay theory, the age of social constructionism. Drawing from labeling and phenomenological theory, and influenced heavily by marxism and feminism, social constructionist perspectives challenged the antithesis of sex and society. Sex was viewed as fundamentally social; the modern categories of sex, most importantly, heterosexuality and homosexuality, but also the whole regime of modern sexual types, classifications, and norms are understood as social and historical creations. Social constructionist perspectives suggested that "homosexuality" or, more appropriately, same-sex experiences, were not a uniform, identical phenomenon but their meaning and social role varied historically. In particular, constructionists argued that instead of assuming that "the homosexual" is a transhistorical identity or a universal human type, the idea that homosexual desire reveals a distinct human type of social identity is said to be unique to modern western societies. Michel Foucault (1980) provided the classic statement:

As defined by ancient civil or canonical codes, sodomy was a category of forbidden acts; their perpetrator was nothing more than the juridical subject of them. The nineteenth-century homosexual became a personage, a past, a case history, a life form . . . Nothing that went into total composition was unaffected by his sexuality. It was everywhere present in him: at the root of all his actions . . . because it was a secret that always gave itself away. (p. 43)

Foucault's thesis of the social construction of "the homosexual" found parallel articulations in the concurrent work of Jeffrey Weeks (1977), Jonathan Katz (1976), Carroll Smith-Rosenberg (1975) and Randolph Trumbach (1977).

Foucault's geneaological studies of sexuality aimed at exposing a whole sexual regime as a social and political event. In this regard, Foucault questioned the political strategy of an affirmative lesbian and gay movement on the grounds that it unwittingly reproduced this regime. Foucault's deconstructionist message fell on largely deaf ears in the context of a politics affirming identity and the prodiguous efforts at lesbian and gay community building in the 1970s. Many so-called social constructionist studies through the early 1980s sought to explain the origin, social meaning, and changing forms of the modern homosexual (e.g., D'Emilio 1983; Plummer 1981; Faderman 1981). As much as this literature challenged essentialist or universalistic understandings of homosexuality, it contributed to a politics of the making of a homosexual minority. Instead of asserting the homosexual as a natural fact made into a political minority by social prejudice, constructionists traced the social factors that produced a homosexual subject or identity which functioned as the foundation for homosexuals as a new ethnic-like minority (D'Emilio 1983; Faderman 1981). Social constructionist studies often legitimated a model of lesbian and gay subcultures as ethnic-like minorities (Epstein 1987).[2]

Social constructionist perspectives have dominated studies of homosexuality through the 1980s and have been institutionalized in lesbian and gay studies programs in the 1990s. Debates about essentialism (Stein 1992) and the rise, meaning, and changing social forms of homosexual identities and communities, are at the core of lesbian and gay social studies. Since the late 1980s, however, aspects of this constructionist perspective have been contested. In particular, discourses that sometimes circulate under the rubric of queer theory, though often impossible to differentiate from constructionist texts, have sought to shift the debate somewhat away from explaining the modern homosexual to questions of the operation of the hetero/homosexual binary, from an exclusive preoccupation with homosexuality to a focus on heterosexuality as a social and political organizing principle, and from a politics of minority interest to a politics of knowledge and difference (see ch. 7). What is the social context of the rise of queer theory?

By the end of the 1970s, the gay and lesbian movement had achieved a level of subcultural elaboration and general social tolerance, at least in the US, that a politic oriented to social assimilation far overshadowed the liberationist politics of the previous decade. Thus, Dennis Altman (1982), a keen observer of the gay movement in the seventies, could speak of the homosexualization of America. And yet at this very historical moment, events were conspiring to put lesbian and gay life into crisis.

A backlash against homosexuality, spearheaded by the New Right but widely supported by neoconservatives and mainstream Republicans, punctured illusions of a coming era of tolerance and sexual pluralism (Adam 1986; Seidman 1992; Patton 1985). The AIDS epidemic both energized the anti-gay backlash and put lesbians and gay men on the defensive as religious and medicalized models which discredited homosexuality were rehabilitated. While the AIDS crisis also demonstrated the strength of established gay institutions, for many lesbians and gay men it emphasized the limits of a politics of minority rights and inclusion. Both the backlash and the AIDS crisis prompted a renewal of radical activism, of a politics of confrontation, coalition building, and the need for a critical theory that links gay affirmation to broad institutional change.

Internal developments within gay and lesbian subcultures also prompted a shift in gay theory and politics. Social differences within lesbian and gay communities erupted into public conflict around the issues of race and sex. By the early 1980s, a public culture fashioned by lesbian and gay people of color registered sharp criticisms of mainstream gay culture and politics for its marginalization and exclusion of their experiences, interests, values, and unique forms of life e.g., their language, writing, political perspectives, relationships, and particular modes of oppression. The concept of lesbian and gay identity that served as the foundation for building a community and organizing politically was criticized as reflecting a white, middle class experience or standpoint (Moraga and Anzaldua 1983; Lorde 1984; Beam 1986; Moraga 1983). The categories of "lesbian" and "gay" were criticized for functioning as disciplining social forces. Simultaneously, lesbian feminism was further put into crisis by challenges to its foundational concept of sexuality and sexual ethics. At the heart of lesbian feminism, especially in the late 1970s, was an understanding of the difference between men and women anchored in a spiritualized concept of female sexuality and an eroticization of the male that imagined male desire as revealing a logic of misogyny and domination. Being a woman and a lesbian meant exhibiting in one's desires, fantasies and behaviors a lesbian feminist sexual and social identity. Many lesbians, and feminists in general, criticized lesbian feminism for marking their own erotic and intimate lives deviant or male-identified (e.g. Rubin 1982; Allison 1981; Bright 1984; Califia 1979, 1981). In the course of what some describe as the feminist "sex wars," a virtual parade of female and lesbian sexualities entered the public life of lesbian culture, e.g., butch-fems, sadomasochists, sexualities of all kinds mocking the idea of a unified lesbian sexual identity (Phelan 1989; Ferguson 1989; Seidman 1992a). If the intent of people of color and sex rebels was to encourage social differences to surface in gay and lesbian life, one consequence was to raise questions about the very idea of a lesbian or gay identity as the foundations of its culture and politics.

Some people in the lesbian and gay communities reacted to the "crisis" by reasserting a natural foundation for homosexuality (e.g., the gay brain) in order to unify homosexuals in the face of a political backlash, to defend themselves against attacks prompted by the plague, and to overcome growing internal discord. However, many activists and intellectuals moved in the opposite direction, affirming a stronger thesis of the social construction of homosexuality that took the form of a radical politics of difference. Although people of color and sex rebels pressured gay culture in this direction, there appeared a new cadre of theorists. Influenced profoundly by French poststructuralism and Lacanian psychoanalysis, they have altered the terrain of lesbian and gay theory and politics (e.g., Sedgwick 1990; Butler 1990; Fuss 1991; de Lauretis 1991; Doty 1993).

Queer theory has accrued multiple meanings, from a merely useful shorthand way to speak of all gay, lesbian, bisexual, and transgendered experiences to a theoretical sensibility that pivots on transgression or permanent rebellion. I take as central to queer theory its challenge to what has been the dominant foundational concept of both homophobic and affirmative homosexual theory: the assumption of a unified homosexual identity. I interpret queer theory as contesting this foundation and therefore the very telos of Western homosexual politics.

Modern western homophobic and gay affirmative theory has assumed a homosexual subject. Dispute has revolved around its origin (natural or social), changing social forms and roles, its moral meaning, and political strategies of repression and resistance. There has been hardly any serious disagreement regarding the assumption that homosexual theory and politics has as its object, "the homosexual" as a stable, unified, and identifiable human type. Drawing from the critique of unitary identity politics by people of color and sex rebels, and from the poststructural critique of "representational" models of language, queer theorists argue that identities are always multiple or at best composites with literally an infinite number of ways in which "identity-components" (e.g., sexual orientation, race, class, nationality, gender, age, able-ness) can intersect or combine. Any specific identity construction, moreover, is arbitrary, unstable and exclusionary. Identity constructions necessarily entail the silencing or exclusion of some experiences or forms of life. For example, asserting a black, middle-class, American lesbian identity silences differences in this social category that relate to religion, regional location, subcultural identification, relation to feminism, age or education. Identity constructs are necessarily unstable since they elicit opposition or resistance by people whose experiences or interests are submerged by the assertion of identity. Finally, rather than viewing the affirmation of identity as necessarily liberating, queer theorists figure them as, in part, disciplinary and regulatory structures. Identity constructions function as templates defining selves and behaviors and therefore excluding a range of possible ways to frame the self, body, desires, actions, and social relations.

Approaching identities as multiple, unstable, and regulatory may suggest to critics the undermining of gay theory and politics but, for queer theorists, it presents new and productive possibilities. Although I detect a strain of anti-identity politics in some queer theory, the aim is not to abandon identity as a category of knowledge and politics but to render it permanently open and contestable as to its meaning and political role. In other words, decisions about identity categories become pragmatic, related to concerns of situational advantage, political gain, and conceptual utility. The gain, say queer theorists, of figuring identity as permanently open as to its meaning and political use is that it encourages the public surfacing of differences or a culture where multiple voices and interests are heard and shape gay life and politics.

Queer theory articulates a related objection to a homosexual theory and politics organized on the ground of the homosexual subject: This project reproduces the hetero-homosexual binary which, in turn, perpetuates the heterosexualization of society (Namaste 1996). Modern Western affirmative homosexual theory may naturalize or normalize the gay subject or even register it as an agent of social liberation, but it has the effect of consolidating heterosexuality and homosexuality as master categories of sexual and social identity; it reinforces the modern regime of sexuality. Queer theory wishes to challenge the regime of sexuality itself, that is, the knowledges and social practices that construct the self as sexual and that assume heterosexuality and homosexuality as categories marking the truth of selves. The modern system of sexuality organized around the heterosexual or homosexual self is approached as a system of knowledge, one that structures the institutional and cultural life of Western societies. In other words, queer theorists view heterosexuality and homosexuality not simply as identities or social statuses but as categories of knowledge, a language that frames what we know as bodies, desires, sexualities, and identities. This is a normative language as it shapes moral boundaries and political hierarchies. Queer theorists shift their focus from an exclusive preoccupation with the oppression and liberation of the homosexual subject to an analysis of the institutional practices and discourses producing sexual knowledges and the ways they organize social life, with particular attention to the way these knowledges and social practices repress differences. In this regard, queer perspectives suggest that the study of homosexuality should not be a study of a minority – the making of the lesbian/gay/bisexual/ subject – but a study of those knowledges and social practices that organize "society" as a whole by sexualizing – heterosexualizing or homosexualizing – bodies, desires, acts, identities, social relations, knowledges, culture, and social institutions. Queer theory aspires to transform homosexual theory into a general social theory or one standpoint from which to analyze social dynamics.

Queer theory and sociology have barely acknowledged one another. Queer theory has largely been the creation of Humanities professors (see ch. 7). Sociologists have been almost invisible in the debates around queer theory. Moreover, in its deconstruction of modern Western categories of sexual identity, and in its analyses of the interpenetration of sexuality and society, queer theory has evolved into a distinctive social theoretical tradition that assumes an independence from sociology. Indeed, many queer theorists claim to draw exclusively from poststructuralism, feminism, psychoanalysis, and semiotics for its conceptual resources in understanding the social formation of sexualities. However, as some recent observers have commented (e.g. Epstein 1996; Plummer and Stein 1994), queer theory in fact owes a great deal to sociology, both to general sociological theories such as labeling theory, feminist sociology, the interpretive-ethnomethod-ology of Garfinkel and Goffman, functionalism, and conflict theory, and to the sex studies of sociologists such as Gagnon and Simon, McIntosh, Plummer, and Weeks.

The mutual isolation and indifference of queer theory and sociology is beginning to change. There is increasingly a sense that the emphasis on discourse, intertextuality, and knowledges in queer theory, though important for critical social analysis and politics, is one-sided (see ch. 7). Efforts to rearticulate queer theory giving it a stronger institutional or social structural grounding are underway, often drawing on the traditions of sociology. For example, Cindy Patton (1995) has sought to rework the category of identity drawing on Bourdieu's idea of cultural capital; Michael Warner (1993) draws on Giddens and others to propose rethinking queer theory as a social theory; Donald Morton (1996) and others are reinventing marxism one more time in an effort to formulate a materialist queer theory.

Paralleling efforts to sociologize queer theory, some sociologists are attempting to queer sociology. Not surprisingly, these efforts have largely been initiated by sociologists working in the area of sexual studies. At one level, sociologists are drawing on queer theory to criticize existing sex, and especially lesbian/gay, studies. Sociologists are criticized for taking-for-granted the universality of modern categories of sexuality, for example, assuming the universality of categories such as homosexuality and hetero-sexuality. Similarly, a queer influence is evident in criticisms of sociological research which focuses exclusively on homosexuality and fails to analyze heterosexuality as a social organizing force, not just a category of identity. Ki Namaste writes:

Both mainstream sociological perspectives (e.g., labeling theory) and (mainstream) gay studies . . . neglect the social production of heterosexuality, choosing instead to focus on gay and lesbian communities. Poststructuralism [i.e. queer theory] is particularly useful in this light because it considers the relations between heterosexuality and homosexuality. It addresses not only the emergence of and development of homosexual communities, but also the intersection of these identities within the broader context of heterosexual hegemony. (1996, p. 204)

Some sociologists are beginning to sketch a queer sociology of sexuality. This would mean expanding social inquiry beyond the formation of sexual identities and communities. Steven Epstein suggests the following expanded focus: "How are complex, often internally contradictory, and ambiguous systems of sexual meaning constructed and challenged in different cultures . . . Which institutions are central to the production or contestation of sexual codes and beliefs? How do sexual belief systems and patterns of sexual conduct and identity formation intersect with other markers of social difference and sytsems of oppression, such as class, race, and gender (1996: 157–58; cf. Stein and Plummer 1996)? Sociologists have gone beyond making programmatic statements to giving some empirical articulation to the notion of a queer sociology of sexuality. For example, drawing heavily on the work of Butler, Kristin Esterberg (1996) studied how lesbian identities are fashioned or performatively enacted through their everyday actions and interactions. Similarly drawing from a queer perspective which asserts the constructed, multiple, fluid character of identity, Amber Ault (1996) analyzes the way bisexuality troubles the heterosexual/homosexual binary.

Sociologists have only begun to imagine the larger project of queering sociology. Here I can only sketch the contours of what I consider this effort to involve.

First, queering sociology would initially entail a critical aim. Sociologists would examine the history and present role of this discipline in the making of sexual selves and social orders. In particular, queering sociology involves criticizing the way in which sociology has contributed unwittingly no doubt to naturalizing sex and normalizing a normative heterosexuality. Queers should critique sociology for the ways its premises, categories, and thematic perspectives are organized around normative heterosexuality (e.g., Ingraham 1996). This is a critique that assumes a link between epistemology and politics, as it exposes sociology's undoubtedly unconscious rationalization of a heteronormative social order.

Secondly, queer standpoints have the potential to shift the categorical and thematic focus of sociology. They can offer original narratives of society, history, and social change. For example, queer social knowledges can propose that the question of the making and organization of bodies, desires, and sexualities – no less than the question of class, ethnicity, race, or religion – are at the center of the formation of many contemporary societies. Queer pespectives can relate stories of the making of hetero-and-homosexualized bodies, desires, identities, and societies in modern Europe and the United States as master themes analagous to the rise of capitalism, the bureaucratization of social worlds, or modernization as social differentiation.

Thirdly, having denaturalized the body and historicized sexuality, a queer standpoint suggests a rethinking of general societal dynamics. For example, Stein and Plummer (1996) suggest one way of thinking about the challenge and opportunity queer theory presents to the sociology of stratification:

How can sociology seriously purport to understand the social stratification system . . . while ignoring quite profound social processes connected to heterosexism, homophobia, erotic hierarchies, and so forth . . . What happens to stratification theory as gay and lesbian concerns are recognized? What are the mobility patterns of lesbians? How do these patterns intersect with race, age, region, and other factors? What happens to market structure analysis if gays are placed into it? . . . We need to reconsider whole fields of inquiry with differences of sexuality in mind. (pp. 137-138)

Or, as Epstein says, "The challenge that queer theory poses to sociological investigation is precisely in the strong claim that no facet of social life is fully comprehensible without an examination of how sexual meanings intersect with it" (1996: 156).

Fourthly, queering sociology points to reconsidering the sociological canon. Those social thinkers who figure the body, desire, and sexuality as social and historical, and who narrate history and modernity from the perspective of the making of bodies and sexualities merit inclusion in the sociological theory and analysis curriculum. For example, if we describe the classical period of sociology as roughly between the late nineteenth century and early twentieth centuries, why not teach Edward Carpenter and Freud alongside the texts of Marx, Weber, Du Bois or Charlotte Perkins Gilman? And when we turn to current figures and texts, why not place queer theory alongside exchange theory or neomarxism and perhaps teach, along with the texts of say Peter Berger, James Coleman, or Dorothy Smith, the texts of Ti-Grace Atkinson, Adrienne Rich, The Combahee River Collective, Dennis Altman, Jeffrey Weeks, Gayle Rubin, Judith Butler, Eve Sedgwick, and of course Michel Foucault.

5

Difference troubles: the flight of sociology from "otherness"

As a discussant on a panel addressing the issue of conceptualizing "difference" in sociology, I responded to four panelists who *defended* the re-centering of the disciplinary culture of sociology around the notion of social and cultural difference. Despite their intention, however, I argue that these panelists, like most of their colleagues, fail to imagine difference as "otherness" because they do not challenge the core "Enlightenment" premises of their own standpoint. Assumptions such as the unity of the self and "humanity," Western modernization as social progress, and the equation of reason with Western scientific traditions suppress or pathologize difference, render difference into a temporary or transient condition, or figure social differences as stages of development towards a higher, unitary social endpoint.

I reprint this brief critical commentary because it illustrates prominent conceptual approaches to the question of difference among sociologists. I consider this discussion especially indicative of the failure of sociology in this regard in that the panelists I responded to are advocates of a sociology attentive to social difference. I criticize them because, like those they criticize, these sociologists refuse an epistemological de-centering that seems implicit in their own positions.

I have decided to keep the identities of the panelists anonymous since their papers were works-in-progress and they were not given the opportunity to respond to my comments. Moreover, it is less their specific points of view that are of interest than the general positions they stake out on the question of difference. What follows is the text of my critical commentary of four panel presentations.

I begin with a provocation. Sociologists have failed, miserably, in imagining social differences in their own terms and in allowing difference to disturb our dominant assumptions and categories. We have been pre-occupied with developing one set of premises and concepts, one language of the social, one standard and concept of knowledge, and one system of sociology. We have retreated from differences which are threatening to our dominant regime of knowledge either by ignoring them, assimilating them to our episteme, rendering them an instance or variation of a general principle, making them a transient condition or an evolutionary phase destined to disappear. Sociology has been wedded to an epistemology and politics which pivot around "foundational" notions of social unity, historical or evolutionary progress, and Western globalization.

Many sociologists would no doubt consider these criticisms uninformed and wrong-headed. How can I possibly say that sociology has not been attentive to social difference? Didn't Marx recognize – and defend – the (revolutionary) difference that was represented by the working class? Didn't Weber devote much of his sociology to tracing the civilizational differences between the "Occident" and the "Orient"? Didn't Durkheim"s *The Division of Labor in Society* contrast "traditional" kinship-based societies characterized by "mechanical solidarity" with the "organic solidarity" of "modern" differentiated societies?

Marx most assuredly spoke of the working class as holding different interests than the bourgeois class. But did Marx understand the motivations, social interests and values of the working class in terms different from the way he understood Western bourgeois Enlightenment culture? No. The working class were described in the language of the dominant Enlightenment model – as self interested, rational agents, as viewing the world from the standpoint of secular/scientific reason, and as assuming Western superiority and linear progress. In marxism, the working class turns out to be a superior realization of Western Enlightenment ideals – its future, not its negation or contestation.

Consider Durkheim. In the *Division of Labor*, kinship-based societies featuring mechanical solidarity marked out a social space of social difference. But what kind of difference is this? These societies are understood as representing an *early evolutionary phase* of social development which is destined to pass into the universal condition of Western modernity. These kin-based "traditional" social formations amount to an inferior and transient condition, the subordinate term in the opposition to "the modern."

Similarly, in his comparative studies of religion and society, Weber analyzed the ways, for example, China and India are different from the west. However, what marks these civilizations as different, according to Weber, is the absence of Western-styled modernization, for example, the lack of Western "autonomous" cities, modern political parties, and concepts of citizenship and rights. These social differences function then as the inferior contrasting term in the East/West or Orient/Occident binary. Weber leaves little doubt that the East or non-West is a transient social difference which will pass into the universal social identity represented by the modern West. Weber anticipated the globalization of Western culture, the destruction of difference in the name of Western universality – a fact about which he was ambivalent.

Classical and contemporary sociology acknowledges difference but primarily as a *variation or instantiation of the general*, as a *transient condition*, or as *the inferior other*. This is not a difference that contests or disturbs the dominant Enlightenment paradigms of knowledge, society, and history. It is a rendering of difference that takes flight from approaching it as "otherness," a figure that is potentially troubling to dominant models of social knowledge.

What would it mean to acknowledge difference without surrendering its otherness? It would be a difference that refuses assimilation, that resists surrendering its "alien" status, an otherness that cannot be erased by being rendered a mere variation, instance, phase, or inferior subordinate moment.

As I turn to the contributions of the panelists, I want to interrogate the ways they figure difference. How have they constructed difference – as other, or have they submerged difference in an encompassing identity? How open have they been to a difference that disputes the dominant episteme – i.e. Western Enlightenment social knowledges? What would a sociology look like that rendered the dominant frameworks of society and knowledge into a mere "other" or that imagined the social as a decentered space of difference? My sympathies lie with keeping the social center a space of difference and preserving otherness as a terrain of trouble and contestation. The voices of difference need to be heard but they should be disturbing – the screeches and scratching sounds which remind us that our worlds are, if we listen carefully and are willing to see, full of aliens – queers everywhere. Are we prepared to imagine a social space with no center, no ground, no endpoint, or are we simply gesturing toward the "other" to ensure that we do not lose ground to the invasion from the margins?

For panelist "A," the challenge to the dominant Enlightenment model of Western sociology is in the movements of decolonization in Africa, India and south-east Asia. These nationalist movements have contested the claims of Western sociology to have provided premises, concepts, and theories which are universally true. Western sociology is accused of Eurocentrism – of asserting universal validity for premises and perspectives saturated with the particular interests and values of the West. Despite its emancipatory aim, Western sociology is seen as suppressing difference, for example, the unique lives of Africans. As part of decolonization, "A" observes the development of indigenous sociologies in Africa.

"A" affirms the value of difference, in this case the appearance of indigenous nonWestern sociologies. He is aware that Western sociology, with its aspiration to universal knowledge or to articulate one vocabulary of the social, often represses unique aspects of nonWestern societies. However, he worries that the development of these differences might be "at the expense of the goal of universality." He thinks that the championing of difference as sheer multiplicity is dangerous. "A" wants a universal language of the social but one that is respectful of difference. Unfortunately, he sacrifices difference in the quest to preserve the universal.

How does "A" erase difference despite his intention to preserve it? He argues that the appearance of African sociologies should not be interpreted as opposed to Western sociology. Rather, both African and Western sociologies are variations of an evolving universal sociology whose roots are in the modern West. Moreover, while the shape or form of sociology in Africa is still undecided, "A" holds that African sociologists should draw on their distinctive social histories to contribute to a universal sociology. African sociologists would accommodate general, transhistorical concepts, models, and explanations to take into account the unique aspects of African societies. This is a retreat from difference because "A" does not allow that African sociologists might feel the need to craft an alternative conceptual or epistemic standpoint, one irreducible to, and troubling to, dominant Enlightenment paradigms (cf. Asante 1987; Collins 1990). In addition, "A" appeals to an evolutionary model of historical development and social knowledge. I quote: "Through evolution these specific differences will give way to more genuine universal and unifying expressions at the meta-cultural level." In other words, different sociologies will give way to "a truly universal, one-world sociology." Difference turns out to be transient. The epistemological politics of social and historical unity and identity triumphs.

Just what makes the defense of a universal sociology so important that it justifies sacrificing difference? "A" never directly says but I suspect that it has to do with the belief that a culture which upholds the belief in the unity of humanity and an ideal of universal knowledge is necessary for preserving a democratic society. This is of course neither an uncommon nor an unreasonable position but it needs to be explicitly defended in light of perspectives which have traced the entanglement of the Enlightenment culture in the history of colonization and the subjugation of nonWestern peoples (e.g., Said 1979, 1993; I. Turner 1978; Young 1990). Undefended appeals to truth, reason, and progress, especially as they are wedded to foundational and universalizing strategies, cannot be accepted at face value in light of histories and social analyses which implicate the Enlightenment in dynamics of domination, discipline, and normalization (e.g., Adorno and Horkheimer 1972; Foucault 1978, 1979).

Panelist "B" takes into account the role of dominant Enlightenment knowledges in power struggles, for example, in the domination of Europeans over non-Europeans, capital over labor, men over women, and whites over people of color. "B" is suspicious of scientific claims to foundations and universality because they have masked ethnocentric perspectives and have functioned to silence or marginalize subordinate populations. "B" intends a sociology attentive to difference, not as mere variation or instantiation of the general but as true "otherness" or as a voice of dissent and opposition. I do not think, however, that she ultimately eludes the seductive charms of "the universal." Moreover, her rhetoric of difference is belied by an undisturbed feminist politic of identity.

The claims of Western sociology to speak an objective, value-neutral, universal language of the social masks its involvement in the making of hierarchies of class, race, and gender. The very structure of Western sociology, its subject-object dualism, its model of the rational actor, its abstracted individualism, and its focus on the public institutional sphere, register a European, middle-class, and masculinist standpoint. The lives of women, people of color, and laborers are either excluded or rendered inferior within the dominant perspectives of Western sociology. "B" aims for a sociology which can give voice to these subjugated lives. Difference is imagined as troubling to the center. For example, women are viewed by many feminists, including "B," as representing a unique approach to knowledge, social action, and society. For example, women are said to experience the self as embedded in dense relations of daily life, to favor processual and egalitarian values, and to approach knowledge as involving, centrally, feelings, values, and dialogue. Drawing on feminist critiques of masculinist knowledges (e.g., Harding 1986; Jagger and Bordo 1989; Smith 1987), "B" aims to affirm difference – for example, between men and women, without, however, abandoning generality. Her strategy is to rely upon a standpoint epistemology.

There is much to be said in favor of standpoint theory. I will not make that case here (cf. Harstock 1983; Smith 1987). There are though complications, instructive ones, some of which I will allude to. Consider the issue of difference in relation to standpoint theory (cf. Butler 1990; Clough 1994; Lemert 1995; Flax 1987; Mohanty 1988; Spelman 1990). "B" thinks in global binary oppositions – women/men, European/nonWestern, white/people of color. Do women mark an identity? Do men? Do Europeans? "B" knows that neither women nor men signify a unity but that they signal an endless diversity or multiplicity depending on the ways gender intersects with class, race, sexuality, nationality, and so on. Her binaries, with their implied essentialism and dualistic logic, suggest the kind of exclusionary and hierarchical strategy that she criticizes as Eurocentric and androcentric. "B" is trapped in the dominant binary. Her response does not go beyond reversing the values of the terms, rendering the second, previously subordinate term – women, people of color, nonWestern – superior. In this way, "B" reproduces – and perpetuates – the binary and its multiple exclusions and hierarchies. To avoid this position, she could have made a "deconstructive" move. The latter aims at displacing the authority of the binary and releasing the signifiers – women, men, European, nonWestern – from a logic of identity to permit a wider play of difference and critical opposition (e.g., Butler 1990; Cornell 1991; Fuss 1989; Riley 1982; Spivak 1987; Nicholson 1995).

If standpoint theory fails "B" in making the case for difference, it is also suspect in making the case for general social knowledge. "B" wishes to avoid both the repressive universalism of the Enlightenment and the relativism of postmodernism which is said to undermine the possibility of social critique. Standpoint theory is her alternative. Social knowledge is produced by people whose social identity and location is determinate. Knowledge may be situated and partial but it is general and can claim validity (cf. Haraway 1988; Collins 1990). Standpoint theory stands and falls on the plausibility of its "foundational" categories – e.g., women, men, lesbian, European, African-American, African. My doubts have already been registered: to the extent that such categories serve to ground or warrant a claim to knowing and therefore a politics, they are exclusionary and normalizing. There is, moreover, no nonarbitrary basis for restricting the proliferation of possible standpoints. This renders virtually meaningless any gesture to conceptual authority based on standpoint theory claims to validity. Identity categories can no more bear the foundational weight than can the categories of instinct, labor, rational self-interest, intentionality or communicative action. Surrendering truth claims to social knowledges that rely on images of mirroring or strong notions of coherence does not mean giving up generality and critical knowledges; it suggests the substitution of pragmatic for realist justifications (e.g., Lyotard 1984; Rorty 1982; Williams 1985).

Sociology has refused difference, at times, by assimilating or repressing difference or approaching it as a transient condition or evolutionary phase to be superseded. Sociology has also resisted difference by, at times, figuring difference as deviant and dangerous. Of course, the figure of the "oriental," the "single or sensuous woman," the "black," the "immigrant" or the "delinquent/criminal" has at times been imagined in sociological narratives as dangerous. In the figure of "the homosexual," panelist "C" discovers all of these failed tropes of difference.

The lives of homosexuals have been excluded or marginalized in a heteronormative sociology (see ch. 4). "C" observes, for example, the absence of research, until very recently, on lesbian and gay movements in the "social movement" literature or on lesbian and gay households in the "family" literature. Fields of research such as social stratification or the sociology of education have proceeded as if homosexuality was not an axis and intersecting aspect of social inequality or as if lesbian and gay men were not part of educational institutions. Moreover, sociologists, even some who have studied homosexuality as a field of research, have typically reproduced in their own knowledges the dominant sexual categories and sexual hierarchies.

In this regard, queer theory represents a challenge to sociology. It not only neutralizes threatening images of "the homosexual" by "normalizing" homosexual desire but takes lesbian and gay desires and identities as productive of new social knowledges (e.g., Butler 1991; Sedgwick 1990; Warner 1993). Claiming a unique standpoint towards knowing the social world linked to the experience of "the closet" and " coming out," queer theory approaches sexuality as deeply social and political, historicizes sexual categories, problematizes minoritizing frameworks (gay people as an ethnic minority) in favor of placing the hetero/homosexual binary at the center of social dynamics, and contests assimilationist political strategies in favor of a politics which affirms difference and challenges the normalizing controls (social control through judgements about what is normal) or a disciplinary society (Berlant 1993; Duggan 1992; see chs. 6 and 7 in this volume).

"C" views queer theory as disturbing to sociology. Queers press sociology to reexamine its assumptions about the self, the sexual, and the social. By placing questions of the formation and politics of the body and desire at the center of social analysis, queer studies challenges sociologists to reconsider issues of social control, stratification, social organization, the state and social change. Sociology has much to learn from queer theory (see Plummer and Stein 1996; Epstein 1996; Gamson 1996; Ingraham 1996; Irvine 1996; Namaste 1996), not least its complicity in reproducing a social system organized around the norm of heterosexuality.

"C" is aware that queers can be decidedly unruly and famously ill behaved. Some queer intellectuals mock the dominant episteme. Many queer theorists, for example, have abandoned "foundationalism" and universalism; they have disrobed Reason to discover a will to (heterosexual) power. Some queer theorists champion deconstructive or genealogical moves aimed at contesting grounds and essences and exploding unities and identities into a multiplicity of differences over legislative efforts aimed at establishing foundations, securing identities, or constructing theoretical systems. "C" however retreats from this disruptive gesture. She describes, and dismisses, this epistemic acting out as "anti-rationalist." This, of course, is a classic Enlightenment strategy for resisting difference – that is, mark it as irrational and inferior. "C" has not contested the rational/irrational, science/fiction binaries. She is trapped in the duality of either affirming or denying reason, in gesturing for or against science. Queer theory is a difference then that ultimately can be tamed and absorbed into the dominant disciplinary episteme. "C" promises that if queers behave and straights listen, we will all benefit because "it will make for better sociology." The ghost of the Enlightenment still prowls about in the collective unconscious of the Western mind, even the queer mind.

"D" wishes to smash the grip of Enlightenment legislative reason on sociology. Efforts to legislate rules of knowledge are criticized as authoritarian and exclusionary (cf. Bauman 1987, 1991). In principle, "D" champions epistemological pluralism; in practice, he makes a case for a social issues-and-community-based sociology.

Relying on the poststructural or postmodern subversion of the reason/unreason, science/ideology, knowledge/power, and scientist/citizen binaries, "D" assumes the lack of a central authority or standpoint to legislate epistemic rules. He does not wish to engage the current epistemic fray. He is convinced that the expansion of the rules of discourse has been accomplished. Enlightenment legislative reason has been dethroned. Its time to go beyond the politics of epistemology. We must shift our focus from struggles over the rules of knowledge production and authorization to its content. "D" sees this as a shift to real social issues as they affect actual communities in contrast to epistemic struggles which are merely "academic."

"D" is a genuine trouble maker. He charms me, but has not entirely won me over. I register two kinds of reservations. If Derrida or Foucault are to be believed, the struggle over epistemology, over the rules of knowledge, is permanent because knowledge is always implicated in power relations. Hence, we cannot move beyond the politics of epistemology. We must contest dominant knowledges, recover subjugated knowledges, and deconstruct foundationalist justifications, not only to expand the rules of discourse but because knowledge is entangled in the making of subjects and social worlds. Epistemological struggle is central to cultural politics and the politics of institutional orders.

Defending epistemological struggles does not exclude or devalue a social issues-based advocacy type of sociology. It does assume, contrary to the position of "D", that sociologists have a critical social role separate from engaging the social problems of communities. The image of a social problems oriented sociology in which the boundaries between us and ordinary folk are erased, is moreover, appealing but puzzling. What would such a sociology look like? How would the validity claims of a problem-oriented, community-based sociology be justified? How would this type of sociology promote the goals of freedom better than, say, genealogy, deconstruction, ideology critique, or pragmatically driven narratives? "D's" proposals to make sociology more public-centered and politically engaged lack moral and intellectual force in part because of his epistemological agnosticism.

We are all, at least us "Westerners," in the grip of a culture of the Enlightenment. This is a culture that is preoccupied with certainty and legislating order, uniform rules, unity, and secure grounds of belief and judgement (Bauman 1990). Its authorized knowledges have privileged science, the quest for foundations, theoretical systems, and a universal language of the natural and the social. This regime of truth, whatever its social hopes and even beneficient legacy, has also contributed to creating selves and social orders controlled by a normalizing disciplinary system (Foucault 1980).

Sociology is a carrier of this disciplinary power/knowledge system of social control. Those of us who belong to the tribe of sociologists, but who dwell on its margins because of our subject positions or because our desires or identities or knowledges threaten the prevailing disciplinary conventions, must turn against the center or all claims to be positioned at the center. We must contest sociology's disciplinary center – its foundationalism, universalism, the privileging of science, and its dualisms of fact/value, science/ideology, and scientist/citizen. A politics of the margins should renounce assimilationism or its own re-positioning as a center in favor of decentering epistemic and social authority and rendering the center, and all claims to occupy a center, into mere points or positions in a social space of meaningful differences. We must empty out the epistemological closet to release all of the silenced and censored subjugated knowledges and social voices which are mired in shame, fear, and despair. We must be champions of difference, of the proliferation of social languages and knowledges. Let's declare a war against the center, against all centers, all authorities in the name of difference, multiplicity, in the name of a democratic society which does not create ghettos and closets.

Let our critics take note: we are not embracing chaos but a new order of multiple identities and knowledges, situationally negotiated norms, and pragmatic justificatory strategies. The anticipation of a culture centered on difference and tolerance should be the hope that inspires a politics of the margins, not a bland assimilationism nor the millenasian dream of the end of domination.

PART II

Engaging difference: from lesbian and gay studies to queer theory

6

Identity and politics in a "postmodern" gay culture

Contemporary lesbian and gay male cultures evidence a heightened sensitivity to issues of difference and the social formation of desire, sexuality, and identity. As individuals "we" know what it means to be treated as different, to be rendered as a deviant other by folk and expert cultures, and to approach our bodies, desires, and identities with a deliberateness often lacking in mainstream straight society. Nevertheless, this existential awareness of the cultural politics of otherness has not necessarily been reflected in our dominant theories. For example, the new sociology and history of same-sex intimacies has been narrowly focused on the social origin and development of lesbian and gay male identities and communities among almost exclusively white, middle-class Europeans or Americans.

The theoretical and political limits of the post-Stonewall culture have become apparent. Scholars seem to be rehearsing a monotone history of gay identity to the point of pointlessness. The arcane polemics between constructionists and essentialists has evolved into a sterile metatheoretical debate increasingly devoid of moral and political import. Much of current lesbian and gay studies remains wedded to a standard Enlightenment scientistic self-understanding that, in my view, is inconsistent with its social constructionist premises. Gay identity politics moves back and forth between a narrow single-interest-group politic and a view of coalition politics as the sum of separate identity communities, each locked into its own sexual, gender, class, or racial politic.

I hold the view that the currents of thought that now routinely go under the rubric "postmodern" offer a cultural resource to imagine rethinking identity and politics. I approach postmodernism as a broad cultural and intellectual standpoint that aims to decenter or destabilize unitary concepts of the human subject, foundationalist and objectivist views of knowledge, and totalizing perspectives on society and history. Furthermore, in place of the millenarian politics of marxism, radical feminism, or gay liberationism, I view postmodernism as imagining its politics in terms of multiple, inter-secting struggles. Its aim is less "the end of domination" or "human libera-tion" than the creation of social spaces that permit the widening of choice, the proliferation of social differences and multiple solidarities, and expanded democratization through the deconstruction of naturalized and normalized social norms, the creation of multiple public spheres, and so on.

I hesitate, however, to assume that postmodern thinking marks an epochal shift to "postmodernity" or to a new socio-historical era. I situate postmodern turns of social thought in relation to the evolution of the left-wing of the new social movements. This is a claim I intend to initially press. Specifically, I make the case that postmodern strains in gay thinking and politics have their immediate social origin in recent developments in the gay culture. Specifically, in the reaction of people of color, Third-World-identi-fied gays, poor and working-class gays, and sex rebels to the "ethnic model" of identity that achieved dominance in the lesbian and gay cultures of the 1970s, I locate the social basis for a rethinking of identity and politics.

Postmodernism and the new social movements

Postmodernism has come to signify, among other things, a phase of his-torical development (Baudrillard 1981, 1983, 1984), a stage of late capital-ism (Harvey 1989; Jameson 1992), a new aesthetic sensibility (Huyssen 1986), an epistemological break (Rorty 1979; 1982), the end of grand nar-ratives (Lyotard 1984), and a new political juncture (Rorty 1991; Eagleton 1986; Haraway 1985; see also Connor 1989). These disparate descriptions of the postmodern reflect divergent social standpoints and agendas. Postmodernism is, to put it simply, a rhetorical figure whose meaning is linked to the use to which it is put in a particular social context.

In this chapter, I approach postmodernism as a general theoretical or intellectual standpoint. I situate it in relation to the history of the new social movements (NSM) in the 1970s and 1980s focusing on the US (see Castells 1983; Cohen 1985; Crighton and Mason 1986; Eder 1985; Habermas 1981; Melucci 1980; Touraine 1981). I argue that postmodern cultural politics in the US have been prompted by the struggles between the NSM and mainstream American society. Furthermore, the conflicts between the NSM and the social mainstream have been mirrored, in some important respects, within the NSM. It is this dual conflict that has formed at least one social base of the rise of postmodern ways of thinking and pol-itics (see ch. 11; Foucault 1980; Huyssen 1986; Bordo 1990).

The immediate context of the appearance of postmodernism in the United States is the break of the left from marxism. I interpret postmodernism, at least one prominent current of it in the US, as the standpoint of a post-marxist left whose politics are tied to the NSM.

The shift in left politics in the 1970s and 1980s from the politics of class and labor to the post-marxian social criticism of the NSM forms a pivotal social setting for the rise of a left postmodern social discourse. In the US, the social base of marxism has been significantly narrower than in Europe. Yet marxism was, for many postwar leftists, the dominant language of social criticism and political strategizing. Virtually all of the NSM, at least in their liberationist strains, initially (in the late 1960s and early 1970s) deployed marxism as a model for a critical theory and politic. However, in each case, in the black, feminist, and gay liberationist movements, in the New Left and countercultural movements, the dominant conceptual and political strategies broke away from marxism or in many cases abandoned it entirely. Marxism may have initially facilitated social criticism and political mobilization in the NSM, but its epistemic and political privileging of working-class politics rendered racial, gender, sexual, and other nonclass struggles secondary and marginal.

In the course of the 1970s the liberationist movements often abandoned marxism as both a language of social criticism and an organizing political strategy. Thus, while early radical feminists such as Millet and Firestone articulated their critique of sexism in the language of marxism, many of their radical feminist successors (e.g., Adrienne Rich, Andrea Dworkin, Mary Daly) elaborated a decidedly non-marxist, cultural critique of sexism. By the mid-1970s, the left was socially, ideologically, and politically decentered. It was composed of a plurality of movements, each focused on its own particular project of building an autonomous community, evolving its own language of social analysis, and forging an oppositional politic.

The social fracturing of left politics was accompanied by a theoretical decentering. This entailed not only the narrowing of marxism to a local sociopolitical and discursive project but a broader strategy of historicizing and politicizing all social discourses, including the social knowledges of the human sciences.

To establish their own sociopolitical space, the NSM had to contest marxism's status as *the* science of society. Left critics challenged the marxist claim to have revealed the essential social conflicts and laws of history. In particular, leftists criticized the marxian notion that class struggle anchored in economic inequalities is the primary social division and site for political organizing. For example, feminists disputed the validity of applying a marxist economic and class analysis to premodern kinship-based societies (e.g., Rubin 1975; Rosaldo and Lamphere 1974; Ortner and Whitehead 1981). Indeed, many feminists contested the marxian analysis of modern societies on the grounds that its organizing concept of production excluded sexual and household reproduction and failed to address the gendered texture of private and public life (e.g., Balbus 1982; Flax 1981; Nicholson 1986; Young 1982). Marxism had the effect, moreover, of marginalizing gender struggles. Socialist-feminist efforts to graft a gender analysis onto marxism have proved unsuccessful (e.g., Young 1982). In the course of the 1980s many feminists have repudiated marxism, at least as a general theoretical standpoint; they have evolved their own critical discourse and politics that centers on gender dynamics. The feminist critique had the effect of narrowing marxism to a local conceptual and political project, one centered on labor and the dynamics of class.

These new oppositional movements have not been unified by any post-marxist social theory. Totalizing efforts by neo-marxists such as Althusser or Habermas have not proved compelling, at least in terms of generating a meaningful level of theoretical consensus. Social criticism has splintered into a myriad of local discourses mirroring the social fracturing of the American left.

The relativizing of marxism was part of a more general confrontation with the Enlightenment heritage. The NSM contested the claim of science to universal knowledge and its rationale that it promotes social progress through enlightenment. In fact, a central struggle of the NSM has been against science as a discourse that carries cultural and institutional authority. Unlike the oppression of labor, which is linked directly to political economic and class dynamics, cultural political struggles are pivotal to the NSM. The ways in which women, gays, lesbians, people of color, and the differently abled are oppressed is centrally tied to stigmatizing, polluting public discourses and representations. These groups are, to be sure, oppressed by economic discrimination and social policies enforced by the state. However, whereas social oppression for blue-collar workers is rooted in economic and class arrangements, the oppression of gays, the disabled, many women and people of color is anchored in cultural representations. In particular, the human sciences – psychiatry, psychology, criminology, sociology – have played a key role in shaping social hierarchies by fashioning normalizing models of identity and social norms and by becoming part of the social practices enforcing disciplinary social control e.g., therapy, prisons, criminal justice practices.

The struggle over cultural production and representation has been central to the NSM. They have not only challenged particular constructions of identity that carry the authority of science but have contested the claim of science to epistemic authority. Thus, many in the NSM have disputed scientific constructions of women as biologically destined to be wives and mothers; they have raised suspicions about representations that, under the sign of science, project women as primarily emotional, nurturing, and other-directed – a characterization that warrants socially subordinate caretaking and service roles (e.g., Ehrenreich and English 1979; Millet 1969; Weisstein 1973). Similarly, lesbians and gay men have had to struggle against scientific-medical constructions of same-sex desire as symptomatic of an unnatural, abnormal, socially pathological human-type – the homosexual (e.g., Bayer 1981; D'Emilio 1983; Weeks 1985; Watney 1987; Patton 1990; Crimp 1988). At the heart of both the feminist and gay movements has been a politics that targets science and its institutional carriers – schools, hospitals, psychiatric institutions, prisons, scientific associations, the state – as important creators of oppressive models of identity and social norms.

As the NSM have contested the authority of science, we can observe postmodern strains in their discourses. The claim of science to value-neutrality and objectivity has been disputed; the privileging of science as a carrier of Truth has been challenged. Enlightenment legitimations that authorize science on the grounds of promoting social progress through eliminating prejudice and ignorance have been questioned. In at least certain strains of NSM thinking, science has been reconceived as a culture-bound social practice that bears the mark of its sociohistorical embeddedness and the social interests of its producers. Viewed as a normative social force, science has the effect of drawing moral boundaries, shaping social hierarchies, and creating identities. Science is imagined as a discursive strategy implicated in heterogeneous power struggles.

The confrontation between the NSM and the social mainstream is only one social dynamic that has been productive of postmodern knowledges. There are internal dynamics within these movements that reproduce this external struggle and that have been equally productive of a postmodern point of view – specifically, the struggles by individuals and groups who have been marginalized within these movements. They have contested the particular models of identity, community, and politics that have achieved sociopolitical dominance in these movements and that project their own interests as universal. The clash between the periphery and center *within these movements* is a key source of postmodern thinking and politics (see chs. 7, 9, 11).

In the remainder of this essay, I wish to at least partially redeem the claim linking the rise of postmodern social discourses to the internal dynamics of the NSM by focusing on the evolution of gay intellectual culture. My hope is that this approach might provide a useful standpoint from which to grasp

the social and political significance of the rethinking of the politics of identity and difference that goes under the name of postmodernism and poststructuralism.

A brief resume of my argument. My starting point is gay liberation
theory. I argue that liberation theory moved on a conceptual terrain decidedly different from its predecessor and successor. Liberation theory presupposed a notion of an innate polymorphous, androgynous human
nature. Liberation politics aimed at freeing individuals from the constraints
of a sex/gender system that locked them into mutually exclusive
homo/hetero and feminine/masculine roles. Liberation theory and politics
exhibit a kinship with what is now called postmodernism. Instead of evolving in this direction, however, liberationism gave way in the late 1970s to an
ethnic model and political agenda. Although this model proved effective in
socially mobilizing lesbians and gay men, its emphasis on a unitary identity and community marginalized individuals who deviated from its
implicitly white, middle-class social norms. Moreover, its narrow single-
interest-group politic proved ineffective in response to the antigay backlash
in the late 1970s.

In the 1980s, there was a reaction to this ethnic model by marginalized
social interests (e.g., gay people of color and sex rebels), by activists wishing
to renew a more radical gay politics, and by a new cadre of intellectuals
trumpeting the politics of difference. While the ethnic model that grounded
gay identity politics for two decades was under assault, a poststructuralist
version of postmodern gay theory stepped forward as one successor project
to a fading liberationist agenda. To the extent that poststructuralism, like
its political counterpart, Queer Nation, edges into a post-identity politic,
its exquisite intellectual and political impulse draws its power more from its
critical force than any positive program for change.

From the politics of liberationism to ethnic separatism

In the years preceding gay liberationism, mainstream homosexual thought
(represented in the publications of the Mattachine Society and the
Daughters of Bilitis) highlighted homosexuality as a condition of only
some people (see D'Emilio 1983; Marotta 1981; Martin and Lyon 1972).
Homosexuality itself was described as a basic character trait. Indeed, many
in the homophile movement, as it was often called, viewed homosexuality
as symptomatic of a minor or secondary personality disorder. However, the
underlying shared humanity of homosexuals and heterosexuals was
thought to warrant the abolition of the legal supports of prejudice and discrimination.

Although many in the mainstream homophile movement described homosexuals as a minority, this social difference was not celebrated. The project of building an autonomous homosexual culture proposed by Harry Hay was decisively rejected. Instead, these homophile organizations interpreted the minority condition of homosexuals as an unfortunate consequence of social discrimination. Homophile activists sought to abolish the homosexual as a distinct social identity. They desired social assimilation.

Gay liberation and the lesbian-feminist movement challenged mainstream homophile thinking. They contested the notion of homosexuality as a status of a social minority. They repudiated the idea of homosexuality as symptomatic of a psychological disorder or of an inferior social status. And they rejected a politics of assimilation (Adam 1987; see also D'Emilio 1983; Marotta 1981; Martin and Lyon 1972).

In the early years of gay liberation (1969–73), gay theory was divided. For the purpose of this essay, I distinguish gay liberation and lesbian-feminist theory. Gay liberation theory was not necessarily produced by and for men. Many lesbian-identified women participated in its creation. In contrast, lesbian-feminism was created by and for women. It emerged, in part, as a reaction against gay liberation, which was criticized as reflecting the values and interests of men. It also developed in response to liberal and radical feminist orthodoxy, whose priorities were said to be those of heterosexual women.

Lesbian-feminists repudiated the view of lesbianism as simply a type of sexual desire or orientation. They interpreted lesbianism as a personal, social, and political commitment to bond with women. A lesbian is, as the classic manifesto of lesbian-feminism, "Woman-Identified Woman," declared, woman-identified (Radicalesbians 1973; Myron and Bunch 1975; Atkinson 1974; Tanner 1971). The lesbian recognizes her unique kinship with female experiences and values. She makes a choice to center her life around women.

For lesbian-feminists, lesbianism is not a condition or trait of some women; it is not a sexual preference that marks women off from each other. Quite the contrary, lesbianism or being women-identified is said to be a condition of all women to varying degrees. If some women fail to realize this, it is because in a male-dominated society they have absorbed male-imposed definitions that wed womanhood to heterosexual relations and social roles.

Lesbianism is viewed as a political act. The decision to form primary bonds with women challenges male dominance that is said to be maintained through the institution of heterosexuality. To the extent that a woman's personal and social worth is defined by her relation to men (e.g., her role as wife and mother), she cedes control over her life to men. Lesbianism projects women as autonomous and equal to men. Lesbian-feminism encourages women to become aware of their ties to other women; it intends to promote the growth of female values and modes of being by building an autonomous "womansculture."

In the early years of the liberation movements, lesbian-feminism was pioneered by women such as Sidney Abbott, Barbara Love, Rita Mae Brown, Ti-Grace Atkinson, Martha Shelley, and the women around the Radicalesbian and the Furies collectives. While lesbian-feminism lost much of its organizational authority within the women's movement by the mid-1970s, it achieved an ideological prominence among feminists and lesbians as it was elaborated into what has come to be called "cultural feminism." Many of the leading cultural feminists had their personal and ideological roots in lesbian-feminism, for example, Adrienne Rich, Robin Morgan, Susan Griffin, Andrea Dworkin, Mary Daly, and Kathleen Barry.

Gay liberation theory materialized in the post-Stonewall period between roughly 1969 and 1973. Liberation theory appeared in newspapers such as *Come Out!*, *Rat*, and *Fag Rag*. In contrast to feminist theory, there were few attempts to provide a sweeping historical theory from an affirmative gay standpoint.

Dennis Altman's *Homosexual Oppression and Liberation* (1971) was perhaps the only statement of liberation theory that compares to, say, Millet's *Sexual Politics* or Shulamith's *Dialectic of Sex*. Although the author is Australian, he reported an extensive involvement in the American gay liberation movement. The book reflects, moreover, a decidedly American point of view, as it carried on a dialogue with the New Left, American feminists, and gay writers.

Altman offered a grand narrative of the struggle of the homosexual subject for liberation against social oppression. Although he featured the theme of homosexual oppression and the movement for liberation, the homosexual subject turns out to be a sociohistorical event. Humanity is not naturally divided into heterosexuals and homosexuals. The homosexual, as we know this figure in the postwar Western world, is not a universal human type but an historical product.

Although Altman rejected the essentialist premise of a transhistorical homosexual subject, he does not avoid a social ontology. Drawing on the Freudo-marxism of Marcuse's *Eros and Civilization*, he assumes "the essentially polymorphous and bisexual needs of the human being" (1971: 74). In this primeval condition, the self takes pleasure from all the parts of his/her body and from both genders. Altman maintains that societies impose upon humanity a repressive regime that channels our polymorphous eroticism into a narrow genital-centered, procreative-oriented heterosexual norm.

Gay liberation is characterized as a movement of human sexual liberation. It aims to institute a sexual regime in which sexuality is not defined by a mutually exclusive gender preference. A political strategy that centers on legitimating a homosexual identity perpetuates a divided sexual self and society. It does not contest a sexual regime that reduces eros to a genital-centered, penetrative sexual norm. Accordingly, sexual liberation should involve struggling against circumscribing eros to a romantic, marital, genital-and-penetrative sexual desire. Altman envisions a liberatory ideal that defends a diffuse body eroticism, the eroticization of everyday life, sexual exchanges that go beyond a romantic coupling, and approaching sex as a medium of procreation and love but also pleasure and play.

Altman argues that gay liberation is more than a movement to liberate eros; it is a gender revolution. The struggle against the homo/hetero dichotomy is intertwined with the struggle against a sex-role system that views masculinity and femininity as mutually exclusive categories of gender identity. Altman views the binary sex and gender system as mutually reinforcing. "There is a marked connection in our society between the repression of bisexuality [the creation of the homo/hetero roles] and the development of clearly demarcated sex roles" (1971: 80). The gender system is said to posit heterosexuality as a primary sign of gender normality. A true man loves women; a true woman loves men:

Sex roles are a first, and central, distinction made by society. Being male and female is, above all, defined in terms of the other: men learn that their masculinity depends on being able to make it with women, women that fulfillment can only be obtained through being bound to a man. In a society based on the assumption that heterosexuality represents all that is sexually normal, children are taught to view as natural and inevitable that they in turn will become "mummies" and "daddies." (Altman 1971: 81)

To challenge the tyranny of the homo/hetero classification system and to assert our innate bisexuality involves a challenge to the bipolar gender system.

Although liberation theorists did not share all of Altman's ideas, there was a common core of liberation theory. For example, Allen Young's manifesto "Out of the Closet, into the Streets" described gay liberation "as a struggle against sexism," where sexism means "a belief or practice that the sex or sexual orientation of human beings gives to some the right to certain privileges, powers, or roles, while denying to others their full potential.

Within the context of our society, sexism is primarily manifested through male supremacy and heterosexual chauvinism" (192: 7). In American society, sexism is said to be responsible for the creation of a homosexual and heterosexual identity and a masculine and feminine identity that privileges heterosexual men.

Liberationists reasoned that sexism denies the innate universality of homosexual and heterosexual, masculine and feminine desires and feelings. These roles – heterosexual and homosexual, man and woman – alienate us off from parts of ourselves, divides us, and structures sexual and gender hierarchies. Gay liberation is said to be a struggle against heterosexism and sexism, as we would say today. Its agenda is to liberate humankind's innate homosexual and heterosexual, masculine and feminine desires in order to become whole.

According to Allen Young, the deep meaning of the term "gay" suggests a new *human* ideal. This is an ideal of realizing in free, expressive and equal relationships humankind's inherent bisexual, androgynous nature. "Gay is good for all of us. The artificial categories 'heterosexual' and 'homosexual' have been laid on us by a sexist society. Children are born sexual. To protect the power of straight men in a sexist society, homosexuality becomes prohibited behaviour" (1972: 29). Young imagined lesbians and gay men as a vanguard pioneering sexual and human liberation. "Homosexuals committed to struggling against sexism have a better chance than straights of building relationships based on equality because there is less enforcement of roles. We have already broken with gender programming" (1972: 29; see also Wittman 1972).

Between 1969 and 1973 a new body of gay theory accompanied the rise of the gay liberation movement. It departed from previous homosexual theory which often mirrored dominant medical-scientific ideas by conceiving of homosexuality as symptomatic of an abnormal personality characteristic of a segment of humanity. Liberationists rejected the notion that gay politics should aim at merely social acceptance and assimilation. Instead, liberation theory posited humans as innately bisexual and polymorphous. Homosexuality and heterosexuality were not seen as mutually exclusive desires, psychic conditions, or human types; they were described as universal aspects of humankind. Societies create regimes that make homo/hetero gender preference mutually exclusive master categories of sexual identity. Some societies create a stigmatized, polluted homosexual desire and an oppressed homosexual minority. Moreover, this sexual regime is said to be implicated in a gender system that divides humans into masculine and feminine roles. The aim of gay liberation was to abolish a sex/gender system that privileges heterosexuality and men.

There are some key similarities between gay liberation theory and "postmodern" ideas. Liberation theorists view the validity of their own discourse as tied to their particular sociohistorical identity and interests. They do not write as universal intellectuals, to use Foucault's term for the standpoint of many modernist intellectuals (Foucault 1980). The liberationist theorist Allen Young declared: "Because I am a white male homosexual, a New Yorker, a leftist, most of what I say is from that perspective. There are other homosexuals – Third World People, lesbians, transvestites – about whom I can say little. They speak for themselves" (1972: 7). Gay liberation theorists viewed themselves as local intellectuals speaking to specific experiences of sexual and gender oppression that are mediated by conditions of class, race, nationality, and so on. Their own discourse was understood as moral and political.They intended to reconfigure the everyday language of sex and gender, to challenge conventional perspectives that maintain an oppressive sex/gender system, and to offer alternative visions of personal and social life. Although they retained a residue of essentialism in their notion of an original bisexual, polymorphous, and androgynous human nature, their accounts of sexual and gender dynamics are decidedly constructionist.

Their vision of liberation, moreover, parallels somewhat a postmodern concept that frames freedom as the proliferation of sexual desires, pleasures, and consensual forms of intimate life. However, liberationists retained a millennarian notion of a liberated humanity free from constraining normative structures that would be foreign to most postmodern texts. Most postmodernists, moreover, would not share the strong vanguardism in these liberationist discourses. In a word, gay liberation theory may be described as a post-marxist left discourse that leans in a postmodern direction yet retains much of the modernist legacy, in particular its salvationist hopes and vanguardism.

Between the early 1970s and the mid-1980s, there transpired a shift in lesbian and gay male culture (Altman 1979, 1983, 1982b; Bronski 1984; Lee 1979; Faderman 1991). Gay men and lesbians went their separate ways. The tensions in the early gay liberation days evolved into a full-blown separatism, even though some lesbians still identified with an inclusive gay movement. A gay subculture was created largely by and for men. Moreover, many lesbians either identified with the women's movement or with the lesbian separatist project of forging a womansculture.

Interestingly, the developments in the lesbian and gay male subcultures during this time reveal important similarities. In particular, there was an emphasis on community building around the notion of a unitary sexual identity. Gay men created an institutionally elaborated subculture. Although lesbian-feminist subcultures were typically less institutionalized, their dense, informal, network-based character and their blending with feminist institutions gave to them a socially developed texture. Similarly, in both the gay male and lesbian-feminist subcultures, a focus on personal identity and lifestyle became central. In the gay male subculture, newspapers such as *The Advocate*, with its promotion of consumerism and expressive-hedonistic values, symbolized the personalistic emphasis of this community. Although the lesbian-feminist culture was much more self-consciously ideological and radical, it too exhibited a preoccupation with lifestyle concerns, for example, female values and spirituality. Finally, in both the lesbian-feminist and gay male subcultures we can detect a movement away from a liberationist framework toward an ethnic model, with an emphasis on cultural difference, separate community building, and identity-based interest-group politics.

From the solidarity of identity to the politics of difference

As a movement committed to liberating humanity from the mutually exclusive and limiting roles of the heterosexual/homosexual and the feminine/masculine, gay liberation came to an end by the mid-1970s. From a broadly conceived sexual and gender liberation movement, the dominant agenda of the male-dominated gay culture became community building and winning civil rights. The rise of an ethnic model of identity and politics in the gay male community found a parallel among lesbian-feminists who increasingly emphasized the building a womansculture based on unique feminine values. However, whereas gay men represented themselves as an ethnic group oriented toward social assimilation, lesbian-feminists presented themselves as the vanguard of a separatist cultural politic.

As an ethnic identity model acquired cultural dominance in the gay male and the lesbian-feminist communities, previously muffled voices of dissent began to be heard in the cultural mainstream of these communities. Specifically, individuals whose experiences and interests were not represented in the dominant gay and lesbian identity constructions criticized the ethnic model as exhibiting a white, middle-class bias. Simultaneously, the ethnic identity model was under attack by scholars who underscored the immense sociohistorical diversity of meanings and social arrangements of same-sex desire. Finally, the emerging prominence of poststructuralism provided a language to deconstruct the category of a gay subject and to articulate the dissenting voices in a postmodern direction.

The challenge to the dominance of an ethnic model, with its notion of a unitary gay identity and its emphasis on cultural difference, surfaced from individuals whose lives were not reflected in the dominant representations, social conventions, and political strategies. A revolt transpired of the social periphery against the center, only this time the center was not mainstream America but a mainstream gay culture. From minor skirmishes in the mid-to-late 1970s to major wars through the 1980s, the concept of a unitary lesbian or gay male subject was in dispute. Three major sites of struggle against the gay cultural center have been the battles around race, bisexuality, and "nonconventional sexualities."

Conflicts around gender were divisive in the early years of the gay movement. For example, the Gay Liberation Front was initially composed of both men and women. Yet conflicts between gay men and lesbians, heightened by the feminist critique of male domination, led some lesbians to withdraw from liberation organizations. Many of them, along with feminists who were disenchanted with liberal-feminism, were central in pioneering radical-feminism. Ultimately, the tensions between straight and gay radical feminists contributed to the rise of a lesbian-feminist movement. Gender conflicts have continued to be a divisive issue for the gay movement. In the 1970s and early 1980s, however, this tension was "resolved" by a split into two separate movements – one predominantly gay male and the other exclusively lesbian and heavily lesbian-feminist.

Gender conflicts have not challenged the ethnic model since this division was dealt with by the evolution of separate gay male and lesbian communities. The race issue, however, has posed a major challenge to the construction of a gay subject and to the ethnic assimilationist and separatist tendencies of the gay male and lesbian-feminist communities respectively.

Much of the discussion of race through the early 1980s was pioneered by women of color and had the women's movement as its primary reference. Yet, lesbian women of color played a pivotal role in this discussion and implicated the lesbian community in the discussion of racism and anti-racist struggles. For example, in the important anthology by radical women of color, *This Bridge Called My Back*, the primary focus of its contributors was the racism of the women's movement. However, in a section entitled "Between the Lines: On Culture, Class, and Homophobia," the racism and classism of lesbian-feminism was central (Moraga and Anzaldúa 1983).

In a discussion of lesbian separatism, Barbara Smith underscores the class- and race-based character of lesbian-feminism: "Separatism seems like such a narrow kind of politics . . . [It] seems to be only viably practiced by women who have certain kinds of privilege: white-skinned privilege, class privilege" (Smith and Smith 1984: 121). Smith goes on to say that many lesbian women of color will not find separatism a viable strategy not only for economic reasons but because of the racism of many lesbian-feminists. Moreover, to the extent that lesbians of color must struggle simultaneously against the racism of white women, separatism impedes the building of alliances with men of color. Race is said to place lesbian women of color in a different relation to men than white lesbians. "You see white women with class privilege don't share oppression with white men. They're in a critical and antagonistic position whereas Black women and other women of color definitely share oppressed situations with men of their race" (Smith and Smith 1984: 121). Smith maintains that being an African-American lesbian is not a minor variation of an essentially common lesbian experience. To grasp the experience of black lesbians it is not enough to merely add racial to sexual oppression. Rather, *race is said to alter the meaning and social standpoint of being a lesbian.*

In the early 1980s, lesbians and gay men of color made the racism of the women's movement and the homophobia of their own ethnic communities a focus of their social criticism. By the late 1980s, it was the gay culture that was the focus of critical scrutiny. For example, in 1986, the first black gay male anthology, *In the Life*, appeared (Beam 1986). In the "Introduction," Joseph Beam protested the invisibility of the black gay male experience in gay culture:

It is possible to read thoroughly two or three consecutive issues of the *Advocate* . . . and never encounter, in words or images, Black gay men. It is possible to peruse the pages of *212 Magazine's* special issue on Washington D.C. and see no Black faces. It is possible to leaf through any of the major gay men's porno magazines . . . and never lay eyes on a Black Adonis. Finally, it is certainly possible to read an entire year of *Christopher Street* and think that there are no Black gay writers worthy of the incestuous bed of New York gay literati . . . We ain't family. Very clearly, gay male means: white, middle-class, youthful, Nautilized, and probably butch; there is no room for Black gay men within the confines of this gay pentagon. (1986: 14)

Beam identified a major problem, black invisibility in gay public life and the social cause: racism. The invisibility of black gays in the gay community was paralleled by their invisibility in the African-American community. *In the Life* was intended to "end the silence that surrounded our lives" (1986: 17). By giving voice to their experience, black gay men hoped to create a public presence, a community within the gay and African-American communities.

The success of *In the Life* spawned a second black gay male anthology, *Brother to Brother* (Hemphill 1991). In his introduction, Essex Hemphill echoed Beam's view that the gay community reproduces the invisibility and devaluation of black gays in the African-American community and in mainstream America. "The post-Stonewall white gay community of the 1980s was not seriously concerned with the existence of black gay men except as sexual objects . . . It has not fully dawned on white gay men that racist conditioning has rendered many of them no different from their heterosexual brothers in the eyes of black gays and lesbians" (1991: 14). Hemphill argued that the dominant gay male culture does not express the experience of black men. It represents the lives of mostly white, middle-class, urban men organized around their personal concerns – sex, consumerism, and civil rights.

Lesbian and gay men of color have contested the notion of a common or identical gay subject and the idea that the meaning and experience of being gay are socially uniform. Indeed, some people of color have argued that a discourse that abstracts a notion of gay identity from considerations of race and class is oppressive because it typically implies a white, middle-class standpoint. The Latino activist, Charles Fernandez, put it this way: "Reflected in the general public's image of the typical homosexual, in the lesbian and gay media's depiction of its target audience, in the movement's agenda and strategies, in the academy's methodology and theorizing, and in the lesbian and gay community's own self-understanding, is this move-ment's subject and protagonist: a white and middle-class person" (1991: 9). Moreover, many gay people of color contend that the remedy to the eth-nocentric character of dominant – white and middle-class –gay construc-tions of identity and politics involves more than acknowledging racial or class variations. Race is said to be as deeply embedded in the formation of a person's identity or as elementary in the shaping of social interest as sexuality (e.g., Moraga 1983; Beam 1986; Gomez 1988; Almaguer 1991; Trujillo 1991).

Gay people of color have challenged the dominant model of sexual iden-tity. This model assumes that individuals who share a same-sex preference in a homophobic society share a common experience, set of values and interests, and political agenda. Gay people of color have objected arguing that there is no core gay identity around which race or class adds mere social nuance or variance. Rather, individuals are simultaneously gay, male, African-American, Latino, or working-class, each identification being shaped and shaping the others.

The notion of a unitary gay identity has been fundamental to the evolv-ing gay communities of the late 1980s. *Even more basic to the framing of the gay community as an ethnic group has been the assumption that gender prefer-ence defines sexual orientation.* The very possibility of framing homo-sexuality as a site of identity and ethnicity presupposes the reduction of "sexual orientation" to "sexual object-choice" or gender preference. Gay culture took over from mainstream America the privileging of hetero-sexuality and homosexuality as master categories of sexual and social identity. Even lesbian-feminists who redefined lesbianism as a social and political act of woman-identification did not contest the identification of sexual orientation with a hetero/homo gender preference. In discussions over bisexuality and nonconventional sexualities, the privileging of a hetero-sexual/homosexual definition and the coding of sexuality by gender preference are questioned – a questioning that goes to the very heart of the ethnic model of homosexuality.

In their introduction to the anthology *Bi Any Other Name: Bisexual People Speak Out*, Lorraine Hutchins and Lani Kaahumanu criticize the gay culture for perpetuating a sexual code that privileges gender preference as definitive of sexual identity and that assumes individuals neatly fold into heterosexual or homosexual selves (Hutchins and Kaahumanu 1991). This code erases or stigmatizes the experiences of those individuals for whom gender preference is not a mutually exclusive choice and does not adequately describe their sexual lives. "We're told that we can't exist, that we're really heterosexual or really gay, that nothing exists except these two extremes" (1991: xx).

Some individuals who identify as "bisexual" do not contest a social system that organizes sexual identity in terms of gender preference. They aim to legitimate a bisexual desire as a legitimate identity alongside a heterosexual or homosexual identity. For others, however, bisexuality is said to challenge the very privileging of gender preference. They intend to render gender preference just one aspect of, but not necessarily defining of, sexual orientation.

Gender is just not what I care about or even really notice in a sexual partner. This is not to say that I don't have categories of sexual attraction . . . I have categories, but gender isn't one of them. I'm erotically attracted to intelligent people, to people with dark/colored skin and light eyes and hair, to people with a kind of sleazy, sexy come-on, to eccentrics. In some of those categories I am homoerotic . . . in others I am hetero-erotic . . . To be perfectly frank, I can barely imagine what it's like to be a lesbian or a straight woman, to be attracted to women because they are female . . . I feel like . . . I am color blind or tone deaf to a gender-erotic world. (Hutchins and Kaahumanu 1991: 5).

In "My interesting condition," Jan Clausen contests the privileging of gender preference as the basis of sexual identity (Clausen 1990). She recounts the process of fashioning an identity and a social life around same-sex desire. She emphasizes the virtues of a lesbian life – the dignity it confers, the friendships,the sense of purpose, and the political empowerment. She describes her turmoil when, after having established a lesbian identity, she discovered her own heterosexual passions (1990: 13). From the vantage point of a lesbian culture that imagines a sociopolitical sexual identity on the grounds of an unequivocal same-sex desire, Clausen became "radically Other through the deceptively simple act of taking a male lover" (1990: 13). She is reluctant however to affirm a bisexual identity. In part, this reflects her general disenchantment with identity politics. "Throughout much of my adult life, the insights of identity politics have shaped my world view, informed my activism, my writing, and in many respects the conduct of my most intimate relationships . . . On the other hand, I've often felt uneasy about the intensity of the lesbian feminist focus on identity. It sometimes leads into an obsessive narrowing of perspective" (1990: 17). Clausen has an additional problem with embracing a bisexual identity:

I have a second problem with 'identifying' as bisexual . . . I do not know what "bisexual" desire would be, since my desire is always for a specifically sexed and gendered individual. When I am with a woman, I love as a woman loves a woman, and when I am with a man, I love as a woman loves a man. So bisexuality is not a sexual identity at all, but a sort of anti-identity, a refusal . . . to be limited to one object of desire, one way of loving. (1990: 18-19)

Clausen connects her ambivalence towards identity with an "anti-identity politics" or a politics that resists identity on behalf of an affirmation of "being all the parts of who I am" (1990: 21).

Leaving aside, for the moment, the coherence of an "anti-identity politic," Clausen registers reservations many lesbian-and-gay-identified individuals share about the ethnic framing of same-sex desire (for a different perspective on ethnicity and gay identity, see Epstein 1987). The ethnic modelling of gay desire has presupposed the privileging of gender preference to define sexual and social identity, which, in turn, has been the basis upon which a gay community and politics are forged. Although this model can claim some major social accomplishments, it has reinforced "normalizing" social norms that devalue desires, behaviors, and social bonds that involve attraction to both sexes. In challenging gender preference as a master category of sexual and social identity, the bisexual critique suggests the possibility of legitimating desires other than gender preference as grounds for constructing alternative sexual identities, communities, and politics. This brings us to the third site of the debate: "nonconventional sexualities."

In the late 1970s and 1980s, the so-called sex debates served as a major locus for contesting the ethnic model. In these debates, the privileging of gender preference for defining sexual identity and the notion of a unitary sexual identity came under assault. The battles varied somewhat between the lesbian and gay male communities (see Seidman 1992b; Ferguson 1989; Phelan 1989).

In the lesbian context, protest was aimed at the ideological prominence of lesbian-feminism and its cultural feminist variant. The cultural feminist perspective posits a unique and unitary female sexual nature (across the hetero/homosexual divide) as the ground of a sexual ethic. Sex was defined as an expression of intimacy, as a mode of sharing and showing love. Sexual behavior was supposed to exhibit its essentially nurturing, tender, person-centered, and diffusely erotic nature. Legitimate sex should accordingly be embedded in long-term, intimate, loving, and committed relationships. Sex that is body-centered, motivated by carnal pleasure, casual, involves role-playing, or is promiscuous was defined as male-identified and therefore unacceptable or deviant.

The cultural feminist sexual ethic was viewed by many lesbians as narrowly reflecting the experience of a small segment of the lesbian community, namely some white, socially privileged women who were committed to lesbian-feminism. A cultural feminist sexual orthodoxy was experienced as oppressive to lesbians whose sexual values differed. Their desires, behaviors, and relationships were rendered marginal and deviant from the cultural feminist perspective.

In the early 1980s, discontent with lesbian-feminism and its cultural feminist elaboration surfaced in a series of public skirmishes. The chief battle sites were around pornography and sadomasochism (S/M), but the central issue was the meaning of eros for women and for feminism. Cultural feminists seized the initiative. Their antiporn anthology *Take Back the Night* alerted women to the dangers of eros – of a carnal, aggressive, male-identified desire (Lederer 1980). Critics responded with *Women against Censorship* and the "Sex Issue" of *Heresies*, in which eros, as an aggressive, carnal, and lascivious desire, was owned as feminine and feminist (Burstyn 1981, 1985; see also Feminist Anti-Censorship Task Force 1986). In conferences, journals, magazines, newspapers, and novels, feminists and many lesbians owned desires that had been culturally claimed as masculine and, by lesbian-feminists, as dehumanizing. A proliferation of dissenting sexualities found a voice, a feminine, indeed feminist, voice that shattered the notion of a unitary female sexual subject. For example, lesbians, who also spoke as feminists, stepped forward as advocates of S/M. How does lesbian identity politics accommodate women whose primary attraction is to women but whose chief sexual orientation is S/M and whose primary sexual political alignments are with gay and straight men? Whereas S/M advocates, such as the San Francisco group "Samois," defended discipline and bondage games for their erotic and spiritual qualities, voices surfaced that rationalized gender role-playing in the butch-fem mode as another, frequently misunderstood, erotic genre (Samois 1982; Nestle 1981, 1984; Clark 1987). With publications such as *Pleasure and Danger, The Powers of*

Desire, Heresies, On Our Backs, and in the writings of such self-identified lesbians and feminists such as Pat Califia, Gayle Rubin, Dorothy Allison, Amber Hollibaugh, Susie Bright, and many others, the notion of a unitary female or lesbian sexual subject was replaced by a female and lesbian subject who is prolific and heterogeneous in her sexual desires, behaviors, lifestyles, and values (e.g., Allison 1981, 1983, 1985; Bright 1984; Califia 1979, 1980, 1981; Hollibaugh 1983, 1984; Rubin 1982; English, Hollibaugh and Rubin 1987).

There was nothing comparable to the lesbian-feminist sexual ethic in the gay male subculture of the 1970s. Its sexual code leaned toward a strident libertarianism. There did materialize, though, a dominant intimate norm within at least some urban subcultures – couple-centered but non-monogamous (Seidman 1991). This sexual regime tolerated a great deal of diversity – for example, marriage-like arrangements but also the social acceptance of casual sex, public sex, sex with multiple partners, sex between friends, and paid sex.

There were, however, limits to sexual choice, even if these were not spelled out as clearly as they were in lesbian-feminist circles. By the early 1980s these limits were clarified as marginalized sexualities began to speak the very language of identity and legitimacy that mainstream gay men voiced a decade prior. While a myriad of submerged sexual interests clamored for public recognition, affirmative identities and communities materialized around S/M and man/boy love, only to meet with a great deal of opposition (Weeks 1985).

I will confine my remarks to S/M. By the early 1980s, there appeared gay male S/M bars, clubs, newsletters, magazines, and advocacy organizations (Califia 1982; Mains 1984; Kantrowitz 1984). They demanded that the dominant gay culture recognize their legitimacy, for example, by including them in public events and by representations that accorded their lives complexity and integrity. Whereas S/M advocates shared with the broader gay community a status as sexual minorities struggling for rights and legitimation, they were, in fact, a threat to the gay mainstream. S/M challenged the privileging of gender preference in defining sexual identity. Gay men who practice S/M may have exclusive sex with men, but they often define their sexual identity primarily in relation to their S/M practices. Although the gay male subculture may be more tolerant of S/M than the social mainstream, S/M practices in gay communities were often no less closeted. Gay critics ironically recycled arguments used against homosexuality to discredit S/M, for example, S/M was said to be a sign of unnatural, abnormal, immoral desires, or a symptom of social decline, cultural narcissism, or homophobia (e.g., Johnson 1985; Kleinberg 1982).

As lesbians and gay men succeeded in building elaborate subcultures, as they have obtained a measure of public legitimacy, they have met with resistance not only from outside forces but from within. Perhaps this very success has allowed for the surfacing of internal discord. In any event, as a dominant sociocultural order materialized in the lesbian and gay male communities, individuals who felt excluded or marginalized formed their own subcultural identities, networks, and political agendas. They challenged a hegemonic culture. The dominant ethnic model of identity and community was accused of reflecting a narrow white, middle-class, Eurocentric experience. The very discourse of liberation, with its notion of a gay subject unified by common interests, was viewed as a disciplining social force oppressive to large segments of the community in whose name it spoke.

Parallelling the assertion of a discourse of sexual difference by gays of color and sex rebels, a constructionist scholarship placed in doubt the rather commonplace assumption that "gay" connotes a unitary, transhistorical meaning. This scholarship aimed to relativize the concept of gay identity. In the late 1970s and early 1980s, writers such as Jonathan Ned Katz, Jeffrey Weeks, Carroll Smith-Rosenberg, John D'Emilio, and Lillian Faderman argued that the late twentieth-century Western experience of same-sex intimacies, and the terms used to describe it, are historically unique (see Foucault 1978; see also Katz 1983; Smith-Rosenberg 1985; Weeks 1977). A central claim was that in the late nineteenth and early twentieth centuries, sex, including same-sex experience, became the basis of a sexual and social identity. The deployment of sex as a core identity facilitated the historically unique formation of a distinctively "gay" identity, community and politics. Thus, modern terms such as "homosexual," "lesbian," and "gay" presuppose an historically specific sexual and social system – one in which gender preference is the basis of a core self identity.

According to this new history and sociology of sexuality, the categories of homosexual, gay, and lesbian do not signify a common, universal experience. The gay subject invoked in subcultural discourses and representations is seen as an historical product. Thus, Carroll Smith-Rosenberg in her classic essay, "The Female World of Love and Ritual: Relations between Women in Nineteenth-Century America," maintained that there was no category of homosexuality in the nineteenth century and that sexual orientation at that time did not signal a sexual or social identity (Smith-Rosenberg 1985). Moreover, she claimed that same-sex intimacies, including open, romantic involvements, were widely accepted, at least among middle-class women. It was not uncommon for intimate bonds between women to be maintained simultaneously with heterosexual marriage, without carrying a stigma or personal shame (see also Faderman 1981).

Similarly, in his pioneering documentary histories and commentaries, Jonathan Katz insisted that same-sex experiences of intimacy in nineteenth-century America were not the same phenomena as what is meant in postwar US by a homosexual or gay experience (Katz 1983). Katz documents the absence of a category of homosexuality – or heterosexuality – in American popular culture until the early twentieth century. A multiplicity of meanings were attached to same-sex desire, some signifying less a sexual than a gender phenomenon (see also Chauncey 1985). Although a great deal of debate has transpired around the precise dating of the origin of a homosexual identity, the general claim that the modern concept of the homosexual is implicated in a historically specific sociocultural configuration seems compelling.

Social constructionism was proposed as a conceptual or epistemological strategy (see Stein 1992; Mass 1990). Nevertheless, it carried definite social and political resonances. It alerts us to the repressive consequences of imposing current Western perspectives on non-Western experiences. In an effort to advance contemporary intellectual and political agendas, many intellectuals generalized recent Western categories. Lists of famous "lesbians" and "gay men" and their contributions to culture and social progress were intended to document the universality of homosexuals and their positive social role. Constructionists, though, criticized this conceptual strategy as ethnocentric and as having the undesirable consequence of erasing diverse social and historical experiences.

Yet, social constructionism exhibits an ambivalent relation to the ethnic identity model. On the one hand, as we have seen, constructionism featured the social and historical formation of sexual meanings, and thereby challenged the supposed universality of current models of sexual identity. On the other hand, constructionism reinforced the ethnic model by framing its project as investigating the historical rise and social formation of gay identity-based communities and politics. Indeed, social constructionism, at least the historical scholarship of the late 1970s through the 1980s, often served as a kind of celebration of the coming of age of a gay ethnic minority (e.g., D'Emilio 1983).

At the core of both the sociopolitical and intellectual (constructionist) assertion of difference is, at least implicitly, an assault upon a modernist culture – straight and gay – whose controlling logic of identity exhibits an intolerance toward particularity or difference. In its compulsion to classify, order, and generalize, to find grounds or foundations for its categories, forms of life, and conceptual strategies, gay culture – like the broader social mainstream – strains toward erasing difference, even as it prides itself on its celebration of the individual (Bauman 1991). In its affirmation of the particular against the general, of difference against the power of identity, the social and intellectual developments I have identified exhibit a post-modern edge.

The politics of contesting identity

Social constructionism recalls the standpoint of gay liberation. For example, by asserting the social and historical character of sexuality, it encourages, at least implicitly, a culture of social activism. If sexual conventions are social in origin, they can be changed through movements of political mobilization. In addition, constructionism provides a language highlighting social differences that lesbians and gay men who are marginalized can appeal to in order to legitimate their demands for social recognition and inclusion.

Viewed from the standpoint of gay liberationism, however, social constructionism appears suspect in certain regards. Unlike liberation theory, which was closely aligned to the politics of the movement, constructivist perspectives are increasingly disconnected from the political impulses of the movement. Indeed, gay constructionist knowledges have become almost the exclusive concern of academic intellectuals engaged in mostly rarefied discussions. For example, the seemingly interminable debate between "constructionists" and "essentialists" over such unresolvable issues as the respective role of "nature" versus "history" in the origin of homosexuality or the division between "realists" and "nominalists" in debating the meaning and application of "sexual" categories. Moreover, if the debates are not mired in such a metaphysical quagmire, they are often preoccupied with an equally sterile historical scholasticism that revolves around tracing the appearance of homosexual subcultures or dating the rise of a homosexual identity.

Furthermore, whereas liberation theory assumed an explicitly moral and political understanding of its own discourse, social constructionists are often wedded to a scientistism or objectivism, claiming for their own approach a true objectivity and evidentiary-based truth. Indeed, many intellectuals view a constructionist approach as superior precisely because it obtains true representations of reality in contrast to the ethnocentric distortions of essentialist conceptual strategies. While constructionists have uncovered ethnocentric bias in gay scholarship that universalizes present-centered, culture-bound perspectives, they have not applied the same suspicion to their own discourse. If categories of same-sex intimacies are marked by the sociocultural context of their origin, is not the same true of categories of sociohistorical analysis? And, if representations are embedded in broad national or civilizational environments, are they not likewise stamped by the more particular social traits of their producers, for example, their class, race, ethnicity, nationality, age, or gender? Gay social constructionists have been enthusiastic in taking over Foucault's historicism but decidedly less so when it comes to his understanding of the interconnection of social knowledge and power (see Seidman 1994b).

Many activists and intellectuals discontented with mainstream lesbian and gay male culture are looking back fondly to the agenda of gay liberation. Indeed, many who embrace the rhetoric of social constructionism do so, in part, because they see in it a warrant for radical social activism.

I share this discontent with mainstream lesbian and gay male cultural politics. I wish to recover the expansive social and political potential of liberation theory. Nevertheless, we need to be clear about its limitations. As I noted earlier, liberationists viewed their movement as one of sexual and gender liberation. Unfortunately, they understood emancipation as a release from homosexual/heterosexual and masculine/feminine roles. They challenged the dominant sexual and social regime by juxtaposing to it a polymorphous, androgynous ideal of a liberated – constraint-free – humanity. Wouldn't a liberated humanity, however, require stable identities, social roles, and normative constraints? Liberationists conflated the critique of rigid roles and identities with the critique of all identities and roles as indicative of social domination. In a word, liberationists projected a radically individualistic, antinomian utopian concept of emancipation. They lacked, moreover, a credible strategy to transform a stable, socially anchored system of sexual identity into a post-identity liberated social order.

Liberationist theory emerged as a gay identity and community were coalescing. It assumed the social dominance of a system of mutually exclusive roles around sexual orientation and gender; it formed as an opposition movement to this regime but reinforced it by narrowing its agenda to abolishing this system.

Today lesbians and gay men find themselves in a very different situation. Their standpoint is that of an elaborated culture founded upon an affirmative identity. Many individuals who are self-identified as lesbian and gay men have built coherent and meaningful lives around this identity. Moreover, although such individuals still encounter serious opposition in the social mainstream, they have gained considerable social legitimacy. The liberationist strategy of juxtaposing a post-identity model to an existing oppressive system of sexual identities would seem to lack credibility today.

The present condition of sexual subcultures and communities organized around affirmative gay/lesbian identities yet exhibiting heightened conflicts around those very identities should be the starting point of gay theory and politics. Where gay liberation confronted a dialectic of identity and difference that revolved around straight/gay and man/woman polarities, today these oppositions are multiplied a hundredfold as we introduce differences along the dimensions of race, ethnicity, gender, age, sexual act, class, lifestyle, and locale. Thus, the dominant liberationist opposition between gay/straight and gay/lesbian passes into divisions between say, white/black gay, black/Latino gay, middle-class/working-class gay, or lesbian/lesbian S/M, and on and on. Contemporary gay culture is centered on social difference and the multiplication of identities.

The standpoint of sexual theory and politics today must address the following question: How can we theorize and organize politically our multiple differences in light of the suspicions surrounding the dominant ethnic model of identity politics? One strategy has called for the abandonment or destabilization of identity as a ground of gay politics. In poststructuralist theorizing, a shift in focus is urged from the politics of personal identity to the politics of signification. In particular, a poststructural or "queer" theory has articulated this politics of signification in terms of the deconstruction of a hetero/homosexual cultural code that structures the "social text" of daily life (see Fuss 1991; Butters 1989; Boone and Cadden 1990).

Reflecting on the recent history of the exclusions and conflicts elicited around identity constructions, a poststructural perspective suggests abandoning efforts to defend or reconfigure identity politics. Appealing to one's sexual, gender, or ethnic identity as the ground of community and politics, even if such formulations allow for multiple and interlocking identities, is questioned because of its inherently unstable and exclusionary character. Diana Fuss describes a poststructural perspective on identity as follows: "Deconstruction dislocates the understanding of identity as self-presence and offers, instead, a view of identity as difference. To the extent that identity always contains the specter of non-identity within it, the subject is always divided and identity is always purchased at the price of the exclusion of the Other, the repression or repudiation of non-identity" (Fuss 1989: 102-103). In other words, preferring a view of identity as a relation rather than an essence, poststructuralists propose that the identity of an individual is therefore always implicated in – needs, produces, yet excludes – its opposite. "Heterosexuality" has meaning only in relation to "homosexuality"; the coherence of the former is built on the presence and the repression or repudiation of the latter. These two terms form an interdependent, hierarchical relation of signification.

From a poststructural perspective, gay identity constructions maintain the dominant hetero/homosexual code, including its normative heterosexuality. If homosexuality and heterosexuality are a coupling in which each presupposes the other, each being present in the invocation of the other, and in which this coupling inevitably assumes hierarchical forms, then the epistemic and political project of affirming a gay subject reinforces and reproduces this hierarchical figure. Poststructuralists recommend that this discursive figure itself – the hetero/homosexual definition – become the focus of a "deconstructive" analysis in place of the construction of the gay subject. In effect, poststructuralists urge an epistemic shift from the humanistic standpoint of the individual subject creating himself or herself to the standpoint of a "semiotic" cultural order.

The proposal to shift gay theory and politics from a preoccupation with "the gay subject" to the heterosexual/homosexual symbolic figure as a sort of semiotic order suggests a parallel shift from a minority discourse to a general social theory. Some poststructuralists view the heterosexual/homosexual code as at the very center of Western culture – as structuring the core modes of thought and culture of Western societies. This is the chief contention of Eve Kosofsky Sedgwick.

Epistemology of the Closet proposes that many of the major nodes of thought and knowledge in twentieth-century Western culture as a whole are structured – indeed, fractured – by a chronic, now endemic crisis of homo-heterosexual definition . . . The book will argue that an understanding of virtually any aspect of modern Western culture must be, not merely incomplete, but damaged in its central substance to the degree that it does not incorporate a critical analysis of modern homo/heterosexual definition. (Sedgwick 1990: 1)

Sedgwick conjectures that the homo/heterosexual figure is a master cultural trope marking not only sexual definitions but categorical pairings such as secrecy/disclosure, knowledge/ignorance, private/public, masculine/feminine, majority/minority, innocence/initiation, natural/artificial, same/different, health/illness, growth/decadence, urbane/provincial (1990: 11, 71–72). She urges an epistemological shift from a focus on the resisting gay subject to the analysis of the homosexual /heterosexual code and its pervasive structuring of culture and social practices.

The surfacing of a poststructural standpoint may be interpreted, in part, as a response to the impasse of current gay politics and theory. In particular, the ambivalent positioning of gay politics between radical separatism and assimilationism seems closely tied to its centering on identity. Poststructuralists aim to destabilize identity as a ground of politics and theory in order to open up alternative social and political possibilities. If this view is plausible, poststructuralism may be interpreted as a kind of theoretical wing of Queer Nation. Both appeal to a disruptive politic of subversion against the normalizing, disciplining norms and social processes within the straight and gay mainstream.

To what end is poststructural critique directed? If the premier collection *Inside/Out* is exemplary of the poststructural turn in gay theory, the chief domain of struggle is the multiple sites of cultural production, in particular, high-brow literary and popular culture (Fuss 1991). The principal aim is to document the presence of the hetero/homosexual figure, to chart its discursive power effects and culturally contagious character, and to deconstruct it by revealing the mutual dependency of the polar terms and its susceptibility to be reversed and subverted. Underlying this politics of subversion is a vague notion that this will encourage new, affirmative forms of personal and social life, although poststructuralists are reluctant to name their social vision. The poststructuralist move seems troubling, moreover, to the extent that social practices are framed narrowly as discursive and signifying, and critical practice is confined to deconstructive textual strategies. Insofar as poststructuralists narrow cultural codes into binary signifying figures, insofar as discursive practices are not institutionally situated, there is an edging toward textual idealism.

An additional doubt about the poststructuralist turn: who is the agent or subject of the politics of subversion? The poststructuralist critique of the logic of identity ends in a refusal to name a "subject" or agent of critique. Indeed, I detect a disposition in the deconstruction of identity to slide into viewing identity itself as the fulcrum of domination and its subversion as the center of an anti-identity politic. For example, although Judith Butler often elaborates complex understandings of identity as a disciplining force she at times conflates identity with domination and a politics of subversion with a politics against identity. "If it is already true that 'gay men' and 'lesbians' have been traditionally designated as impossible identities, errors of classification, unnatural disasters within juridco-medical discourses . . . then perhaps these sites of disruption, error, confusion, and trouble can be the very rallying points for a certain resistance to classification and to identity as such" (Butler 1991: 16). Butler's politics of subversion at times becomes little more than a kind of disruptive repetitive performance that works "sexually *against* identity." But to what end?

Poststructuralist gay theory edges beyond an anti-identity politics to a politics against identity *per se*. Implicit in this subversion of identity is a celebration of liminality, of the spaces between structures or outside structure itself. A strong parallel with Queer Nation is, once again, apparent. Like the poststructuralist refusal of identity, Queer Nation assumes that under the undifferentiated sign of Queer are to be united all those heterogeneous desires and interests that are marginalized and excluded in the straight and gay mainstream. Queers are not united by a unitary identity but only by their opposition to normalizing social forces. Queer Nation aims to be the voice of all who are disempowered by virtue of being subjected to disciplinary social control. In its resistance to social codes that impose unitary identities, in rebelling against forces imposing a repressive coherence and normalizing order, Queer Nation affirms an abstract unity of difference without wishing to name and fix these. This positioning resembles the poststructuralist refusal to name the subject, as if any anchoring of the flux and abundant richness of experience marks the beginnings of domination and hierarchy.

This refusal to anchor experience in identifications ends up, ironically, denying differences by either submerging them in an undifferentiated oppositional mass or by blocking the development of individual and social differences through the disciplining compulsory imperative to remain undifferentiated. Poststructuralists, like Queer Nationals, hope to avoid the self-limiting, fracturing dynamics of identification by an insistent disruption of identity. Yet, their cultural positioning, indeed their subversive politics, presupposes these very identifications and social anchorings (see ch. 7).

I have noted a strain in poststructuralist gay theory to go beyond a critique of identity politics to a politics against identity. The latter seems driven by its centering on a politics of identity subversion and draws from romantic, antinomian, and anarchistic traditions for its cultural resonance. Its limit, if you will, is the continuing practical efficacy of the resisting gay subject. In other words, it fails to theoretically engage the practices of individuals organized around affirmative lesbian and gay identities. Although poststructuralists acknowledge that affirmative gay identities have developed in resistance to an administrative-juridical-medical institutional rendering of same-sex desires as a site of deviance and social regulation, their focus on subverting identity seems to abstract from this institutional struggle and the social origin and efficacy of identity politics (see Warner 1994). Identity constructions are not disciplining and regulatory only in a self-limiting and oppressive way; they are also personally, socially, and politically enabling; it is this moment that is captured by identity political standpoints that seems untheorized in the poststructural critique.

If the issue is not identity versus nonidentity, if subjects and social formations cannot elude categories of identity, if, indeed, identity categories have personal and socially enabling and enriching qualities, then the issue is less their affirmation or subversion than analyzing the kinds of identities that are socially produced and their manifold social and political significance. In this regard, I would support the poststructuralist proposal to view identity as a site of ongoing social contestation rather than a quasi-natural substance or an accomplished social fact. Identities are never fixed or stable, not only because they elicit otherness but because they are occasions of continuing social struggle. Yet, I would not privilege, as many poststructuralists seem to, signifying practices but would connect these to institutional dynamics. I would, moreover, follow the poststructural emphasis in framing identities as social structuring forces or, to use the Foucauldian terms, as disciplining forces whose consequences for the individual, social relations, and politics should be critically analyzed. However, to the extent that some poststructuralists reduce the disciplining force of identity constructions to modes of domination, I would object. This rendering edges toward a politics against identity, to a sort of negative dialectics. As disciplining forces, identities are not only self-limiting and productive of hierarchies but are self-enabling and productive of social collectivities, moral bonds, and political agency. Although the poststructuralist problematization of identity is a welcome critique of the essentialist celebration of a unitary subject and separatist politic, its troubled relation to identity edges toward an empty politics of gesture or disruptive performance that forfeits an integrative, transformative politic.

The recent proliferation of critiques of identity politics, particularly under the guise of poststructuralism, gives expression to the sociopolitical assertion of difference that I sketched previously. In its critique of identity politics as normalizing and exclusionary, in its disruption of an illusory unity that masks difference and normalizing control, in pressuring a view of identities as political artifices, poststructuralism is valuable. To the extent, however, that poststructuralist perspectives edge toward an anti-identity or post-identity standpoint, to the extent that they fold into a politics of the disruptive gesture, they lack coherence. At another level, insofar as poststructuralism encourages us to focus less on the formation of gay identities as grounds of an ethnic minority and urges us to analyze cultural codes, it pushes our inquiries beyond a sociology of a minority to a study of the structure and tensions of modern culture. Yet to the extent that poststructuralists reduce cultural codes to textual practice and to the extent that these practices are abstracted from institutional contexts, we come against the limits of poststructuralism as social critique.

Foregrounding the social

Identity politics has assumed that a politic can be erected on the presumption that all individuals who have in common a certain trait (e.g., a particular gender, sexual orientation, race, or ethnicity) share something essential and defining about themselves, something which marks them off from others and which can serve as the basis for creating a community of interest. However, every assertion of a social identity, no matter how much it strains to be inclusive, produces boundaries of inside/outside and functions as a normalizing, disciplinary force. Moreover, identity politics has strained either towards an interest-group politic aimed at assimilationism or an equally troubling ethnic-nationalist separatism. Poststructuralism suggests a reverse or, if you wish, deconstructive social logic. It dissolves any notion of a substantial unity in identity constructions leaving only rhetorics of identities, multiple "subject positions," and performative enactments of identity. Whereas identity politics offers a strong politics on a conceptually weak, politically exclusionary basis, poststructuralism offers a thin politics as it problematizes the very notion of a collective in whose name a movement acts.

I sense the battle over identity politics beginning to grow tiresome, or perhaps it is my own weariness. The terms of the discussion are in need of a shift. In both defenders of identity politics and its poststructural critics there is a preoccupation with the self and the politics of representation. Institutional and historical analysis and an integrative political vision seems to have dropped out. Perhaps as the politics of backlash comes to an end, we can begin to entertain more affirmative social and political visions (cf. Nicholson and Seidman 1995). Central to a renewal of a political vision will be approaches that emphasize viewing identity as a social positioning, as marking a social location in the institutional, administrative, juridical organization of society, and as an axis of social stratification. As much as race, sexuality, gender, or class mark a site of self-definition and therefore implicate us in a politics of identity and representation, these categories serve as social and political markers. Sexual status positions the self in the social periphery or the social center; it places the self in a determinate relation to institutional resources, social opportunities, legal protections, and social privileges; it places the self in a relation to a range of forms of social control. Conceptualizing identity in a multidimensional social space features its macrosocial significance; we would be compelled to relate the politics of representation to institutional dynamics.

In framing identity as a social positioning we will need to avoid assuming that all individuals who share a social location by virtue of their gender or sexual orientation share an identical history or social experience. The notion that a hetero/homosexual social positioning creates two antithetical unitary collectives, the former positioned as one of privilege while the latter is positioned as an oppressed and resisting subject, lacks coherence. While appealing to a collective interest is a condition of political mobilization, it is unnecessary and undesirable to invoke a substantialist understanding of group life (cf. Young 1995).

A major shortcoming of sociological essentialism is that it assumes that each axis of social constitution – gender, sexual orientation, ethnicity, class – can be isolated. However, as many feminist and gay people of color have argued, these axes of social positioning cannot be isolated in terms of a set of common attributes and experiences since they are always intersecting and mutually inflecting. Individuals experience sexual orientation in a particular class, race, or gender mediated way, and only so. While we may wish, from time to time, to differentiate these axes of social positioning and identification for specific intellectual and practical reasons, we must avoid reifying what are analytical and political moves.

Unfortunately, I can do no more at this point than offer these rather sketchy proposals. However, the general direction of my thinking should be clear. Let me give a quick forward-looking résumé.

I urge a shift away from the preoccupation with self identity and representations that is characteristic of identity politics and poststructuralism to an analysis that embeds the self in institutional practices. Queer intellectuals need to imagine a politics of resistance that is guided by a transformative and affirmative social vision. This suggests an oppositional politic that intends institutional and cultural change without, however, being wedded to a millenarian vision. In a "postmodern" culture, anticipation of the "end of domination" gives way to multiple, sometimes intersecting, on-going struggles for democratization, social justice, and expanded control and choice over one's body, desires, pleasures, and communities of solidarity.

Academic intellectuals have an important role in these struggles. Our struggles over knowledges are crucial to the extent that knowledges, especially disciplinary knowledges, are entangled in dynamics of social and political power. Additionally, academics are a crucial source of critical perspectives which can provide cultural resources for movements of political mobilization. The relationship between intellectuals, especially academic intellectuals, knowledges and power is a central theme of chapter 7.

7

Deconstructing queer theory, or, some difficulties in a theory and politics of difference

From at least the early 1950s through the mid-1970s, the idea was widespread in American society that what was called homosexuality was a phenomenon with a uniform meaning across histories. Both mainstream America and the homosexual mainstream assumed that homosexuality marks out a common human identity. Public dispute has centered on the moral significance of this presumed natural fact. Whereas the post-World War II scientific, medical, and legal establishment routinely figured homosexuality as signaling a psychologically abnormal, morally inferior, and socially deviant human type, homophile groups and their supporters defended the "normality" of "the homosexual." Even the mainstream lesbian and gay movements of the 1970s primarily contested stereotypes of homosexuality, not the notion that "the homosexual" is a distinct human type. Public struggles easily folded into friend-versus-foe of "the homosexual."

Since the late 1970s, the terms of the struggle over "homosexuality" have changed dramatically. The assumption that "homosexuality" is a uniform, identical condition has given way to the notion that the meaning of same-sex sexual desire varies considerably within and across societies (e.g., by class, race, ethnicity, or subcultural identity). By the early 1980s, it had become conventional wisdom among many intellectuals at least that the meaning and therefore the experience of same-sex sexuality articulates a social and historical, not a natural and universal, logic.

One consequence of the "constructionist" questioning of "essentialism" has been the loss of innocence within the gay community. The presumption of a lesbian and gay community unified by a common baseline of experience and interest has been placed into seemingly permanent doubt. The struggle over homosexuality has been grudgingly acknowledged to be a struggle among lesbian, gay, bisexual, and queer individuals and groups who hold to different, sometimes conflicting, social interests, values, and political agendas. A new cynicism has crept into lesbian and gay intellectual culture. Representations of homosexuality produced within these subcultures evoke similar suspicions with regard to their disciplining role and their regulatory power as representations issuing from a heterosexist cultural mainstream. No discourse or representation of homosexuality, no matter how sincerely it speaks in the name of liberation, can escape the suspicion that it exhibits particular social interests and entails definite political effects. All images of homosexuality have, to use Foucault's term, power/knowledge effects or are perceived as productive of social hierarchies. The simple polarity between friend and foe of homosexuality has given way to a multivocal cultural clash that is so disconcerting to some intellectuals that they have retreated into the presumed certainties of a naturalistic ontology, e.g., the gay brain.

I write today with a sense of the end of an era. The sex and race debates exposed deep and bitter divisions among lesbians and gay men; AIDS has threatened the very desires by which many of us have defined and organized ourselves into a community with the spectre of disease and death; a relentless politic of coming out, being out, and outing, has failed to deliver on its promise of liberation from fear and prejudice; the growing crisis of lesbian-feminism and the dubious gains of the gay mainstream surrendering to a single-interest group politic of assimilationism suggest the exhaustion of the dominant templates of lesbian and gay politics. Solidarity built around the assumption of a common identity and agenda has given way to social division; multiple voices, often speaking past one another, have replaced a defiant monotone which drowned out dissonant voices in favor of an illusory but exalted unity.

If we are witnessing the passing of an era, it is, in no small part, because of the discrediting of the idea of a unitary, common sexual identity. The troubling of identity was instigated initially in the sex and race debates. Sex rebels protesting the consolidation of a gay and lesbian-feminist sexual ethic, and the resounding public voices of people of color contesting the writing of the lesbian and gay subject as a white, middle-class figure, were crucial discursive junctures in the growing sense of crisis in the lesbian and gay mainstream. I view the assertion of a queer politics and theory as both a response to, and further instigation of, this crisis. Although many meanings circulate under this sign, queer suggests a positioning as oppositional to both the heterosexual and homosexual mainstream. I take the critique of "the homosexual subject," perhaps the grounding idea of modern Western images of homosexuality, as central to queer interventions. Both queer theory and politics intend to expose and disturb the normalizing politics of identity as practiced in the straight and lesbian and gay mainstream;

whereas queer politics mobilizes against all normalized hierarchies, queer theory put into permanent crisis the identity-based theory and discourses that have served as the unquestioned foundation of lesbian and gay life. Queers disrupt and subvert in the name of a politic of difference which moves back and forth between anarchism and a radical democratic pluralism. My focus will be on the theory side of queer interventions.

Queer theory represents a powerful force in rethinking homosexuality as a culture and politics. It might seem odd to think of mostly academic theorists as shaping a movement of cultural change. Yet their placement in prestigious universities, their growing prominence in gay intellectual culture, and their influence in the radical politics of Queer Nation and HIV/AIDS activism suggests that they have become an important force shaping lesbian and gay culture and politics. Indicative of their social influence is their critical reception from old-guard humanistic intellectual elites. For example, Jeff Escoffier (1990) registers concern about the depoliticization of gay intellectuals as they are converted to deconstruction. Similarly, in a brief review of the 1991 lesbian and gay studies conference, Simon Watney (1992) criticizes queer theory for marginalizing AIDS politics in favor of the high ground of theory. These criticisms evidence a cultural clash among elites who represent divergent intellectual and political standpoints. Such cultural collisions should not be discounted as mere ideological obfuscation. Cultural elites produce representations and discourses which shape images of self and community and political strategies. Although news reporters, novelists, artists, and film makers may have access to more people, academic intellectuals influence these media and cultural elites directly and exert a broad public influence through teaching and writing. Just as an earlier generation of liberationist theorists shaped gay cultural and political life, today it is a new movement, a generation of queer theorists, who are shaping lesbian and gay intellectual culture.

To grasp the social and political significance of queer theory, I wish to situate it historically. I sketch the historical contours of the development of lesbian and gay intellectual culture from the early 1970s to the present. This sketch is intended to be merely suggestive. This is followed by a characterization of the basic ideas of queer theory and its social and political meaning. Finally, I expose its own silences while appreciating its important connection to a politics of knowledge.

Situating post-Stonewall gay intellectual culture

A first phase of lesbian and gay intellectual culture spanned roughly the years between 1968 and 1975. In 1968, there was only the beginnings of a gay community and that only in a few major urban areas. A lesbian and gay cultural apparatus, if one can speak of that in 1968, was the product of a previous generation which organized around the Mattachine Society and the Daughters of Bilitis. Reflecting the local and clandestine character of these organizations, there were no national public lesbian- or gay-identified newspapers, magazines, or presses; no institutionalized gay art or theatre, and only a few gay-identified writers who mostly wrote in isolation. Homosexual theory moved back and forth between a view of homosexuality as a secondary psychological disorder characteristic of a segment of the population and a normal desire present in varying degrees in the human population. The beginnings of a theory of homosexuality as an oppressed minority was voiced by radicals such as Harry Hay but largely ignored. Gay politics was overwhelmingly oriented to civil rights with the aim of social assimilation (D'Emilio 1983).

A lesbian and gay liberationist movement emerged in response both to the forced heterosexualization of society and to the assimilationist politics of the homophile movement (Adam 1987; Altman 1982; Faderman 1991). At its cultural forefront were mostly young, educated, white individuals who identified themselves as gay liberationists or lesbian-feminists. They criticized the heterosexism and sexism of the social mainstream. Inspired by the new left and feminism, they substituted a transformative politics for the politics of assimilationism of the Mattachine Society and the Daughters of Bilitis. Liberationist thinking exhibited several major strains. For example, homosexuality was often viewed as a natural, universal condition. Protest was aimed at the pathologizing of homosexuality. Homosexuality was being reclaimed as natural, normal, and good without challenging a sexual regime organized around hetero/homosexuality. However, some liberationists struggled against a system of mutually exclusive sexual and gender roles; they envisioned an androgynous, polymorphous ideal of humanity liberated from the roles of heterosexual/ homosexual and man/woman and from a narrow genital-centered sexuality. Other liberationists, especially lesbian-feminists and the "radical fairie movement," assumed and celebrated the difference between heterosexuals and homosexuals; radically nationalistic, they aimed to build a new community and culture. Some proposed a separatist agenda while others appealed to liberal pluralistic images of the American mosaic.

By the early 1970s, we can observe the beginnings of a lesbian and gay national cultural apparatus. Liberationists were pivotal in shaping this intellectual culture. They published journals, magazines, newsletters, and newspapers; national publications cropped up circulating lesbian and gay art, literature, and theory. Although many lesbian- and gay-identified intellectuals had ties to academia – indeed many were graduate students or professors – their writings were squarely anchored in movement culture and politics. In part, this position reflected their weak ties to academia (as junior faculty in a fiercely hostile setting) and their strong ties (e.g., through self-definition and community affiliation) to the evolving movement. With their primary personal and social roots in the movement, gay liberationists and lesbian-feminists were able to merge the roles of intellectual and activist (e.g., Altman 1971; Bunch 1975). The style and language of their writing is indicative of the interests of movement activists, e.g., critiques that typically took the form of short essays, poems, pamphlets, manifestoes, memoirs, short stories, and autobiographical statements rather than analytical or theoretically oriented books. Their work appeared in inexpensive newsletters, newspapers, pamphlets, or books and anthologies written for general public consumption. In short, in the early years of gay liberation and lesbian-feminism, lesbian/gay intellectual culture was firmly rooted in movement concerns and public struggles. Liberationists were, if you will, public intellectuals, spokespersons for a social movement and community-in-the-making.

A second phase of lesbian and gay culture spans roughly the mid-1970s to the mid-1980s. This was a period of community building and the political maturation of the lesbian and gay movements. A fully elaborated and institutionalized gay community dotted the social landscape of virtually all major cities across the United States. A pivotal part of this social development was the creation of a national, public lesbian and gay cultural apparatus that included newspapers, periodicals, publishing companies, and artistic and literary associations. A national gay and lesbian culture existed for the first time in the United States by the mid-1980s.

Although gay liberationists were pivotal in this community-building effort, their ideas and agenda were marginalized in the new lesbian and gay mainstream. Liberationist visions of creating a new humanity gave way to ethnic nationalistic models of identity and single-interest group politics inspired by either a liberal assimilationist ideal or, in the case of lesbian-feminism, a separatist ideological agenda. Being lesbian and gay was celebrated as a distinctive sociocultural identity.

A new intelligentsia appeared. With the institutionalization of lesbian/ gay communities across the nation, a new stratum of lesbian- and gay-identified cultural workers (e.g., writers, news reporters, artists, and knowledge producers) could be supported by newspapers, magazines, book publishers, and theatres. Moreover, the expanded tolerance for homosexuality in mainstream United States allowed for the rise of a new stratum of gay academic intellectuals who made homosexuality into the topic of their research and theorizing. Many of these academics had roots in gay liberationism or lesbian-feminist communities. They were, in general, critical of the view of homosexuality as a transhistorical condition. They disputed attempts to frame homosexual identity as a fixed, universally identical phenomenon without, however, breaking away from identity politics. They approached homosexuality in social and historical terms. In particular, the merging of homosexuality and identity was analyzed as a recent Western historical event, not a natural, universal condition.

Unlike a previous generation of lesbian- and gay-identified intellectuals, this generation (e.g., Weeks 1977; D'Emilio 1983; Boswell 1980; Faderman 1981) were much more academically anchored. Mostly historians, they often were tenured faculty; they wrote for academic journals or published books in university presses; they were the first generation of intellectuals who could succeed in academia despite assuming a lesbian or gay identity. Although many of these intellectuals were academics, their work was not divorced from movement culture and politics. In part, this unity reflects the fact that as historians they generally wrote in a style broadly accessible to the lay community, even as they aimed for recognition by their colleagues. Moreover, many had a history of social activism and were politically and socially integrated into lesbian and gay life; these lay communities were a chief audience for this new intelligentsia. Perhaps most importantly, their work, which focused on the social formation of a homosexual identity and community, reinforced the heightened minoritization of lesbian and gay life in the late 1970s. Thus, although many of these intellectuals wrote as academics seeking collegial status, their strong ties to the history and current politics of the movement, and their identification with disciplines that valued public education, allowed them to merge the roles of academic and public intellectual.

The third phase of an evolving lesbian/gay intellectual culture spans the period between roughly the mid-1980s and the present. Community building continued as the lesbian and gay communities assumed the form of fully institutionalized subcultures. Moreover, while the previous period witnessed dramatic social and political successes, a drive to become mainstream dominated movement politics in this period. Indeed, the antigay backlash of the late 1970s through the early 1980s might be read as evidence of the very success of mainstreaming. Mainstreaming is evident in the marketing of blatantly gay-identified fashion; in the inclusion of gays in the Rainbow Coalition as an integral partner; in the diminished danger social and cultural elites felt in being associated publicly with lesbian and gay causes. Perhaps the most dramatic illustration of mainstreaming occurred in the realm of intellectual culture. Mainstream high-brow journals, magazines, and presses opened up to lesbian- and gay-identified writers, especially in academically oriented publishing. Journals such as *October*, *Social Text*, *Socialist Review*, *Radical America*, *South Atlantic Quarterly*, *differences*, *Oxford Review*, and *Raritan* have published major statements on lesbian/gay themes. Important presses, from Routledge and Beacon to university presses such as Chicago, Columbia, Duke, Minnesota, and Indiana, have developed strong lists in lesbian and gay studies. Gay studies programs and research centers are being established in major universities.

The mainstreaming of lesbian and gay intellectual culture means that the university has become a chief site for the production of lesbian and gay discourses. To be sure, discourses of same-sex experiences continue to be produced by nonacademic cultural workers, e.g., film makers, journalists, novelists, poets, essayists, pornographers, political activists, and writers. Yet it is increasingly gay-identified academics who are controlling the production of lesbian and gay knowledges. And while this development suggests that lesbians and gay men will have a voice in the struggles over the production and circulation of knowledge, it also means that gay intellectual culture is now more divided than ever between an academic and nonacademic sector. Moreover, as the gap widens between an academically dominated discourse of homosexuality and everyday gay culture, there is the distinct possibility that gay theory and politics will have only a feeble connection. As theorists and activists are socially positioned differently, as they speak in different languages to divergent publics, their relations may be strained and weak; for example, theorists might invoke activists for political correctness while activists appeal to theory for cultural respectability.

The third phase has seen the rise of a new force in lesbian and gay intellectual culture: queer theory. An older intellectual elite of self-taught interpreters of lesbian and gay life (e.g., Katz 1976; Martin and Lyon 1972; Rich 1980) and professional historians and social scientists (e.g., D'Emilio 1983; Trumbach 1977; Weeks 1977; Smith-Rosenberg 1975), whose roots and chief public were the lesbian and gay community, are losing ground in the struggle over defining knowledges of "homosexuality" to a new cultural elite of academics who increasingly deploy the sign of queer to describe or position their approach. The most conspicuous strain of queer theory draws heavily on French poststructural theory and the critical method of deconstruction. Producers of queer theory are integrated into academia more completely than previous generations who produced gay knowledges; they are mostly English professors who pursue collegial status as well as recognition from the lesbian and gay nonacademic cultural elite, e.g., public writers, editors of magazines and newspapers, commercial publishers, and political elites. Queer theorists have often come of age during a period of the renewed activism of HIV/AIDS politics and share a spirit of the renewal of transformative politics with groups like ACT-UP or Queer Nation. Queer theory is profoundly shaping gay intellectual culture, at least that segment previously controlled by independent scholars, academic historians, and social scientists.

Queer theorists are positioned to become a substantial force in shaping lesbian and gay intellectual culture. Frequently unified by generation and by academic affiliation, sharing a culture based on common conceptual and linguistic practices, and capturing the spirit of discontent toward both the straight mainstream and the lesbian and gay mainstream, queer theory is an important social force in the making of gay intellectual culture and politics in the 1990s. I wish to contribute to understanding and assessing this cultural movement.

Deconstructing gay identity: queer theory and the politics of knowledge

Despite an antigay backlash, the lesbian and gay movement made giant steps towards community building and social mainstreaming in the 1980s. In urban centers across the United States the lesbian and gay community staked out a public territorial, institutional, cultural, and political identity. From this social base, lesbians and gay men campaigned, with a great deal of success, for social inclusion, as evidenced by civil rights legislation, political representation, legal reform, and the appearance of affirmative media representations.

Social success may, ironically, have allowed for hitherto-muted differences to surface publicly. Differences that were submerged for the sake of solidarity against a heterosexist mainstream erupted into public view. In particular, clashes over sexuality and race served as key sites for differences to coalesce socially. Local skirmishes over sexual ethics and political priorities escalated into a general war over the social coherence and desirability of asserting a lesbian and gay identity.

The dominant ethnic nationalist model of identity and politics was criticized for exhibiting white, middle-class, hetero-imitative values and liberal political interests. On the political front, parallel criticisms of the lesbian and gay mainstream surfaced among HIV/AIDS activists (e.g., ACT-UP) and Queer Nation activists who positioned themselves in opposition to the normalizing, disciplining cultural politics of the lesbian and gay social center. They challenged the very basis of mainstream gay politics: a politics organized on the premise of a unified subject. By calling themselves queer, and by organizing around broad issues of controlling the body or access to health care, a new post-identity cultural political force coalesced in the 1980s. On the intellectual front, a wave of lesbian- and gay-identified people of color and sex radicals attacked the unitary gay identity construction as normative and as a disciplining force which excludes and marginalizes many desires, acts, and identities of lesbian- and gay-identified individuals. They evolved various alternative proposals for rethinking identity and politics, for example, the notion of interlocking subject positions and sites of oppression and resistance. Nevertheless, it has been the movement of queer theorists, drawing on French poststructuralism, who have theoretically articulated this challenge to identity politics and whose ideas have moved into the center of lesbian and gay intellectual culture.

Poststructural theory frames literary criticism less as a matter of defining or contesting a canon, engaging in a dialogue on presumably universal questions of literary form, or as delineating the formal structures of a text, than as a type of social analysis. Literary texts are viewed as social and political practices, as organized by social and cultural codes, and indeed as social forces that structure identities, social norms, and power relations. In particular, texts are viewed as organized around foundational symbolic figures such as masculine/feminine or heterosexual/homosexual. Such binary oppositions are understood as categories of knowledge; they structure the way we think and organize experience. These linguistic and discursive meanings contribute to the making of social hierarchies. Deconstruction aims to disturb or displace the power of these hierarchies by showing their arbitrary, social, and political character. Deconstruction may be described as a cultural politics of knowledge. It is this rendering of literary analysis into social analysis, of textual critique into social critique, of readings into a political practice, of politics into the politics of knowledge, that makes deconstruction and the queer theory inspired by it an important movement of theory and politics.

Who are the queer theorists? Some names may serve as initial markers: Eve Sedgwick (1990), Diana Fuss (1991), Judith Butler (1990, 1991), Lee Edelman (1994), Michael Moon (1990), Teresa de Lauretis (1991), Thomas Yingling (1990), and D. A. Miller (1991). Key texts include Sedgwick's *Epistemology of the Closet* (1990), Butler's *Gender Trouble* (1990), and Diana Fuss's *Essentially Speaking* (1989). A central statement is the anthology, *Inside/Out: Lesbian Theories, Gay Theories*, edited by Diana Fuss (1991). Let me be clear. I am not speaking of an intellectually and politically unified cultural movement. Queer theorists are a diverse lot exhibiting important disagreements and divergences. Nevertheless, they share certain broad commitments – in particular, they draw heavily on French poststructural theory and deconstruction as a method of literary and social critique; they deploy in key ways psychoanalytic categories and perspectives; they favor a de-centering or deconstructive strategy that retreats from positive programmatic social and political proposals; they imagine the social as a text to be interpreted and criticized towards the aim of contesting dominant knowledges and social hierarchies.

I intend to sketch what I take to be the dominant intellectual and political impulse of queer theory. I do not intend to provide detailed analyses of key texts. My aim is to make the project of a particularly influential cultural movement intelligible and to begin to assess its importance. In the remainder of this section, I wish to state, as clearly as I can, the guiding impulse and core ideas of this body of work.

Homosexual theory – whether essentialist or constructionist – has favored a view of homosexuality as a condition of a social minority. Although essentialist and constructionist perspectives may assume that homoeroticism is a universal experience, both viewpoints simultaneously aim to account for the making of a homosexual social minority. For example, an essentialist position might hold that only some individuals are exclusively or primarily homosexual. Holding to this assumption, the analyst might proceed to explain how this homosexual population has come to speak for itself as a social minority. A social constructionist position might assume that, though same-sex experiences are a universal condition, only some individuals in some societies organize their lives around homoeroticism. A social analyst who assumes constructionist premises may wish to trace the social factors which have transformed this universal homoerotic desire into a homosexual identity. Despite differences between so-called essentialist and constructionist assumptions regarding same-sex experience, lesbian and gay analysts have been preoccupied with explaining the social forces creating a self-conscious homosexual minority. Both essentialist and social constructionist versions of lesbian/gay theory in the 1970s and 1980s have related stories of the coming of age of a collective homosexual subject.

Queer theorists have criticized the view of homosexuality as a property of an individual or group, whether that identity is explained as natural or social in origin. They argue that this perspective leaves in place the heterosexual/homosexual binary as a master framework for constructing the self, sexual knowledge, and social institutions. A theoretical and political project which aims exclusively to normalize homosexuality and to legitimate homosexuality as a social minority does not challenge a social regime which perpetuates the production of subjects and social worlds organized and regulated by the heterosexual/homosexual binary. Minoritizing epistemological strategies stabilizes a power/knowledge regime which defines bodies, desires, behaviours, and social relations in binary terms according to a fixed hetero/homo sexual preference. Such linguistic and discursive binary figures inevitably get framed in hierarchical terms, thus reinforcing a politics of exclusion and domination. Moreover, in such a regime homosexual politics is pressured to move between two limited options: the liberal struggle to legitimate homosexuality in order to maximize a politics of inclusion and the separitist struggle to assert difference on behalf of a politics of ethnic nationalism.

To date, the dominant logic of lesbian and gay politics has been that of battling heteronormativity toward the end of legitimating homosexuality. As important as that project is, queer theorists have exposed its limits. A binary sex system, whether compulsively heterosexual or not, creates rigid psychological and social boundaries that inevitably give rise to systems of dominance and hierarchy – certain feelings, desires, acts, identities, and social formations are excluded, marginalized, and made inferior. To the extent that individuals feel compelled to define themselves as hetero-or-homosexual, they erect boundaries and protective identities which are self-limiting and socially controlling. Moreover, identity constructions developed on the basis of an exclusively hetero-or-homo desire are inherently unstable; the assertion of one identity category presupposes, incites, and excludes its opposite. The declaration of heterosexual selfhood elicits its opposite, indeed needs the homosexual in order to be coherent and bounded. In fact, the very consciousness of "the homosexual other" cannot but elicit suspicions of homosexual desire in oneself and others across the range of daily same-sex interactions, friendships, dreams, fantasies, and public images. Heterosexuality and homosexuality belong together as an unstable coupling, simultaneously mutually productive and subverting.

Beyond producing a series of psychological, social, and political oppositions and instabilities, a binary sexual regime places serious limits on sexual theory and politics. To the extent that sexual (and self) identity is defined by sexual orientation equated with gender preference, a vast range of desires, acts, and social relations are never made into an object of theory and politics. To equate sexual liberation with heterosexual and homosexual legitimation presupposes an extremely reductive notion of "the sexual" since it leaves out of consideration any explicit concern with the body, sensual stimulation, and sex acts and relations other than in terms of gender preference. Implicit in the texts of the queer theorists is the claim that the mainstream focus on legitimating a homo-sexual preference and identity betrays middle-class, conventional intimate values. By focusing politics exclusively on legitimating same-sex gender choice, the lesbian and gay movement leaves politically uncontested a range of particular sexual and intimate values that may be marginalized or devalued in other respects. In other words, the gay mainstream often takes for granted the normative status of long-term monogamous, adult-to-adult, intraracial, intragenerational, romantic sexual and intimate values. If a person's sexual orientation involves, say, same-sex S/M or interracial or commercial sex, s/he would be resistant to reducing the politics of sexual orientation to gender preference and the legitimation of a homosexual identity. The gay mainstream, including gay theory, is criticized as a disciplining, normative force, one unwittingly reinforcing dynamics of exclusion and hierarchy.

Queer theorists argue that homosexuality should not be treated as an issue of the lives and fate of a social minority. Implicit in this approach is the notion that the identity of the individual is the ultimate foundation for gay theory and politics. The gay community and its politics is imagined as the summation and mobilization of individuals who are self-defined as gay or lesbian. Queer critics urge an epistemological shift. They propose to focus on a cultural level. Their field of analysis is linguistic or discursive structures and, in principle, their institutional settings. Specifically, their object of analysis is the hetero/homosexual opposition. This is understood as a category of knowledge, a way of defining and organizing selves, desires, behaviors, and social relations. Through the articulation of this hetero/homosexual figure in texts and social practices (e.g., therapeutic regimes or marital customs and laws), it contributes to producing mutually exclusive heterosexualized and homosexualized subjects and social worlds. Just as feminists claim to have discovered a gender code (the masculine/feminine binary) which shapes the texture of personal and public life, a parallel claim is made for the hetero/homosexual figure. Queer interventions urge a shift from a framing of the question of homosexuality in terms of personal identity and the politics of homosexual oppression and liberation to imagining homosexuality in relation to the cultural politics of knowledge. In this regard, queer theory places the question of homosexuality at the center of society and social analysis. Queer theory is less a matter of explaining the repression or expression of a homosexual minority than an analysis of the hetero/homosexual figure as a power/knowledge regime that shapes the ordering of desires, behaviors, and social institutions, and social relations – in a word, the constitution of the self and society.

The shift from approaching homosexuality as an issue of individual identity (its repression, expression, and liberation) to viewing it as a cultural figure or category of knowledge is the central claim of Eve Sedgwick's *Epistemology of the Closet* (1990). Her opening paragraph announces a framing of homosexuality in terms of a cultural politic of knowledge.

Epistemology of the Closet proposes that many of the major nodes of thought and knowledge in twentieth-century Western culture as a whole are structured – indeed, fractured – by a chronic, now endemic crisis of homo/heterosexual definition . . . The book will argue that an understanding of virtually any aspect of modern Western culture must be, not merely incomplete, but damaged in its central substance to the degree that it does not incorporate a critical analysis of modern homo/heterosexual definition. (Sedgwick 1990: 1)

From the turn of the [nineteenth] century "every given person . . . was now considered necessarily assignable . . . to a homo-or-a-heterosexuality, a binarized identity . . . It was this new development that left no space in the culture exempt from the potent incoherences of homo/heterosexual definition" (Sedgwick 1990: 2). The homo/heterosexual definition is said to shape the culture of society, not just individual identities and behaviors. It does so, moreover, not only by imposing sexual definitions on bodies, actions, and social relations, but, perhaps more significantly, by shaping broad categories of thought and culture whose thematic focus is not always explicitly sexual.

I think that a whole cluster of the most crucial sites for the contestation of meaning in twentieth-century western culture are consequently and quite indelibly marked with the historical specificity of homo-social/heterosexual definition . . . Among those sites are . . . the pairings secrecy/disclosure and private/public. Along with and sometimes through these epistemologically charged pairings, condensed in the figures of "the closet" and "coming out," this very specific crisis of definition has then ineffaceably marked other pairings as basic to modern cultural organization as masculine/feminine, majority/minority, innocence/initiation, natural/artificial, new/old, growth/decadence, urbane/provincial, health/illness, same/different, cognition/paranoia, art/kitsch, sincerity/sentimentality, and voluntarily/addiction. So pervasive has the suffusing stain of homo/heterosexual crisis been that to discuss any of these indices in any context, in the absence of an antihomophobic analysis, must perhaps be to perpetuate unknowingly compulsions implicit in each. (Sedgwick 1990: 72)

Sedgwick insists that these categories of knowledge are unstable.. Modern Western sexual definitions move between contradictory positions. For example homosexuality may be viewed as specific to a minority of the human population (i.e., some individuals are exclusively homosexual) or understood as universal (i.e., all people are thought to have homosexual desires). The instability of the homo/hetero sexual definition makes it a favorable site for deconstructive analysis. "One main strand of argument in this book is deconstructive . . . The analytic move it makes is to demonstrate that categories presented in a culture as symmetrical binary oppositions – heterosexual/homosexual, in this case – actually subsist in a more unsettled and dynamic tacit relation" (Sedgwick 1990: 9-10). Sedgwick wishes to reveal the instability of this symbolic trope and to disrupt its hierarchical structuring for the purpose of displacing or neutralizing its social force.

In the collection *Inside/Out* (Fuss 1991), the figuring of society as a social text and of social analysis into deconstructive analysis is made into the programmatic center of queer theory. Departing from Sedgwick, who attends exclusively to the canonized texts of academic "high" culture, the contributors to this volume deploy a deconstructive critical method on the "texts" of popular culture, e.g., Alfred Hitchcock's film *Rope* (Miller 1991), the 1963 horror movie, *The Haunting* (White 1991), or popular representations of Rock Hudson (Meyer 1991).

In her introduction to *Inside/Out* (1991) and in *Essentially Speaking* (1989), Diana Fuss sketches a framework for a deconstructive or queer cultural political of knowledge. She contrasts conventional approaches to identity which view it as a property of an object with a poststructural approach which defines identity as a discursive relational figure. "Deconstruction dislocates the understanding of identity as self-presence and offers, instead, a view of identity as difference. To the extent that identity always contains the specter of non-identity within it, the subject is always divided and identity is always purchased at the price of the exclusion of the Other, the repression or repudiation of non-identity" (Fuss 1989: 103). In other words, persons or objects acquire identities only in contrast to what they are not. The affirmation of an identity entails the production and exclusion of that which is different or the creation of otherness. This otherness, though, is never truly excluded or silenced; it is present in identity and haunts it as its limit or impossibility.

Fuss applies this deconstructive approach to the hetero/homosexual figure:

The philosophical opposition between "heterosexual" and "homosexual" . . . has always been constructed on the foundation of another related opposition: the couple "inside" and "outside." The metaphysics of identity that has governed discussions of sexual behavior and libidinal object choice has, until now, depended on the structural symmetry of these seemingly functional distinctions and the inevitability of a symbolic order based on a logic of limits, margins, borders, and boundaries. Many of the current efforts in lesbian and gay theory, which this volume seeks to showcase, have begun the difficult but urgent textual work necessary to call into question the stability and ineradicability of the hetero/homo hierarchy, suggesting that new (and old) sexual possibilities are no longer thinkable in terms of a simple inside/outside dialectic. But how, exactly, do we bring the hetero/homo opposition to the point of collapse? (1991: 1)

The point of departure for queer theory is not the figure of homosexual repression and the struggle for personal and collective expression or the making of homosexual/gay/lesbian identities but the hetero/homosexual discursive or epistemological figure. The question of its origin is less compelling than a description of its social textual efficacy. Thus, virtually every essay in *Inside/Out* searches out this symbolic figure in a wide range of publicly circulating social texts. To the extent that Fuss's Introduction is intent on making the case for shifting theory away from its present grounding in identity concepts to a cultural or epistemological centering, she intends to underscore, and indeed contribute to, the destabilizing of the hetero/homo code and the limits of a politics organized around the affirmation of a homo-sexual identity. She rehearses the standard deconstructive critique: the hetero/homo code creates hierarchies of insides and outsides. A politics organized around an affirmative homo-sexual identity reinforces this code and creates its own inside/outside hierarchy.

Deconstructive analysis aims to expose the limits and instabilities of a binary identity figure. "Sexual identities are rarely secure. Heterosexuality can never fully ignore the close psychical proximity of its terrifying (homo) sexual other, any more than homosexuality can entirely escape the equally insistent social pressures of (hetero) sexual conformity. Each is haunted by the other . . . " (Fuss 1991: 4). Deconstructive analysis reveals that the hetero/homo presuppose each other, each is elicited by the other, contained, as it were, in the other, which ultimately accounts for the extreme defensiveness, the hardening of each into a bounded, self-protective hardcore and, at the same time, the opposite tendency toward confusion and collapse. "The fear of the homo, which continually rubs up against the hetero (triadic-style), concentrates and codifies the very real possibility and ever-present threat of a collapse of boundaries, an effacing of limits, and a radical confusion of identities" (Fuss 1991: 6). The collapse of this binary identity figure as a cultural social force and as a framework of opposition politics as identity politics is the aim of the deconstructive project. Fuss advocates a politics of cultural subversion. "What is called for is nothing less than an insistent and intrepid disorganization of the very structures which produce this inescapable logic" (1991: 6).

The limits of queer textualism

From the beginning of the homophile movement in the 1950s through gay liberationism and the ethnic nationalism of the 1980s, lesbian and gay theory in the United States has been wedded to a particular metanarrative. This has been a story of the formation of a homosexual subject and its mobilization to challenge a heteronormative society. Gay theory has been linked to what I wish to call a "politics of interest." This refers to a politics organized around the claims for rights and social, cultural, and political representation by a homosexual subject. In the early homophile quest for tolerance, in the gay liberationist project of liberating the homosexual self, or in the ethnic nationalist assertion of equal rights and representation, the gay movement has been wedded to a politics of interest.

Queer theory has proposed an alternative to, or supplement of, the paradigm of an identity-based politics of interest. Abandoning the homosexual subject as the foundation of theory and politics, queer critics take the hetero/homosexual discursive figure as its object of knowledge and critique. This binary is said to function as a central category of knowledge which structures broad fields of Western culture and social conventions. Queer social analysts expose the ways this epistemological figure functions in Western culture and social practices. The hetero/homosexual definition serves as a sort of global framework within which bodies, desires, identities, behaviors, and social relations are constituted and regulated.

Queer theorists, or at least one prominent strain, may be described as proposing a cultural "politics of knowledge." Their aim is to trace the ways the hetero/homo figure structures discourses and representations which are at the center of Western societies. They aim to make gay theory central to social theory or cultural criticism, rather than approach it as a minority discourse. Parallelling the Marxist or feminist claims about the bourgeois/proletariat and masculine/feminine oppositions, queer analysts claim for the hetero/homo binary the status of a master category of social analysis. They wish to contest this structure of knowledge and cultural paradigm. They intend to subvert the hetero/homo hierarchy not with the goal of celebrating the equality or superiority of homosexuality nor with the hope of liberating a homosexual subject. Rather, the deconstructive project of queer theory and politics aims at neutralizing and displacing the social force of this cultural figure. But by what means and to what end?

As I consider the politics of queer theory, I will register some reservations. We have seen that, as I read this intervention, queer social critics are clear about their aim and strategy: they wish to trace the cultural operation of the hetero/homo hierarchical figure with the aim of reversing and disturbing its infectious and pervasive social power. But how? What force is claimed for deconstructive critique and what is its ethical and political standpoint?

Fuss insists that the aim of queer analysis is to "question the stability and ineradicability of the hetero/homo hierarchy [and to bring] the hetero/homo opposition to the point of collapse" (1991: 1). But how? Fuss calls for an "analysis interminable, a responsibility to exert sustained pressure from/on the margins to reshape and to reorient the field of sexual difference to include sexual differences" (1991: 6). Fuss does not assume that this "analysis interminable" is sufficient to subvert the hetero/homo hierarchy. Cultural critique must be wedded to a politics of interest. Fuss assumes that only social agents challenging institutional arrangements and relations of power can effect a major cultural and social change. However, she also believes that current social movements such as the lesbian and gay and women's movements are organized around the assertion of unitary, essentialized identities which perpetuate and stabilize the hetero/homo figure. This is her dilemma: the very subjects positioned to trouble the hetero/homo hierarchy are invested in it. Deconstructive critique cannot disavow identity, as it is the very subjects who claim identities as men, women, lesbian, and gay who are the only agents of change. Thus, the queer project aims to deconstruct and refigure identities as multiple and fluid with the hope that "such a view of identity as unstable and potentially disruptive . . . could in the end produce a more mature identity politics . . . [and] stable political subjects" (Fuss 1989: 104). Unfortunately, there is no analysis of what such subjects might look like or what configuration of interests and social will might propel them to instigate the kinds of changes Fuss wishes. Indeed, there is no account of the social conditions (e.g., changes in the economy or state or class, gender, or racial formation) that make her own critique of identity politics possible. What social forces are producing this political and discursive pressuring on the center? This under-theorization of the social is even clearer in Eve Sedgwick.

Sedgwick is no idealist. She is keenly aware of the limits of deconstructive analysis. Sedgwick holds that "there is reason to believe that the oppressive sexual system of the past hundred years was if anything born and bred . . . in the briar patch of the most notorious and repeated decenterings and exposures" (1990: 10). The staying power of the hetero/homo figure rests, in no small part, on the fact that it has been rearticulated in a dense cultural network of normative definitions and binaries such as secrecy/disclosure, knowledge/ignorance, private/public, natural/artificial, wholeness/decadence, domestic/foreign, urbane/provincial, health/illness, and sincerity/sentimentality. In other words, the hetero/homo figure is woven into the core cultural premises and understandings of Western societies. At one level, Sedgwick's project is to identify the ways the hetero/homo definition has been sustained by being written into the cultural organization of Western societies. Here we may raise an initial concern about the politics of knowledge. If the exposure of the instabilities and contradictions of the hetero/homo structuring of Western cultural configurations does not effectively displace or decenter this figure, deconstructive critique would seem to have surrendered much, if not all, political force. Sedgwick seems to be acknowledging that the social force of the deconstructive critique is contingent upon its being connected to a politics of interest. However, the only politics of interest she alludes to is the varied movements of homosexual politics, which assume the validity of the hetero/homo figure while challenging its particular hierarchical ordering. It would seem that the logical move for Sedgwick is to link cultural to social analysis and to couple a deconstructive critique of knowledge to a constructive politics of interest. Unfortunately, Sedgwick's analysis remains at the level of the critique of knowledge and the decentering of cultural meanings, an intervention which by her own account has been going on for a century. This uncoupling of cultural from social analysis is a departure from at least the original intention of Derrida, who insisted on linking discursive meanings to their institutional settings and thereby connecting deconstructive to institutional critique. "What is somewhat hastily called deconstruction is not . . . a specialized set of discursive procedures . . . [but] a way of taking a position, in its work of analysis, concerning the political and institutional structures that make possible and govern our practices . . . Precisely because it is never concerned only with signified content, deconstruction should not be separable from this politico-institutional problematic" (Derrida, quoted in Culler 1982: 156). Queer theory has largely abandoned institutional analysis. In Sedgwick, the hetero/homo definition functions as an autonomous cultural logic, prolifically generating categories and fields of knowledge. These cultural meanings are never linked to social structural arrangements or processes such as nationalism, colonialism, globalization, or dynamics of class or family formation or popular social movements. Lacking an understanding of the ways cultural meanings are interlaced with social forces, especially in light of Sedgwick's analysis of the productive and infectious character of the hetero/homo figure, greatly weakens the political force of her analysis.

Queer theory is a response to the hierarchies of sexual and homosexual politics. No less than liberationist or lesbian-feminist theory, queer analysis is responding to the damaged lives and suffering engendered in a compulsively heterosexual society. The former approach homosexual politics by asserting a homosexual subject struggling for liberation against oppression. By contrast, queer theorists approach homosexual politics in relation to a power/knowledge regime organized around the hetero/homo hierarchical figure which is said to function as a master framework for the constitution and ordering of fields of knowledge and cultural understandings which shape the making of subjectivities, social relations, and social norms. I perceive a parallel with many feminist discourses in the 1980s. In the face of the staying power of male domination and resistance to change, many feminists in the 1980s turned away from learning theory and sex-role theory to psychoanalytic theory and to a quasi-naturalistic gynocentric or cultural feminism. Queer theory suggests a deep cultural logic to explain the staying power of heterosexism. The roots of heterosexism are not socialization, prejudice, tradition, or scapegoating, but a basic way of organizing knowledges and fields of daily life which are deeply articulated in the core social practices of Western societies.

Queer theory analyzes homosexuality as part of a power/knowledge regime rather than as a minority social identity. It hopes to contribute to destabilizing this regime, to disrupt its foundational cultural status. But to what end? What is the ethical and political standpoint of queer theory?

The deconstructive critique of the hetero/homo hierarchical figure is tied to a politics of difference. Its goal is to release possibilities for bodily, sexual, and social experiences which are submerged or marginalized by the dominant regime. Queer theory's social hope is allied to proliferating forms of personal and social difference. The queer politics of difference is, I believe, different in important respects from the assertion of difference that surfaced in the race and sex debates. In the latter case, the assertion of difference often remained tied to a politics of identity; the aim was to validate marginalized subjects and communities. For example, the cultural criticism of people of color did not deconstruct or contest identity categories but sought to multiply identity political standpoints. Deconstructive queer theorists affirm the surfacing of new subject voices but are critical of its identity political grounding in the name of a more insistent politics of difference. Despite its critique of methodoligical individualism or the view of the individual as the source and center of knowledge, society, and history, much queer theory, at least its deconstructive currents, is wedded to a social vision whose ultimate value lies in promoting individuality and tolerance of difference; where queer theory does not edge into an anarchistic social ideal it gestures towards a democratic pluralistic ideal.

The tie between queer theory and a politics of difference needs to be at least provisionally queried. What kind of politics is this and what kinds of differences are intended and with what ethical force? Unfortunately, we must proceed obliquely since queer theorists have not directly engaged such questions. Consider Eve Sedgwick. If one of her aims is to explain the persistence of compulsive heterosexuality by reference to the hetero/homo figure as productive of cultural fields of knowledge, her other aim is to expose the ways a multitude of desires have been muted, marginalized, and depoliticized by this power/knowledge regime. Sedgwick exposes the monumental constriction involved in defining sexual orientation primarily by gender preference. Revealing the immense condensation entailed in rendering the gender of sexual-object choice into a mastery category defining sexual and social identity is a main pivot of her work.

> Historically, the framing of *Epistemology of the Closet* begins with a puzzle. It is a rather amazing fact that, of the many dimensions along which the genital activity of one person can be differentiated from that of another (dimensions that include preference for certain acts, certain zones or sensations, certain physical types, a certain frequency, certain symbolic investments, certain relations of age or power, a certain species, a certain number of participants, etc. etc. etc.), precisely one, the gender of object choice, emerged from the turn of the century, and has remained, as the dimension denoted by the now ubiquitous category of "sexual orientation" ... *Epistemology of the Closet* does not have an explanation to offer for this sudden, radical condensation of sexual categories; instead ... the book explores its unpredictably varied and acute implications and consequences. (Sedgwick 1990: 8-9)

As hetero/homosexuality become master categories of a sexual regime, as sexual desires, identities, and politics are comprehended by the hetero/homo object choice, a whole series of possible sites of individuation, identity, pleasure, social definition, and politics (e.g., sex act, number of partners, time, place, technique) are suppressed or depoliticized. the moral and political force of Sedgwick's critique of the hetero/homo figure, as I read her, draws on the cultural capital of a politics of sexual difference. Against the sexual and social condensation of the hetero/homo power/knowledge regime, Sedgwick implicitly appeals to an order of sexual differences. This is a social ideal where desires, pleasures, bodies, social relations, and sexualities multiply and proliferate. But what would such an order of difference look like? What ethical guidelines would permit such sexual innovation while being attentive to considerations of power and legitimate normative regulation? Not all self and social expressions would be tolerated; we cannot evade the need for a sexual ethic and regulation, including structures of discipline and moral hierarchy. What would such a normative order look like? Sedgwick's silence on these matters is, I think, indicative of a refusal on the part of many queer theorists to articulate their own ethical and political standpoint and to imagine a constructive social project.

In *Gender Trouble* (1990) and elsewhere (1991), Judith Butler proposes a variant of deconstructive analysis but one which gestures towards a constructive politics. Butler's focus is a system of compulsive heterosexuality which is said to contribute to the formation of a bipolar sex/gender system. In this power/knowledge regime, a rigid natural order is posited that assumes a causality that proceeds from a bipolar sexed subject (male or female), to gender bipolarity (men and women), and to a heteronormative sexuality. Butler aims to show that instead of a natural sex/gender system underwriting heterosexuality, the latter is the unconscious compulsion behind figuring a natural, dichotomous sex/gender system as an order of truth. In a deconstructive move, Butler aims to trouble this power/knowledge regime by suggesting that this presumed order of nature is a contingent, politically enacted social order. To illustrate this point, she analyzes drag as a practice which disturbs the sex/gender/sexuality system by presumably exhibiting the performative character of sex and gender and its fluid relation to sexuality. Butler is not suggesting drag or a performative politics as an alternative to the politics of interest; rather she is proposing, as I read her, that the current Western sex/gender/compulsively heterosexual system is maintained, is part, because it functions as a configuration of knowledge. This power/knowledge regime needs to be exposed as social and political; drag or performative disruptions are practical counterparts, as it were, of deconstructive critique. They do not replace the politics of interest but supplement it.

For Butler, deconstructive analysis takes aim at a system of compulsive heterosexuality which is said to underpin the production of bipolar sexed and gendered subjects. Her critique aims to undermine this sex/gender/sexual order for the purpose of ending the compulsion to enact a rigid bipolar gender identity and conform to a normative heterosexuality. Butler's critique is inspired by an ideal of difference – by the possibilities of a social space where selves can fashion bodies, gender identities, and sexualities without the normative constraints of compulsive heterosexuality and bipolar gender norms. In this regard, drag serves as more than an exemplar of cultural politics; it prefigures a social ideal – of a porous, fluid social terrain that celebrates individuality and difference. Her appeal to difference, however, lacks an ethical reflection. For example, which differences are permissible and what norms would guide such judgements? Moreover, I detect in Butler the suggestion of a post-identity order as part of a social ideal characterized by minimal disciplinary and constraining structures. But what would such an order look like? What concept of self or subject is imaginable in the absence of a strong identity concept? Moreover, are not such identities productive of rich experiences, subjective stability, and social bonds? If self identities were not regulatory, what structures would serve to organize subjectivities?

The university and the politics of knowledge

Deconstruction originated in France in the late 1960s. A reaction to both structuralism and the social rebellions issuing from new oppositional subjects (e.g., prisoners, students, cultural workers, women), deconstruction exhibited the spirit of rebellion of a post-Marxian left. It advocated a politics of negative dialectics, of permanent resistance to established orders and hierarchies. Animating the spirit of May 1968 was a politics of difference, a vaguely anarchistic, aestheticized ideal of fashioning a social space of minimal constraint and maximum individuality and tolerance of difference. However, deconstruction presupposed subjects with bounded identities who conformed to normative orders which made discipline and political mobilization possible as a condition of their own critique and a transformative politics. Moreover, deconstructive critics have been notorious in refusing to articulate the ethical standpoint of their critique and politics making them vulnerable to charges of nihilism or opportunism. As we have seen, many of the same limitations are evident in queer theory.

Queer theory originated in the United States, amongst mostly English and Humanities professors in the 1980s. It would be a mistake, however, to dismiss queer theory as merely academic. Its roots are, in part, the renewed activism of the 1980s associated with HIV/AIDS activism and the confrontational, direct-action, anti-identity politics of Queer Nation. Moreover, I wish to suggest that much queer theory can be viewed as a response to the development in the postwar United States of the university as a chief site in the production and validation of knowledge. The university and its disciplinary knowledges have become a major terrain of social conflict as knowledge is viewed as a key social power. Knowledges were of course politicized in the social rebellions of the 1960s. For example, feminists criticized the social sciences for producing knowledges which constructed and positioned women as different, inferior, and socially subordinate to men. In the 1980s, debates over canons and multiculturalism have rendered the sphere of knowledge a key arena of politics. Accordingly, the housing of queer theory in the university should not, as some critics fear, be interpreted as necessarily depoliticizing theory. To the contrary, its academic positioning makes a cultural politics of disciplinary knowledges possible. Such a politics is important precisely because such knowledges are a major social force shaping subjects and social practices. Although we need to interrogate the politics of knowledge in terms of how it articulates with a politics of interest, it would be a mistake to dismiss its key role in current social struggles.

The persuasive force of the queer project depends on the extent to which one assumes that the dominant models of lesbian and gay politics presuppose the hetero/homo binary. Queer interventions aim to expose their unconscious complicity in reproducing a heteronormative order and an order that condenses sexual freedom to legitimating same-sex gender preference. Yet queer theorists have often surrendered to a narrow culturalism or textualism; they have not articulated their critique of knowledge with a critique of the social conditions productive of such textual figures; they have not provided an account of the social conditions of their own critique. The "social" is often narrowed into categories of knowledge and culture while the latter is itself often reduced to linguistic, discursive binary figures. The "historical" is similarly reduced to an undifferentiated space, e.g., the modern West or the period 1880–1980 in modern Western societies. Finally, the ethical standpoint of their own discourses is veiled. Queer critics have refused to give social and moral articulation to the key concepts of difference as they invoke it to critique the compulsiveness to identity in modern Western societies. If we are to recover a fuller social critical perspective and a transformative political vision, one fruitful direction is to articulate a politics of knowledge with an institutional social analysis that does not disavow a willingness to spell out its own ethical standpoint.

PART III

Democratic prospects: the politics of knowledge and identity

8

Transfiguring sexual identity: AIDS and the cultural politics of sexuality and homosexuality, 1981–1986

AIDS appeared during a period of significant change in American sexual conventions. A series of movements in the 1960s and 1970s pointed in the direction of expanded sexual choice and diversity. The women's movement struggled for women's sexual autonomy. Feminists demanded that women be able to define and control their own sexuality, and that included choosing a lesbian alternative. Less visible were the struggles by sexually disenfranchised groups such as the disabled or the elderly to be accepted as full sexual beings. The counterculture made a more open and expressive eroticism a prominent part of its social rebellion. Furthermore, changes in US sexual norms that reflected long-term trends became more palpable. For example, the norm that legitimated sex only as an act of love or a sign of fidelity was challenged. Sex discourses and representations (e.g., pornography, sex manuals, sex radical ideologies) appeared that constructed sex as a sphere of pleasure and self-expression with its own intrinsic value and justification (Seidman 1991). Some of these discourses defended a libertarian ethic which permitted sex in virtually any context of mutual consent and respect. This expanded the types of relationships in which sex was acceptable. Indeed, the exclusivity of marriage as the proper site for sex gave way to more pluralistic conventions that permitted sex in varied social settings. In short, while it would be misleading to assert that a revolution occurred, there did transpire important changes in US sexual norms and behavior during this period (D'Emilio and Freedman 1988; Seidman 1991a, 1992).

Indicative of the liberalization of US sexual culture was the increased tolerance for homosexuality.[1] By the mid-1970s lesbian and gay subcultures were visible in virtually every major urban center (Altman 1983; D'Emilio 1983). These provided gay people with institutional protection, a source of social support and a collective base for a sexual politic. Within these gay spaces a cultural apparatus emerged that included publications (books, magazines, newspapers), theatre groups, art, literature, and scholarship. Of particular importance is that this new lesbian and gay intelligentsia articulated affirmative images of homosexuality. Constructions of "the homosexual" as a morally perverse, deviant or pathological figure were challenged. New models viewed homosexuality as an alternative sexual or affectional preference, as an affirmative social identity and as the basis of an oppressed social minority. Finally, gay people made important gains towards political empowerment and social inclusion. For example, by the mid-1970s more than half the states in the US repealed their sodomy laws; dozens of cities passed anti-discrimination ordinances; the civil service commission eliminated its ban on hiring homosexuals and so on (D'Emilio 1983).

A trend towards sexual liberalization in postwar US, which included an expanded tolerance of lesbians and gay men, encountered on-going resistance and hostility. In the late 1970s this tolerance narrowed considerably as antigay themes became integral to a revived conservative politics. The explanation for this lay, in part, in social developments that paralleled sexual liberalization. Specifically, the conjunction of a series of events including an economic recession, political legitimation problems stemming from Watergate, military setbacks in Vietnam and Iran, and social turmoil stemming from the various civil rights, protest and liberation movements, produced a pervasive sense of social crisis. A series of purity crusades swept across the country (Rubin 1984; Califia 1980). This was one way Americans responded to perceptions of social danger and sought to gain control over their social fate. Phenomena such as pornography and groups such as "paedophiles" were blamed for the crisis. However, gay people in particular were singled out. This was not entirely fortuitous. The trend towards the acceptance or at least tolerance of homosexuality challenged the exclusive legitimacy of a heterosexual, marital and patriarchal norm. Moreover, the visibility and political assertiveness of homosexuals coupled to the symbolic association of homosexuality with social decline in a context perceived by many Americans as one of family breakdown and national deterioration made homosexuals an easy target for scapegoating.

The anxiety and hostility many Americans felt towards recent social developments was, in part, displaced onto homosexuals. They were portrayed as a public menace, as a threat to the family, and as imperiling the national security by promoting self-centered, hedonistic and pacifist values. An anti-gay backlash crystallized that was initially centered around local and state campaigns to repeal gay rights ordinances. Gradually, it expanded to include national legislation, the resurgence of anti-gay discourses, and escalating discrimination and violence (Altman 1983; Bush and Goldstein 1981; Seidman 1992a; Tucker 1981). Its aim was to deny legitimacy to homosexuality, dismantle gay subcultural institutions, return gays to a condition of invisibility and marginality, and to reassert a discourse of the dangers of homosexuality.

By the early 1980s the conservative offensive against homosexuality appeared to be losing some momentum. The Family Protection Act, initially introduced in 1979 and resubmitted in 1981, failed to gain congressional approval. The Briggs initiative, a major piece of anti-gay legislation, was defeated. Existing gay rights ordinances were successfully defended against the right. Unfortunately, the marginalization of the anti-gay campaign suggested by these defeats did not come to pass. The appearance of AIDS and the recognition of its epidemic proportions by 1983 reinvigorated a waning anti-gay politic. Anti-gay themes assumed a new prominence in New Right politics. AIDS was seized upon to promote a conservative social agenda. The political ramifications of AIDS have been widely commented upon (Altman 1985; Patton 1985; Goldstein 1985). I want to press a different point: AIDS has given rise to a far-reaching, perhaps unprecedented, public discussion of homosexuality. AIDS was invoked to advocate changes in normative images of "the homosexual" and the place of homosexuality in American society.

Specifically, I argue that AIDS has provided a pretext to reinsert homosexuality within a symbolic drama of pollution and purity. Conservatives have used AIDS to rehabilitate the notion of "the homosexual" as a polluted figure. AIDS is read as revealing the truth of male homosexual desire and as proof of his dangerous nature. In particular, conservatives pointed to the divorce of desire from intimacy as the very root of the perverse and promiscuous nature of homosexuality. It is this uncoupling of desire and affect which links homosexuality to danger and death.

The reverse side of this polluting of homosexuality is the purification of heterosexuality. However, it is a specific normative form of heterosexuality: A monogamous, marital sexual ideal. Moreover, by linking AIDS intrinsically to the permissiveness of the 1960s, many conservatives interpreted AIDS as a symbol of the failure of social liberalization. Many liberals read AIDS as the failure of the radical impulse of the sixties.

AIDS served as a battleground between conservatives and liberals. The (straight) liberal media typically criticized enlisting AIDS to promote an anti-gay politics. Indeed, many liberals highlighted the extreme intolerance of the conservative reaction to AIDS in order to discredit the broader social and political agenda of the right. This does not mean, however, that liberals reacted to AIDS simply as a medical fact. Liberals also used AIDS to promote a specific moral and political agenda. Many liberals were prepared to describe homosexuality as falling within the moral boundaries of American society only if it approximated a "middle-class" intimate ideal. In this regard, they enlisted AIDS in their campaign to construct an image of the "respectable homosexual," and to legitimate a monogamous, marital sexual ethic where eros is justified only in this context. Liberals frequently used AIDS to legitimate a sexual and social order that allowed for "liberalization" within a fairly limited range of normalized social control. They defended their ethic of choice and constraint against both "conservative repressiveness" and left liberationist politics.

These liberal themes were conspicuous in a gay male controlled media. Gays seized on AIDS to advance their own program of sexual and social reform. AIDS was read by many gays as marking the failure of a way of life, namely, the "fast-lane, free-wheeling" sexual lifestyle of the 1970s urban subculture. AIDS was said to signal, like Stonewall, a critical turning point in the coming of age of gay men. For some gay reformers, AIDS prompted a new era of maturity and social responsibility among gay men. Taking issue with this assimilationist impulse were others who saw in AIDS not the failure of their sexual values and lifestyle, but of society. AIDS was understood as a symbol of the failure of a heterosexist and homophobic society. For these social critics, AIDS anticipated a renewal of an agenda of broad social change. In particular, gay men were counselled to resist control by straight-dominated institutions and to defend subcultural lifestyles while shifting erotic behavior to safe sex practices. Between 1981 and 1986, discourses in the gay media were then divided between critics who imagined AIDS as marking the failure of subcultural sexual values and critics for whom AIDS symbolized the horrors of a illiberal culture of normative heterosexuality.

AIDS and heterosexual constructions of homosexuality

In the "heterosexual media," the identification of AIDS as a gay disease was made early and lingered in the public, despite indisputable evidence to the contrary available as early as 1982. In part, the medical establishment was responsible for this labeling. Although Center for Disease Control (CDC) researchers knew as early as August 1981 that homosexual men were not the only population afflicted by Kaposi's Sarcoma and a range of unusual opportunistic infections, they labelled the new syndrome "Gay-related immunodeficiency" (GRID) early in 1982. Motivated no doubt by genuine public concerns, as well as by the sensationalist aspects of the story, the national media, with virtually no critical scrutiny of the medical-scientific experts, declared the existence of a "homosexual cancer," a "gay plague," or a "gay epidemic."[2] These terms strongly suggested an intrinsic tie between homosexuality, disease and death.

The two most prominent epidemiological theories through the mid-1980s connected GRID (renamed AIDS in 1983) to homosexual behavior in an intimate way. Proponents of the so-called "Overload Theory" held that "the gay lifestyle," by which was meant a pattern of multiple sexual partners, drug abuse, a history of sexually transmitted diseases, and poor health habits, was responsible for the collapse of the immune system. In 1983 the Human Immunodeficiency Virus was discovered, which is now considered to be the primary cause of AIDS. HIV breaks down the body's resistance to disease leaving it vulnerable to a host of infections. The virus is transmitted through blood and body fluids, including semen. For example, the introduction of semen into the body during sex releases the virus into the blood stream. Sex is thus implicated in AIDS. Homosexual men who practice anal intercourse are especially vulnerable to HIV since the delicate tissue of the anus is easily torn. This allows the semen, and therefore the virus, of the infected person to pass directly into the "passive" partner's blood system.

Both the Overload and the Viral theory emphasized the tight link between sexual behavior and AIDS among homosexual men. Indeed, these two theories highlighted the role of sexual "promiscuity" as the intermediary causal link to both disease and death. The Overload theory posited an ironic and insidious dynamic: the immediate sensual pleasures of "promiscuous" sex sets in motion a hidden causality of disease and death. The very act of sexual union – with its cultural resonances of love and the production of life – is turned into an act of death. Although a viral hypothesis does not view AIDS as the very signature of homosexual desire, it asserts an indirect tie between promiscuity and AIDS among homosexual men. It is, after all, primarily through non-monogamous sex that sex threatens viral infection.

Prompted by medical research or perhaps merely sanctioned by it, "promiscuity" became the focal point in the heterosexual media. The media exhibited a seemingly endless fascination with the sexual aspects, and especially the quantitative aspects, of homosexual behavior. A widely reported study by a CDC task force in 1981 provided the initial medical justification for this preoccupation.[3] Assuming, quite reasonably, a connection between their sexual behavior and the large numbers of male homosexual AIDS cases, CDC researchers compared their sexual patterns with a homosexual control group free of the disease. They reported that the AIDS group had approximately twice as many sex partners. Although the precise nature of the connection between the number of sex partners and AIDS was unclear, the researchers asserted a tight causal tie.

Serious doubts have been raised about this study (Martin and Vance 1984). A central flaw was the study's failure to define what counts as a "sex act." When does an act between two men count as a sex act? Does the number of "sex partners" suggest a common reference for heterosexual and homosexual men? If gay men count sexual behavior in which there is no exchange of semen as sex acts (e.g., mutual masturbation, body rubbing, kissing, anal intercourse without semen exchange), then the number of sex partners by itself is irrelevant to AIDS. If the key factor is the bodily exchange of semen, the pertinent information is the number of sex partners with whom there occurred sex acts of this type. In this regard, the comparisons between the AIDS cases and the control group along the key dimension of exposure to semen revealed no statistically significant differences in the CDC study. Whatever the causal link between homosexual sexual behavior and AIDS the 1981 CDC study provided few credible clues.

Despite the flaws and tentativeness of the early CDC research linking "sexual promiscuity" to AIDS among gay men, the heterosexual media seized upon this as the explanation. An unintended consequence of this reporting was that representations of homosexuality as an amoral, perverse, and dangerous sexual desire were widely circulated. Headlines and feature stories in virtually all the major national media dramatized a gay lifestyle that amounted to little more than a relentless quest for sexual pleasure. For example, a report in *The San Francisco Examiner* interpreted the high percentage of homosexual men with AIDS as confirming the conventional wisdom that homosexuals are "a population whose lifestyle is based on a freewheeling approach to sex" (1982: 14). John Fuller in *Science Digest* observed that the victimization of homosexual men by AIDS was further proof of what science has told us about homosexual men. "Sociologists and psychologists had long noted that the constant search for new sexual partners is a persistent pattern among many gay males" (Fuller 1983: 85).

I want to underscore a key point regarding this discourse: the "promiscuity" of homosexual men is not considered an historically specific characteristic of same-sex behavior or a trait of some men who have sex with men. Rather, "promiscuity" is viewed as essential to homosexuality. In other words, this discourse revitalizes an image of the male homosexual that was in decline – namely, as a type of person with unique physical, emotional and behavioral traits whose essence is an insatiable, uncontrollable sex drive. Homosexual men are said to sexualize themselves and others; they reduce persons to eroticized bodies; they frame sex as mere physical release or pleasure-seeking. "Promiscuity" is thought to manifest the true amoral nature of the homosexual. Homosexual desire is restrained only by the quantitative limitations of physical exhaustion and social convention. It is this compulsive, hyper-active desire that is thought to compel the male homosexual to eroticize the forbidden and to transgress all moral boundaries – thereby making him a profound social danger. "The homosexual" was constructed in much of the straight media as the very antithesis of "the heterosexual" who is said to connect sex to intimacy, trust, and the nourishment or production of life.

Conservatives invoked AIDS to authorize a moral order that de-legitimated homosexuality. The juxtaposition of the figure of "the life-giving heterosexual" and "the promiscuous, deadly homosexual" specifies a moral order which privileges the former as healthy, good, right, and socially beneficial while discrediting the latter as abnormal, wrong, perverse, and socially dangerous. In many conservative discourses, AIDS was said to not only reveal the truth of homosexuality as unnatural but to be its just punishment. "The poor homosexuals – they have declared war upon nature, and now nature is exacting an awful retribution," declared Patrick Buchanan (1983: 31). Reverend Charles Stanley, head of the 14.3 million member Southern Baptist Convention announced: "It [homosexuality] is a sinful lifestyle, according to the scripture, and I believe that AIDS is God indicating his displeasure and his attitude towards that form of lifestyle" (*Times Union* 1986). Articulating the same moral judgment but within a medical-scientific language, Dr. James Fletcher concluded: "If we act as empirical scientists can we not see the implications of the data [AIDS and STD's among homosexual men] before us? Might not these 'complications' be 'consequences' [of homosexuality]? Were it so a logical conclusion is that AIDS is a self-inflicted disorder . . . Indeed from an empirical medical perspective alone current scientific observation seems to require the conclusion that homosexuality is a pathological condition" (quoted in E'Eramo 1984: 9).

In the above moral rhetorics, AIDS represents a just punishment for homosexuals for violating a normative order, whether legislated by God or Nature. There is, however, another more subtle logic of moral judgment insinuated into these conservative discourses. AIDS is seen as the male homosexual's death wish turned upon himself. In postwar American culture, homosexuality was often imagined as symbolizing an unconscious wish to destroy society. Images of subversion surround the homosexual. The near-ubiquitious association of homosexuals with the corruption of children – the very symbol of social purity – is indicative of this symbolism. It is, I believe, precisely because homosexuality is often constructed as a social danger evoking resonances of decline and chaos that AIDS has been construed as the truth of homosexuality and its just punishment. AIDS symbolizes the wish for the annihilation of "the other" being turned against the homosexual. It is because homosexuality symbolizes for many Americans a threat to life and society that even in the face of homosexuals' enormous suffering and the loss of lives in the AIDS epidemic, the public reaction has often been complacent, indifferent, and vengeful. For threatening society and killing "the innocent," homosexual men are thought to have received their just punishment in AIDS.

AIDS has been used by conservatives to revive the notion of "the homosexual" as a dangerous and polluted figure. AIDS has been invoked as proof of the diseased, contagious and dangerous nature of homosexuality. AIDS has allowed backlash forces to claim that homosexuals are, in fact, a public health threat. It has provided a pretext to attack gay institutions and to push homosexuality back into a state of public invisibility and marginality. After the defeats of many of the backlash initiatives of the late 1970s, AIDS revived efforts to remedicalize and recriminalize homosexuality. For example, the Dallas Doctors Against AIDS issued the following declaration: "Such a sexual public health concern must cause the citizenry of this country to do everything in their power to smash the homosexual movement in this country to make sure these kinds of acts are criminalized" (quoted in Patton 1985: 3-4). Conservative perspectives on AIDS contributed to the social oppression of lesbians and gay men. Such views legitimated and shaped a public response to persons with AIDS which was nothing short of inhumane. Persons with AIDS were denied medical and dental care; funeral parlors would not bury them; many were fired from their jobs, evicted from their homes, and stigmatized by society – abandoned by straight society and made to feel guilty and ashamed for their illness.

The heterosexuality media has not been uniform in its construction of AIDS and homosexuality. Many liberals interpreted AIDS less as disclosing the truth of homosexual desire than as revealing the failure of the "sexual revolution." Instead of criticizing a reified homosexual desire, liberals faulted the urban male gay subculture and its libertarian sexual ideology as the key causal link between homosexuality, "promiscuity" and AIDS. At times, it must be said, the line between liberal "historicism" and conservative "essentialism," and the line between tolerance and repression, collapses. For example, after criticizing conservative attempts to enlist AIDS in a repressive politics, Charles Krauthammer (in his liberal days) alluded to a possible natural link between homosexuality and disease. "In reality no one knows whether AIDS is accidently a homosexual disease or intrinsically so" (1983: 21). Without an historical perspective on the development of the gay subculture, the liberal perspective simply shifts the reification of the "promiscuous homosexual" from an abstract homosexual desire to an ahistorically conceived gay subculture. Liberals did though consistently oppose backlash efforts to use AIDS to reinstitute a harsh regime of social oppression.

Although the liberal media sought to avoid politicizing AIDS, they seized on AIDS to defend a sexual ethic that binds sex to intimacy and monogamy, although expanding the range of normalized lifestyles to include both heterosexual and homosexual cohabitating couples. The liberal media used AIDS to rehabilitate a pre-gay liberation ideal of the "respectable homosexual": discreet, coupled, monogamous, and bound by shared responsibilities and property.

For example, the *New York Times* virtually campaigned to create and legitimate this ideal of "the respectable homosexual."[4] Its coverage of AIDS regularly included interviews with prominent figures in the gay community or "experts" who uniformly criticized the immature and irresponsible lifestyle of gay men in the 1970s. The *Times* reported changes in homosexual behavior and attitudes. Key indicators of the "fast-lane" gay lifestyle (e.g., numbers of sex partners, STD's, bathhouse attendance) were scrutinized to detect a retreat from "promiscuity." Statements by gay community leaders observing a new emphasis on dating, courting, and nonsexual socializing were interpreted as indicating a social trend. This newspaper did more than report these events. By enlisting select experts and gay community leaders to serve as spokespersons for social reform, the *NYT* became an influential social force advocating changes in the norms and ideals of gay intimacy and identity.

This advocacy role was obvious in several human interest stories featuring homosexual couples who were clearly intended to serve as role models. One such story, entitled "Homosexual Couple finds a Quiet Pride" (Dullea 1984), focuses on two white professional men who lived together for some forty years. They are, in appearance, indistinguishable from conventional professional heterosexuals. In other words, there is no trace of a more unconventional gay subcultural style to their self-presentation. There is an implied discreetness to their homosexuality and their demeanor exudes an almost exaggerated 1950s sense of staid respectability. They are described as preoccupied with typical middle-class heterosexual concerns such as career, family, home, hobbies and anniversaries. The "success" or longevity of their relationship is summed up by the remark, "You have to work at it." Quite clearly, the *NYT* was offering a construction of this couple that was intended to serve as a model of an ideal homosexual identity and intimate values. With moral codes and identity models in flux, and with homosexuality itself assailed by backlash forces, this image of a discreet, monogamous, coupled and conventional homosexual life was endorsed as an alternative to the more unconventional intimate lifestyles of the 1970s. In fact, the principal thesis of the story was that a "heterosexual model" was being adopted by homosexuals. "In recent years, some homosexual couples have begun to adopt many of the traditions of heterosexual marriage. Beside having wedding and anniversary parties, couples are exchanging vows . . . in religious services known as 'gay unions.' They are drawing up contracts, wills . . . to provide legal, protections for themselves and their partners. They are adopting children" (Dullea 1984). Setting aside the veracity of this statement, the message was clear: AIDS is a positive catalyst encouraging homosexual men to adopt the more mature and responsible intimate patterns of heterosexuals. AIDS is said to have prompted gay men to discover the charms, civility, security and safety of romance and monogamy. Liberals, no less than conservatives, exploited AIDS for their own moral and political purpose. Whereas the latter enlisted AIDS as part of their backlash politics, the former used AIDS to relate a moral tale of the virtues of middle-class models of identity and lifestyle.

AIDS and the crisis of homosexuality in the gay community

There is a common theme running through the straight liberal and gay AIDS discourse. AIDS was said to evidence the failure of an ideology and way of life. Indeed, AIDS assumed a redemptive significance. AIDS was described as a principal catalyst in the reformation of the gay community. It instigated a period of personal and social awakening and maturation.

Gay men were among the earliest defenders of the Overload theory. This might seem odd since the basic message of this theory was that homosexual men brought AIDS upon themselves through their own profligate lifestyle. In a much discussed early piece in the gay press, "We Know Who We Are," Michael Callen, Richard Berkowitz, and Richard Dworkin asserted, despite the flimsiest of evidence, "that there is no mutant virus and there will be no vaccine. We must accept that we have overloaded our immune systems with common viruses and other sexually transmitted infections. Our [promiscuous] lifestyle has created the present epidemic of AIDS among gay men" (Callen 1982). The full moral weight of this self-incriminatory rhetoric was partially deflected by targeting the subculture as the source of "the gay lifestyle" and therefore of AIDS. Callen criticized the conventions and values of a sex-obsessed urban gay subculture. "Throughout ten years of promiscuity, I have tried to be a good gay and wear my STD's as red badges of courage in a war against a sex-negative society" (Callen 1983: 93). Callen's harsh judgment of the gay subculture was not exceptional. For example, writing in *The Village Voice*, Stephen Harvey remarked:

For years, gay men have been prey to a brand of propaganda perpetrated among themselves which, in its subtle way, has been scarcely less insidious than the harangues aimed at the community from without . . . Co-ghettoists have implied . . . that there was something stunted and incomplete in the lives of any gay men who couldn't get into those obligatory Saturday nights of mass euphoria in the dark . . . To cast doubt on any aspect of the way we habitually behave has been decided out of hand as reactionary . . . In this town at least . . . what gay solidarity means is the high times you have with regulars of the bar, disco, bathhouse of your choice. (1982: 21)

Many gay men interpreted AIDS as signalling the failure of a gay sub-culture – in particular, its libertarian sexual values.

Although the sexual norms and values of the gay subculture were targeted as the main causal tie between "promiscuity" and AIDS, the individual was not absolved from all guilt but was often implicated in his own victimization. Thus Callen appealed to those "promiscuous" gays "who know who they are to acknowledge and change their lifestyle. "We have remained silent because we have been unable or unwilling to accept responsibility for the role that our own excessiveness has played in our present public health crisis. But, deep down, we know who we are and we know why we're sick" (Callen 1982). David Goodstein, one-time owner and editor of *The Advocate*, insisted that AIDS is the responsibility of individual gay men. "As gay men, AIDS is our responsibility. By responsibility I mean that we are the cause of who we are, what we have and what we do" (1985). The claim that gay men must bear some of the moral burden was a constant theme in the wave of newspaper and magazine reports whose stories were narrated as an individual odyssey from "promiscuity" to AIDS.

Sexual "promiscuity" stands at the center of the gay media interpretation of AIDS. It was explained as a product of an historically unique gay subculture. A direct causal relation was asserted between "promiscuity," the epidemic and the anti-gay backlash. For homosexual men who supported conventional middle-class intimate values, for older men who were comfortable with a culture of concealment, for those uncomfortable with their sexuality or gay liberationists whose ideals were perceived to have faded behind a focus on self-fulfillment, AIDS, symbolized the failure of current gay life and was an occasion to voice their discontents.

I am suggesting that for many "heterosexuals" and "homosexuals," AIDS served as a pretext to reconsider the meaning of homosexuality and to press for changes in the models of gay identity and subculture. I believe that many gay men felt that the suffering and heightened oppression they experienced in the AIDS crisis could be somewhat neutralized or even made self-confirming by imagining AIDS as a great moral drama. AIDS came to signify in many gay discourses the beginnings of a period of renewal and rebirth.

The notion that AIDS marks a turning point was neatly captured in the apocalyptic imagery of Larry Kramer's angry and moving piece "1112 and Counting." Kramer framed AIDS as an ordeal of collective survival. "Our continued existence as gay men . . . is at stake . . . In the history of homosexuality we have never been so close to death and extinction before" (Kramer 1983). In order for gays to survive AIDS, Kramer counseled a shift from the current hedonistic preoccupations of gay men to a new ethic of sexual and social responsibility. Where Kramer edged toward apocalyptic symbolism, others spoke in an oddly upbeat, even millenarian, tone of the epidemic initiating a new era of maturity and respectability. Toby Marotta observed that "most gays share my view – that [AIDS] is the most profound, maturing incident for the gay community in its history" (Quoted in Morganthau 1983: 33). David Goodstein coupled a critical view of pre-AIDS gay life to the prospects for renewal and reform initiated by AIDS. "During the last half of the 1970's, it wasn't chic in gay male circles to place a high value on life-companions or close friendships. Now [i.e., with AIDS] we have another chance for progress: to acknowledge the value of intimate relationships" (Goodstein 1985). Stephen Harvey was even more direct in voicing the redemptive possibilities of AIDS. "It's a perverse and maybe tragic irony that it took the AIDS outbreak . . . to at last . . . integrate [our] sexual natures with the rest of what [we] are" (Harvey 1982: 21).

Central to this image of a coming era of personal and community maturity among gay men is the legitimation of the intimate ideals and rituals of middle-class heterosexual culture. "Indiscriminate sex with phantom partners in backrooms is beginning to diminish. The grunge and filth bars are losing their appeal. Fistfucking is fading. Barbarity is on the way out. Romance [is] . . . on the way in" (Bell 1982). Stories abounded in the gay press of men rediscovering the quiet joys and healthy lifestyle of romantic love and monogamy. Typically, such narratives describe a pre-AIDS period of immaturity and indulgence, with AIDS marking the great turning point where, after a protracted period of soul-searching, one is reborn, and the profligate, self-destructive ways of the past given up for a new morality of health, monogamy and romance. Typical was the story by Arnie Kantrowitz, "Till Death Do Us Part" (Kantrowitz 1983). His story begins by recalling the liberating experience of sexual promiscuity. "My experiment in sexual anarchy was a rare delight, a lesson in license, an opportunity to see both flesh and spirit glaringly naked. I will never apologize to anyone for my promiscuity" (p. 26). Yet, that is exactly what he does as he narrates his odyssey of personal growth. From the standpoint of a post-AIDS sexual morality his early sensual delights now appear to him as compulsive and narcissistic. The endless cycle of excitement, release, and exhaustion left him empty. "I decided to trade self-indulgence for self-respect" (p. 26). Having personally witnessed the guilt-ridden, self-destructive ways of his pre-AIDS days, he "decided to get healthy." Exercise and proper diet replaced drug abuse and late nights. With health and self-respect accomplished, there could be only one proper dramatic finale. "Finally, I rediscovered the difference between lust and love and began an affair" (p. 26). The transfiguration of AIDS into a moral drama of reformation and renewal has allowed some individuals to be so emotionally distant from the enormity of suffering it has brought that the current period was defined as one of social hope. The journalist Steve Martz observed, in what was a common motif, that "the energy formerly reserved for the sexual hunt [can now be] channeled into the community in other ways [such as] . . . the growth of gay community centers, sports clubs, choruses, and a host of other groups." He concluded by remarking that "all of which I believe makes 1983 a time for optimism and joy" (Martz 1983: 23).

Criticisms of gay sexual culture were at times coupled to a critique of the broader social response to AIDS. In *And the Band Played On*, Randy Shilts criticized both gay leaders, especially gay entrepreneurs and sex radicals, for trading in the high ideals of gay liberation for a sexualized and commercialized ideal of self-fulfillment and assailed the mainstream public response to AIDS (Shilts 1987). He accused the medical, scientific, governmental and media institutions of failing to respond effectively to AIDS because of their fear and loathing of homosexuality.

In at least one genre of discursive politics, the strategy was to criticize social homophobia while dropping the critique of the gay culture. In these discourses, the framing of AIDS as a moral tale of the failure of gay life was itself criticized. AIDS symbolized the failure not of the gay subculture but of US (heteronormative) social institutions. AIDS was framed as part of a tale of homosexual oppression. The tardy, reluctant, and ineffective social response to AIDS was said to document the social intolerance towards homosexuality that lurks beneath the liberal surface of US political culture. AIDS provided a (hopeful) occasion to reactivate a liberationist agenda with its renewal of radical gay activism.

An example of this discursive genre is the essay, "AIDing Our Guilt and Fear," by the gay activist and journalist Michael Bronski (1982). He observed that in spite of the extremely provisional medical information available, the straight media described AIDS as a gay disease that threatened all Americans. AIDS prompted, moreover, the renewal of constructions of the promiscuous, immoral homosexual who threatens society with disease and death. AIDS made it legitimate to publicly express antigay feelings. Unfortunately, says Bronski, this stereotyping of "the homosexual" by the straight media has been echoed by the gay media to the extent that it has blamed AIDS on a "fast-lane" lifestyle. Bronski cites two leading gay newspapers which ran pieces by physicians who asserted, on the basis of quite provisional medical information, that AIDS among homosexual men is caused by "promiscuity." Bronski quotes an anonymous gay physician: "Perhaps we've needed a situation like this to demonstrate what we've all known all along: Depravity kills!" Bronski criticized perspectives which interpreted AIDS as a judgment on gay life. Such views make gay men responsible for their own victimization. It may, moreover, lead gays to surrender control over their lives to those heterosexual institutions (e.g., medicine and science) which have been oppressive in the past. Bronski discerned a surfacing of guilt and internalized homophobia among gay men in their susceptibility to a view of AIDS that blames themselves.

Although Bronski interpreted the social response to AIDS to be inadequate, he did not make the public reaction itself a focus of social criticism. Instead, he proposed that we treat AIDS as a medical event or disease, not an occasion for moral and social commentary. Interestingly, this was the position advanced by Dennis Altman. In "AIDS: The Politization of an Epidemic" (1984) Altman criticized both straights and gays for using AIDS as a pretext for social criticism. Sensing that AIDS was prompting an escalation of antigay sentiments, he advocated the "de-homosexualization of AIDS." "I would like to see the discussion of AIDS shift to one that sees it as a test of . . . medicine and health care, rather than a metaphysical judgment of lifestyles" (p. 108).

It was a mistake to imagine that it was possible to frame AIDS solely as a medical fact. Indeed, Altman's more elaborate statement, *AIDS and the Mind of America* (1985), imbued AIDS with moral significance. Not only does he see in the ineffective social response to AIDS in the US a sign of homophobia, but at times he takes AIDS as entailing a judgment of sexual morality. He cautiously suggested that AIDS indicates the errors of a libertarian sexual ethic that he helped to shape and legitimate. "It is difficult in view of . . . AIDS to escape the feeling that those of us who argued for liberating sex . . . were wrong" (p. 172).

The reluctance to seize on AIDS as an occasion for social criticism was absent in Cindy Patton's *Sex and Germs* (1985; cf. Watney 1987; Goldstein

1989; Crimp 1987). She framed AIDS as a story of the failure of liberal America. She argued that the straight media seized upon AIDS to attack trends toward a more sexually open and pluralistic culture. In particular, AIDS was used as a pretext to initiate a far-reaching assault on the gay community. The public hysteria surrounding homosexuality prompted by AIDS was taken as a sign of the enhanced social influence of the New Right and their conservative social agenda. In other words, Patton described AIDS as a major site of sexual political struggles between sex-negative, antigay forces and defenders of eros and sexual and social liberation. She defended a gay sexual culture which celebrates eros while reconfiguring pleasures to conform to safe sex practices.

The genre of AIDS interpretation represented by Patton shifts the blame from individuals to social institutions. Although Patton is too reductive in interpreting the social response to AIDS as one of homophobia and antigay backlash in order to illustrate American illiberalism, she is right in underscoring the prejudices and parochial politics informing the US social response. This genre of AIDS discourse does not further victimize persons with AIDS by rendering the disease a failure of "the gay lifestyle." Instead, this approach features America's failure to live up to its liberal ideals of respecting social difference. Finally, by viewing HIV as requiring only a change in sex practices, and not a wholesale cultural shift, Patton leaves life-style options open to individual choice rather than mandated by hygienic, public health imperatives.

Patton's claim that AIDS does not require, on the grounds of public health alone, a wholesale break from past sexual conventions found strong echoes in the gay culture. As we have seen, while some in the gay community seized on AIDS to advocate major subcultural reform, others defended their sexual culture and proposed a shift *only* in specific sexual practices. This position was staked out nicely by Tim Vollmer (1985).

Vollmer did not dispute the claim that a unique gay subculture materialized in the 1970s that affirmed "libertarian" sexual values. He defended this sexual culture for providing positive images of homosexuality and for its sheer erotic brilliance. Vollmer did not deny the seriousness of AIDS. The epidemic not only left an almost unthinkable trail of personal tragedies in its wake but has threatened to unravel gay communal life. Vollmer believed that sex was a primary basis of gay male identity and community. AIDS threatened to make sex the bearer of disease, death and social disintegration. In this perilous situation, Vollmer advised gays to resist homophobic images of "the profligate homosexual." Gays must not relinquish control over their lives to heterosexual medical or media authorities. Vollmer counseled gays to avoid a mindless emulation of heterosexual intimate models, and instead to innovate new models of sexual and interpersonal relationships that build upon existing gay culture. Vollmer defended a pluralistic sexual ethic that accepts self-designed and diverse sexual and intimate lifestyles so long as safe sex guidelines were followed.

AIDS and homosexuality: the limits of a discourse

The straight and gay media response to AIDS between 1981–1986 shared a common moral theme: the dangers of "promiscuity" which was said to be a defining feature of homosexuality today. The former frequently derived "promiscuity" from the very essence of homosexual desire. The latter often traced it to the contemporary gay male subculture. However, even this more "historicist" approach is suspect. By positing an abstract relationship between the gay male subculture and "promiscuity," the suspicion remains that a universal immoral homosexual desire is at work. Neither straight nor gay AIDS discourses, in the main, offered historical perspectives on the social factors that shaped gay life and could explain, and make understandable, its distinctive configuration of sexual values and patterns.

Viewing homosexuality within an historical and sociological framework suggests an alternative perspective on AIDS and homosexuality. For example, historians and sociologists have documented the rise of a unique gay male community in the 1970s in which sex functioned as a primary source of gay identity and community (see Seidman 1991). An elaborate system of sexual exchanges materialized, along with discourses and representations that imbued sex with meanings related to the celebration of the body, pleasure, a sexualized gay identity, sexual and social rebellion, and a gay brotherhood. Moreover, anal sex became a legitimate and widely engaged sexual practice. Indeed, it served as a symbol of a new masculine gay pride. This gay male subculture unfortunately provided a favorable milieu for the rapid spread of HIV unbeknownst to those who carried and spread it. This sociological approach avoids simple-mindedly blaming individuals, a reified homosexual desire or "the gay subculture." It makes possible strategies of behavioral change in light of HIV that may be both effective and preserve the integrity of gay male cultural values.

Notwithstanding widely publicized announcements of changing sexual patterns among gay men, the available research is much less unequivocal (Turner et al. 1989). To be sure, studies report a decline in certain indicators of non-monogamous sex, e.g., bathhouse attendance or STD's. However, this may simply mean that non-monogamous sex is occurring in different locations and is confined to safe sex acts. Indeed, the appearance of sex clubs organized around safe sex and the recent prominence of forms of eroticism centered on visual stimuli, sex talk or role-playing suggests that their may be little change in many gay men's sexual values and practices, even as there has been a shift to safe sex acts. To reiterate a point made above, any discussion of changes in sexual patterns that focuses narrowly on the number of sex partners without considering their sociological context and meaning is limited. For example, a discussion of changing sexual patterns would need to take into the account the unique gender dynamics of an all-male community. Many social analysts have argued that in such a culture, which exhibits fairly conventional masculine attitudes and values, sexual expression will exhibit certain unique patterns that depart in some significant ways from dominant heterosexual and lesbian patterns, e.g., permitting more slippage between desire and affect or sex and intimacy (see Altman 1983; Seidman 1991). Defending the exclusive legitimacy of a "marital" intimate ideal that binds sex to love in a monogamous relationship may be an ineffective message to gay men responding to HIV. There is, in fact, a good deal of evidence that while gay men have altered their behavior in light of HIV, the turn to sexual monogamy is the choice of only a minority (Turner et al. 1989; Martin 1986; Jones et al. 1987). If reducing the risk of HIV infection among gay men is the goal, the more effective message might be to emphasize safe sex practices – whether monogamous or non-monogamous.

To return to the question of numbers, even if we assume that many gay men have fewer partners in the post-AIDS era than in the 1970s, this does not amount to a significant change in sexual patterns. The latter is not defined solely by whether one is monogamous or not. Such a definition omits the qualitative, meaningful aspects of sex, e.g., its normative and emotional content and its interpersonal dynamics. Moreover, this one-sided quantitative view of sex implies an equally simplistic sexual ethic suggesting that monogamy by itself can serve as the normative standard for evaluating sexual behavior. The conceptual and moral muddle of this discourse is strikingly revealed in the loose and ambiguous way the concept of "promiscuity" is used in AIDS discourses.

In both the heterosexual and gay media, "promiscuity" is taken as the decisive link between homosexuality and AIDS. Yet, one looks in vain for a definition or a serious analysis of its meaning. Its sense, however, is conveyed by references to having many sex partners. This definition, however, is misleading. Promiscuity cannot be defined only by the sheer number of sex partners. For example, a serial monogamous pattern which involves a sequence of changing partners would not, I think, be considered promiscuous behavior. Similarly, promiscuity is not the same as non-monogamy. We would not consider promiscuous a wife who had one extramarital affair, though we might if her nonmarital sex partners changed frequently and lacked "intimacy." Promiscuity would seem to involve more than multiple sex partners since such behavior would perhaps not be considered promiscuous if relationships of intimacy and responsibility were established with each partner. Promiscuity would seem to suggest a pattern of multiple sex partners in which the sex partners change frequently and with each there is an absence of "intimacy" and "responsibility." In this regard, the line between serial monogamy, polygamy, sexual pluralism and promiscuity cannot always be drawn in a hard and fast way. A serial monogamous pattern involving a sequence of short-lived, emotionally distant relationships has a promiscuous aspect. A polygamous pattern involving one primary long-term relationship and sex with anonymous others suggests a more salient promiscuous element.

At stake is more than a matter of conceptual clarification. The categories used to describe sexual behavior carry moral and practical implications. Homosexuality cannot be characterized as promiscuous in some generic or essential way. Studies of homosexual behavior over the past few decades in the US highlight a diversity of sexual or intimate patterns ranging from a monogamous, marital model to promiscuity (e.g., Bell and Weinberg 1978). Any attempt to frame homosexual desire as some abstract, universal and homogeneous entity whose essence is promiscuity will not find support in behavioral research. For example, researchers agree that a more typical pattern for at least some gay men in the 1970s was to combine a primary committed relationship with secondary affairs centered on sex (Peplau and Gordon 1983; Harry and Duvall 1978; White 1980). These secondary involvements ranged from having a few erotically-centered relationships involving extended responsibilities and intimacy to having high numbers of changing, anonymous sex partners. To the extent that the latter was more common then the line between polygamy and promiscuity is blurred. In fact, according to some observers, this more promiscuous style characterized a segment of the urban gay population in the 1970s. Surveys of sexual behavior show that during this period gay men had, on the average, a much higher number of sex-partners – many of whom were anonymous – than heterosexuals and lesbians (Jay and Young 1977; Blumstein and Schwartz 1983). It is reasonable to assume *some* connection between this behavior and AIDS among gay men. The error is to assume a genetic causal tie between homosexuality, promiscuity, and disease or to take AIDS as evidence of the pathological nature of homosexuality.

There is a series of wrong moves here. Patterns of multiple sex partners is *not* the cause of AIDS but a risk-factor. To be even more precise, it is a risk-factor if one engages in high-risk sex and if one does so in circumstances where HIV is widely circulated. Gay men do not have to be non-monogamous to acquire AIDS. It is not legitimate to take AIDS as indicative of a particular type of sexual pattern or lifestyle. Furthermore, given its appearance among heterosexuals and, in some nations it afflicts predominantly them, it is wrong to interpret AIDS as a homosexual disease. There is no evidence that AIDS is congenital or that it is produced by homosexual behavior or that it favors homosexual men. The only statement that can be endorsed unequivocally is that *specific* same-sex sexual acts are today high-risk in *specific* social environments. This observation does not, however, require that gay men adopt any particular lifestyle or sexual ethic. It mandates only safe sex practices but how these are incorporated into a life style or pattern of intimate relationships is open to diverse morally legitimate choices (Seidman 1992).

Conclusion

Foucault has shown how the original intent and political purpose of a sex discourse can be reversed. For example, the scientific-medical discourse of "the homosexual" as a perverse or pathological human type promoted new forms of social control. Yet, by taking the question of homosexuality out of a religious context and placing it in a scientific one, it allowed an appeal to empirical evidence to be used to discredit religious constructions and, ultimately, to contest the scientific-medical model itself. Moreover, this scientific-medical discourse contributed to creating a common homosexual consciousness and culture that eventuated in a politic aimed at legitimating homosexuality.

If there is a hopeful sign in the AIDS crisis, it is in the potential unintended consequences of making homosexuality a public issue. AIDS has forced public officials to gather and publicize knowledge about homosexuality. The acquisition of detailed empirical knowledge of homosexuality is deemed essential for public health reasons. The medical profession and the lay public must rely upon social researchers and knowledgeable observers of the homosexual scene for information which is considered vital to controlling AIDS. Much of this research will undoubtedly be done by gay people. It is likely that this research will yield perspectives that will discredit stereotypes. Moreover, there will be a need to disseminate credible information about homosexuality in order to facilitate behavior that reduces risks of contacting AIDS. The enormous expansion of public talk about homosexuality (in newspapers, radio and television programs, in books, plays, advertisements and ordinary conversations), may contribute to making homosexuality more socially acceptable, especially if stereotypes lose credibility. It is likely that AIDS will prompt renewed efforts at sex education. In so far as AIDS education is part of this effort, the discussion of homosexuality will become more routine. At the very least, these developments would provide a context in which to challenge normative heterosexuality.

It is, then, possible that AIDS may have a long-term beneficial effect. AIDS requires credible empirical knowledge of homosexuality. This will stimulate and legitimate research on homosexuals, much of which will challenge stereotypes. Finally, this knowledge will be disseminated throughout society and taken seriously because of its link to a health crisis. This could provide a favorable setting for legitimating homosexuality and re-negotiating the moral boundaries of US sexual and political culture. In the end, this will not result from merely a process of mass enlightenment. Rather, it will require political mobilization to shape these public discussions. Gays must have a political presence if they expect to contribute to public policy decisions that arise from the AIDS crisis.

9

From gay ethnicity to queer politics: the renewal of gay radicalism in the United States

For whatever reason, society rejects the homosexual . . . above all simply because he is homosexual. He is seen first and foremost as a homosexual . . . The homosexual then becomes a victim of the same kind of thinking . . . Before change can be effected in others, . . . the homosexual must accept himself first as a man or woman more alike than different from other men and women. He will then discover that he can be accepted by others . . .

These words, printed in the *Mattachine Review* in December 1957, express a theory and politics of homosexuality widely shared among Americans involved in the so-called homophile movement. Homosexuality was viewed as a defining aspect of an individual's identity but it was not assumed to mark out a distinctive psychological and moral human terrain. Indeed, it was widely believed – and still is by many who are self described as homosexual – that a politics anchored in a concept of homosexual difference has the effect of perpetuating demeaning and disempowering images of "the homosexual." For most members of the Mattachine Society and the Daughters of Bilitis, the legitimation of homosexuality pivoted on the claim that homosexuals share a common humanity with heterosexuals. Was this strategy a failure of nerve on the part of these homophile organizations? I do not think so. In the context of the 1950s in America, where homosexuality was framed as a difference that signified a deviant, polluted identity, it was not unreasonable, nor ineffective, for individuals to legitimate homosexuality by asserting a common, universal humanity. This approach defined the individual's primary identity as a human while classifying homosexuality as a secondary identity. This figuring of homosexuality remains a credible strategy of legitimation, particularly in the context of a strong individualistic civil rights tradition in the United States and for individuals who wish only to normalize homosexuality.

The assertion of a common humanity unifying "homosexuals" and

"heterosexuals" was not the only strategy in the 1950s proposed to construct and legitimate homosexuality. There was an alternative, somewhat
submerged, perspective which figured homosexuality as marking out a
social difference. What did difference mean? A weak concept alluded to the
differences socially created by practices of discrimination and prejudice –
differences that would disappear as discrimination diminished. There was
another, stronger concept of difference. For the originators of the
Mattachine Society, in particular Harry Hay and Chuck Rowland, for
whom their political coming of age occurred in the ideological politics of
the American Communist Party, homosexuals were viewed as a group
oppressed by their sexual difference. Difference here signifies a social and
cultural difference that was said to be deeply rooted in biological or historical conditions and therefore more or less permanent. Moreover, instead of
refusing this difference, they advocated the making of homosexuals into a
self-conscious political and cultural minority. Homosexual's difference was
to be proudly and defiantly announced. Harry Hay imagined a sociopolitical project in which homosexuals would develop their own culture and
institutions.

There was then a major division over the meaning and politics of homosexuality at the very moment in which a gay movement was taking shape in
the United States. Is homosexuality to be conceived of as a minor variation
of an essentially common human nature or is it a distinctive but positive
version of being human? Should a homosexual movement assert a common
humanity to legitimate homosexuality or should it highlight the unique
social character and contributions of homosexuals? The former points to
what I will call a politics of respectability. It gets its political and moral
credibility from an Enlightenment culture that authorizes appeals to a
common, universal humanity and does not otherwise challenge the social
and moral boundaries between respectable and deviant society. The latter
gestures towards a politics of difference. It does not deny a baseline of
common humanity but appeals to the social value of human difference. A
politics of difference emerged briefly in the early fifties in the concept of a
homosexual minority; it resurfaced in the radical fairie movement, in
lesbian-feminism, and in the ethnic modeling of homosexuality that has
come to dominate the gay mainstream.

The politics of respectability declined somewhat in the 1970s and 1980s.
The rise of a politic of group identity in black and women's liberation and
the nationalist movements of decolonialization in Third World societies
favored the rise of an ethnic nationalist concept of homosexuality. The idea
was simple enough: Like Jews or Blacks in the United States, homosexuals
are said to share their own unique values, beliefs, and political agenda by

virtue of their distinctive common experience, in particular, that of oppression and resistance in a heterosexist society (Cory 1951; Hoffman 1968; Martin and Lyon 1972). The ways in which gay public culture signifies its difference from the straight mainstream is valued. Of course not all differences are affirmed – not the difference of the closet and internalized homophobia – but those that reflect the willful self-creation of homosexuals in the form of a unique lifestyle and culture.

I will have more to say about the ethnic modeling of homosexuality but before I pursue this theme, we need to recall that in the United States in the late sixties and early seventies this version of the politics of difference was not the only one. At odds with the ethnic concept of homosexuality were perspectives that surfaced in gay liberationism (e.g., Altman 1971; Jay and Young 1971), in marxist gay theory (e.g., Fernbach 1981; Gay Left 1981), and to some extent in the poststructuralism of Foucault (1978). Despite the risks of any summary statement, I would like to propose the following broad characterization of these varied perspectives: homosexual identity was imagined as a sociopolitical event. Claiming homosexuality as an identity, even as a valued different identity, was said to function as a form of social control; it regulated and constrained the range of legitimate sexual, personal, and social expression. The aim of homosexual politics was not to legitimate homosexuality but to liberate all individuals from the roles or identities of hetero-and-homosexuality as part of a broader emancipatory project of freeing the self from all unnecessary social constraints. In Dennis Altman's classic *Homosexual Oppression and Liberation* (1971) this erotic politic pivoted on an idealization of a bisexual, androgynous, eroticized body and culture. Foucault's *History of Sexuality* (1978) gestured towards an emancipatory ideal of bodies and pleasures released from disciplinary regimes.

It was neither the politics of respectability nor one of the above versions of radical gay politics that won out in the United States. Rather, it was an ethnic identity politic that triumphed by the mid-70s. To repeat, the key idea was that homosexuality is at the core of personal experience; a community was to be built around this identity; politics aimed at legitimating a homosexual identity and community (see ch. 6; also Epstein 1987). This ethnic identity politics has been articulated within a civil rights assimilationist social ideal – a version of the politics of respectability – and a separatist, nationalist social model, e.g., lesbian-feminism (e.g., Bunch 1975; Johnston 1973).

The success of an ethnic group politic of identity is not, for reasons I indicated above, surprising. Nor am I of the opinion that this has been a necessarily undesirable development. Opposition to normative heterosexuality seems unthinkable without a homosexual subject. And a homosexual movement *is* unthinkable without the creation of a community which is almost unthinkable without invoking a common homosexual identity. At a minimum, it seems that an appeal to a collective homosexual subject unjustly victimized has provided some of the affective and ethical drive for the extraordinary acts of courage, risk taking, and sacrifice that has fueled the movement. At a more personal level, many of us in the United States have felt compelled to leave our families and neighborhoods in order to live openly and with integrity as lesbians and gay men. We needed safe nurturing spaces to fashion positive identities and to forge alternative communities. The ethnic enclaves we imagined and constructed replaced the families and neighborhoods that no longer welcomed us. Let us not forget that, whatever the limits of these imagined communities, they have allowed many of us to craft coherent, meaningful lives protected from the violence directed to being lesbian or gay in a heteronormative world.

The heyday of the ethnic modeling of homosexuality was the period roughly between the early 1970s and the early 1980s. Dense networks of bookstores, political organizations, intimate ties, cultural festivals, and women studies gave a definite shape to a lesbian-feminist culture (Kreiger 1983; Wolf 1979). The making of institutionally elaborated, mostly male, gay subcultures, typically territorially and culturally bounded, suggested an ethnic enclave (Humphreys 1979; Lee 1979; Levine 1979; Murray 1979). The institutionalization of lesbian and gay desire was accompanied by a cultural ferment. This was a period of great intellectual creativity. In particular, we can observe the rise of social constructionist approaches to homosexuality (e.g., Katz 1976; Plummer 1975; Smith-Rosenberg 1975; Trumbach 1977; Weeks 1977). These perspectives emphasized the historical, socially produced character of homosexuality. Intellectuals, often academic intellectuals, initiated a new research program excavating the sociohistorical conditions involved in the making of homosexual identities and communities. To say it in very sketchy terms, parallelling the consolidation of public homosexual cultures anchored in a concept of a common identity, there surfaced discourses tracing the rise and formation of homosexual identities and communities. For example, John D'Emilio's *Sexual Politics, Sexual Communities* (1983) had the telling subtitle: *The Making of a Homosexual Minority in the United States*. If Emilio's book legitimated the ethnic turn of the gay mainstream, Lillian Faderman's *Surpassing of the Love of Men* (1981) legitimated lesbian-feminism by crafting a story of the rise of lesbians in the model of ethnic nationalism.

I detect a shift or perhaps simply the surfacing of new voices and dynamics in the public culture of gay America. There are cracks in the dominant ethnic model of homosexuality. I want to identify some of these fissures, to take seriously the possibility that the recent surfacing of a public language of queer politics and theory is indicative of important changes in homosexual culture and politics.

What events are challenging the ethnic model and with what implications for queer lives in the United States as we approach the end-of-the-century?

At the very historical moment at which an ethnic model of homosexuality was consolidating as a dominant cultural and political template, something happened – well actually many things were happening in the early eighties to trouble the coherence of this model. Events challenged the fundamental premises of what had become mainstream lesbian and gay politics and pointed, often not very clearly, to alternative ways of thinking about self and politics.

What happened? First, a well-organized anti-gay campaign was launched in the late 1970s responding in no small part to the political successes of the gay movement, to the new public visibility of homosexuality, and to the growing acceptance of lesbian and gay identities by many mainstream cultural and political elites (Adam 1987; Rubin 1983; Seidman 1992). As city after city adopted gay rights laws, as politicians pursued gay votes, and as opinion makers normalized homosexuality, a sense of change was in the air. Thus, Dennis Altman (1982), always an acute observer of the American scene, could speak, with a sense of heady optimism, of "the homosexualization of America." Like many of us, Altman may have underestimated the extent and strength of public support for the anti-gay backlash. He surely did not anticipate the coming of the plague. While AIDS may have allowed the Hollywood crowd to go public in supporting homosexuals, the anti-gay forces – trumpeting their message of diseased, deviant, and dangerous homosexuals – were far more successful in capturing the American mainstream (see ch. 8). The noble humanitarian response of gays to the plague was not matched by an equally impressive political response. The truth is that gay America was not prepared for the enormity of the anti-gay effort nor for the often hostile public sentiment fueled by AIDS. From the early 1980s lesbians and gay men were increasingly on the defensive, responding to a multi-pronged offensive by anti-gay forces. Of course, much of our energies had to be channeled into the care of the sick. Yet I want to underscore a crucial point: in the face of a hostile Reagan administration, in the face of a well-organized backlash against us as well as against gender and race-based movements, in the face of a plague ravaging our community, the gay movement was simply unable to draw on solid alliances with gender-or-race-or-class-based communities. This was so, in part, because the ethnic identity model – with its isolation of a homosexual identity and community and with its single interest group politic – had rendered our bonds to other oppressed communities fragile. We lacked the kinds of emotional, social and political ties necessary to mobilize an effective coalitionally based response to the backlash forces.

The ethnic model seriously impeded our ability to draw on alliances with other oppressed communities in the face of the twin crises of the backlash and the plague. By isolating an abstract homosexual subject who was assumed to have singular homosexual interests, the ethnic model contributed to insulating the homosexual community. Moreover, the very unity that this model claimed as one of its chief accomplishments was unraveling. And this fracturing of social solidarity was, ironically, an effect of the ethnic model itself. Let me explain.

The ethnic identity model implicitly endorsed the idea of a common homosexual experience, identity, and interest. However, what counted as *the homosexual experience* were the experiences of individuals who assumed a particular class, racial, and gender standpoint. To simplify, the concept of the homosexual that was dominant in the gay mainstream – and what was taken as the interests and ideals of the homosexual – expressed the standpoint of white, middle-class, sexually respectable, fully able-bodied, often conventionally gendered men and women. All those individuals who were self described as gay but who were not white, not middle-class, not able-bodied, not sexually or gender conventional, did not have their distinctive experiences, interests, and political will expressed in the gay mainstream. In short, the ethnic model marginalized and silenced a multitude of differences among lesbians and gay men (see ch. 6). Perhaps the very successes of the seventies permitted these hitherto submerged differences to surface, but surface they did in the early eighties. This period witnessed a virtual explosion of difference into public gay life. The major sites for the assertion of difference were in the spheres of race, gender, and sexuality. For example, there was the formation of public subcultures of lesbian and gay people of color; hitherto submerged and silenced non-conventional sexualities – from butch/fem to S/M and man/boy love – materialized claiming their own identities, organizations, and political agendas; lesbians and gay men for whom gender transgression was crucial in their lives and politics were not struggling against the codes of normalization and respectability *within* the gay mainstream.

My point is simply this: the gay mainstream – now organized around an ethnic model anchored in a concept of a unitary homosexual identity – was criticized by lesbians and gay men for functioning as a mode of social control by means of the very mechanism that straights used against gays, namely "normalization" which controls through silencing, marginalizing, and pathologizing difference. While the combination of the backlash, the plague, and the fracturing of gay solidarity led many lesbians and gay men to retreat into a dogmatic essentialism and biological defense of gay ethnicity (e.g., the biologism of the gay brain), it simultaneously encouraged a new radicalism.

The social impetus and shape of this gay radicalism is inseparable from its roots in a new generation coming of age in the late 1980s and nineties. The sons and daughters of the sixties generation, these young queers take for granted the gains of their elders. Homosexuality is normalized quicker and easier. Coming out begins at fourteen or sixteen, not twenty-five or forty-five and in the context of an institutionalized gay life anchored in affirmative identities. This is a generation impelled by rage. They are angry at straight society – their parents, peers, schools, media, and government – for its intolerance; furious at the obscene loss of lives to the plague as a result of social prejudice and neglect, critical of the gay mainstream for its guarded politics of respectability, its insularity, and its conventional normalization of homosexuality. Some of this anger has been channeled into the renewal of gay radicalism.

The ethnic model of homosexuality that has been dominant in American gay culture and politics is perhaps in crisis. The backlash has exposed its limits. Moreover, the eruption of internal differences, the appearance of a postmodern language of de-centered, multiple identities and the foregrounding of coalitional politics stretch to the limits the coherence of the concept of gay ethnicity. A younger generation resistant to "ghettoization" and a politics of respectability imagine a political cultural ideal beyond assimilation or separatism. The crumbling of empire – both the Soviet and the American – the assertion of national autonomy, and the rise of a multicultural politics of difference has inspired new forms of gay radicalism.

In place of orthodoxy there is a new political heterodoxy. There is the model of coalitional politics proposed, in particular, by people of color who conceive of composite or hybrid identities – of identities that fuse sexuality, gender, race, and class – and view these aspects of identity as simultaneously marking interlocking axes of social formation and politics (Anzaldua 1987; Combahee River Collective 1983; Moraga 1983). There is the politics of ACT UP – radical in its confrontational style, in its coalitional strategies, and in linking representations and knowledges to institutional seats of power (Aronowitz 1995; Crimp 1987; Gamson 1989). Similarly, the politics of outing gestures towards a new radicalism as it views the closet not as a personal experience enforced by prejudice or ignorance but as an institution central to the power structure of American society (Gross 1993; Signorile 1994). We know we're in a different political terrain, one closer in spirit to gay liberationism than to gay ethnicity, when we read the following words of Michelangelo Signorile.

There exists in America what appears to be a brilliantly orchestrated, massive conspiracy to keep all homosexuals locked in the closet. This conspiracy forces many of us to live in shame and tremble with fear. Anyone who dares venture out of that closet is threatened with destruction. The vast majority heed the warning . . . The conspiracy is a relatively unconscious one, ingrained in our culture . . . [Even] straight liberals who . . . champion gay rights . . . aren't aware how vigorously they enforce the closet in America, but they do enforce it, every day.

Perhaps no event announces a new era of politics as dramatically as the appearance of Queer Nation. I want to briefly comment on the meaning of the language and politics of queer.

Queer carries multiple meanings in American gay public life. For some, it is a shorthand for the terms gay, lesbian, and bisexual. For others, it is a style, at once personal and political marked by a certain brashness – a refusal to apologize or to account for homosexuality and a refusal to accept either intolerance or mere tolerance.

As a distinctive political movement, Queer Nation is said to have originated in April 1990 in New York. Whatever its precise origin, Queer Nation emerged, in part, out of the renewed confrontational politics of ACT UP, and, in part, in response to the heightened everyday violence against lesbians and gay men at a time when homosexuality had become normalized in urban gay subcultures (See Chee 1991; Duggan 1992). Although Queer Nation is characterized by direct action strategies, nonhierarchical, non-bureaucratic organizing, local political interventions, and a playful subversive media politics, these features do not define its political logic. While the imagery of queer nation might suggest a version of gay ethnicity, Queer politics is in many respects antagonistic to ethnic identity politics.

To grasp the logic of queer politics we must comprehend its departure from the theory of gay ethnicity. Queer politics disputes the ethnic concept of homosexuality as simply an identity of particular individuals and a particular community. Queers criticize a politics exclusively aimed at legitimating a homosexual identity – a politics organized around the struggle for rights and political and cultural representation for that collectivity making claims under the sign of the homosexual. A Queer perspective conceives of modern homosexuality not only as a desire or identity of some individuals and communities but as present – even if unacknowledged – in the lives of straight people and in the social organization of straight America.

Homosexuality is said to be an invisible force shaping the visible forms and functioning of heterosexually based lives and institutions. Homosexuality is the repressed but present other that silently shapes its

noisy, arrogant heterosexual counterpart. Is not homosexuality present –
often as that which is to be guarded against, as that which is thought to be
threatening to nature and civilization – in the codes and rituals of friendship, romance, and family, in sports, in property law, in the military, in state
policies from marriage to immigration, in disciplinary knowledges, literature, the mass media, and in therapeutic regimes and medical practices?
The notion that homosexuality always shadows heterosexuality is pivotal
to so-called queer theory. Queer theorists aim *not* to account for the rise of
a homosexual identity and community but to uncover homosexual meanings and desires in what are considered straight contexts – in television
sitcoms, in disciplinary knowledges and literature, in concepts of citizenship and nationalism as well as in the operation of the state (see ch. 7).
Queer politics and theory press beyond a minority-based politic and theory
to become a theory and politic of the social center.

By conceiving of homosexuality as an identity, gay ethnic politics reinforces the silencing and the invisibility of homosexuality in all but the
periphery of society. Queer politics aims to end that silence, to make that
which is invisible visible, to expose the dependency of heterosexuality on
homosexuality. Queer politics wants to show how American institutions,
culture, and politics are shaped by homosexuality – though this homosexual presence is refused in a heteronormative order which has the arrogance to not only censor and pathologize homosexuality but to deny its role
in the making of straight America.

Queer politics is then a refusal to be comfortable on the social periphery
– in the ghettos of gay America, in the security of a street legal identity, in
the bars that come alive when the straight world is safely tucked in, and in
the subcultural enclaves which are protectively walled off from straight
America. Queers refuse the gesture of tolerance extended by straights – and
accepted by the gay mainstream – which holds so long as gay people remain
on the periphery and so long as they conform to a code of respectable
sexual and gender behavior. Queers contest mainstream public space as
exclusively straight space. When Queers organize actions in straight frater-
nities and bars, in malls and High Schools, and on the main streets of
America, they are contesting spaces that are officially enforced as for
straights only. Queers claim this space for themselves, as space already
organized by the invisible force of homosexuality – sometimes in the sense
of closeted queers who literally made the space and traverse it daily – and
as space to be visibly occupied by the homosexual other. Queer politics is
scandalous politics; queers materialize as the dreaded homosexual other
imagined by straight society that had invisibly and silently shaped straight
life but now do so openly, loudly, and unapologetically.

Queer politics is neither illiberal nor liberal. It exposes the lie of the politics of liberal tolerance. Tolerating homosexuality as a discrete and segregated identity and community conceals the authoritarian expulsion of homosexuality from the social center and the intolerance of America towards differences that truly stretch the cultural boundaries of personal and public life. Gay ethnic identity politics is criticized for reinforcing the norm of heterosexuality. The political logic of gay ethnicity permits a tolerance of homosexuality but only as a minority identity, only as a segregated and marginalized subculture, and only as it leaves normative heterosexuality intact.

Just as gay people are finally gaining some recognition and respect as a legitimate minority, a new radicalism is making its presence felt and disturbingly so to both the straight and gay mainstream. This new radicalism speaks with many voices. Yet whether we are listening to radical gays of color or to those exposing the closets of power or to queers noisily crashing the straight party, there are some common markers – most notably, a perspective asserting that oppression lies *less* in laws, stereotypes, ignorance, or lack of exposure to homosexuals than in the very structure of our key institutions and in the core cultural codes of our societies. Homosexual oppression is said to be a fundamental part of the organization and functioning of American society, rather than a more surface or peripheral phenomenon that can be dealt with through education, legal reform, or coming out. The new radicals depart from mainstream lesbian and gay politics not only in viewing heterosexism as more deeply structured into society; they are abandoning the goal of gaining tolerance for a homosexual identity and community as its chief aim in favor of agendas such as the abolition of the "closets of heterosexual power" or the formation of a coalitional block linking the opposition to heterosexism to the struggle against patriarchy, capitalism and racism. In certain versions of queer politics, I detect a radical agenda that takes as its object of critique not heterosexism, not homophobia, and not the closet, but the sexual regime organized around a sexual and social binary and hierarchy along the axis of gender preference, i.e. a regime which makes a hetero-and-homo-gender preference master categories of sexual and social identity and organization. Queer politics aims to expose – and ultimately abolish – this regime as a mode of social control. In this regard, queer politics gestures towards a radical politics of difference that anticipates, however vaguely, a postdisciplinary ordering of bodies, pleasures, identities, and social relations. Here I can do no more than sketch this current of queer politics and theory.

Queer politics is, well, a queer sort of politics. Queers criticize the conceptual cornerstone of the gay movement: the idea of the homosexual as a unitary experience and identity. Queers have proposed not only that homo-sexuality is a heterogeneous experience varying (say) with race, class, or gender, but that these differences are all there is. Every appeal to a common homosexual identity not only misrepresents some people's lives but neces-sarily creates boundaries of insider/outsider similar to the hetero-sexual/homosexual hierarchical division. The very identity in whose name we struggle for our rights and freedom is criticized as functioning as a mechanism of social control, creating boundaries of respectability and deviance or insider/outsider within gay life. In part, queer politics is about exposing the disciplining role of identity politics. Queer politics gives voice to the multiplicity of lives – African-American queers, S/M queers, fems, and transgendered queers – which have been silenced, marginalized or pathologized by both the straight and gay mainstream. Queers aim to shape a culture and movement that values differences, multiple voices, protean identities, and hybrid coalitional subjects.

As I interpret certain of its impulses, queer politics suggests an even more radical agenda – the linking of a gay politics to a more encompassing politics of the body and desire. Gay politics, at least in its ethnic identity version, has focused on legitimating same-sex preference, i.e. homosexual desire, identities, intimacies, and communities. Queers do not deny the importance of this politics but criticize the ways it unintentionally rein-forces the very sexual regime that scandalizes homosexuality. A politic intent on legitimating same-sex preference implicitly acknowledges the nor-mative status of heterosexuality. Moreover, to the extent that gay politics aims exclusively or chiefly at normalizing a homosexual preference, this sexual politic leaves the dominant normative ordering of bodies, pleasures, identities, and social relations undisturbed. If gender preference is author-ized as *the* master category of sexual and self identity, so that bodies, desires, and identities are organized and framed chiefly as heterosexual or homosexual, a wide range of experiences that pertain to the body and desire – but not chiefly to gender preference – are marginalized, patholo-gized or simply de-politicized in public culture e.g., S/M, transgendered practices, multiple partner sex, butch-fem eroticism, intergenerational, interracial intimacies, public sex, erotic play between children and between teens, or intimacies that depart from the norm of long-term, cohabiting, nuclear units. The gay movement has largely surrendered its claim to being a movement of sexual and gender liberation in favor of a one-dimensional agenda of legitimating a homosexual gender preference. This is painfully obvious in the seemingly perpetual battles around whether to include bisex-uals, transgendered folk, sadomasochists, man/boy lovers, and transvestites in the Pride Marches. For individuals – whether straight or gay – whose desires and intimacies involve practices that depart from conventional norms – their struggles are not those of the lesbian and gay mainstream. Indeed they may be as much in a relation of opposition to the gay as the straight mainstream. Queer politics presses for a transgressive politic of the body, desire, and identity against the normalization of "sexuality" enforced by the straight and gay mainstream.

I want to conclude with a quick look backwards and some hopeful thoughts for the future of queer politics.

For many Americans born in the 1940s or early 1950s and coming of age in the seventies, we readily embraced the idea of gay ethnicity. Growing up in families and communities that scandalized us, living much of our lives in shame, secrecy, loneliness and public anonymity, the idea of being part of a public community, of being like Jews, Blacks, or Italian Americans has been very alluring. Moreover, this generation has created a public collective life; we built affirmative identities and communities – safe, nurturing environments that provided us with positive personal and public identities. We should be proud because very much like our parents and grandparents we created a new world for ourselves, a world where we belong. Intellectuals have memorialized this experience by crafting ennobling stories – with heroes, villains and often happy endings where individuals put their lives together, where communities fought to gain their rights, where a nation found a place for us. But these stories are just that, stories aimed at celebrating and shaping a collective life and politic. And while this story and the life we created merits praise and celebration, we must recognize that this public gay culture is a social event which emerged and proved important at a very specific historical period. It provided safe, affirmative psychic and social spaces in a terribly heterosexist and homophobic society. It did so, however, at some cost, namely the price of excluding and pathologizing internal differences, impeding coalition building, and leaving the reign of heterosexuality intact. This price is now too high to pay for the promise of safety and comfort, a promise which, in any event, can no longer be redeemed.

The terrain of gay life and politics in the United States is changing. A new era is perhaps dawning in queer America. A generation has come of age which lacks the experiences of its elders and faces a new America – an America in a world without empires; an America lacking a clear social center and cultural consensus; and America in the throes of cultural wars; an America where the plague seems a permanent fixture. Queers are changing with the times. While some have surrendered to despair or consumer absorption, many other queers in America are channeling their rage and perception of social hope into a new gay radicalism. This radicalism speaks in many voices but what cannot be missed is its disavowal of gay ethnicity – its refusal to retreat into a safe identity and insular community. There are no safe spaces – gay bashing, the plague, internal division and the exclusionary politics of identity means that the gay community is no longer a haven in a homophobic world. Identities and communities must be fought over. Queer bodies have become the site of power struggles but so too have the bodies of straights. The struggles have intensified – hatred is on the surface; gay bashing and violence is an everyday reality but now queers are bashing back, defending their bodily, psychic, and public territories and claiming those of straight America as their own. There is a new radical spirit in queer America – confrontational, unapologetic, experimental, intolerant towards a homophobic straight America – queers are refusing to take their place on the margins, in the slightly opened closets that most gays still inhabit.

One thing seems clear, at least to me: these changes are indicative of shifts in the broader American culture of homosexuality. We are experiencing the making of new homosexualized bodies, desires, and public cultures. These are perhaps changes as momentous as those of the sixties – changes in the way we think and experience ourselves and society. Identities are imagined as plural and protean; our politics is insistently coalitional; the social field is approached as a field of difference, meaning, and contestation; emancipation is imagined less as the end of domination than as the permanent struggle against certitude, hierarchy, uniformity – and for a world respectful of individuality and social difference, ambiguity and playfulness, democratization and consensual pleasures. These changes are coalescing into a politic against normalization, a politic of incessant rebellion, a politic linking representations, meanings, institutions, and the state. This is perhaps the dawning of a new gay radicalism, or so I hope.

10

Postmodern anxiety: the politics of epistemology

Chapter 2 of this book, "The End of Sociological Theory", was the basis of a symposium in *Sociological Theory*. It initially received four critical responses. Lemert (1991) and Richardson (1991) responded as friends of "the postmodern turn." I did not directly respond to their comments. Instead I focused my reply on clarifying the social meaning of postmodernism and further articulating its significance for sociology. I did this by means of responding to at least the key objections raised to my position by Alexander (1991) and Antonio (1991). I reprint this reply, edited and somewhat revised, because it states, as clearly as I have been able to, my perspective on the social sources of postmodern theory in the US and defends a strong notion of discursivity from a "postmodern" standpoint.

The new social movements, postmodern and democratic pluralism

I begin on a personal note. Lemert (1991) rightly points out that my views on theory have changed between *Liberalism and the Origins of European Social Theory* (1983) and my current writing. In the late 1970s, I believed in the notion of science as truth and in general theory as a type of social reason that must be defended as part of the defense of a democratic society. I sought to legitimate a particular sociological project: a comparative historical sociology of modernity. I was greatly influenced by my teacher, the late Benjamin Nelson, as well as the commitment to general theory I found in Habermas and in the postpositivism of my friend Jeff Alexander (1982).

By the time my book appeared in 1983, I was already moving towards a semiotic approach to science as a symbolic political practice. The move from semiotics to a "postmodern" perspective was in no small part the result of my identification as a gay man and activist. The connection between this event and my turn to postmodernism tells a story that is, I believe, central to current discussions of social knowledge and power.

As a gay activist, I found myself in a struggle with science and ultimately with some key features of modernist culture. From the early decades of the twentieth century through the present, the human sciences have been important producers and carriers of a discourse on homosexuality that constructed same-sex desire as a sign of a unique, inferior, and dangerous human type: the homosexual.

Science had not only helped to create a polluted homosexual identity but also had helped to bring into existence an elaborate apparatus of homosexual oppression. Science justified incarceration; science justified curative therapies that aimed at great psychic alteration; science justified legal criminalization; science promoted medical surveillance and control. The point is not that I learned that science is an evil social force. I knew otherwise. I was aware that science helped to displace religious concepts of same-sex desire as sinful and immoral. I knew that I could enlist science to combat religious opponents of gay rights. I knew, indeed, that I could use science against its own stereotypical, stigmatizing constructions. I knew that many brave souls had campaigned under the banner of science for social respect and rights for "homosexuals."

The point is that I came to view science as a powerful practical-moral or social force. I learned that science's claim to truth carried a social authority that made it productive of forms of personal and social life. Its power lay not only in its capacity to rationalize the denial of moral legitimacy for same-sex desire or to justify the denial of civil rights or claims to social inclusion. Through its cultural and institutional authority, science could inscribe in our bodies and minds a sexual/social regime – one that made desire into an identity, one that made gender preference into a master category of sexual and social identity, one that made hetero/homosexual identities mutually exclusive, and one that purified a heterosexual life while polluting a homosexual life. Although the social productivity of the human sciences left a trail of damaged lives, it also made possible the elaboration of affirmative gay identities and communities.

Whatever I might think of the evolution of the gay culture, I know that insofar as I think of my homosexuality as an identity, I am still under the authority of science. Science was a pivotal, but my no means the only, social force in making heterosexuality and homosexuality the master categories of the sexual self. I live under this sexual regime. I may decide to accept that framework and work within it to legitimate a homosexual identity, or I may decide to challenge it; the point is that either choice puts me in a practical, social relation to science.

As it turns out, I have deployed science regularly in my advocacy role. Yet I have done so in a deliberately rhetorical fashion; that is, I am aware of the legitimating authority science carries even while remaining in a cynical relation to the truth it is said to reveal – for example, that homosexuality is normal or natural or the basis of a social minority. These "truths" may indeed legitimate the possibility of individuals choosing a homosexual life, but it is a *life* that one now must choose – that is, an identity, a cultural and social community, and a way of defining and relating practically to one's body, desires, self, and others. The social legitimation of homosexuality, as we now frame same-sex desires and intimacies, would not signify human or sexual emancipation, but the fuller elaboration and consolidation of a particular sexual and social system. Although I believe that the struggle to elaborate this sexual social order is important at this time, I have abandoned the "modernist" interpretation of this struggle as one of human liberation or as the emancipation of "the homosexual." It is not a process of liberation that transpires in the acquisition of gay rights or the legitimation of gay lifestyles; rather, it is the full articulation of a socially formed sexual and social system that has produced the very sexual subjects who now speak in the language of legitimacy provided by that system. By abandoning the narrative of the "liberation" of the "subject" – the homosexual or the woman or the working class – I have abandoned a core premise of modernist culture and social knowledges.

By the mid-1980s, at a time when the gay community had achieved the status of an institutionally elaborated subculture, many of us in the community began to raise some questions about the limits of the sexual regime we were helping to create. Curiously, our struggles focused not only on the heterosexual norm enforced by the social mainstream but also on the gay community.

The development of affirmative gay identities and communities allowed a new set of tensions and struggles to surface. The fashioning of affirmative identities and communities around same-sex desire did not necessarily entail challenging the core assumptions regarding sexuality of the broader social order. Therefore, those desires and practices that were marginalized and censored within the dominant sexual system for reasons unrelated to homosexuality remained suppressed and devalued. The legitimation of homosexuality could coexist easily with the oppression of other non-conventional sexual and intimate lifestyle choices. Indeed, a politic aimed solely at the legitimation of homosexuality reinforced a social order that defined sexual desire and identity by gender preference, thus relegating to a depoliticized status all other desires and sexual choices.

In the early 1980s, skirmishes broke out *in* the gay community around the issue of marginal sexualities – e.g., bisexuality, butch/fem lesbian practices, and S/M. Bisexually identified individuals protested the tendency among gay men and lesbians to reinforce the bipolar sexual regime of the dominant culture, which oppressed those individuals whose desires were directed to both genders. Whereas some simply wished to make space for bisexuality as a legitimate sexual choice, others aimed to challenge the very rendering of gender preference as a master category defining sexuality and social identity. The latter challenge found expression as well among lesbian feminists, who not only opposed the dominant heterosexual regime for reducing lesbianism to a sexual identity but also criticized the gay movement for not challenging male domination.

A similar critique issued forth from an emerging gay and lesbian S/M movement. The S/M movement protested the reinforcement of gender preference as the master category of desire and identity by the gay community, which marginalized and devalued their own desires, identities, and communities. Indeed, the S/M movement found itself frequently at odds not only with the dominant heterosexual community but also with the gay community, whose moral boundaries often converged with dominant social norms in categorizing S/M as deviant, abnormal, or perverse. In other words, legitimating homosexuality within the dominant social order left intact a sexual regime which continued to marginalize and devalue many desires, pleasures, identities, and solidarities that did not fall neatly into an exclusive hetero/homo binary or that centered around or privileged sexual choices other than gender preference (e.g., number of partners or particular sex acts or the place of sex).

Internal divisions surfaced as well around normative constructions of gay identity and politics. A dominant gay cultural apparatus projected ideals of body type, self presentation, lifestyle choices, and so on. Critics charged that these normative constructions reflected the largely white, middle-class, and conventional values of those who controlled gay social, political, and cultural institutions. People of color, working class gays and lesbians, the disabled and others who did not find their experiences or values reflected in dominant representations of being gay voiced their discontent. They argued that their oppression in the broader heterosexual mainstream was being reproduced in the gay community. The assumption that homosexuality was a primary sexual and social identity, which rendered gender, race, ethnicity, class, ableness or nationality as secondary, minor variations of an individuals principal gay identity, was contested as a multiplicity of submerged selves and communities began to speak languages of desire and identity that did not marginalize these differences. Again, the "modern" foundational notion of a gay or homosexual subject was contested.

As an activist, I found myself in a difficult situation. I could hardly deny the social and political value of a narrative construction of the gay subject and his/her liberation. Yet I had concluded that the "gay subject" was not, in fact, a transhistorical or historically emergent entity but a social construction that had proved productive in shaping desire and behavior and in fashioning social bonds and facilitating political mobilization. Whatever the practical gains of asserting a universal gay subject, this strategy had the effect of silencing or marginalizing many who described themselves as lesbian or gay. The gay community thereby reproduced the forms of oppression many of these marginalized groups – people of color, working-class people, those with disabilities – experience in the broader social mainstream.

Insofar as new affirmative gay constructions projected being gay as a core, essential identity, it blinded individuals to differences due (say) to race, class, gender, age, or ethnicity. These non-sexual aspects of the self were often considered secondary characteristics producing minor variations around the primary identity of being gay. I believed, as did other activists and intellectuals, that this view promoted an insular community and narrowly focuses interest-group politics. This "ethnic model" of homosexuality may have been fruitful, even necessary in the 1970s for the purpose of community building and political mobilization. By the 1980s, however, as internal social differences exploded into gay public life, and as the community came under attack by anti-gay crusaders, the gay social and political agenda seemed to require a shift away from an ethnic model with its narrow interest-group politics. The gay and lesbian community needed to break down the isolation between themselves and racial, ethnic, feminist, and disabled communities. This was not simply a matter of forging a rainbow coalition by encouraging gays to understand that they shared common interests with, say, African-Americans or Latinos. They needed to grasp that they were not simply gay while others were women, Latino or African-American. Gay men and lesbians needed to see that they were simultaneously identified by their racial, ethnic, gender, and class status, and that, like African-Americans or women, gays were simultaneously implicated in heterogeneous sexual, gender, racial, ethnic, and class struggles. To make this social and political shift required a shift towards a concept of the self as exhibiting multiple, criss-crossing identities, social roles, and interests.

I do not think that it was merely coincidental that the early 1980s simultaneously saw the rise of coalition politics in the gay community and social constructionism and deconstruction. Framing gay identity as an emerging sociohistorical event and as an unstable, contestable institutional and discursive production, prompted gays to begin to define themselves as having multiple identities, recognizing multiple, sometimes contradictory positions of social power and oppression, and approaching their own battles for social empowerment as connected to struggles around gender, race, ethnicity, class, and so on.

As I came to reflect upon my experiences in a more theoretical way, I found myself contesting a whole series of assumptions that I knew to be central to the tradition of the Enlightenment. Assumptions about the duality of scientific knowledge and power, the link between science, truth and social progress, an essential unified subject, millenarian notions of human liberation, the course of history as a odyssey from repression to emancipation – all seemed to be a crumbling faith. Challenging modernism was not easy. These were assumptions held not only by the dominant institutional elites in the US but by many friends and leaders in the gay movement and a broader progressive culture that I was a part of.

If my point is not already clear, let me be direct: postmodern social ideas emerged, at least in part, out of the development of the new social movements. The intellectual and social historical meaning of postmodernism *in the US* needs to be grasped in relation to the evolution of these movements. Unfortunately, critics, even friendly ones like Antonio and Alexander, often fail to socially situate postmodernism. For example, although Antonio rightly observes that there are many versions of postmodernism, he repeatedly – and wrongly – identifies my own standpoint with Baudrillard's "radical postmodernism." In this radical version, according to Antonio, postmodernism is a cultural critique of modernity, a pessimistic social vision in many ways reminiscent of the Frankfurt School. Postmodernism is described as a symptom of a demoralized, anomic culture in which critical reason is in retreat as a vital public realm and an autonomous moral subject has been eviscerated by mass culture and consumerism. Much of Antonio's paper is a polemic against what he calls "radical postmodernism," which has little bearing on the views I advanced in "The End of Sociological Theory." Similarly, Alexander assumes that my postmodern critique of modernist social science is necessarily tied to what he takes to be *the* postmodern critique of contemporary Western societies. This critique is, in his view, another version of romantic antimodernism and antiliberalism. Yet nowhere do I connect my critique of sociological theory to a substantive view of contemporary America or "the modern West."

Antonio should have remained true to his own understanding of the varieties of postmodernism. There are many different versions of postmodernism and, in particular, many different ways of relating its critique of science to its analysis of social history. If Baudrillard edges towards one extreme of left cultural critique, Rorty's (1991) postmodernism represents a liberal social vision. My own view is sympathetic with Rorty's affirmation of contemporary Western societies while pushing his liberalism in a decidedly stronger pluralistic and democratic direction. "Democratic pluralism," roughly speaking, is the standpoint of the later work of Foucault (1980) and Lyotard (1984) as well as that of many postmodern feminists and queer theorists. For my part, I do not see postmodernism as entailing a complete break from contemporary Western modernity. I reject the view that dismisses postmodernism as a form of romantic antimodernism. American postmodernists generally stand opposed to those left critiques that reduce modernity to instrumental reason, technocracy, or capitalist domination. Indeed, as I have argued elsewhere (Seidman 1991), at least one current of postmodernism emerged, in part, as a left critique of the marxist tendency to reduce modern societies to economistic/class dynamics. These postmodernists have criticized the marginalization in marxism of nonclass dynamics and struggles. They have criticized marxism's disposition to dismiss liberal Western developments such as the rule of law, a tradition of civil rights, democratic process, the establishment of a relatively autonomous sphere of civil society, and so on as little more than functional facades masking the iron rule of capital or the bourgeoisie. If at least some postmodernists are decidedly more affirmative towards liberal Western democracies than many in the marxist or romantic traditions, many of us are decidedly more critical than liberals towards the intellectual and social heritage of Western modernity.

Postmodernism, at least the version of those who articulate it as standing in a positive relation to the new social movements (e.g., Huyssen 1986), view it less as a complete break from contemporary Western liberal modernity than some of its critics apparently imagine. In this regard, the criticism advanced by Antonio and Alexander – that postmodernists necessarily abandon discursivity, which, in turn, is understood as essential for a democratic society – seems once again to reflect less a reading of my position than stereotyped image of postmodernism held by critics.

My critics offer two main objections to abandoning a modernist theoretical standpoint in favor of a "postmodern" social narrative with a moral intent. First, they argue that as a postmodern approach jettisons essentializing, totalizing categories and explanations, as a postmodern critique of essentialism decomposes all unitary categories, postmodernism forfeits its constructive role as a mode of social analysis. It becomes, to quote Antonio, "a subversive strategy for decentering and deconstructing not for precisely representing conditions." (1991: 9). Alexander makes the claim that the postmodern critique of theory as ethnocentric and local destroys the possibility of social theory, which presupposes theory's ability to make claims to truth. "To make a claim to reason is to suggest, however, that sociological theory can achieve a perspective on society that is more extensive and general than the theorist's particular lifeworld and the particular perspective of his or her social group" (1991: 2).

Secondly, these critics contend that in forsaking a general theoretical standpoint, I surrender the possibility of offering anything like a cogent critical standpoint towards social realities. They contend that a postmodern critique of general standards as local and ethnocentric undermines any basis beyond particular interests for recommending social reform. Because all discourse is said to be an ethnocentric projection, I am said to ultimately render discourse impotent as a tool of social critique. Postmodernism perhaps unwittingly legitimates the role of force and power in social affairs by conflating knowledge and power. The postmodern surrender to interest is seen by Alexander as promoting an irrationalist illiberal politics. Antonio sees in the postmodern emasculation of discourse an equally ironic result: the further decline of a public realm of political and moral engagement by enthroning the reign of interest. Therefore, these critics conclude that my intention to make sociological theory a positive moral force in society is undermined by advocating a postmodern turn.

These are important points. I want to respond directly to them. Before I do, however, I wish to draw attention to certain unexamined assumptions in both Antonio's and Alexander's defense of modernism.

The Enlightenment project, which posits a link between science and emancipation through its rationality or truth producing power, is uncritically assumed by Antonio and Alexander. They never address criticisms of this project by feminists, anti-racist theory, lesbian and gay theorists, the early Frankfurt School, and by poststructuralists, who questioned the role of a foundationalist, scientistic concept of reason in promoting social progress. Indeed, against the presumed postmodern threat of illiberalism, Alexander invokes the Enlightenment "theoretical project to humanize the world" (1991: 6), as if the history of that project has not been subject to enormous suspicion and critique.

What I find curious and objectionable in these defenders of modernism is that in the face of what they perceive to be the enormity of a postmodern threat to science, reason, liberalism and a democratic society, they appeal to a socially purified, transcendent image of science. Their appeal to the impersonal, rational character of science reveals a reverence for science. Why is science or theoretical reason so immune to criticism? Why does their commitment to a critical, reflexive reason seem to lapse when they think about science? Antonio speaks of the power of theoretical reason to produce standards of criticisms and to falsify "ineffectual theories." What truths, what standards of critique, and what examples of falsifying ineffectual theories is he referring to in the context of sociology? Antonio invokes an image of science as "nurturing the cool detachment of the self" (1991: 14). Does he have in mind Marx or perhaps Weber or Daniel Bell or Habermas? Moreover, this imagery of a detached self suggests a decidedly Eurocentric, masculine self. Why is there no reflexivity here? Similarly, in his sacralizing of science, Alexander speaks of the human sciences as creating a "tradition of reason" (1991: 3). Curiously, or perhaps not so, he identifies this tradition of reason with societies that guarantee universal rights and the rule of law. Any guesses as to which civilization has created a tradition of reason?

I conclude this brief digression with this observation. It would not be difficult to show that in their very defense of the Enlightenment project, Alexander and Antonio perpetuate Eurocentric, androcentric values and interests that marginalize and oppress non-Europeans and many women. The sacredness with which they surround science, the conflation of the appeal to reason with science, seems to blind them to the values and social interests projected under the guise of reason.

Discursivity in modern and postmodern contexts

Does a postmodern perspective, as I have proposed, commit one to the view that all categories and arguments reflect only individual or group interests, a position which makes social inquiry and criticism impossible? Alexander maintains that social inquiry presupposes an ability to make claims to reason or truth for our discourse. By this he means the capacity to develop general perspectives or traditions of discourse which go beyond individual or group experiences and interests or which are decentered and constitute, in his own words, a "tradition of reason." This, of course, has been the dominant self-understanding of science and one which, not incidentally, confers on it cognitive and social authority. It is the claim to truth, he argues, which produces a tradition of rationality – that is, a tradition which allows us to have interpersonal discourse that includes specifying normative standards to adjudicate interpretive conflicts.

I would not of course deny that traditions of discourse have developed in the West and elsewhere, if by this we mean the formation of public conventions that guide social conversations. I depart from Alexander, though, first, in his claim that these are traditions of rationality. If by rationality he were to mean only a set of social and discursive conventions by which we can carry on conversations about the world, I would have no problem. Unfortunately, Alexander seems to imbue rationality with standard modernist assumptions of a privileged type of knowledge. Moreover, when he connects this tradition of rationality to specifically Western social conditions, it becomes clear that he is privileging not just a type of discourse but a civilization. It is precisely this type of conceit – which under the banner of universal or general reason authorizes a particular social experience, set of values, and interests – that is symptomatic of the failure or limits, as I see it, of the Enlightenment project.

In my view, these traditions of discourse which, as Alexander rightly says, promote interpersonal standpoints or public languages to talk about the social, are stamped by a series of heterogenous and particularistic or ethnocentric values and interests. These interpersonal standpoints, in other words, are not innocent of social, political, and moral meanings. Their claims to universality mask local social entanglements and social projects – projects, which I may wish to defend, but not by concealing their social particularity or by wrapping them in a language of universal reason. The history of social thought from at least Marx through Freud, Nietzsche, Weber, Mannheim, critical theory, feminism, anti-racist theory, and poststructuralism has made a compelling case for the social entanglement of social knowledge. Marx, we recall, made us suspicious of the class structuring of social discourse; feminists have alerted us to the gender projects informing discourse; African-Americans have revealed the national/ethnic structuring of discourse, and so on. Exhibiting the particularistic aspects of social discourse does not entail reducing discourse to individual or groups specific meanings and interests. Discourses may and typically do articulate beliefs, values, and social interests that go beyond a particular group. I would argue, however, that given the history of skepticism towards the claims of discourse to universality, and given a history of the social entanglement of disciplinary discourses, these discourses might advisedly be approached with an eye not only to their communicative role but to their relation to social interests and social hierarchies. I urge only that we do not create discourses as if they represent an ongoing human quest for the truth of "the social." Instead, I favor approaches to social knowledge which view them as social interventions into social conflicts and as embodying a interest to shape human affairs.

Insofar as we approach social discourses and knowledges as interventions into public life, I urge that we reconsider evaluating knowledges exclusively in terms of either a correspondence or coherence principle of truth. In chapter 2, I outlined some drawbacks to a culture which narrows judgment into empirical-analytical standards of representational correctness: the social role of science and knowledge is neglected; science and its producers are privileged, thereby creating a vast realm of submerged, discredited discourses, knowledges and communities. As we understand social discourse narrowly as a cognitive practice, its moral and political significance is concealed; we create a stratum of experts and authorities of the social, thereby weakening the public realm of social debate. Finally, the placing of social discourse under the sign of science produces compulsively metatheoretical, universalizing discourses that render it insular and socially irrelevant. I prefer to approach disciplinary discourses as public conversations about society. In this description I would not make truth into the sole standard by which such conversations should be judged. This does not mean replacing scientism with an equally one-dimensional "practical" or ethical-political standard. Questions of empirical and analytical adequacy remain central. They would, however, be recognized as social conventions valued for the ways they enhance communication or for their social utility. We would, moreover, need to acknowledge that in many disputes empirical-analytical considerations do not suffice to adjudicate between conflicting interpretations.

I am recommending that we refashion a scientistic, disciplinary culture around a notion of "social narrative," which would be connected to a pragmatic discursive culture. What kind of narratives do I imagine, and how does a "pragmatic turn" preserve an elaborated discursivity? In chapter 2, I criticized the major stories of social evolution advanced by the classical sociologists. These grand narratives projected highly Eurocentric, androcentric, chauvinistic national values. I objected to the essentializing and universalistic assumptions of much classical theory, which function, often quite unintentionally, to naturalize social events, to repress social differences, and to perpetuate social hierarchies. I raised doubts about the flattened concepts of liberation and domination that were used, which conceal and obfuscate heterogeneous struggles. I argued for densely contextual, ethically motivated "local" narratives.

If, however, social narratives or discourses should be judged in part by the purposes they serve and their social consequences, why exclude general, even transnational, evolutionary social narratives? Nancy Fraser and Linda Nicholson (1990) propose that there can and should be many types of stories depending on the particular purpose in mind. For example, highly general stories of gender construction or domination that are said to structure a society or societies and may operate across centuries may serve the purpose of legitimating gender as a category of social analysis or give credibility to the notion of women's oppression. Their point is well taken. Given pragmatic criteria, social narratives of different scope would be expected.

If, moreover, social knowledges are not to be evaluated exclusively by their empirical-analytical "adequacy" or truth value, how do we evaluate them? Are we left, as my critics think, with the mere proliferation of stories, with no normative standards beyond social and political self-interest? By questioning the Enlightenment project, with its quest for theoretical foundations and objective analytical or conceptual standards, and, in its scientistic version, with its norms of theory testing, empirical falsification, and so on, am I abandoning discursivity and surrendering to a narrow *Realpolitik*?

Does rendering empirical-analytical moves conventional and "local" undermine the possibility of a critical social reason? My suggestion, in short, is to propose a stronger pragmatic approach to social knowledge. Instead of relying exclusively on an appeal to reality to judge the value or worth of social discourses, I propose that we consider the intentions and consequences of our social stories, in addition to conventionalized empirical-analytical strategies. This would entail assessing our discourses in light of both their own aims and their social implications, logically speaking. For example, we might adopt a rational choice model with the intention of producing social explanations which enhance conceptual economy and quantitative predictive precision. These would become the chief internal standards by which to judge the adequacy of this conceptual strategy. It would be irrelevant to criticize this approach by claiming that it did not, say, consider society in its modality as symbolic meaning. This "intentionalist" approach appeals to internal standards. Does the discourse do what I intended? The advantage of this strategy is that it sets up its own standards of criticism. Moreover, it does not take conceptual conflict as an occasion to go metatheoretical in order to impose intellectual and social order.

If a pragmatic approach were to stop with this strategy, it would be seriously limited. Social knowledges need to be evaluated not only by their internal aims but by their intellectual and social effects. Insofar as we think of our discourses as social interventions that are productive of personal and social forms of life, we need to ask, "What are the social consequences (ideally or in principle) and therefore the moral significance of our stories?" What forms of life are projected or constructed in our stories? What values, identities, social norms, and with what social consequences are promoted?" Accordingly, it would be legitimate to ask, "What is the broader social and moral meaning of a rational choice model?" This model might indeed prove to be very useful in producing conceptually and quantitatively precise social analyses but what constructions of self, society, and nature are projected in it and what, if any, are its political implications? What if such social discourses promote a one-dimensionally instrumental view of individuals and social relations that devalues the expressive, relational communicative aspects of our personal and social lives? What if we find that a particular rational choice model is consistently used to rationalize elite decision-making arrangements? It would be legitimate, from a pragmatic standpoint, to criticize this conceptual strategy on ethical and political grounds. In a pragmatic discursive culture, elaborating on the moral and political meaning of our stories and discourses would become a way to *expand the discursive character of sociology* beyond, not in place of, a narrow empirical and analytical focus (see the epilogue).

Critics, of course, would want to know what kind of moral analysis or discourse is possible if we surrender an objectivist standpoint. What normative basis can we appeal to in order to defend particular values, social norms, or form of life? My reply, in brief, is that, in the absence of ethical first principles or a transcendent moral reason, what remains are pragmatic arguments whose persuasive force is necessarily contingent on a wide range of social considerations, such as the degree to which conventions of argumentation and social interests are shared, the extent of common values, the openness to difference and negotiation. Instead of appealing to a pure ethical rationality, for example, a Kantian or Utilitarian ethic, appeals that increasingly lack social force in societies in which a deconstructive suspicion has become part of a national culture, we would justify particular social norms and arrangements by appealing to values and ideals that are embodied in specific cultural conventions and practices. Ethical argumentation would occur in a language of gains and losses, advantages and disadvantages, comparative benefits, a language of purpose, utility, and consequence. It is no doubt true that this strategy will permit clear, settled, uncontested, unambiguous moral consensus only rarely, if at all. Moral rules, boundaries, and hierarchies will almost always be sites of social conflict. The form of this contestation, ideally, would be elaborated arguments about what kind of society we have and want.

Is this pragmatic strategy susceptible to being manipulated for narrow, self-interested ends? Yes, but the same is true of the objectivist or universalistic-rationalist strategy, in which self-interest rules in the name of reason or moral virtue. At least in the pragmatic strategy, the interpretive and therefore the interested character of our moral claims is evident. Such claims will be contested more readily if they are viewed as interpretive accomplishments than if one envelops them in an aura of transcendent reason. A pragmatic strategy would encourage a more open, democratized public realm.

As scientists and other so-called experts who claim the authority to speak in the name of reason lose their privileged voice in the conversation about society, other voices can claim the right to be heard. This does not mean that sociologists would lack a social rationale. Obviously, our legitimacy would not rest on our claims to provide objective knowledge or Truth; rather the value of sociology would revolve around our role in encouraging an open, reflexive, elaborated culture of public debate on the meaning and moral character of our social arrangements. The hope of a discourse that breaks away from a stultifying empirical/analytical compulsivity to reclaim a public vitality is, for me, the utopian moment, if you will, of the "postmodern" sensibility.

11

The politics of sexual difference in late twentieth-century America

It has become commonplace to observe that sex, as much as the economy or education, is a political battleground. Whether our focus is nineteenth-century conflicts in the US around masturbation, sodomy, women's sexuality, prostitution, and the free love movement, or recent conflicts over reproductive rights, gay marriage, pornography, child abuse, and sex education, these aspects of personal life are, as feminists have insisted, indeed political. Moreover, as queer theorists have similarly insisted, sexuality is not only a personal issue that is politicized but is itself a social force. Whatever sexuality might mean for the individual, it functions as a social code, normative framework, principle of social organization or simply put, a way of defining, regulating, and organizing bodies, selves, and populations which produce identities, solidarities, and relations of domination. Hence sexuality may be approached as an analytically autonomous sphere of individual and social determination – a site of desire, identity, social organization, and politics.

But how to interpret conflicts over sexuality? At a minimum I suggest distinguishing two levels of sexual politics. First, there are conflicts over rights, resources, and representations. For example, Americans are divided over sex education, civil rights for homosexuals, funding for family planning, and the legitimacy of public sexual representations. Such divisions point to a sexual stratification system in the US – for example, a system that socially privileges heterosexuality, marriage, two parent families, romanticized sexuality, monogamy, the privatization of sexuality, and so on. Such sexualities and intimacies receive social benefits, juridical-administrative recognition, symbolic esteem, social legitimacy, and a normalized, morally valued status. Much of sexual politics involves struggles to alter and maintain this sexual hierarchy through battles around rights, resources, and representations.

These conflicts have been analyzed in the language of social movement literature – in terms (say) of resource mobilization, social interests, the formation of social and political organizations, grassroots and elite support, the role of the media, and so on. A key site of conflict however is at the level of sexual-intimate meanings and morality. For example, at the very center of the politics of sex education are contrasting views of the meaning of sexuality, clashes over whether sex education is or should be a private or public responsibility, and, most fundamentally, a conflict over sexual values, that is, over what sex means, what norms are appropriate to guide sexual behavior, and how to fix the place of sex in personal and public life.

I aim to analyze sexual conflicts at the level of the politics of meanings and morality. Such cultural conflicts being into relief divisions that bear on basic, core aspects of American culture – for example, disagreements about how to establish moral boundaries with regard to sexual behavior and representations in public life, divisions with regard to interpreting and assessing sexual meanings and norms, and conflicts over what counts as a family. Although divisions over sexual-intimate meanings will likely remain contested and unsettled for some time (for example, it is hard to imagine a resolution to disagreements over whether sex is fundamentally about pleasure, procreation, or love), norms, rules, and conventions still must be established to govern intimate and public life. How are such normative conflicts to be settled? How, in fact, do Americans justify their sexual and intimate practices? What "moral logics" operate in this realm? These cultural and normative disputes will be the main focus of this chapter, as they underlie not only struggles over rights and resources, but point to broader societal divisions and potentially far-reaching sociocultural shifts.

I argue that Americans are divided with regard to the moral logics they deploy to authorize sexual norms, to delineate the moral boundaries of legitimate and illegitimate intimate arrangements, and therefore to establish hierarchies of sexual and intimate practices. On the one hand, Americans appeal to a substantive sexual ethic or what I call a "morality of the sex act" which assumes that sexuality has an inherent meaning, social purpose, and moral status. Some sexual and intimate practices are said to be intrinsically right, good, normal, healthy, while others are unnatural, abnormal, wrong, immoral. On the other hand, more recently, especially with the rise of the counterculture and its evolution into a new age and human potential culture, and with the formation of feminist, lesbian and gay, bisexual and S/M movements, there has appeared a moral logic that does not assume that particular sex acts and intimacies have intrinsic social and moral meaning. Such a "communicative sexual ethic" holds that social agents make sex meaningful and ethical judgment is to be determined by the moral qualities of the social exchange or communication. The two moral logics do not collapse into a simple political or ideological binary. For example, a morality of the sex act is often used to not only condemn but to justify homosexuality (by the claim that it is natural and therefore, given the folk culture of America, morally good). Although a morality of the sex act can legitimate sexual-intimate differences, its logic of natural/ unnatural and normal/abnormal inevitably produces classes of "deviant" or outsider sexualities. On the other hand, a communicative sexual ethic breaks from the logic of natural/unnatural and normal/abnormal. It still functions of course as a regulatory force, but this takes the form of providing general normative guidelines, not moral imperatives. Such an ethic permits a wide range of sexual choice, tolerance and affirmation of intimate differences, while also being less productive of deviant identities.

I will suggest, moreover, that to the extent that a communicative sexual ethic is becoming part of the folk culture of the US, it renders the clash over sexualities and intimacies much more divisive and socially charged. This is so because a communicative ethic legitimates a range of choices and practices that challenge currently dominant modes of organizing sexual and intimate life, for example, normative heterosexuality, marriage-based families, families based on blood ties, romanticized sexuality, intimacies organized around shared residence, and so on. Indeed, to the extent that substantive sexual and intimate values and practices such as normative heterosexuality, marriage, and nuclear families, have been defining of American national identity, these cultural clashes take on the weight of struggles over the very meaning of America.

Consider, for example, the politics of homosexual rights. Whether posed in terms of the debate over homosexuals in the military, gay marriage, or antisodomy legislation, the conflict over homosexual rights is at the center of US public life. But how to interpret this political conflict? At one level, it is surely about the politics of individual choice and social inclusion. Hence, advocates and opponents of homosexual rights argue over which sexual choices and practices are legitimate and which sexual identities should be accorded full citizenship rights. At another level, the debate can be interpreted as addressing the character of America's societal community. Thus, some advocates argue that granting homosexual rights will strengthen national unity while denying such rights weakens it by fomenting social discontent. By contrast, some critics maintain that granting homosexual rights legitimates a "lifestyle" that undermines a heterosexual based marital-familial institution which is said to be the basis of American national community.

I want to underscore two key points. First, Americans defend or oppose against homosexual rights by arguing over the meaning and morality of sexuality. Thus, advocates will speak of the naturalness and normality of homosexuality, interpret sexuality as having multiple purposes beyond procreation, appeal to the consensual character of same-sex intimacies, and emphasize the role of homosexuality today as a social identity providing personal coherence and social solidarity. By contrast, opponents of homosexual rights often justify their position by appealing to the perverse or unnatural, and pathological nature of homosexuality, its uncoupling from procreation and a concept of family based on marriage and blood ties, and its immoral, promiscuous lifestyle. In short, the struggle over homosexual rights is engaged on the terrain of sexual meanings and values. And, in the end, to the extent that the clash of sexual meanings and values cannot be resolved discursively (there has been no resolution to the dispute over whether homosexuality is natural or unnatural, normal or abnormal), this ongoing discursive division evolves into a conflict over moral logics or principles which are appealed to in order to legitimate social norms. The second point I wish to emphasize is that the homosexual rights debate is about more than which "groups" or populations deserve rights or state protection from discrimination and harassment; its about which social practices are legitimate, what kinds of intimacies and families are valued, the place of new sexual communities in public life, what range of behaviors are to be covered under privacy laws, and what kind of community and nation America imagines itself to be.

I intend to map out key conflicts around sexuality in late twentieth century US. I proceed by initially providing an historical perspective that describes some of the major changes and patterns of sexual diversity in the US. Based on this perspective, I argue that although conflicts over rights, resources, and political and cultural representations are important, these clashes evidence struggles over "foundational" or core sexual beliefs and norms, over the logics that establish the moral boundaries of sexuality, and the status and social role of sexual identities and communities, that are even more significant as indicators of social division and cultural conflict in contemporary America (sections II and III). Moreover, in the emergence a communicative sexual ethic which assumes that practices have no intrinsic sexual meaning or moral status but that these emerge in social exchanges, I see the beginnings of both a new perspective viewing sexuality as a principle of social organization and a new politic contesting this organizing principle. I take this development to be the most radical impulse of current sexual politics – an impulse issuing from the social periphery but finding powerful articulation in critical knowledges and in social movements (see section IV). For example, the rise of a queer and transgendered movement politicizing the sexualization of bodies, contesting essentialized constructions of identity and the organization of selves around the binaries of male/female sex, masculine/feminine gender, and heterosexual/homosexual sexuality, and challenging the normative regulation of self in terms of the binary of normal/abnormal, anticipates ·a major reorganization of American intimate culture.

In the concluding section of this chapter, I consider some of the ethical-political implications of these cultural conflicts. In particular, in the shift to a communicative sexual ethic, I highlight possibilities for the depolitization of many intimate choices. Such an ethic suggests approaching many sexual choices in the language of aesthetic preference or in a language involving ethical judgments that would be less normalizing and therefore less productive of deviant, outsider sexual-intimate practices. In part, the depolitizing of intimate choices, of sexual and gender practices, are in my view integral aspects of a democratizing sexual politic for late twentieth century America. Of course, there are still many spheres of intimate life such as sex education, family planning and funding, childcare support, anti-violence legislation, and so on where expanded state intervention should remain a vital component of a democratic sexual politic.

The 'new sexual pluralism' in historical perspective

The mid-nineteenth-century US will serve as an historical baseline. My comments draw on research focused very broadly on white middle America and angled towards the north-east and urban, nonimmigrant populations (Seidman 1991). I have no reason to think that my observations on sexual-intimate patterns in this century are not relevant to broader populations, but I would not want to preclude the possibility that certain nonwhite, non-middle-class populations exhibit somewhat different patterns and sites of sexual conflict.

Historians tend to agree that the core of the social organization of mid-nineteenth-century intimate life in the US was marriage (e.g., Degler 1980). As proscriptions in popular medical and advice literature against masturbation, fornication, adultery, youth sexuality, premarital sexuality, and sodomy make abundantly clear, marriage was the only legitimate institution for sex. Moreover, within marriage a procreative ideal was normative. To be sure, erotic pleasure was expected to accompany procreative behavior, but valuing sex for its sensual pleasures was considered demeaning to the ethical-spiritual essence of a love-based marriage. The dominant contrasts in mid-nineteenth-century America were between marriage and nonmarital sexualities, between procreative and erotic behavior, and between ethical-spiritual love and a sensual, animal-like desire. The range of proscriptions in this normative literature point to a world of lived sexual difference – from the sexualities of youth and single Americans to the underworld of pornography and prostitution that flourished in major cities. These differences though lacked social legitimation.[1]

Elsewhere (Seidman 1991, 1992), I have described two major changes that occurred in American culture in the course of the twentieth century: the "eroticization of sex," which was linked to the "sexualization of love," and the rise of a "new sexual pluralism" connected to the making of a culture of sexual identities. I would today add a third development: the rise of movements challenging the very "system of sexuality" that took shape in the last two centuries.

As many historians have recently argued, our Victorian ancestors were not against sex or sensuality (Gay 1986; Lystra 1989; Rothman 1987). They disapproved of sexual pleasure as an end in itself and were convinced of the undesirable consequences of such pleasures. The power of sex was such that sensuality threatened to engulf marriage in a sea of lust and animal desire, thereby debasing its spiritual core. The seductive power of sensual pleasure required a social regime that channeled the "sexual instinct" into a reproductive imperative organized around a marital ideal of ethical-spiritual companionship.

The sexualization of love signaled the end of this aspect of Victorian culture. Relying on popular medical literature, novels, and autobiographies, I traced a shift in the meaning and normative role of sex (Seidman 1991; cf. D'Emilio and Freedman 1988). In particular, nonprocreative notions of sex became central to normative concepts of love and marriage. Moreover, as sex was approached as a legitimate way to sustain love and marriage, its erotic or expressive-sensual aspects became the focus of social interest and value. In a word, the giving and receiving of sexual pleasure became a legitimate way to express love. This facilitated the making of a culture organized around the cultivation of the erotic aspects of sex. Sexualized love gave birth to a culture of eroticism which by the 1960s, ironically, staked claims to legitimacy by virtue of its individualizing and communicative aspects independent of love and marriage. As an expressive, pleasurable, and communicative practice, sex became an autonomous value sphere.

One major consequence of these changes is that sex has become a site of multiple meanings and conflicting social norms. Although some Americans criticize this culture by appealing to an ethical-spiritual ideal of sex and love, few oppose eroticized sex. Social dissension revolves around the balance of the erotic and nonerotic aspects of sex and love, around the individualizing versus the communitarian aspects of eroticism, and around the social form of sexual expression, for example, marriage, cohabitation, and committed or casual relationships.

The American culture of eroticism contributed to the rise of sex as a basis of self identity. As sex was valued for its expressive, pleasurable, and communicative aspects apart from marriage and love, individuals were able to focus on particular sexual pleasures. This made possible the fashioning of new sex-based identities around specific sexual practices such as S/M or homosexuality. In fact, historians have argued that in the early decades of the twentieth century a national culture was taking shape that made sexuality into a basis of social identity. This is the second major change I wish to briefly address, as it made possible a "new sexual pluralism."

As I mentioned above, the dominant contrasts in mid-to-late nineteenth-century middle America were between marital and nonmarital sex, procreative and nonprocreative sexualities, and between ethical-spiritual love and sensuality. Although these oppositions have retained a cultural resonance for subsequent generations of Americans, the legitimation of sex outside marriage (even if this is still contested), of nonprocreative sex (even if the issue of which nonprocreative sexualities are acceptable remains contested), and of eroticism (even if its role in intimacy and society is contested) has made these tensions peripheral. The major sexual dramas in postwar America are staged in the binary oppositions of normal/abnormal and heterosexual/homosexual. This shift in the site of tension indicates a reorganization of American sexual culture, with questions of identity and normality moving into the center of social conflict.

Historians have made a compelling case that in the United States in the nineteenth century, sexuality was not a category of social identity. For example, the concepts of heterosexuality and homosexuality were absent (Duberman 1986; Faderman 1991; Katz 1983; Rotundo 1989; Seidman 1991; Smith-Rosenberg 1985). The closest approximation to a category of sexual identity was sodomy, which functioned to classify a multiplicity of sexual acts, including bestiality, masturbation, fornication, and anal or oral sex. Sodomy gained its coherence on account of being defined against procreative sex within marriage. The sodomite was not someone with an autonomous sexual identity but a person convicted of violating a social norm or law. Moreover, all Americans were considered potential sodomites. Sodomitical behavior was interpreted as a weakening of self or social control, perhaps a flaw in character or a momentary surrendering to temptation. It did not reveal a distinctive sexual identity.[2]

Jonathan Katz (1995) has proposed that it was not until the twentieth century that "heterosexuality" was invented. Previously, Americans organized intimacies around opposite-sex affections, but heterosexuality, as it evolved initially in medical-psychiatric discourses and later in popular culture, referred to a unique complex of ideas: the assumption of two distinct sexes, sex uncoupled from reproduction, the normality of opposite-sex desire, and opposite-sex desire forming the basis of an exclusive sexual identity. What seems indisputable is that homosexuality, as a category of personal identity, did not become part of American society until the early decades of this century (Chauncey 1994; D'Emilio 1983; Faderman 1991; Katz 1983). This points to a far-reaching change in American intimate culture: particular sexual desires are now organized as the basis of primary social identities.

In the course of this century, an event whose history we cannot trace here, sexuality moved from an act to an identity determining, in many instances, the fate of the individual. It was as if the exotic catalogue of sexual personages that occupied the pages of Krafft-Ebing, Havelock Ellis, and Sigmund Freud stepped onto the stage of history. This century witnessed the public appearance of a virtual parade of new sexual identities: the heterosexual, homosexual, pedophile, fetishist, sadist, masochist, and so on. Henceforth, sexual conflict revolved around the meaning and social regulation of sexual identities.

Recent scholars have told a complex story of sexuality in America involving a cast of characters, from the vice squad, scientists, psychiatrists, lawyers, news reporters to the new sexual subjects themselves (D'Emilio and Freedman 1988). A leading motif of this story is that the new sexual subjects who stepped into public view in the first half of this century eventually mobilized to achieve a normalized moral and social status. The paradigmatic case is that of the homosexual. Vilified and made into a deviant, pathological figure by medical-scientific-juridical practices, positioned on the margins but periodically exposed to reinforce the norm of heterosexuality, the homosexual fought back deploying the tools of the oppressor-science and the appeal to normality. One consequence of this politicization is that today the homosexual is no longer just a personage but a social identity (D'Emilio 1983). As the story of the homosexual goes, so goes the tale of the bisexual, the hysterical female, the sadomasochist, and so on. Many of the very sexual identities that were scandalized by medical-scientific discourses are now claiming legitimacy, in part, deploying a revised version of the discourse of their oppressors. Sexual conflict is today centered around identities and the clash of communities.

Let me try to clarify the implications of these social developments for the question of sexual diversity. Sexual conflicts in contemporary America may be approached along at least three interrelated dimensions. First, the shift from a Victorian culture organized around a procreative marital norm to a culture based on the legitimacy of nonprocreative and nonmarital sexualities has produced societal conflicts around sexual meanings and values. How are the boundaries of legitimate sexual expression fixed in a society where sex has acquired multiple meanings and social roles? Secondly, sexual conflict occurs around the issue of identity. How to determine which sexual identities are legitimate? To the extent, moreover, that sex-based identities have been elaborated into cultural communities, should they be recognized in their differences in public and institutional policy? Thirdly, conflicts focus on the system or regime of sexuality itself – with its sexualization of bodies, typologies of sexual identities and norms of normality and health. What are the impulse and implications of movements that imagine an order of bodies, desires, and intimacies beyond sexuality?

The conflict over sexual ethics

Sexual conflicts are not new to contemporary America. As the proliferation of purity campaigns, struggles around prostitution, age-of-consent laws, abortion, and pornography indicate, sex was a site of considerable social tension in the nineteenth century. Nevertheless, at least among the white, nonimmigrant middle classes, as evidenced in the normative literature but also in diaries, memoirs, and in the few available surveys of sexual beliefs and practices, there was a general consensus that sex had its proper place in marriage and that its principal role was reproductive. Sexual pleasure may have been an acceptable consequence of procreation, but it was not valued in itself. Indeed, even by the turn of the century, as love was sexualized and sensuality legitimated, sex was still valued only in marriage. It was only gradually in the course of this century that love was legitimated apart from marriage and sex acquired value apart from marriage and love.

It was in the 1960s and 1970s that this century-long change fully emerged into public view and became the focus of major social conflicts. The language of sexual revolution in this period captured less a reality of an abrupt shift than a gradual reorganization of intimate culture in America. Moreover, while public conflict was often riveted on issues of rights (e.g., reproductive or gay rights), underlying these important political struggles were conflicts over the very meaning and social role of sex. In other words, once sex was no longer exclusively tied to a procreative marital or romantic norm, social division surfaced around determining its moral and social coordinates. Battlelines were drawn, for example, between those who defended a tight alignment of sex, love, and marriage and defenders of a slippage between not only sex and marriage, but between sex and love.

Moreover, if sex carried multiple legitimate meanings, how could its social parameters be defined? What range of interactions, with what social and moral characteristics, legitimated sexual expression? And what is to be the appropriate public interest in sex as it is no longer tightly linked to marriage and love – a question that has become more urgent with AIDS, the rise of single-parent households, and the sexualization of youth culture.

Although these diverse sexual conflicts have been analyzed as struggles over individual rights and "group" social interests (e.g., in the case of the women's movement the struggle for reproductive rights), this political struggle also goes on at the level of "sexual ethics." Thus the struggle over reproductive rights is in part a struggle by women to be sexually autonomous, which includes the right to uncouple sex from procreation, marriage, and indeed, for some women, from love. Whether the site of conflict is reproductive rights, gay rights, or youth sexuality, one aspect concerns the meaning and normative regulation of sex.

How can we characterize this normative conflict over sexuality? At one level, Americans are divided over the very meaning of sex. Is reproduction, love, pleasure, self expression, health, or communication the essential meaning of sex? Available evidence suggests that although some Americans continue to assign a primarily reproductive meaning to sex, many more view sex as an expression of love (see Seidman 1991). And while there is much evidence that Americans overwhelmingly value sex as a way to express love (which itself is the site of conflicting meanings), there is division over whether sex is also to be valued as a practice of pleasure, self expression, or communication apart from love. To simplify this picture, I think the basic conflict in this regard is between Americans who believe that the essential meaning of sex is as an expression of romantic love and others who hold that sex carries multiple meanings. This conflict becomes especially consequential when we consider its normative implications. If sex is defined primarily as an act of love, only relationships that exhibit the culturally specific social characteristics of being "loving" will be normative, even though what is an appropriate relationship for "love" is itself in dispute. By contrast, if sex has multiple meanings, social norms will be defended that allow for sex in varied social arrangements, including those that are nonmarital and nonromantic.

This is not the place to try to map out the range of normative sexual conflicts. Instead, I wish to comment on one aspect of this conflict which is at the core of American sexual politics.

My thesis is that there is a division around the moral or justificatory logics that ground sexual ethics. This refers less to a value conflict, for example, the conflict between sexual autonomy and social welfare, than the logic of authorizing social norms. Specifically, Americans are divided between what I will call a "morality of the sex act" logic and a "communicative sexual ethic." In the former, sex acquires a determinate moral and social meaning as part of a cosmology, which may be understood in the language of religion, natural law or secular reason. From this perspective, sexual practices have an *inherent moral significance* which determines their appropriate social status. An example of this moral logic would be a perspective which justifies sex only as a procreative or loving act in a heterosexual marriage, while proscribing nonprocreative, nonloving, nonheterosexual, and nonmarital sex, by appealing to a Christian cosmology. Or, a psychiatric perspective that appeals to a scientific model of normal psychosexual development to justify norms of heterosexuality and a love-centered marital or quasi-marital arrangement on the grounds of what are taken to be universal standards of normality and health illustrates the logic of a morality of the sex act. By contrast, a communicative sexual ethic assumes that sex acts have no inherent meaning but *gain their moral coherence from their interactive context*. It is the qualities of the social interaction that are appealed to as ethical standards. This justificatory strategy judges sex practices by considering (say) the consensual, responsible, caring, reciprocal, and mutually respectful aspects of the social interaction.

To illustrate the difference in these two moral logics, consider the issue of lesbian and gay rights. From the vantage point of the logic of a morality of the sex act articulated in a Christian framework, homosexuality might be considered inherently sinful or immoral. Hence, extending rights to homosexuals to protect them against job or housing discrimination would be opposed on the grounds that society has an inherent interest in protecting itself against an immoral practice. On the other hand, an alternative Christian perspective might hold that homosexuality is just another divinely created form of human expression. These Christians might oppose discriminatory practices by insisting that the only issue of moral significance should be "responsible behavior," that is, can an individual do his/her job and pay the rent. From this communicative ethical standpoint, an individual's "sexual orientation" would be irrelevant for establishing social norms.

As this example suggests, we have two different moral logics at work in authorizing sexual norms. Each standpoint has its own language, logic of justification, and metatheory that gives it coherence and ethical force. Each logic moreover has its own stress points. The appeal to an "order of things" or a transcendent foundation to ground sexual ethics is subject to the suspicion that today surrounds "foundational" claims in general – namely, that they conceal particular interests and values or express a metaphysic or

world view of a particular tradition or community. Moreover, while such a
moral logic might have propped up a liberal intimate culture at one time,
today it seems at odds with the multicultural character of the US. The communicative sexual ethic exposes weaknesses relating to its formalism and
minimalism. Not only can the general values it appeals to such as choice
or consent be contested (e.g., in the feminist debates over consent), but such
values (e.g., responsibility and respect) are so general that they often
cannot provide guidance on specific disputes. For example, invoking the
general value of individual choice, providing it does not involve coercion,
to justify tolerance towards homosexuality may be effective for establishing certain "negative freedoms" (e.g., protection against job discrimination) but it does not necessarily provide guidance in determining "positive
freedoms," such as whether homosexual marriages should be legalized or
whether homosexuality should be taught as a valued lifestyle choice. These
are matters of substantive social values and ideals which a minimalist language of choice, consent, responsibility, etc. does not provide much, if any,
guidance.

To the extent that conflicts over sexual ethics are metatheoretical or arise
from contrasting world views, a resolution appears unlikely. It seems fanci-
ful moreover to anticipate an overarching or integrative moral logic emerging from this division. The differences of moral logics will continue to be
part of sexual politics. My sense is that conflict at this normative level has
ambivalent social and political significance. On the one hand, these conflicts are typically local in two ways. First, the focus of conflict rarely leads
to broader social divisions or alignments, and therefore to global civic
polarization. For example, the field of conflict over pornography is not
necessarily reproduced in divisions over say abortion or homosexuality
(witness the feminist critique of pornography). Thus, many sexual conflicts
are issue-specific and limited as sources of social division. Secondly, even
within these issue-specific conflicts, the differences are usually quite specific and occur within a network of shared beliefs, values, norms, and argumentative styles and rhetorics. For example, divisions over abortion
usually boil down to disagreement over when life begins, not on a woman's
right to have sex, not on the value of her life and the life of children, and
not on broader social and sexual values such as the individual's right to
choose to be sexual, the linking of sex to affection or love, the importance
of family, and considerations of public or social welfare. On the other
hand, these conflicts, especially along their outer edges, evidence a division
over the legitimate boundaries of sexual expression and the standards
guiding rule-making decisions. This conflict is potentially socially polar-
izing, as it may involve a clash of ultimate values, norms, and institutional

forms of sexual-intimate life, and contrasting visions of national identity. It is though especially when such normative conflicts get connected to clashes between social groups that they acquire enhanced societal importance.

The conflict between sexual communities

It would be misleading to assume that the division in moral logics reflects an ideological division between conservatives and liberals. Indeed, the meaning of conservative and liberal in the sphere of sexual politics is unclear, especially in light of the feminist sexuality debates (Ferguson 1989; Jeffreys 1990; Seidman 1992). Moreover, as we have seen, a morality of the sex act can be deployed to oppose or support gay rights. Thus, advocates often justify gay rights by appealing to a psychiatric model which defines homosexuality as normal. Similarly, critics might deploy a communicative sexual ethic by arguing that it is precisely the qualities of "the homosexual lifestyle," its "promiscuity," "pleasure-seeking," and "transient relationships," that warrant social repression. While there is no one-to-one logical correspondence between moral logic and political ideology, it is nevertheless the case that historically the communicative sexual ethic has been closely aligned with movements defending sexual pluralism, while the morality of the sex act logic has often been used to resist such movements. It is this linkage of moral logics to social movements that has made this normative division into an important source of social tension.

I have already commented on the limits placed on the expression of legitimate sexual differences in nineteenth-century America. However, in the course of the present century the links between sex, love, and marriage loosened and a wider range of sexual practices acquired legitimacy. Moreover, sexual desires or behaviors became the basis for establishing social identities. Some of these new sexual figures responded to their deviant status by creating quasi-ethnic communities akin to the European immigrant communities established in the first half of the twentieth century. The paradigmatic case is the homosexual community, but parallels are to be found in feminist communities, and more recently in communities which have evolved around S/M, bisexuality, and sex workers. In the remainder of this section, I consider some of the implications of these new sexual communities for the issue of social diversity.

My comments will focus initially on the lesbian and gay community as this is the most organized sex-based community. I assume a vast historiography and sociology of the making of these communities (e.g., Adam 1987; Chauncy 1994; D'Emilio 1983; Faderman 1991). I will overlook the many differences within these communities, focusing on some very general normative and political divisions.

Let me state the obvious. The mainstream of the lesbian/gay movement is in the social mainstream of America. Whether struggling against discriminatory laws, antigay violence, or media and popular stereotypes, the chief agenda of this movement has been social integration, which includes gaining equal civil rights, equality of opportunity, freedom from harassment from the state and citizens, and so on. Moreover, the social values of the chief organizations (e.g., National Lesbian and Gay Task Force, Human Rights Campaign) mirror mainstream America. For example, the struggle for domestic partnership legislation or lesbian/gay marriage, as Andrew Sullivan and Bruce Bawer rightly insist, endorse a quasi-marital, familial social norm. I would argue that it is precisely the integration of many lesbian/gay Americans in every way but their homosexuality that is the chief pathos driving this movement. To justify an agenda of social inclusion this movement has typically deployed the morality of the sex act logic – for example, defending the normality of homosexuality by appealing to "modernized" medical-scientific knowledges.

A "mainstream," however, makes sense only in relation to an "opposition." Thus, as much as the mainstream agenda aims at social inclusion by asserting the normality of homosexuality, and by trying to normalize a national identity that includes homosexuals, movements of opposition to both the straight and lesbian/gay mainstream have favored a communicative sexual ethic. In particular, for individuals whose sexual-intimate values depart from mainstream culture, or for whom their homosexuality is only one way their sexual-intimate lives are rendered deviant, they have preferred a communicative sexual ethic. Moreover, efforts to legitimate their sexual differences have often meant contesting the social norms that regulate sexuality.

In short, as unique sexual values and patterns have evolved in the lesbian/gay community, reflecting, among other considerations, a history of marginalization and oppression and the same-sex basis of their communities, there has emerged an oppositional sexual politics contesting the moral boundaries and hierarchies of sexual and intimate life.[3] Two brief examples will have to suffice.

First, sadomasochism is hardly unique to lesbian/gay culture. What is distinctive is the development of a public S/M community, with its own organizations, publications, knowledges, styles of self presentation, and so on (Califia 1982; Kantrowitz 1984; Mains 1984; Rubin 1982). For individuals who are part of an S/M community their practices and identities are typically defined as deviant – pathological or perverse – by the heterosexual and often by the homosexual mainstream. Although some advocates appeal to the naturalness and normality of S/M for legitimation, such normative strategies have limited plausibility given the tight moral association of sex with affection and love exhibited in gentle and tender behaviors. Accordingly, its not surprising that S/M practitioners prefer a communicative sexual ethic that appeals to, for example, the consensual, mutually responsible, respectful and pleasurable qualities of this social practice (e.g., Samois 1982; see Seidman 1992).

Secondly, consider the practice of multiple sex partners which again is hardly unique to the gay community. In a society in which sex acquires an independent value as a medium of pleasure, self expression, and communication, multiple sex partner practices are to be expected. Nevertheless, even during the height of sexual liberalization in the 1960s and 1970s, the evidence is clear: gay men exhibited patterns of multiple sex partners that suggest a unique social formation (Seidman 1991). In the era of AIDS, there has been some alteration in specific sex practices (e.g., less anal intercourse and more non-penetrative practices) and perhaps a reduction in the number of sex partners, but the general pattern of multiple sex partners among gay men has not significantly changed (Martin 1986; Turner 1989). Given this population's high risk status for sexually transmitted disease, this further supports the notion of a somewhat unique gay male sexual-intimate culture. Parenthetically, in light of the institutionalization of this pattern, and discourses that give it moral coherence and value, it is hardly plausible to dismiss its moral credibility by interpreting it as a pathological symptom of oppression. For gay men who have adopted this pattern, even if for a limited period of their lives, claims to its moral legitimacy ultimately invoke its "communicative" aspects, for example, individual choice or its consensual and responsible behavioral qualities. The legitimation of this practice, like the legitimation of S/M, involves contesting the logic (morality of the sex act) and the specific rules that now govern the social organization of sex in America.

Of particular importance in these two examples is that normative conflict is not simply between individuals, experts, or social elites, but *between sexual communities*. Conflict is driven by the demand of historically emergent oppressed sexual communities to have their particular nonconventional or different social practices recognized by society. This entails contesting the dominant sexual order – indeed renegotiating the rules that govern establishing normative boundaries or rules and the system of sexual hierarchy itself. Thus, in the case of S/M communities, contesting moral boundaries and rules involves struggles at the level of sexual meanings (e.g., to legitimate consensual pleasure-centered sex while aestheticizing judgments of specific sex acts), struggles at the level of moral logics (e.g., against a morality of the sex act), and struggles at an institutional level (e.g., to change laws and cultural representations).

The conflict over the system of sexuality

It is but a small step, though of huge significance, to trace this struggle over moral logics, boundaries, and hierarchies *to conflicts around the system of sexuality itself*. In order to understand the full import of this social event, I need to clarify the broader analytical and historical perspective on sexuality that underpins this discussion.

For the past decade or so, a scholarly archive has accumulated which contests the conventional view, still dominant in public and academic discourses, that defines sexuality as a natural fact. Although sexuality may be said to vary historically with regard to the meaning and social form of its practices, the conventional view still leaves intact the assumption of a human sexual nature. Scholarship in this field supports the view that sexuality is to be understood as a sociohistorical event. This does not mean that the understanding of the nature of sexuality is a recent historical event. Nor does it mean a recognition that social forces shape human sexuality. Instead, the idea of sex as a natural order is understood as an historical event. Moreover, what creates this notion of sex is sexuality, which is viewed as a social organizing principle. If sex can be said to be universal, sexuality is a mode of social organization to be found only in some societies.

A more or less conventionalized version of this perspective proposes that sexuality emerged as a social organizing principle only in some European nations in the eighteenth and nineteenth centuries. Scholars argue that before "modernity" there were sex acts, intimacies, prohibitions and regulations, but not sexuality which is said to refer to an historically unique social organization of sex. There was sodomy and sodomites but not homosexuality and homosexuals (Bray 1995; Foucault 1978; Goldberg 1992; Katz 1983; Weeks 1977), opposite-sex intimacies but not heterosexuality (Brown 1988; Katz 1995; Laquer 1990), marriages and intimate unions, including same-sex unions, but not romantic love (Boswell 1994), and violators of moral boundaries who were punished but there were not deviant *sexual* identities such as the homosexual or the paedophile (Foucault 1978). Many historians claim that modernity gave birth to sexuality as an imagined unity of desires, acts, and sexual types and as an order with a developmental logic exhibiting normal and aberrant developments. Sexuality is then approached as a social organizing principle creating identities and social hierarchies, regulated by normalizing social norms enforced by the state and social institutions, and contested by movements of sexual affirmation and rights.

To elaborate the above perspective, I turn to Foucault (1978) who, more than anyone else, has linked an historicizing argument regarding the making of sexuality to a nonWhiggish sociology of sexuality. Foucault speaks of a shift in European societies in the seventeenth and eighteenth centuries in their social structure and mechanisms of power from the "deployment of alliance" to the "deployment of sexuality." The former refers to a type of society in which kinship is crucial in determining social roles, statuses, and the organization of wealth.

Accordingly, marriage and procreative behavior, as practices pivotal to the organization of kinship, are the focus of an elaborate system of laws and social norms. All intimacies outside of marriage, and all desires within marriage that exceed a procreative imperative, are subject to a host of prohibitions and punishments. In such a society, power operates through the authority of sovereigns (patriarchs, kings, nobles) to stabilize kinship systems, and thereby the political economy, by enforcing a procreative marital norm by means ultimately of their power to take life. The shift to the deployment of sexuality involves a change from a form of social organization centered on the rules governing marriage and kin relations to rules governing sex everywhere but especially outside marriage – for example, among children, between men and women, and on peripheral sexualities such as sexual fetishes. In the course of the nineteenth century sex became an object of knowledge and basis of social regulation. A system of sexuality emerged within which a range of particular excitations, pleasures, and acts were constructed as manifestations of "sexuality." Every conceivable form of sexual desire and practice was classified; clearly marked boundaries were fixed between normal and abnormal sexuality; new sexual figures were invented – the hysterical woman, the pervert, and the homosexual; new authorities were charged with knowing and regulating the sex of its citizens (e.g., doctors, lawyers, state administrators, criminal justice personnel, and psychiatrists). The deployment of sexuality involved a shift in the chief mechanisms of power from juridical to disciplinary power. Instead of power operating through the authority of sovereigns to take and give life, disciplinary power operates to manage life. It is centered on the body and the sex of the individual (anatomo-politics) and species (biopolitics). Power works not through denial or censorship, but through the production, administering, and optimization of the utility of bodies, and their subjection to normalizing social controls.

According to Foucault, the shift to the deployment of sexuality reflects the new importance of the body and sex in a society where the productivity of labor and the fertility and health of a huge, mobile population become key national concerns. One effect of the deployment of sexuality is the creation of the idea of sex as a unitary force, as the ground of the self and society, and as the basis of national well-being. For those of us whose lives are organized by the deployment of sexuality, we are compelled to know our sexuality, announce our sexual identity, and fulfill its nature. Whatever other effects are produced by this sexual self assertion, we are operating within the logic of the system of sexuality (Foucault 1978: 157).

Approaching sexuality as a sociohistorical event and an organizing social force offers a distinct analytical vantage point from which to critically understand issues of sexual diversity and conflict. For example, instead of assuming "sexuality" as a natural or sociological fact, this perspective offers an account of the very possibility of a politics and discourse of sexuality by explaining the sociohistorical transformation of bodies, desires, and intimacies or "sex" into "sexuality." If we understand sexuality as a social regime in the above sense, simple-minded ideas of sexual progress would give way to analyses of the kinds of differences such a regime allows. This perspective makes it possible to ask what kinds of emotional-sensual-intimate differences are suppressed and indeed superseded by "sexuality," with what consequences for the lives of individuals and communities.

Approaching sexuality as a principle of social organization points a double edged critical vantage point. On the one hand, this perspective suggests the limits of the politics of sexual rights, pluralism, and liberation. To the extent that movements of sexual affirmation, from those that assert an ideal of orgasmic sexuality to feminist struggles to affirm women's sexuality, assume the deployment of sexuality and articulate its grammar and logic, they contribute to its enforcement. For example, as important as the lesbian/gay rights movement is for expanding tolerance and social inclusion, this movement reinforces the system of sexuality – for example, by isolating an order of sex out of a field of feelings, desires, excitations, actions, and intimacies, by assuming that same-sex affections mark out a distinct sexual and social identity, by framing sexual identity in terms of the hetero/homosexual binary, and by assuming that sexual identity reveals the hidden truth of the self. The legitimation of lesbian/gay rights, moreover, does not end power over the homosexual but transfers it from scientific-medical-juridical institutions to the lesbian/gay community or to those who construct normative and normalizing models of lesbian/gay identity.

At the same time, this perspective makes it possible to recognize the critical potential of movements that challenge the deployment of sexuality and imagine an order "beyond sexuality." This was the critical standpoint that Foucault seemed, at one point, to advocate:

It is the agency of sex that we must break away from, if we aim . . . to counter the grips of power with the claims of bodies, pleasures, and knowledges, in their multiplicity and their possibility of resistance. The rallying point for the counterattack against the deployment of sexuality ought not to be sex-desire, but bodies and pleasures. (1978: 157)

Writing in the early 1970s, Foucault was directing his remarks, in part, to gay liberationism, a movement which he valued for its normalizing of homosexuality and criticized precisely because this normalization reinforced the deployment of sexuality. From the vantage point of the 1990s, it is possible to see in movements such as Queer Nation, ACT UP, in the transgendered and S/M movements, in the emergence of postmodern or hybrid models of identities, intimacies, and families, in the shifts from a morality of the sex act to a communicative sexual ethic, and in feminist deconstructions of the sexualization of the body, self, and intimacy, developments that are troubling to the deployment of sexuality, to use Foucault's terms. To the extent that such developments contest the reduction of sexuality to gender preference, challenge a bipolar hetero/homosexual grid as master categories of sexual and social identity, challenge the tight alignment of sex, gender and sexuality, and contest normalizing norms that classify desires into normal/abnormal, they point to an order beyond sexuality.

Two examples are the rise of queer politics and the appearance of a transgendered movement. Although Queer Nation came and went in a flash, a queer politics, perhaps more as an impulse than an organized movement, remains a vital presence in lesbian/gay communities. Queer politics pivots upon an opposition to sexuality as a system for producing, organizing, and disciplining selves that operates through the power of normalizing social norms and knowledges. While acknowledging the gains of sexual liberalization in postwar America, including the importance of homosexual rights, a queer perspective argues that such developments have reinforced a system of sexuality. Queers contest this sexualizing and disciplining of bodies and selves by challenging normalizing social norms such as the imperative to assert or liberate a sexual identity or to affirm or realize a norm of sexual fulfillment. The knowledges, experts, institutions, and communities that enforce this disciplinary order of sexuality have been made into a site of politics. In this regard, queers struggle for an order of bodies, desires, pleasures, and intimacies beyond sexuality, an order that would be fluid, protean, and productive of differences, and tolerant of expansive sexual-intimate choices between consenting adults.

The transgendered movement is sometimes taken as exemplary of queer politics. With strong roots in the lesbian/gay movement, yet critical of the latter's enforcement of normalizing gender norms that render trans-gendered individuals deviant, the queer impulse of this movement lay in criticizing dominant norms of gender and sex. In particular, transgendered people (e.g., transsexuals, transvestites, drag queens, and gender benders) challenge norms that enforce a rigid alignment of sex, gender, and sexual expression – that is, norms of normality and health that assume that sex (an assigned status of female or male depending primarily on genitalia) dictates correct gender identity (socially appropriate feminine and masculine traits) which, in turn, dictates a correct (i.e., normal, natural, healthy, or right) sexuality, i.e., heterosexuality. Thus, individuals who are said to be born male will and should (if healthy and normal) exhibit the correct masculine roles and behaviors, one of which is an exclusive hetero-sexual orientation. From a transgendered standpoint, this alignment of sex, gender, and sexuality is an historically created, socially enforced order closely inter-twined with a system of sexuality that produces dichotomously sexed bodies, genders, and sexualities. Hence, the aim of this movement is not to legitimate more sexual and gender identities, but to change the very system that produces only male/female sexed bodies, selves gendered as either men or women, and mutually exclusive heterosexual/homosexual identities (Bornstein 1994; Feinberg 1993).

Ethical-political implications

To recapitulate, I have argued that at one level social conflict involves chal-lenges to aspects of a system of sexual hierarchy. There are, for example, struggles over civil rights (e.g., to enact anti-discriminatory legislation to protect sexual minorities or reproductive rights), political and cultural representations (e.g., regarding media and popular images of sexual minor-ities), and resources (e.g., sex education programs, HIV preventation pro-grams, funding for family planning and birth control practices). Many of the most publicized social conflicts in the sphere of sexuality, from gay mar-riage, the porn wars, sex education programs, to efforts to legitimate diverse types of families are struggles of this sort. Although these conflicts are socially divisive, they are not a threat to a system of sexual hierarchy as they sustain the sexualization of selves and identities, normative heterosexual-ity, and the tight alignment of sex, gender, and sexuality.

As conflict ensues at the level of moral logics and sexual values, as it involves clashes between sexual communities and challenges to the very sexualization of bodies and identities, such conflicts suggest challenges to hegemonic social norms and institutions that organize and regulate sexual-intimate practices. By way of a conclusion, I wish to consider some of the potential political and ethical implications of these latter cultural conflicts and developments.

I have suggested that a key site of sexual conflict concerns the moral logics that justify social norms, rules, and therefore a system of sexual hierarchy. I proposed that in contemporary America there is an opposition between a morality of the sex act and a communicative sex ethic. The former appeals to some notion of a fixed or transcendent social and moral order that gives to sexual desires and practices an inherent meaning and social role. The latter asserts that sexual-intimate practices have no intrinsic social and moral meaning; their meaning is given by agents in a social context and the moral status of particular sexual practices hinges on the presence or absence of certain formal qualities of the social interaction, for example, consent, respect, and reciprocity. In the communicative sexual ethic, transcendent moral imperatives or norms are replaced by broad ethical guidelines that leave a lot of room for individual discretion, judgement, and ambiguity.

A communicative sexual ethic has potentially significant political-ethical implications. If sexual practices have no intrinsic meaning, if their moral sense involves understanding the contextualized meaning and social role of such practices and appealing to formal aspects of the communicative practice, such an ethical standpoint legitimates a plurality of sexual practices and patterns of intimacy, including different kinds of families. To say it differently, a communicative sexual ethic suggests that many sexual-intimate acts would lose their broader social and political significance. If, for example, S/M was not interpreted from a Christian standpoint as immoral or as abnormal from a psychiatric standpoint, if S/M was approached as an act judged solely by whether the agents found it meaningful (as pleasure, love, or for its spiritual or therapeutic effects) and whether the practice was consensual and responsible, its symbolic function as a marker of the moral state of the agents or society would diminish considerably. In effect, consensual S/M between adults would become a matter of aesthetic taste, not ethical judgement and therefore not the site of dense social regulations, for example, laws, cultural pollution, public harassment and violence, and medical stigmatization. Accordingly, in so far as a communicative sexual ethic becomes an integral part of American culture and institutional practices, such that everyday judgements are focused on particular acts and are guided by contextually informed, minimalist, and consequentialist reasoning, we would anticipate a sexual-intimate culture less organized around normalizing judgements and therefore less likely to create populations of deviant identities and outsider sexual communities. This would be a culture where large stretches of social practice related to bodies and intimacies would lack moral and political weight. Indeed, this cultural logic implies a social logic anticipating the end of "sexuality" – that is, the end of a regime that enforces a uniform sexualization of bodies and selves, a tight alignment of sex, gender, and sexuality, and a normal/abnormal moral binary. For underpinning or implicit in a communicative sexual ethic is a view of the historical and sociopolitically constructed character of sexuality. The critique of naturalization and normalization makes possible a political project of not only challenging particular aspects of a system of sexual stratification but the very regime of sexuality. If the lesbian and gay movement represents a paradigm case of the former, the queer and transgendered movements imagine an order of bodies, desires, selves, intimacies, and solidarities "beyond sexuality."

The issue I wish to conclude with addresses the credibility and coherence of such a sexual ethic and culture. Is there a compelling logical basis or argument to be made in defense of what has been presented as a sociocultural fact? Would such a culture have the resources to establish moral boundaries and rules and is such an ethical position logically defensible? If we abandon a transcendent standpoint or some notion of an order of things disclosed through the medium of secular reason or religion which provides grounds of judgement, standards of assessment, and substantive ideals and ends, what are we left with to provide guidelines, standards, and ends?

A chief feature of the morality of the sex act is that it makes assumptions about what sex is and, on that basis, proscribes sexual norms. For example, if we assume that the meaning and purpose of sex is to express and consolidate "love," only those sex acts and social interactions are legitimate which exhibit the qualities of love. Although such an ethical position provides strong normative and regulatory guidance, it also devalues and sometimes pollutes or stigmatizes a wide range of very different kinds of behaviors that deviate from such social norms. In other words, a morality of the sex act inevitably suppresses, devalues, pathologizes, and renders immoral a heterogeneous cluster of practices, many of which seem freely chosen, involve only adults, are meaningful to the agents, and lack any obvious "harm" to the individual or to others. This hostility to difference, especially in a sexual culture characterized by a plurality of sexual values, patterns, identities, and communities has made it less credible. Indeed, from the vantage point of a reflexible, pluralistic culture, the presumption of a nonsituated, objectivist moral position has diminishing plausibility. Any sexual ethic that relies for its normative clout on the assumption that sexuality has a determinate, fixed meaning and therewith an ideal social form and role is today suspected of ethnocentrism and imperial designs. It is as if only a moral logic which abstracts from the clash over sexual meanings and values has compelling logical force.

This is precisely the basis of the claim to moral authority of a communicative sexual ethic. It assumes that sex acquires diverse, often conflicting social meanings and purposes. Moreover, its proponents hold that the clash of sexual values is inevitable and irresolvable, as such conflicts are implicated in a conflict of world views. Accordingly, a communicative sexual ethic intends to find a normative standpoint beyond this clash of values that can provide guidance and yet preserve the integrity of many sexual differences. Ethical judgement would focus on the communicative context of the sexual exchange, not on the sex act itself. Consensus is said to be more likely achieved if minimal normative conditions are sufficient to legitimate social practices. Such a formalistic and minimalist ethical standpoint has the advantage of being nonjudgmental with regard to substantive sexual values or respectful of a wide range of sexual differences, yet providing guidance and establishing moral boundaries (see Seidman 1992; Weeks 1995).

A communicative sexual ethic intends to avoid basing its judgements on particular sexual values such as the claim that sex is or should be about love or procreation or pleasure. The sex act itself is assumed to have no intrinsic moral significance; nothing about the sex act per se carries moral weight. It is entirely the social exchange or some general features of the interaction that give to sex practices their moral import. But which features of the social interaction are to carry moral significance and how to justify those decisions? In order to avoid grounding a sexual ethic on substantive values, only formal, minimal aspects of communication can serve as normative standards, not the intentions, motives, or ends of the interaction. Such formal normative considerations must be able to provide general guidelines and yet permit many differences. Hence, the task is to identify some general, formal aspects of communicative practice that can function as normative standards, such as the consensual, responsible, and reciprocal dimensions of communication which might be said to carry normative weight in abstraction from the meaning and qualities of the practices themselves.

Although I think that some form of a "communicative ethic" best resonates with a society increasingly organized around differences, some of which "run deep" and will persist in the long term, there are some difficulties. The formalism of this ethical position, an inevitable consequence of shifting the site of normative judgement from the "content" to the "form" of social practices, renders it weak as a normative guide in many instances. Thus, while a communicative sexual ethic would be effective in proscribing rape, sexual coercion, sex between children or sex between adults and children, and legitimating a range of presently proscribed sexualities (e.g., same sex intimacies, S/M, bisexuality, bondage, fetishisms, non-monogamy), it provides only very weak, if any, guidance with respect to (say) conflicts over pornography, abortion rights, and has virtually nothing to say about broader value conflicts that relate to normative questions about the place of sex in a good society. For example, conflicts over whether pornography should be allowed in public places and, if so, which pornography, and questions about the morality of sex industry workers are largely outside the purview of a communicative sexual ethic. In a word, some of the most important conflicts over sexuality involve a clash over sexual and social values. Of course a communicative sexual ethic does not exclude public comment on such issues, but it does assume that they will ultimately be resolved at the level of interest and pragmatics.

Perhaps the above concerns simply mean that there will be areas of conflict where strong notions of reason-based consent will give way to forging a culture of pragmatic accommodation. There is though an additional difficulty: A communicative sexual ethic does not avoid substantive value commitments. Does not an appeal to consent, responsibility, or reciprocity presuppose a particular sociocultural standpoint ("modernity" or a secular, reflexive, culture) and a particular set of substantive values (individualism, autonomy, choice, mutuality)? A communicative sexual ethic assumes the credibility and normatively compelling character of these substantive values.

Although this argument does not in my view undermine a communicative sexual ethic, it does mean that such an ethic cannot pivot its claim to legitimacy on the basis of lacking any substantive value commitments. Its cultural currency revolves around articulating general standards that provide rough normative guidelines while respecting a wide range of sexual choices and differences. However, to the extent that these general standards (e.g., consent, responsibility, reciprocity) imply substantive values and particular sociohistorical conditions, such an ethic must provide a rationale for these values and conditions. Today, several options are available if not, in my view, equally compelling. Least credible, at least in Anglo-American and many European nations, is a transcendent appeal to human nature or reason or natural law to provide a decontextualized and presumably non-ethnocentric justification. Rorty (1979, 1991) and others (e.g., Williams 1985; Fleischacker 1995), have proposed strategies of ethical justification which are antifoundational and ethnocentric, though without imperial designs. In place of foundational or transcendent justifications of normative standards, they propose community-and-tradition based and pragmatic types of rationales. Unhappy with both transcendent and pragmatic justifications, a Habermasian inspired position has emerged which advances a discursive ethic underpinned by an evolutionary theory of history (e.g., Benhabib 1992; Honneth 1996). Whereas the latter offers a strong defense of general norms and a weak defense of difference, pragmatics has the reverse strengths and liabilities (see the exchange between Rorty, Benhabib, Hoy, and McCarthy 1996). Perhaps the details of these disagreements are less important than the sociocultural shift they indicate. Whether or not these debates mark some type of broad or global shift in the social terrain, one point seems compelling. The question of how to handle differences of sexuality, race, nationality or ableness without assuming they occupy a social and moral position of inferiority, transience, the past, or irrationality, is a central part of American culture and politics.

Difference and democracy: group recognition and the political cultures of the US, Holland, and France

The question of how societies accommodate social differences is not of course a new issue. Nations composed of multiple cultural communities are not a recent development. However, in the past century or two, at least in Anglo-American nations and the countries of southern Europe, the politics of difference has often been associated with illiberal ideologies such as racism or anti-semitism. Fascism, for example, fashioned demonic images of a threatening "Other" which was invoked to mobilize this movement. The marking of difference as a social danger remains a pivotal strategy in right-wing movements in the West, only today it is less likely to be "the jew" or the communist than "the black" or "the homosexual" or "the muslim" that energizes a hateful politics.

As the social influence of the New Right in the US and England or the National Front in France indicates, a conservative politic anchored in images of a dangerous "Other" continues to be a force in the political landscape of Western nations. However, in the past two decades or so, movements and discourses have surfaced which couple a politics of difference to democratization. This new politics of difference aims to redefine the social meaning of public life and democracy. Moreover, whereas in the past liberalism made its case against a conservative politics of difference, today a democratic politics of difference is pressing its agenda against a now dominant liberal ideology that is often hostile to a politics that affirms a strong concept of democracy and pluralism.

I come then to the questions which will be addressed in this chapter. Should differences of race, gender, religion, ethnicity, language or sexuality be considered in determining, say, educational policy or the distribution of state funds? Should our particular cultural identities as men or women, black or white, Asian-American, Muslim or Christian, straight or gay publicly matter? What are the social and ethical implications of making such differences an organizing principle of public life in a democratic society?

I begin by sketching three ways of thinking about difference and public life that have been at the center of debate in many Western societies.

First, a broadly liberal position holds that the individual is and should be the basis of political society. Every individual is said to be of equal moral worth. The government is obligated to treat all individuals equally as citizens. For example, individuals are to be accorded the same civil rights and social opportunities. From the standpoint of the liberal state, all individuals who qualify as citizens are equal members of a national political community.

This liberal position recognizes that individuals are not only members of a national political community but have particular cultural identities and multiple group affiliations. However, a liberal state is said to have no obligation to recognize these different cultural communities in its laws and public policies. Indeed, state recognition of particular cultural communities would threaten its legitimacy, as it would align the government with a particular group and its particular social values and goals. This would violate the principle of the ethical neutrality of the political community, i.e. the notion that all citizens as citizens stand in an identical and equal relation to the state. To the extent that discriminatory practices impede an individual from exercising his or her civil rights, the state can legitimately act to prevent such practices. However, anti-discriminatory legislation is legitimate only if it applies equally to all individuals. To enact anti-discriminatory policies that single out particular social groups for protection would be a breach in the liberal social contract. It would violate the principle of the equal moral worth and political rights of all citizens.

Indeed, a state that singles out individuals for the ways they are different risks creating a nation composed of hierarchically ranked groups. This points to a second, "conservative" position on the issue of difference and public life. This view endorses a notion of society that is organized around sharp social and moral boundaries between different groups. Individuals are defined by the state as members of a particular social group; to each group is attached different and unequal moral worth, social status, and therefore political rights. The national political community is organized as a hierarchy of groups. This position brings to mind, of course, the *ancien régime* with its hierarchy of estates – the very order against which liberalism defined itself. This concept of society and polity also recalls the racial caste system of the American South or the patriarchal states of the modern west that constructed women as a distinct human group positioned in a subordinate social and legal status. The conservative position values group differences but only as they are arranged in a rigid social and political hierarchy.

Historically, liberals have been vocal critics of conservatives who argue for a very limited view of democracy by insisting on the social imperative of structuring differences hieararchically as a necessary condition of a stable, coherent society. Liberals have though frequently, and wrongly, believed that *any* polity which incorporates difference into law and public policy would be illiberal and anti-democratic.

There is however a third theoretical position which affirms group difference but as part of the democratization of society. For purposes of this essay, I distinguish two such models of democracy. First, there are so-called "consociational democracies" (Barry 1975; Daalder 1971; Driesi 1990; Lijphart 1969). Such societies are divided into socially separate and relatively autonomous communities which are organized less by a majoritarian politics than by elite accommodation. Consociational democracies such as Belgium, Switzerland, and the Netherlands suggest a political system that both assigns to social differences a directly political status and are democratic in that they protect individual rights and establish a principle of consensual rule. There is a second model of a democratic polity that acknowledges "group" rights. This model cannot be identified with any particular society but is presented as a theoretical defense of a "radical democratic polity" (Laclau and Mouffe 1985; West 1990; Young 1990). I would contrast a "radical democratic" model with consociational democracies by the former's strong participatory concept of democracy, and its more consensual, open-ended view of social groups. Radical democrats maintain that the challenge facing Western nations in today's multicultural world is to both preserve individual rights and to construct a democratic polity that incorporates group or social differences into its model of public life.

In this chapter, I aim to make plausible a notion of public life and democracy that recognizes group-based differences, administratively and juridically. I proceed by initially criticizing a "liberal individualistic model," as it has been elaborated and defended in the United States. I next turn to the Netherlands where I argue that, contrary to many American liberals who cannot imagine group-based differences and democracy coinciding in a polity, the Dutch system of "pillarization" illustrates one such model. However, this system enforces unnecessarily restrictive forms of both democratization and pluralism. A process of "depillarization" has opened debate about the future of the Netherlands. While some Dutch intellectuals look to the US, despite its somewhat foreign tradition of radical individualism and the privatization of difference, others are more sympathetic to a West European model. The French "civic republican model," with its coupling of individualism and national solidarity and its highly professionalized and generous welfare state, appears as a desirable choice. Indeed, in the face of multicultural critiques of liberalism, some Americans are also looking to France as a model of a democratic polity. I briefly glance to France suggesting that its model of maximizing sociopolitical unity and civic individualism at the expense of recognizing social difference makes it neither consistent with Dutch or American traditions nor defensible as a model of democratic pluralism.

I intend to offer a sociological sketch of the way three nations have organized or imagined the right way of organizing differences in relation to private and public life. Moreover, I suggest that to the extent that some differences become the basis of communities and therefore function as a social source of autonomy, solidarity, and self respect, sociological and ethical considerations provide compelling reasons to reconsider group-based models of democracy.

The United States: the failed case for civic individualism

According to the sociologist and public policy analyst Nathan Glazer (1984), the Civil Rights Acts passed in 1964 and 1965 expressed a virtual article of faith: America "was to be a . . . nation of free individuals, not a nation of politically defined ethnic groups" (p.11). The American political community was ideally to be made up of individuals who, regardless of their particular cultural identity, would be eligible to be citizens enjoying equal rights. "In the phrase reiterated again and again in the Civil Right Act of 1964, no distinction was to be made in the right to vote, in the provision of public services, the right to public employment, the right to public education, on the grounds of race, color, religion, or national origin" (Glazer 1984: 12). An individuals particular cultural identity as say a woman, African-American, or disabled person was to be considered irrelevant to being an American citizen.[1]

American liberals such as Glazer concede that social differences have not always been privatized. Differences pertaining to race, religion, and gender have been public in that they have structured law and public policy. Blacks, women, the disabled, and Catholics were, until fairly recently, second-class citizens denied the rights enjoyed by whites, men, the able, and Protestants. A public life evolved in the United States that was very definitely group structured and hierarchical. American liberals grant this point but argue that such differences reflect a regrettable historical legacy and have posed a major challenge to American democracy. Moreover, here is a case, liberals argue, which underscores the *dangers* of allowing the state to treat individuals as different – it risks creating groups of second-class citizens. The state then should not encourage such social differences through public policy but rather aim to make them irrelevant to the organization of public life.

In support of the liberal position it is important to acknowledge two points. First, the liberal principles mentioned above have promoted social justice. For example, in civil rights legislative and court decisions, from Brown *v*. Board of Education in 1954 to the Civil Rights and Voting Acts of the 1960s, liberal ideas were used to strike down legislation that perpetuated racial segregation and inequality. Secondly, the history of the United States suggests that there *is* a considerable risk when governments and public institutions are authorized to take into account the ways individuals are different. Difference can easily be figured as deviance or the making of an outsider status.

And yet against this liberal position, I want to argue that differences pivoting around ethnicity, race, gender, religion or sexuality should, at times, be taken into account by the state and public institutions. To make my case I wish to propose initially that group differences develop and persist not only because of social oppression but also because of "relatively autonomous" culturally specific traditions and practices. Accordingly, one cannot interpret the formation of particular cultural communities as simply a response to oppression. This type of explanation suggests, as I think many liberals believe, that ending domination would result in the gradual disappearance of many cultural communities. For example, while Catholic subcultures in the US developed in response to a dominant, often intolerant, Protestant culture, they also formed in the way they did because of their unique religious and social beliefs and practices. Similarly, black cultures evolved in America very definitely in response to racism but they drew on distinctively African or other non-American cultural traditions as they took shape in the American context. Of course, it would be an impossible task to separate those features of a culture that arise from social oppression and those that do not. In any event, such a distinction is unnecessary since a central feature of many minorities and oppressed racial, gender, ethnic, and religious cultural communities in the US has been a struggle to *both preserve their particular cultural identities and communities while ending their political subordination*. Thus, blacks criticize racial stereotypes as reflecting white prejudice while refiguring being black as desirable, for example, by "inventing" an "African" ethnic heritage or by creating positive black-defined styles of personal and collective life. Moreover, while some blacks anticipate the day when race will disappear as a category of identity and social classification, many wish to preserve an African-American identity and culture, even if conditions of civic equality were realized.

In the US, particular cultural identities such as African-American, Korean-American, Catholic, lesbian, or evangelical Christian, have gone beyond affirming contested identities to elaborating distinctive communities with their own social and cultural institutions, literature, art, scholarship, and worldviews. These cultural communities serve as social spaces that protect its members from modes of oppression and function as social bases for political mobilization. They also provide institutional and cultural frameworks which give social and moral coherence and a sense of self worth to those who participate in them. Thus, evangelical Christians have evolved their own subcultural institutions – from schools to newspapers and tv programs – which aim to both perpetuate these islands of primary Christian identities and communities in a sea of secularity as well as provide the material and cultural resources which make possible an agenda of Christianizing America (Ammerman 1991; Rose 1993). Similarly, feminists have fashioned distinctive communities which, though clearly formed in response to male dominance and sexism, function not only to furnish a safe, woman-affirming space but also to encourage the elaboration of affirmative identities, and new forms of collective life and social solidarity. Postwar America is characterized by the participation in civil and political society of multiple public cultures: African-American, feminist, lesbian, gay, Evangelical Christian, Latino, Asian, and disabled.

It would be misleading to assume that there is no significant cultural overlap among these different public cultures. It would be equally wrong, however, to assume that these differences are superficial or minor variations of a common national culture. The extent and depth of cultural unity is a matter of empirical exploration. I want to suggest though that in some cases these social differences run "deep." Some differences penetrate beyond lifestyle choice or variations in aesthetic and consumer preference; they extend into basic cultural values, for example, views about the purpose of political and social institutions or judgements about standards of truth, beauty and goodness. Thus, African-Americans have created public cultures that have their own culturally specific practices, for example, "black English," a distinctive Afro-American literary tradition, and a unique approach to language which pivots around a vernacular style, the generative power of the word, and a polyrhythmic or call-and-response oral style (Baker, Jr, 1994; Brown 1994; Dawson 1994). Some African-Americans have proposed a distinctively Afrocentric epistemology which, in contrast to Eurocentric knowledges, is said to emphasize the situated character of knowledge, the role of concrete experience, dialogue, and narrativity in understanding the production and justification of knowledge (Asante 1987; Collins 1990). Of course not all African-Americans participate similarly, or at all, in a black public culture. Moreover, there is ongoing conflict over the core meanings and practices of this cultural community. Similarly, feminist public cultures have emerged which, in part, share the values and norms of the broader society but, in part, have evolved their own unique culture and community (Fraser 1992: 123). At least one strand of a public feminist culture has proposed a virtual reversal of what have been dominant national values and understandings but which they have criticized as reflecting a masculinist standpoint. Thus, these feminists have emphasized a unique female psychology or psychic structure, a distinctive feminine moral voice, singularly female sexual, intimate communicative values, and a specifically women's centered view of the structure of knowledge, one that abandons the so-called masculinist dualisms of subject/object, reason/emotion, fact/value, and theory/practice. These cultural identities and communities cannot be explained as merely responses to oppression nor as superficial or transient developments; they are an integral and formative aspect of American public life.

If these social differences are likely to remain a key part of US public life, and if at least some of these differences run "deep," then a basic assumption of American liberalism is placed into doubt: the presumption of the impartiality of the public realm (Appiah 1994; Pateman 1988; Young 1990). This assumes that certain key aspects of public life as they pertain to state policy and practice can be organized by neutral values, knowledges and social norms or rules. "Neutral" refers to values and norms that do not favor any specific group or segment of society but are held in common. However, if there are differences which extend into core moral and cultural values, and if these differences have been institutionally elaborated in multiple public cultures, the state and public institutions (e.g., schools, public radio and television, social service agencies) will not be able to treat all individuals as identical and equal in their relation to the state. The state will not be able to ignore these specific cultural identities. Instead, state enacted legislation and public policy will inevitably favor the cultural values and norms of certain individuals or groups – a principle that violates the liberal creed.

For example, public educational policy has favored those members of society whose values are secular and scientific. The decision to secularize the educational curriculum in the US has been justified principally on the grounds that this avoids the alignment of the state with any specific religious denomination. However, government neutrality with regard to religion can, from a different perspective, be interpreted as displacing religion from public education. In other words, the state is not neutral in educational policy because it is aligned with a culture of secularity (Marsden 1994; McConnell 1993). Privatizing religion may allow the state to treat all individuals equally with regard to their religious cultural identity but the state is privileging individuals whose self-identity, cultural values, and group life is organized around a secular worldview. From the standpoint of an American for whom Christianity is primary in his or her self-identity, a state-enforced secular educational curriculum would be oppressive since it devalues that person's core beliefs and excludes or marginalizes the culture that gives shape and purpose to his or her life. For example, state-enforced secularity compels Christian-identified parents to decide between either sending their children to a public school, and thereby risk the devaluation or survival of their religious culture, or choose a religious school, thereby assuming a financial and social burden which secular parents do not have to shoulder.

A state-supported secular educational system has also been justified on the assumption that only secular knowledges, especially scientifically based knowledges, can secure objective knowledge or truths. However, the thesis of the social construction of knowledge maintains that ideas gain their credibility less from a strictly logical proof of truth than from the secular power of those who produce and authorize knowledge or from the practical and political social role of knowledge (Foucault 1980; Lyotard 1984; Rorty 1982). If secular and scientific knowledges cannot be assumed to be any closer to the language of the natural and social universe than nonsecular, nonscientific knowledges, perhaps educational policy should be rethought. Specifically, such policies should take into account the multiple cultures and knowledges circulating in a society and the democratic imperative to have public institutions express the will of all the people.[2]

If the impartiality of the public sphere is impossible, if, for example, decisions about what knowledges should be taught, indeed what counts as knowledge and what or whose standards should guide such decisions, what language to teach in and whether to use exclusively verbal or sign language are and cannot be neutral, then such decisions about the structure of public life inevitably privilege some individuals and communities and subordinate others. State policies and legislative decisions cannot, it would seem, avoid responding to, or implicating, particular cultural identities. This position does not deny the possibility of consensus on public rules and norms but insists that the public realm cannot escape institutionalizing normative and normalizing practices, for example, making culturally specific norms of (say) dress, deportment, language use, and epistemological and rhetorical styles into general normative rules in public life (Minow 1990). Efforts by the state to deny social differences by claiming impartiality marks its own role in privileging majority or dominant groups.

The discussion over public life in the US needs to seriously consider the extent to which the state should take into account particular cultural identities in its policies, laws, and distribution of public resources as a matter of principled democratic practice. This idea, curiously enough, is not entirely foreign to American political practice. For example, contrary to American liberal doctrine, the aboriginal rights of American Indians have been established in law and public policy:

While the United States is often viewed as a 'melting pot,' without permanently distinct minority cultures, this is clearly not true of the aboriginal population. There is a system of reservations for the American Indian population, within which the members of particular Indian communities have been able . . . to protect their culture . . . The reservations form special political jurisdictions over which Indian communities have certain guaranteed powers, and within which non-Indian Americans have restricted mobility, property, and voting rights. (Kymlicka 1989: 136).

Similarly, practices such as affirmative action, Veterans policies, and bilingual education are examples of recent American public policy which involve recognition of group or minority rights, and which are intended to promote social equality and democracy (Skrentny 1994).

To sum up this section, I have proposed a line of criticism intended to expose the limits or incoherence of a certain liberal view of difference and democracy. The question of difference cannot, at least in contemporary America, be reduced to viewing particular cultural identities or communities as strictly private or as a temporary legacy of oppression. Some differences are chosen or at least consented to and some run "deep" and will likely shape public life for some time. The presumption of an impartial neutral public sphere rests on an untenable sociological base.

Dutch civic pluralism: the limits of consociational democracy

Advocates of a democratic politics of difference have found a public somewhat receptive to their message in postwar America. Its most vocal supporters are affiliated with, or influenced by, the so-called new social movements, e.g., some feminists, anti-racist social critics, postmodernists, and queer theorists.[3] Not surprisingly, critics have been equally, and lately it seems, more strident and noisy. Without distinguishing diverse currents of the politics of difference, they accuse all difference-base politics of creating new social groups who claim special privileges, of dividing the nation into closed quasi-ethnic groups, of undermining the quality of education by introducing political criteria into the classroom and curriculum, and of destabilizing a liberal state by making excessive demands for equality and political participation.

Critics of a multicultural or difference-based democracy often fashion dark images of a nation being torn asunder by the centrifugal force of movements that promote particularistic social loyalties. The future of an America in their grip is said to portend the unraveling of a fragile national consensus. Referring to the Soviet Union and the civil war in the former Yugoslavia, Arthur Schlesinger Jr. (1989) suggests that in the post-Cold War period "ethnicity is the cause of the breaking up of nations" (p. 13). The US has avoided this fate to the extent that it has been guided by an ideal of the melting away of ethnic differences in favor of forging a new and inclusive national identity. This ideal however is currently under attack by a new "cult of ethnicity" propagated by multiculturalists. They denounce the concept of the melting pot and instead promote ethnic separatism. Their success, Schlesinger Jr. says apocalyptically, will bring about the "dis-uniting of America."

Questions should of course be raised about the form and consequences of introducing multicultural democratic standards into public life. Nevertheless, critics such as Schlesinger Jr. refuse to seriously examine the issue of difference and democracy in a way that speaks to a nation in which the hegemony of a Anglo-Protestant elite has given way to sociopolitical division and contestation. Moreover, there is a failure among American liberals such as Schlesinger Jr. to consider that there can be various ways difference may be organized in a democratic society.

To further pursue this theme, I could examine some of the ways a group-based public policy has been enacted in the US. For example, I might consider the social and the political consequences of American aboriginal policy or affirmative action or bilingual education (e.g., Kymlicka 1989; Minow 1990; Skrentny 1994). Alternatively, I could proceed normatively by considering arguments defending, in principle, a group-based multicultural democratic polity (e.g., Kymlicka 1995; Taylor 1994; Young 1990). Instead of choosing either of these plausible strategies, I want to pursue a more sociological option. In the remainder of this chapter, I will further explore the question of difference and democracy by briefly contrasting the empir-ical examples of the Netherlands and France. The former because it is both an exemplary illustration of a group-based multicultural democratic nation. The latter because the combination of statism and civic individual-ism in France presents an alternative position on difference and democracy to both the Dutch group rights and the American "individualist" model.

Some political scientists have distinguished "consociational democracies" from what they call "majoritarian" or "adversarial" democracies. For example, the former is said to be characterized by a multiparty in contrast to a two-party system, by executive power-sharing in broad coalitions rather than the concentration of executive power in a single-party majority and often by a decentralized rather than a centralized government (Lijphart 1984). The crucial feature of consociational democracies (e.g., Austria, Belgium, Switzerland) is that these societies are divided into clearly identifiable "segments" or ethnic, religious, linguistic, or cultural blocs. Each "segment" is autonomous or has its own social and political institutions and is inclusive *vis-à-vis* its members. Consociational democracies are said to achieve stability by virtue of (1) the mutual isolation of social blocs which limits inter-segment contact and potential conflict (2) the proportional political representation of segments and (3) the values and attitudes of the segment elites which are oriented to coalition building, pragmatic negotiation, and political accommodation. The Netherlands has been exemplary of a stable type of consociational democracy.

Contrary to the fears of critics of a difference-based politics, the case of The Netherlands presents a democratic society which has been organized around a strong idea of cultural pluralism and a weak notion of cultural unity. Ultimately, I will argue that, from the standpoint of a strong notion of democratic pluralism, The Netherland's political culture is needlessly restrictive of both pluralism and democracy. However, the case of The Netherlands suggests the merits of reexamining the concepts of private and public life.

Between roughly the early twentieth century through the mid-1960s, a somewhat historically unique social system was established which, though protecting individual rights, assumed the "rights" of collectivities. I am referring to the so-called system of "pillarization" (Goudsblom 1967; Huggett 1971; Lijphart 1975; Tash 1991; van Schendelen 1984). The Netherlands was socially and politically divided into identifiable and inclusive social segments. There were four different blocs: Protestants, Catholics, Socialists and Liberals. The first two groups shared a common religion though members exhibited diverse class positions. The latter two groups were unified by their secular, class-based agendas. Each group was relatively socially closed; interactions between members of the four groups were quite limited, superficial, and potentially conflictual.

These social blocs functioned less like religious denominations, social movements or unions in the US then like the territorially based ethnic immigrant communities of say the Italian Catholics or Jews early in this century. Block membership defined a "life" not just a lifestyle. Each bloc had its own media organizations such as newspapers, television and radio programming, its own union and professional organizations, sporting and social clubs, and political parties. Moreover, the government funded each bloc in its "public" activities (e.g., education, culture and media) proportional to its membership.

To take one example of the social role of these collectivities, consider that each bloc had its own primary and secondary school system. Indicative of the strength of the confessional blocs, 72 percent of the school-aged population in 1957 attended private, mostly religious, schools. Virtually all of these schools were fully state funded. Although there was some standardization in the curriculum, especially at the elementary school level, the differences in the curriculum reflected important bloc differences. In the words of Arend Lijphart (1975):

> The thorough division of elementary education not only separates the children belonging to different blocs physically but also instills different values in them. This goes beyond the teaching of different religious beliefs: the standards emphasized in elementary schools are those of the separate subculture of the bloc rather than an integrated national culture. National history is taught in elementary schools as merely the country's past interpreted from each bloc's point of view rather than a truly national history that is felt as a commonly appreciated and unifying background. (p. 52; cf. Goudsblom 1968: 94-104)

Given the comprehensive reach of these pillars, it is not surprising that citizens identified primarily with their own bloc and secondarily with the national political society. Contrary to what many American social observers might expect however, this system of social segmentation and pluralism neither resulted in endemic social conflict, nor impeded progressive public policy. One reason is that the elites of these four social blocs, drawing on a culture that emphasized pragmatic negotiation and a tolerance of difference, took responsibility for consensus building and political accommodation among the blocs (Lijphart 1975: 197). Morever, despite social fragmentation, an identification with the nation was forged, in part, through a history of struggle against Spanish and French domination. Dutch nationalism has been reinforced by public support for a strong centralized state.

The system of pillarization has apparently been in decline since the mid-1960s (Kriesi 1988; van Mierlo 1986). Observers point to the emergence of political parties, unions, newspapers or broadcast media that are no longer tied to any specific bloc; to the rise of new types of social protest associated with the student movement, the counterculture, the environmental, women's and gay rights movements; and to the decline in religious belief. Moreover, the professionalization and bureaucratization of social service provisions, and the proliferation of advisory and regulatory agencies, have greatly weakened the social and political role of these blocs.

The Netherlands is changing. Moreover, whatever the social and political benefits of pillarization, it was nondemocratic in important ways. The negotiation and consensus building between the blocs was done by elites in secrecy and with little input by ordinary citizens. Democracy amounted to little more than the institutionalization of mechanisms to select bloc leaders who would set social policy; there was only a very weak notion of civic participation and social democratization. Furthermore, the inclusive and sharply bounded character of blocs apparently permitted inter-bloc tolerance but at the price of exacting a high level of conformity and intolerance of difference within each pillar. For example, the blocs enforced fairly rigid gender roles and did little to disturb male domination or a heterosexual norm. Finally, the range of social differences that were permitted to be organized publicly was limited by the pillar system. Hence, while the Dutch pillar system illustrates the case of a democracy based on the sociopolitical status of collectivities, its elitism, mass depoliticization, its system of internal bloc conservatism, and its limited tolerance of publicly organized differences, makes this system fall far short of a desirable multicultural democratic ideal.

Its not clear what the future holds for The Netherlands. Several models seem to be circulating in public debate concerning the future of this nation. One possibility, and to my mind the one most open to a strong democratizing potential, suggests continued de-pillarization but simultaneously a defense of heterogeneous public cultures. The emergence of homosexuals in the 1960s and 1970s as a new kind of voluntary, open-ended cultural community is suggestive in this regard, as is the state policy of promoting immigrant cultural communities.[4] A second possible direction is the US model of civic individualism. However, the extreme individualism and antistatism of the US would likely diminish its appeal to the Dutch. A third possible model of democracy looks to western Europe, specifically to France. The French model might seem consistent with Dutch traditions which emphasize balancing individualism and national solidarity and with the technocratic impulse of the postwar Dutch welfare state. Moreover, some Americans discontented with the turmoil surrounding multiculturalism might also look to a French model.

But does France offer a viable option for The Netherlands or the US? Indeed, does France recommend itself as a model of democratic pluralism? I will argue that it does not because it restricts the public organization of social differences and therefore blocks the formation of a heterogeneous democratic public sphere.

French civic republicanism: solidarity and the suppression of difference in the public sphere

As in the US, the French favor a view of the national political community as consisting of individuals considered as equal, identical citizens, not as members of particular cultural communities. However, France goes beyond privatizing social differences. In contrast to the US, this nation discourages the public elaboration or organization of particular cultural identities, for example, the formation of feminist, gay, or ethnic public cultures. French anxiety about difference has been handled through forging strong links between individual and national identity, through emphasizing national sociocultural unity symbolized by a strong centralized state, and by a culture organized around civic republican ideals of solidarity.

Consider AIDS policy in France. As we would expect in a society in which individualism and group differences evoke a threat to national unity, French public policy has not distinguished persons with AIDS from other sick persons (e.g., there are no separate AIDS units in hospitals) and has not identified or ranked social groups at risk. Everyone is viewed as at risk to contact HIV, despite overwhelming evidence that gay men make up most of the AIDS population in France. To its credit, French AIDS policy which has been inspired by the principle of equality and solidarity has avoided the social victimization of persons with AIDS and the public scapegoating of gay men that has been sadly evident in the US. Nevertheless, this refusal to recognize group identities or distinct cultural communities in the name of national solidarity has encouraged an AIDS policy run by experts with little or no input from an officially nonexistent gay subculture; nor has French policy considered the impact of HIV on gay cultures (Steffen 1992). This contrasts with The Netherlands which has both insisted on public solidarity with persons with AIDS and has incorporated gay men into the making of national AIDS policy (Duyvendak 1996; van Wijngaarden 1992). Indeed, Dutch AIDS policy includes the goal of preserving gay public cultures, something that would be virtually impossible in French political culture. Why this radical privatization of social differences in France?

In the US and The Netherlands the state evolved almost as a "superstructural" institution: the centralization of its authority was not accomplished until well into the present century. By contrast, a powerful, centralized state preceded modern nationhood in France. Moreover, if the US, and to a lesser extent The Netherlands, forged a sense of nationhood against the absolutism of a colonial power, France constructed a modern nation state in opposition to the *ancien regime* with its multiplicity of corporate bodies. Thus, whereas the American revolution was fought against the centralized imperial power of England, the French Revolution was defined less by its opposition to the centralized power of the King than to a system of decentralized, sociopolitical corporate bodies that structured French public life. Revolutionaries criticized Absolutism but less with the aim of destroying the centralized state than with democratizing and disciplining it. Indeed, for many radicals the revolution was intended to complete the centralizing impulse of the Absolutist state by further destroying intermediate social bodies and imposing a uniform national culture on regional social diversity.

We might recall that in contrasting the French and American democratic revolutions, Tocqueville (1970) argued that the former amounted to a legal-constitutional change, not a revolution in everyday practices and customs. France tried to impose democracy from above but left in place a depoliticized, mass public culture. Indeed, Tocqueville saw in the French Revolution less a "pure" democratic spirit than a deeply rooted French impulse to centralize power, to impose substitute uniformity for local diversity, and to fashion an orderly, disciplined society (Tocqueville 1970: 90-91). By contrast, Tocqueville believed that American democracy took hold in the towns and villages of daily life and in the habits and hearts of ordinary Americans.

Keen social observers such as Tocqueville and Durkheim have traced a distinctive French impulse towards social control and disciplinary order to its political history. For example, in his explanation of the unique development of a system of boarding education in the fifteenth and sixteenth centuries, Durkheim (1977) emphasized France's "excessive passion for uniform regimentation" (p. 122). He explained this disciplinary impulse by referring to a tradition of political centralization:

"Well before any of the other countries of Europe, we had a firmly established central power. From the end of the fifteenth century . . . the plethora of small feudal states became merged into the unity which was the French nation; the monarchy began to concentrate all authority in its own hands . . . No European society at this time had such a powerful sense of its own political and moral unity . . . "

Moreover, political centralization went hand in hand with the levelling of the "moral diversity of the country . . . [the] imposing [of] unity on the variety of local institutions and . . . establishing a single code of laws and ethics throughout all strata of society." (p. 122). The centralizing and disciplining spirit of France has been traced, as well, to nonpolitical dynamics. For example, Jesse Pitts (1963) argued that French Catholicism both exhibited and unleashed this impulse towards social rationalization:

We find . . . in what could be called the "doctrinaire-hierarchical" aspect of French Catholicism, a trait that seems fairly specific to French culture. This trait is a commitment to a nexus of authoritative ideas which incarnate the highest spirituality. In religious terms the nexus is the Church, in secular terms the Nation. There is a conviction that all behavior should have a clear, deductive connection to this spirituality through rules, principles, regulations which insure the inherent value to the action. (p. 239)

Pitts argued that French Catholicism helped shape a culture of formalism, centralization and solidarity that is, in part, defined by its hostility to individuality and difference. French Catholicism is at

the root of French formalism, the demand for deductive chains of reasoning and hierarchy, the insistence upon the unity of the power of the center, and formulations where everything and everybody is . . . in its place. Individuality here means finding one's position in the hierarchy . . . Aspects of French social structure that seem to implement this doctrinaire-hierarchical theme are the centralizing and formalistic features of the civil service, and its technocratic tradition. (p. 239)

I cannot tease out the complex ways a French civic republican culture, with its statist traditions, egalitarianism, and solidaristic ideal, articulates with a spirit of centralization, social uniformity, and discipline. Instead, I wish to bring this section to a close by underscoring one key point: unlike the US which allows, indeed encourages group differences to flourish in civil society, and unlike the Dutch state which recognizes groups as political agents, the French state often approaches groups with an eye to privatizing and suppressing them or subjecting social differences to hierarchical, normalizing control. France may be a nation of individuals but before such individuals are men or women, bourgeois or proletariat, straight or gay, Catholic or Muslim, they are, or should be, French (cf. Brubaker 1992: 1).

Group rights and democracy

The case for a multicultural, group-based democracy, or at least one possible argument in support of this position, pivots on two claims. First, the sociological truism that by definition social life is unthinkable without individuals belonging to one or more cultural communities. These social groupings are desirable because they give purpose, self worth, coherence, and a sense of belonging to the lives of individuals. We can further assume that at least contemporary industrial societies will inevitably be composed of multiple cultural communities. Secondly, to the extent that some of the differences between these cultural communities touch on basic cultural values, including morality and epistemology, decisions about the rules and knowledges that structure public life can never be ethically or politically neutral; they inevitably favor certain communities. Hence, in a society committed to a strong notion of democracy, it would arguably be preferable to have a polity that recognizes this multicultural condition. At a minimum, this recognition would seem to presuppose establishing procedures that would allow different cultural communities to participate in making the rules that govern their lives.

But, you ask, would not these cultural communities function as quasi-pillars or quasi-tribal units imposing rigid controls on the individual? I conceive of these communities less on the model of the Dutch pillar than that of lesbian and gay or feminist communities as they have evolved in the US or England. These cultural communities are not pillars or kin units in that one is not born into them but "chooses" them; such communities are "open" in that individuals can voluntarily move in and out of them. Moreover, in principle, they are democratic in a strong sense lacking in the pillar or kin unit in that their internal rules and organization is consensually based. Finally, these communities do not envelop or absorb the individual in the way pillars did or some kin units do. Instead, individuals may choose the extent of their identification and involvement in any particular cultural community.

In a nation characterized by multiple cultural communities, democracy is unthinkable without guaranteeing the participation of these communities. Cultural communities would, in this model, be encouraged to form and function as *public cultures* – with their own social and political institutions and organizations. Privatizing social differences effectively mutes the voices of minority and oppressed cultural communities. It is only when cultural communities function as public agents that the values and interests of these communities can potentially exert a societal influence.

A model of public life organized around the participation of multiple cultural communities would of course heighten the level of political conflict. Thus, the question arises: would not such heterogeneous cultural communities participating in making social rules render political consensus and unity impossible? Is not the cost of multicultural democracy endemic social division and instability? To this I reply, has not the failure of states to recognize multiple cultural communities helped to perpetuate social inequalities and hostilities? Is not an undesirable level of social conflict more likely in a nation in which some cultural communities feel alienated and devalued because they lack societal recognition and a public voice or representation than in a polity in which opportunities exist for these communities to shape the rules that govern society?

To be sure, the kind of multicultural democracy I envision would encourage ongoing social contestation. Although this would be an enormously complex and messy process, I believe that in most western nations, surely in the US, France, and The Netherlands, there are sufficient cultural resources shared in common to fashion agreements on social and national policies, even if such agreements are only temporary and subject to continual dissent and future renegotiation. One likely positive effect would be enhanced levels of individual participation in public life as the cultural communities that represent the varied interests and values of citizens became an integral part of the political culture and process. Individuals might accordingly develop a strong sense of national belonging and identification.

Epilogue: Pragmatism, difference and a culture of strong democracy

If it is true that in many Western nations differences in race, gender, ethnicity, nationality, sexuality, and ableness have been reconfigured from personal matters to public concerns, if, to say it otherwise, differences which were once considered private are now viewed as matters of collective life, this suggests major shifts in the organization of polity and civil society. These shifts have been accompanied by serious reflection about their ethical and political significance. Many critics view these developments and their intellectual defenders as dangerous. The rise of multiple, heterogeneous "quasi-ethnic" collectivities and public cultures is said to threaten civil order and a well functioning, stable democratic polity. Indeed, if some of these differences, as I have suggested in previous chapters, extend into moral and epistemic values, critics rightly ask whether championing a strong sociopolitical pluralism, a public world organized in some significant way in relation to these differences, does not portend endemic moral and social turmoil. Without a core of shared moral and epistemic values, critics wonder, will not a strong defense of social differences turn our national civic and public culture into a moral and political battlefield?

It is this anticipation of a society structured around social difference spiraling into civil war and political crisis that is, for some critics, the principal social logic of undoubtedly a well-intentioned multicultural politics. The raging battles over canons and curriculum in American schools, the censoring implications of the logic of "political correctness," the escalation of mean spiritedness in daily life, and the inability to forge a unified social agenda or vision in public life are taken by some critics as the inevitable social implications of a politics of difference. Not more democracy, not more tolerance, and not a more robust civil society, but the splintering of the US into quasi-ethnic groups and the escalation of mutual suspicion, distrust, and hostility in civic life are the consequences of the new politics of difference.

At the core of this anxiety is the presumption that there must be strong common values and beliefs which provide the intellectual and social base of a nation. In particular, there must be a common stock of knowledge. This means, among other things, common rules for handling interpretive and normative disputes which, in turn, presuppose shared understandings of what passes as knowledge, of how knowledge is produced and authorized. In other words, although a framework of common culture might include shared linguistic conventions or social norms, a crucial element is the notion of a *shared epistemology*. Societies, at least liberal democracies or societies whose institutions are based on high levels of consensus and participation, are said to require common procedures to resolve interpretive and normative disputes, shared logics of inquiry and argumentation, and agreed upon justificatory rationales or strategies.

It is for this reason that the realm of intellectual culture, in particular the university and its knowledges, has assumed such significance in debates over social difference and unity in many contemporary societies. If there is polarization around defining knowledge, if knowledge is dragged into the sphere of social interests and power, the very grounds of civil society are imagined to be shaken. Hence, the debates raging now in the US, and in many other nations, around (say) educational curriculum and canons, the place of religion in public life, and the meaning of art, are viewed as disturbing not only to the school system, the churches, and aesthetic institutions, but to civil and political order in that they indicate disarray in assumptions about knowledge that are thought to be foundational for national stability and coherence. The so-called cultural wars have assumed such importance, especially in the US, because incoherence in the realm of knowledge is thought to lead inevitably to civil and political crisis. If we cannot agree on what knowledge is or what counts as authorized conventions of argumentation and justificatory strategies, there will be no consensus on what should be assumed about the world, what or whom should be believed or listened to, how to peacefully mediate disputes, and so on. The question of knowledge is, in short, considered central to the question of the possibility of social unity and democracy in a multicultural nation.

The critique of a culture of impartial knowledge, in particular, criticisms of the claims of science to represent a privileged knowing – privileged because of claims to being value neutral, objective, and universalistic – that have been proposed on many fronts (from poststructuralists to certain currents of feminism, antiracist theory, postcolonial and postmodern perspectives), have opened the doors, say some critics, to epistemological and therefore civil and political incoherence. Given the alignment of these deconstructive critiques of privileged knowledges to a vision of a multi-cultural democracy, it is ironic, critics say, that their relentless decentering strategies imply either a sociologically naive quasi-anarchistic social vision or a corporate statism as the authority of the state will become the final safeguard of order and progress in the face of anticipated social paralysis and disarray.

But is this a compelling critique? Is a strong notion of impartial knowledge a necessary condition of a pluralistic civil society and a democratic polity? Is the only choice between social unity made possible by a culture of strong "rationalism" and a condition of social incoherence implied in the "radical pluralism" of deconstructive critiques? Must a discourse and politics that defends a strong notion of civic and public difference lead inevitably to social fragmentation? Parallelling my argument in chapter twelve that making difference an axial principle of public life would not necessarily produce civic and political incoherence, I wish to press the thesis that a strong version of bringing difference into the way we think about knowledge does not necessarily lead to an endemic, debilitating social fragmentation.

A crucial question is whether a culture of knowledge which is friendly to difference and multiplicity, in the strong sense that I have implied, can also provide the necessary intellectual resources for democracy. Can a culture which admits that some differences "run deep," that allows for "reason" to more easily slide into uncertainly and ambiguity than would (say) many currents of modern Western rationalism, provide enough shared discursive resources to make negotiations across difference possible, make agreements between communities and traditions possible, and support institutions that protect rights, democratic procedure, and demands for representation and participation?

I want to push a bit further than in the previous chapters the claim that a *pragmatic culture of knowledge* is both friendly towards difference, indeed assumes and encourages differences, and makes possible a strong notion of a socially connecting reason. Pragmatism, or a particular version of it that I will advance, is indicative of a culture of knowledge and communicative practice that seems to me strikingly consistent or resonant with a strong notion of a multicultural democracy. The claim of the friendliness of pragmatism to difference is less in need of defense than the question of whether pragmatism makes possible the kinds of social bonds and civility that allow a democratic society to flourish.

As regards social difference, pragmatism assumes an abandonment of efforts to furnish epistemological foundations. However else pragmatism may be described, it is surely its central claim (to be returned to shortly) that knowledge must be understood in relation to social practices. At a minimum, this means that claims to knowledge are to be justified not by appealing to ultimate grounds or to some theoretical casuistry or first principles, but by relating knowledge claims to particular social purposes and interests. If foundational efforts assume that it is possible and desirable to articulate a common logic of knowing, or unifying procedures for producing and authorizing knowledge, in order to supersede epistemological differences, pragmatism assumes a permanent suspicion toward efforts. A pragmatic approach leaves permanently unsettled or unresolved a social world of ongoing interpretive dispute. If such conflicts, at the deepest level epistemic divisions, cannot be superseded or transcended, ideally, by an appeal to common grounds or impartial principles or configured hierarchically as "stages of knowing," disputes must be routinely negotiated by means of various ad hoc discursive strategies.

Indeed, I wonder whether at least some of the resistance to pragmatism reflects a fear of living with differences that "run deep." That is, in so far as (some) pragmatists assume that some differences are significant enough to throw suspicion on the presumed foundations of one's beliefs, this perspective fosters an awareness of the conventionality and particularity of any specific interpretive position. The suspicion is that what an agent takes to be knowledge is just an interpretive standpoint or a particular mapping of the world, which has no necessary and exclusive warrant from the nature of language, reason, or the world, but rather must in the end be recognized as the perspective of a community, tradition, language game, and so on. In this regard, parallel to Gadamer's project of a post-foundational hermeneutic, pragmatism implies a culture which instills a deep reflexivity concerning the particular sociohistorical conditions of agents' ideas, promotes a view of the tradition-or-community-based character of "reason," and imagines agents willing to risk their deepest convictions in the course of communicatively negotiating interpretive, including epistemic, differences.

The demands of a pragmatic culture of such reflexivity and openness would, it would be anticipated, be fraught with anxiety and fear. The risk, at one level, is continual disenchantment: the repetitive exposure as contingent, immanent, and "local" of what an agent assumes to be firm, secure grounds for his or her ultimate beliefs and values. For some of "us" Westerners, heirs to Plato, St. Thomas Aquinas, Descartes, and Kant, this is tantamount to the triumph of unreason and ethical and social incoherence. At another level, the risk of pragmatism is to live with a level of ambiguity, uncertainty, contingency, and social fluidity that many of us might find psychologically and sociologically challenging. Finally, a pragmatic culture would not only decenter foundational convictions but such a reflexive culture would entail a constant pressure to expose the nexus between knowledge and power. To the extent that pragmatism shifts the question of knowledge from the medium of a metadiscourse of reason, language, or logic to that of purpose and consequences, communities and interests, the question of power becomes a thematized aspect of the culture of pragmatic knowledge.

A key question of course is whether such a relentless decentering, critical reflexivity which is aggressively insistent on difference also makes possible social unity. Does pragmatism provide the requisite conceptual resources to fashion the kinds of agreements and shared understandings that a democratic polity assumes? Or, as critics argue, is pragmatism symptomatic of the loss of a vital culture of reason and common purpose? This is the question I want to conclude on, pushing arguments I have made in previous chapters a little further.

What do I mean by pragmatism? In brief, I use this complex term to refer to a position on the production and justification of knowledge.[1] Pragmatists assert that knowledge or truth is not something about which there can or should be a general theory. Knowledge should not be the occasion to inaugurate a special inquiry – epistemology – which, for example, might take the form of a transcendental argument explicating the conditions of the possibility of knowledge, an empiricist argument accounting for the connection between sense perception and ideas, or a linguistic proposal that assumes the task of linking word and world. Instead, a pragmatic perspective holds that knowledge should be approached as involving a practical relation to the world. Specifically, knowledge is viewed as a way of coping or securing particular purposes or goods. Truth or valid knowledge is the status assigned to those ideas and the strategies for their production that have proved useful or successful in "coping" or achieving a specific aim What is taken for knowledge, in other words, is just another way of acknowledging that certain ways of thinking, inquiring, or interpreting things work or are successful *vis-à-vis* the purpose at hand. Hence, in contrast to epistemic positions that hold that knowledge claims can and should be assessed in relation to a general theoretical matrix, a pragmatic approach insists that the social context and the purposes of the production of knowledge cannot be separated from considerations of justification. In place of a "logic" of knowledge, pragmatists wish to substitute a "pragmatics" that would assess knowledge claims in terms of context, purposes, implications, and consequences.

Does this commit pragmatists to reducing knowledge to questions of power? Are truth claims then "resolved" or reconfigured into a nondiscursive medium of social interest, utility, and material conflict? Or does pragmatism entail neglecting or devaluing cognitive or representational claims and arguments? I do not think so. Pragmatists understand that managing in daily life is impossible without the individual making claims about social reality. Individuals advance truth claims and argue about the makeup of the social world, as we orient and justify our actions based on such understandings. Accordingly, pragmatists do not reject a world "out there" nor do they deny that we can make intelligent, adjudicable claims about the world. Pragmatists do say, however, that interpretive conflicts ought not to be settled by trying to elaborate some general theory of truth or social knowledge. This is because knowledge claims and their redeemability are understood as always related to particular social settings, conventions, and purposes.

If there is no general theoretical matrix to appeal to in order to adjudicate interpretive conflicts, how can we proceed? Pragmatists suggest that we proceed pragmatically – that is, with an aim to managing or getting by disputes by means of whatever discursive resources and strategies prove situationally useful. In the face of interpretive or communicative disputes, pragmatists recommend an inventive, multileveled, flexible, practical approach. Instead of approaching disputes with a formal-analytical matrix or logic in hand, or developing such a matrix as disputants "go metatheoretical," a pragmatics of knowledge encourages agents to handle disputes with a series of loose guidelines, such as the following: "Be attentive to the issue at hand and to what is at stake in the dispute"; "attend to situational considerations such as the particular conventions of argumentation and knowledge assessment that operate in the conversation at hand": "consider possible gains and losses, advantages and disadvantages, implications and consequences, of different positions from a variety of cognitive, ethical, and political vantage points." If disputants follow such guidelines for argumentation, and if they are willing to negotiate and at times live with disagreement – and such willingness can itself only be urged in pragmatic terms – in most instances, pragmatics will lead to a temporary but good enough agreement with regard to the dispute at hand. Accordingly, rather than viewing pragmatism as reductionist and anti-rational, pragmatists in fact push for a more reflexive, elaborated discursivity. Unlike nonpragmatists who wish to restrict argumentation to the appeal to brute fact or general theory, pragmatists suspect such foundational strategies of either masking a power move or, more innocently, of being prompted by anxieties over uncertainty or sociocultural difference. Pragmatists cannot prove the impossibility of a nonlocal, nonperspectival vantage point but take for granted Weber's warring values, Wittgenstein's language games, and Gadamer's traditions as a condition of the disenchantment of the West. Pragmatists do not then give up on "reason" or surrender to power. Quite the contrary, they demand a deeper, thicker, more reflexive, relentless discursivity. If appeals to foundations do not end conversations, "rationality" can only mean recourse to elaborate, multileveled discourses that move back and forth between considerations of situation, purpose, interest, evidence, theory, implication, social consequences, and so forth.

For example, let us consider the implications of this pragmatic approach for interpretive disputes in the human sciences. A pragmatic approach to disciplinary disputes in say sociology or women's studies does not entail a dismissal or devaluation of "empirical" or "theoretical" levels of argumentation. Although pragmatists assume that appeals to "fact" or "theory" cannot furnish a conclusive resolution to an interpretive conflict, in many instances an appeal to evidence or a shared conceptual strategy works. If the parties to a conflict agree with regard to the way a problem is posed, with regard to empirical conventions, conceptual approach, argumentative style, and justificatory strategy, then consensus may easily emerge from conventionalized appeals to fact or theory. Given this general level of discursive consensus, disagreements will likely be local and non-threatening to social, in this case, disciplinary order or coherence. Even in disciplines as divided as sociology or history or women's studies, there are many discursive areas of agreement or sites where dissension is quite specific and limited. For example, in area specialities in sociology such as demography, criminology, or social movements, sociologists may very well share similar ways of posing problems, similar conventions with regard to constructing the empirical, a common conceptual stock, and a shared understanding of which strategies count as authorizing knowledge (e.g., particular empirical "logics," writing styles, or appeals to canonized texts). Accordingly, in these speciality areas of sociology we would expect to find wide patches of consensus. However, even in these specialities, and surely across the discipline as a whole, there are conflicts over what counts as "empirical" and how to measure different kinds of evidence. There are, as sociologists are well aware, also disagreements over the meaning of empirical data, conflicts over interpretive frameworks that sometimes reflect core disciplinary disagreements over which problems count, which themes are important, which general categories and perspectives are "valid," and how "we" are to determine validity or according to which – or whose – standards. In other words, what are we to do as conflicts are more general and foundational? What are we to do when dispute extends to the construction of the empirical, to the core categories of social knowledge, and to the appropriate justificatory rationales or strategies that warrant truth claims?

When appeals to fact or theory fail to win consensus, pragmatists say we have recourse to at least two strategies. First, we should do as we do today – namely, continue arguing over evidence, method, and categories but, instead of being circular and dogmatic or going metatheoretical or foundational, we should be inventive and practical. This might mean restating the terms of the dispute by (say) reformulating a general theoretical or metatheoretical dispute into a specific empirical one, shifting the dispute to a different empirical, analytical or ethical site that might prove more productive of dialogue, or pressing disputants to clarify exactly what is at stake in a dispute, whether it lends itself to resolution, what that might look like, and whether it might be more productive to let stand a particular disagreement and move on to another area of conflict. It seems to me that there are many disputes in the disciplines and daily life that we should simply live with disagreement and move on to other issues, disputes about which nothing significant is at stake, and disputes that can be productively pursued by rearticulating them in another register or shifting the site of dispute (say from an analytical to an empirical level or from one empirical site to another or from an empirical to an ethical level).

There is a second strategy pragmatists recommend in the face of interpretive conflict: We should go "pragmatic" in the sense of pursuing consequentialist arguments. This refers to discursive strategies that consider the implications or consequences of particular truth claims or social interpretations. Consequentialist arguments press disputants to justify their claims or positions not by appealing to a "realist" or "coherence" justificatory rhetoric, but by giving an account of what follows from them. Pragmatists demand that disputants elaborate, in as much detail as necessary to understand the position for what it is and potentially persuade others, the consequences that follow, in principle, from a particular validity claim or interpretive position. Of course, you ask, "what consequences matter in assessing a position and how are they to be assessed?" My reply, reduced to its bare essentials, is that those consequences matter, and those standards of assessment will have force, that disputants are able to make a compelling case for. In other words, a pragmatist cannot say in advance what kinds of consequences, or standards of assessment, will matter in argumentation. We cannot a priori mark out discursive boundaries of inside/outside because only the disputants themselves will or should determine what considerations should count.

Consequentialist arguments suggest the importance of ethical and political considerations in discursive cultures, including of course the human sciences. While pressing disputants to account for the implications of their positions involves elaborating the empirical, analytical, or thematic aspects of their arguments, pragmatists see no compelling reason to restrict consequentialist assessments to this cognitive level. Indeed, to the extent that pragmatists conceptualize knowledge as related to social practices or itself as a practice aimed at managing life concerns or securing particular utilities, to that extent knowledges need to be assessed in light of their possible social and political consequences. This is *not* and *should not* be interpreted as an argument for substituting ethical and political for empirical or analytical arguments. To assess a truth claim or interpretive position in light of its potential ethical and political implications necessarily assumes descriptions of the course of social events or analyses of social realities. The pragmatist does not then deny or devalue empirical analysis but insists that any particular empirical analytical move is compelling only as a convention enabling communication, not by virtue of any stronger epistemological claim (see chapter 1). Hence, the consequentialist emphasis in pragmatism is intended to expand the scope of social reasoning to include ethical and political concerns when such considerations are raised in the course of argumentation. Pragmatists therefore imagine a culture in which social thinkers, including lay citizens, approach daily interpretive conflicts by fashioning thicker, more elaborated, multileveled social perspectives and arguments that move among empirical, analytical, ethical, and sometimes political levels.

Pragmatism is not then about shutting down arguments by invoking utility or interest. Pragmatists do not recommend engaging disputes by reductively asking whose interest or purpose is served by a particular claim, perspective, or judgement. Pragmatism, as I understand it, is not about narrowing, restricting, or abandoning "reason." To the contrary, pragmatists insist on an elaborated discursivity against the power of those whose desires and social interests wish to enforce silence. They understand moreover that claims to knowledge are often entangled in social interest and power. Pragmatists aim to expose the play of interest in discourse while insisting that this nexus itself become part of the elaboration of a critical social reason. In other words, while power and knowledge are understood as closely intertwined, this perception does not signal the "end of rationality" or a shift from discourse to strategic action but, for pragmatists, incites us to deepen and enlarge the scope of our argumentation, to expand and thicken our discourse by "going" consequentialist, and to extend this reflexivity to the productivity of our own knowledge-producing practices.

Does pragmatism however tolerate and encourage a level of dissension that threatens civil life? Pragmatists, at least pragmatists of a certain kind, stand for a relentless but not aimless and socially dismembering discursiv-ity. Although fixed points are disturbed and solid foundations of fact or theory may be exposed as wishful projections, pragmatists insist that there are resting places in argumentation and social conflict. They may be based on stretches of discursive consensus that mark all fields of argumentation or are temporary pauses or rest stops made possible by specific *ad hoc* agreements that disputants negotiate. Moreover, pragmatists hold that many interpretive and normative conflicts have little or no significant intel-lectual or practical import. For example, metatheoretical disagreements in the disciplines, for example, disputes over concepts of agency and structure or materialism and idealism, may be foci for interpretive conflicts but they do not threaten to unravel disciplinary cultures. We live with them, as we have for many centuries, perhaps not always comfortably but such dis-comfort has to do with hopes for certainty or secure foundations. Even as cognitive or normative disputes become more potentially consequential, for example, disputes over epistemological or ethical first principles, most of us, most of the time, live without too much discord with such disagree-ments. Most disagreements that have something significant at stake can be managed by means of temporary, ad hoc strategies. This is the case at least in part because disputants share some things in common and, if they are open to dialogue or motivated to cope peaceably, they will invent ways to negotiate past disputes. Of course, if parties to a dispute are not motivated to settle affairs peacefully, and if appeals to the benefits of ongoing dis-course are rejected, neither pragmatic not nonpragmatic appeals will have much effect. When desire rules behavior, conversation gives way to war. Bosnia would have happened whether parties appealed to a pragmatic or nonpragmatic reason. Such discursive strategies have effect only if they are interwoven into a national culture and if there are institutional safeguards against civil war. Obviously, in the former Yugoslavia that was not the case. But the US, France, England, and indeed most of the world, is not Bosnia. In these societies, disputes occur in fields of common discourse and divi-sions take place in settings where many common goals and norms are shared. If big conflicts are to erupt, I would favor a pragmatic culture com-mitted to a thick, elaborated discursivity, to a discursive and practical inventiveness and willingness to get on with the daily business of getting on.

In a society such as the contemporary US, where differences have crys-tallized into sociocultural differences and where conventions of discourse – styles, logics, categories, epistemologies – are regularly contested, a prag-matic culture of reason that is respectful of difference, comfortable with ambiguity and uncertainty, and oriented toward inventiveness and temporary agreements would seem especially appropriate, encouraging civil, peaceful, democratic modes of daily managing collective life. It is of course hardly surprising that the case of pragmatism is appearing now in the US as social differences have become a central part of US public life. I imagine that as these differences consolidate we will face two options: either enhanced levels of social division, warfare, and policing, of which there are many signs today, or a shift to a more pragmatic culture, of which there are some hopeful signs today as well.

Notes

1 The political unconscious of the human sciences

1 The term "political unconscious" is taken from Jameson (1981). Criticizing various "formalistic" approaches to literary interpretation which emphasize a primarily aesthetic focus, Jameson argued that literary texts, including theoretical interpretations and canon formation, should be seen as having social and political meaning. Specifically, Jameson defended a marxist literary approach which interpreted literature in relation to historically specific, socioeconomic-based, class dynamics. The political unconscious refers to the participation of literary texts in the perpetuation of class domination, a participation that was concealed by the figuring of literature – and typically literary criticism – as an aesthetic practice to be appreciated through formal aesthetic analysis. The political unconscious was the "repressed and buried reality of this fundamental history" i.e., the history of class struggle" that was simultaneously the ground of coherence of the text and concealed in its aestheticization (Jameson 1981: 20). Jameson emphasized the inevitability of the politics of knowledge. Literary texts are political not only because they are implicated in class struggle but because whatever texts get authorized as literature – and this of course implicates literary criticism whose role is in part to demarcate literature/nonliterature and good from mediocre literature – entails silencing or marginalizing other texts, traditions, and knowledges. Aside from Jameson and Foucault, I have profited from the following efforts to frame a politics of knowledge: Aronowitz (1988), Gouldner (1971), Haraway (1989), and Shapin (1994). The recent appearance of new genealogical approaches to disciplinary knowledges promise a serious reexamination of the history and politics of knowledge (e.g., Brown 1993; Graff 1987; Gunnell 1993; Hohendahl 1982; Davidson-Messer, Shumway, and Sylvan 1993; Shumway 1994).

2 Foucault's own position with respect to the dilemma of the role of intellectuals in the face of the exposure of the political unconsciousness of the human sciences was to offer genealogy or studies which expose the role of knowledge in the making subjects and social worlds as a plausible "successor" project to the

various versions of scientism. He called genealogy "anti-science" intending less a disavowal of rigorous methodology or analytical thinking than a repudiation of the innocence of science, its imperial aspirations, and its privileged place in western societies today.

3 Much of modern social theory has related a fairly simple story of the relation of religion and science in modern Western societies. Science was described as antagonistic to religion. The progress of knowledge entailed its scientization. For example, Comte, Marx, Durkheim and virtually all their successors related tales of social advance in which the battle of science and religion and the former's triumph were key motifs. Recent historical studies suggest a more complex story, even if still one of sociocultural conflict. At least with respect to the history of higher educational institutions, it seems that until the late nineteenth century it was less a story of global warfare between religion and science than one of local conflicts combined with efforts at cultural coexistence.

Here I can do little more than gesture toward this more complex story. Modern western universities have their roots in late medieval Europe (roughly from the twelfth and thirteenth centuries). Medieval universities at the time were largely secular in their curriculum. The foundation was translations into Latin of Greek and Arabic scientific and literary texts. The curriculum consisted of grammar, rhetoric, arithmetic, logic, music, geometry, astronomy, and philosophy. In particular, the natural philosophy and ethics of Aristotle were central to medieval universities. How was a curriculum built around pagan knowledges justified in the heart of Christendom? Such knowledges were understood as helping to reveal God's creation and wisdom; and as essential for comprehending theological truths (Grant 1984). In other words, Christianity provided a religious-moral framework for what was fundamentally a secular and "scientific" curriculum. To be sure, there were conflicts over the irreligious implications of pagan knowledges, in particular, the anti-Christian aspects of Aristotelianism. Nevertheless, Aristotle's natural philosophy remained at the core of Western universities until the late seveteenth century. The shift at this point was less anti-Christian than a revolt against an Aristotelian "teleological" Ptolemic cosmology in favor of the new "mechanistic" heliocentric scientific worldview.

Of course the dynamics of modern universities with regard to the relationship between religion and science varied considerably from nation to nation. For example, French universities emerged initially outside the church and, both institutionally and culturally, in antagonism to it. In his brilliant sketch of the history of educational thought and practice in France, Durkheim (1977) refers to the deep hostility of the church toward universities which was based not only on the latter's threat to the authority of the former. "The truth is that religion does not feature at all in the curriculum of the period [thirteenth-fourteenth centuries]." He argues that only after the Reformation did religious education as such appear in the colleges. By the *ancien régime*, with its close link of church and state, the church exercised considerable control over colleges and universities (Anderson 1975; Barnard 1969). Yet the faculties of theology, law, medicine, and liberal arts remained largely secular and oriented to career concerns. Universities virtually disappeared during the French Revolution only to be resuscitated under Napoleon, but formally controlled by the state, not the church. In the course of the nineteenth century, historians emphasize a shift away from the explicitly Christian aims of higher education to an emphasis on nationalism and the making of loyal citizens. The secularization of the moral framework of education, and the diminished role of the church in higher education, explains the efforts by Catholics to create a parallel system of religious education by the late nineteenth century.

In contrast to France, where the state played a major role in founding and shaping modern universities into secular, nationalist institutions, American universities were typically founded by churches and had an explictly Christian mission. Religion was integral to American higher education from the founding of Harvard College in 1636 by English Puritans through the period of expansion in the mid nineteenth century. For example, college presidents – and often faculty – were typically clergymen, attendance at daily chapel service was often compulsory, and Christianity provided the overarching moral framework for education. Nevertheless, the curriculum was largely secular. How did evangelical Protestants justify a Christian institution that promoted the scientization of knowledge? Although conflict was by no means absent, the Protestant elite viewed science as a divine vessel whose value was to provide evidence of the order and perfection of God's creation (e.g., Hovenkamp 1978; Marsden 1994). American Protestantism and science were posed in a harmony, even if, as it turns out, it was fragile and unstable. Indeed, by the late nineteenth century, harmony gave way to antagonism as science increasingly broke free of its religious anchor, and as compulsory chapel service, even Sunday service, was repealed, as sectarian language was expunged from the curriculum, as direct assaults surfaced on key doctrines of evangelical Protestantism such as creationism and miracles, and as positivist epistemologies challenged the authority of biblical revelation (Hovenkamp 1978; Marsden 1994).

In considering the relationship between religion and science in modern Western societies, we should keep in mind that until the late nineteenth century, universities were *not* the major sites of knowledge and cultural production. In France, the Revolution abolished all twenty-two French universities. Higher education did not come to a halt, as the faculties of theology, law, and medicine continued to dispense professional degrees, even if the standards were low and students were scarce (Zeldin 1967). The important scientific, intellectual and cultural work, however, occurred outside universities. Even after Napolean established a state-based, national university system (the "Imperial University"), saloons, learned societies, and scientific academies were the cultural centers and the *grandes écoles* became the major institutions of higher education (Anderson 1975; Vaughan and Archer 1971; Fox 1980).

The primary site then for the struggle between religion and science was in public life – in the saloons and learned societies and in the political conflicts over tolerance and censorship. And, if we are to believe the historian Margaret Jacobs (1988: 105), even as the church exercised considerable control over the universities in the seveteenth and eighteenth centuries, the public cultures of Western European societies were rapidly becoming secularized and scientized (cf. Westfall 1986). Peter Gay offers a slightly more nuanced description:

Not only the poor, not only ignorant country clerics, but also professors and even bishops continued to believe in the Christian God . . . In country after country [in the eighteenth century] social and political conflicts were still fought out on religious issues, and there were many thousands of educated Europeans . . . who believed in the efficacy of prayer . . . Theological debates retained much of their old vigor and much of their popularity. To speak of secularization, therefore, is to speak of a subtle shift of attention: religious institutions and religious explanations of events were slowly being displaced from the center of life to its periphery. (Gay 1966: 338)

The gradual secularization of Western cultures suggests perhaps a far more intense cultural conflict outside the walls of academe, a conflict over the very soul of France – and European – nations.

4 As in France, universities in the US were marginal and secondary to cultural production until perhaps the beginning of this century. Intellectual life was centered in coffeehouses, learned societies, scientific associations, libraries, public lectures, museums, clubs, weekly societies, societies for useful knowledge, and, in the nineteenth century, in a developing culture of weekly and monthly newspapers and magazines (Bender 1987; Greene 1976; Kohlstedt 1976; Oleson 1976). This nonuniversity intellectual culture was decisively shaped by a Protestant elite intent on creating a nation of educated citizens and national cultural respectability (cf. Bender 1984; 1987). Moreover, serious scientific and humanistic studies occurred outside colleges and universities – in institutions such as the American Academy of Arts and Sciences (1780), the Franklin Institute (1824), and the Academy of the Natural Sciences of Philadelphia (1812).

The expansion of higher education in the late nineteenth century, and even through the early decades of this century remained fairly limited in its impact on American intellectual life. As late as 1870 there were only 52,286 students registered in *all* American colleges and universities. This amounts to about 1.68 percent of the population aged 18-21. By 1900, only 4 percent of this college-aged population was enrolled in higher education (Larson 1984: 41). Through most of the nineteenth century, the faculty in even the best universities typically numbered fewer than 10. For example, in Brown University in 1800 there were 6 faculty for a student body of 100 (Barber 1988). In 1817, Yale University enrolled 275 undergraduates with a faculty of 10. As late as 1860, Columbia University awarded just 69 bachelor degrees, but then there were only 13 professors. Stanford University opened its doors in 1869 with 9 faculty and 40 students.

The turn of the century witnessed considerable changes in higher education.

For example, in 1898, Columbia University awarded 274 bachelor degrees, 21 Ph.D.s and its faculty grew to 339. Whereas in the 1890s there were only 20 chairs in political economy in the whole country, by 1900 the figure jumped to 51 (Coats 1988). Indicative of a shift in intellectual culture, the years between the 1880s and 1905 saw the formation of national discipline-based associations, including the American Historical Association (1884), the American Political Associaton in 1903, and the American Sociological Society in 1905 (Haskell 1977: 145). These considerations must be kept in perspective. For example, while the undergraduate student population jumped to over 15,000 in 1920, this was still only 8 percent of the 18-21 population. By 1940, the figure jumped to 5 million (still under 15 percent of the 18-21 population). The major shift occurred in the postwar period as 30 percent of the 18-21 population attended higher education in 1950. Similarly, while the early decades of this century saw a dramatic takeoff in graduate education in the United States, it was dramatic from the perspective of the 1800s, not from the vantage point of the 1960s. For example, 1,500 institutions of higher education offered graduate programs in 1900, but 90 percent of American doctorates were produced by just 14 institutions. Again, by 1920 over 15,000 students were in graduate programs but this amounted to less than 5 percent of the 18-24 population. The figure increased to almost a half million by 1960 or almost 25 percent of the 18-24 population (Larson 1984)

Although the modern university has its roots in the period between 1890 and the 1920s, its development and impact as the above suggests, were rather limited. Consider the institutional evolution of American sociology. The American Sociological Society (ASS) wasn't formed until 1905. By 1920 its membership just barely reached 1000, many of whom were not sociologists. Less than 15 doctoral degrees in sociology were awarded in 1920 (Turner and Turner 1990: 29-30). By 1940, ASS membership had virtually remained the same, while some 50 doctorates in sociology were granted in the same year (Turner and Turner 1990: 63-64). The major takeoff of sociology occurred in the post-World War II period. By 1960, ASS membership grew to about 7000; in 1970, over 600 doctorates in sociology were awarded (Turner and Turner 1990: 139).

Nonuniversity intellectual life remained vital and the lines between the two were considerably blurred at least through the 1950s. The proliferation of magazines, newspapers, journals, book clubs, and mass-produced books as well as a culture of public lectures allowed for the continuation of an independent intellectual – schooled in the human sciences and humanities but self-supporting through writing or public talks. Indeed, some of the most important social thinkers of the day lived as independent intellectuals (e.g., Herbert Croly, Max Eastman, Randolph Bourne, Emma Goldman, Walter Lipmann, Sinclair Lewis, Lincoln Steffens, Lewis Mumford, Edmund Wilson, and Margaret Sanger). Moreover, academics such as John Dewey, Charles Beard, and Charlotte Perkins Gilman, and sociologists such as Robert Park, E. A. Ross, and W. E. B. Du Bois, were not academic intellectuals, as we might currently understand them, but more like what Jacoby (1987) called "public intellectuals," with one foot in academia and the other squarely in public life.

5 The consolidation of the university in the post-World War II United States did not witness the end or even necessarily the decline of the "public intellectual." Nonacademic sites of social knowledge production and distribution, from those forged by the so-called new social movements to public cultures created by evangelical Christians and "neoconservatives" remain a vital part of American public intellectual culture. Critics of American public life such as Jacoby (1987) fail to consider adequately the extent to which a multiplicity of *public cultures* has been institutionalized in postwar America. These cultures function as social bases for cultural production or the making of diverse knowledges – sometimes independent of, sometimes interdependent with, colleges and universities.

Feminist, gay, African American, Latino, Asian American, evangelical Christian, and disabled public cultures have established their own publishing companies, magazines, newspapers, newsletters, journals, and culture of public lectures, media discourses and representations, conferences, and experts. They have sometimes established their own colleges, academic disciplines, departments, television and radio stations. Many of these public cultures have evolved distinctive knowledges – their own epistemologies (e.g., Afrocentrism, radical feminism, queer theory, evangelical Christianity) and their own historical and social knowleges and political ideologies (on African American public cultures, see "The Black Public Sphere," a special issue of *Public Culture* [1994]; regarding lesbian/gay public cultures, see Escoffier 1992). Moreover, in some important ways, these knowledges express the particular experience, distinctive values, and interests of its producers and may not be shared by individuals who do not participate in these public cultures. I am not saying that there is no cultural overlap between public cultures but that we should not assume the extent or depth of such overlap and that we should recognize points of sometimes sharp epistemological divergence, even opposition. I address some of the epistemological implications of this pluralism in the last section of this chapter. I do not have the space to address the social and political implications of conceeding, indeed defending, a strong politics of difference. For efforts to think through a democratic politic of difference, one that would acknowledge that differences run deep (extend into core cultural values) and are not transient, see Appiah 1994; Fraser 1992; Kymlicka 1989; Minow 1990; Young 1990; Taylor 1994.

6 We need to be mindful that Marx could have justified his focus on labor, mode of production, and class without appealing to the epistemic and ontological primary of labor. He could have proposed strictly pragmatic rationales. He might have appealed to what his conceptual strategy can do or what kinds of knowledges and social practices it makes possible. For example, he might have argued that a materialist analysis can spotlight certain economic and class dynamics which are important if one wishes to assess liberal-bourgeois ideology or if one wishes to contribute to the making of a critical working class culture. Marx did not deploy a pragmatic justificatory strategy, in part, because he was as much a part of the Enlightenment culture which designated science as the marker of valid knowledge and which aspired to a universal knowledge as the rivals he criticized.

7 Foundational theorizing among sociological theorists is not of one type. There are differences, for example, with regard to the degree that they are tied to scientism or entail a critique of scientism. For example, Giddens (1984) and Alexander (1982) aim to defend a foundational social discourse that is in some ways troubling to a science/nonscience binary in that they acknowledge nonempirical, theoretical and normative pressuppositions. By contrast, sociological theorists such as Collins (1975) and Blau (1975) press for a concept of sociological knowledge that reproduces a fairly rigid science/nonscience binary. But, and this point needs to be underscored, all foundational sociological theorizing, even when not bound to a rigid science/nonscience binary, has been wedded tightly to a culture of scientific knowledge which pressures theorizing to outline a universal language of the social, to provide a general foundation for knowledge, to delineate legitimate from illegitimate knowledges on the basis of strong notions of truth as correspondence of word and world, and to endorse a notion of the progress of reason and history.

8 In this regard, much sociological theory has assumed not only the constancy or universality of the knowing subject but of the object of knowledge – "the social." It is believed that the object of knowledge is constant or that reflection on the social, if governed by the same scientific logic or sustained "rational" reflection, will encounter a series of identical problems producing a common dialogue across centuries. Sociological theorists have imagined that the problem of action and order, the agency/structure or micro/macro relation, and the division between positivist and interpretive conceptual strategies mark out precisely such a universal terrain of social knowledge.

The rise, or perhaps the "mainstreaming," of social knowledges such as feminism, queer theory, postcolonial studies or cultural studies, which have reconfigured the social, suggest the relativization of sociological theory. By that I mean that the framing of the social and its problems by sociological theorists represent just one tradition of theorizing the social. Consider Western feminists for whom the core controversies, if one can even speak in such broad terms, revolve around the meaning of gender, the origins of male dominance, the interconnection of gender, race, sexuality, and class, the relation between the private and public realm, questions of identity and difference, the unconscious and desire, and so on. Similarly, queer studies is not debating the question of action or order or the micro-macro division or whether knowledge is interpretive or nomological but questions about the social and historical formation of bodies, desires, and identities, of identity and difference, and of the role of nature and history in producing "sexualities." One conclusion is that sociological theory is simply one tradition of speaking of the social, one language of the social – insightful and perhaps useful in addressing certain kinds of questions for particular kinds of purposes but not others. Such a relativizing of sociology does not denigrate or diminish its value, any more than relativizing feminism or British cultural studies would devalue these "traditions." This line of thinking simply registers a large doubt about "theory" being anything more than a tradition and receiving any warrant or authority for its language and conceptual strategies beyond what kinds of things a particular tradition allows one to do or say. For some recent efforts to begin to develop a pragmatic approach to social theory and analysis, see Antonio (1989; 1991), Fraser and Nicholson (1994), Joas (1993), Rochberg-Halton (1986), and Shalin (1992).

9 I recognize that modern foundational theories, including disciplinary theories, are defended, in part, by the claim that they promote human progress, for example, by fashioning a sphere of "reason" or a realm of general standards of truth and morality that allow rational critique and social consensus. I do not wish to deny, moreover, that there are emancipatory consequences to such discourses. My chief point is that such discourses conceal an unconscious political logic that is operative which is inconsistent in *its* operation and consequences with this enlightened aim. This is a repressive politic of identity that is built into the very same premises that are tied to its emancipatory interest. The question between, if you will, "modern" and "postmodern" or pragmatic thinkers is whether or not one believes such foundational moves are necessary to secure an emancipatory epistemological space or whether the costs of such strategies outweigh the benefits.

10 A parallel argument is made by Lyotard (1984). He speaks of the decentering of knowledges, the awareness of the multiplicity of language games and knowledges, and the surfacing of a postmodern scientific culture driven by an agonistic impulse or a focus on innovation, difference, disrupting consensus. Of course, Rorty's (1979, 1982) critique of foundationalism and his exploration of a post-philosophical "pragmatic" culture that is organized around "conversation" and "edification" also points to a reconfigured culture of knowledge. See also the suggestive remarks by Michael McConnell (1993a, 1993b), who defends a consistently "postmodern" or epistemologically pluralistic intellectual culture from a broadly Christian perspective.

11 I read both Rorty and Lyotard as suggesting a logical and social critique. The epistemological critique pivots on the "deconstruction" of a subject-object dualism and a representational view of language while the social critique suggests a culture which relentlessly exposes interest in reason and relativizes truth and moral claims to claims of a group, community, and tradition.

12 The blurring of the disciplines, the shift to pragmatic rationales for knowledge, and a culture of epistemological pluralism, would not mean the delegitimation of the university. We should not forget that for most of the history of the American university, through at least World War I, academic knowledges and the disciplines were justified by their often explicit link to a Christian evangelical culture that valued scientific knowledges as a divine path to the making of a Christian civic republic. With the secularization of American public culture in this century, the disciplines were viewed as tools in the making of a good society. In a pragmatic culture, the university would find its moral justication, not perhaps as a tool in the building of a Christian nation but as building a multicultural democratic nation. For efforts to frame the university in a multi-cultural

context that aims to preserve a "strong" notion of social differences and promote democracy, see Barber (1992), McConnell (1993a, 1993b), Marsden (1994).

3 Relativizing sociology

1 Williams (1961: 41–45) did not abandon a literary-aesthetic approach to analyzing cultural forms. Unlike his successors, Williams retained the belief that one of the tasks of cultural studies was to identify general or universal aesthetic standards which can serve as norms of cultural judgement. See the comments of Stanley Aronowitz (1993: ch. 3).

2 The parallel between French "postmodern" social theory and British cultural studies which I suggested is somewhat forced and perhaps misguided to the extent that the latter have been much more friendly to marxism than the former. Whereas Baudrillard, Lyotard, and Foucault critique marxism and abandon its productivist, totalizing, class based, political economic driven hegemonic model of society, this is not entirely the case with at least much of British cultural studies. As Angela McRobbie (1992) has recently suggested, "it would be wrong to underestimate the extent to which neo-Marxist theory informed a good deal of cultural analysis in the ten-year period between 1975 and 1985" (719; also see Sherwood et al. 1993). It is impossible to read British subcultural studies (e.g., Cohen 1972; Hall et al. 1978; Hebdige 1976; see Brake 1980), for example, without comprehending the centrality of the marxist problematic and analytic. Nevertheless, I do not think British cultural studies managed, even then, a satisfactory or comfortable integration of semiotics and marxism. The late eighties and nineties has seen considerable movement within the discourses of cultural studies away from marxism as a master theory. Marxism is, I think, being positioned as in an equivalent relation to, say, feminism, race-based theory, or postcolonial social criticism (see McRobbie 1992). For a retrospective view emphasizing stress points or a looser relation between marxism and British culture studies, see Hall (1992).

3 The slippage, at least ideally, between class, social structure and culture in much of British cultural studies is commented upon by David Morley.

> In short, the relation classes/meaning-systems has to be fundamentally reworked by taking into account the full effectivity of the discursive level. Discursive formations intervene between classes and languages. They intervene in such a way as to prevent or forestall any attempt to read the level of the operation of language back in any simple or reductive way to economic classes. Thus we cannot deduce which discursive frameworks will be mobilized in particular reader/text encounters from the level of the socio-economic position of the readers. But position in the social structure may be seen to have a structuring and limiting effect on the repertoire of discursive or decoding strategies available to different sectors of an audience. They will have an effect on the pattern of the distribution of dis-

cursive sectors of an audience. They will have an effect on the pattern of the distribution of discursive repertoires. What is more, the key elements of the social structure which delimit the range of competences in particular audiences may not be referable in any exclusive way to class . . . The key sites for the distribution of discursive sets and competences are probably . . . the family and the school . . . Other formations – for example, gender . . . may also have a formative and structuring effect, not only on which specific discourses will be in play in any specific text/reader encounter, but also in defining the range and repertoire of performance codes. (1992: 70).

This was written in the 1990s and is significant in at least two respects. First, it is in part a reaction to the class-driven marxism of at least some British cultural studies despite affirming the autonomy of cultural analysis. In some texts of British cultural studies there has been a tendency to (1) reduce social structure to a political economic concept of class and (2) to read media representations, discourses, and popular culture as an extension or subspecies of class dynamics or as a displaced articulation of class politics or as a way to negotiate class hegemony by voluntary or ideological means. Secondly, this statement shows just how far recent cultural studies, even in Britain, is moving away from marxism. As the autonomy of sign systems is defended, as gender, race, nationalism, or sexuality is installed as a social structuring principle irreducible to the logic of class or capital, it is perhaps not misguided to describe this conceptual terrain as "post-marxist" (see McRobbie 1992).

4 To further clarify this point, I am alluding to a body of social analysis, much of it done by professors of English or film, which often relies heavily on poststructuralist ideas. Texts, whether literary or popular, official documents (census reports) or aesthetic objects, are approached as organized by cultural codes which are understood as forms of knowledge. That is, these codes are said to structure our perceptions and experiences; they define the universe of objects and their "normal" operation and order. Thus, social analysis involves exposing the knowledges that operate in texts which contribute to the construction of normative and normalizing models of self and institutional life. For example, television programs or popular music might be analyzed with an eye to their construction of feminine/masculine or hetero/homosexual or Occidental/Oriental binaries, symbolic figures which are themselves "social forces" no less than, say, law or the control of material resources. For further elaboration of this genre of social analysis, see Seidman (1995).

5 My point, I suppose, is that the category of "the empirical" is hardly one that can or should go uncontested. To say it differently, "the empirical" can never be anything more than "conventional" or in Foucauldian terms implicated in a particular power/knowledge regime. To the extent that "the empirical" serves in some western societies as a marker of the real and the true, such that to claim a belief has an empirical basis is to give a "rational" warrant for that belief, and alternatively, to describe belief as nonempirical is to withhold such a warrant or

is to assume that the belief is held for nonrational considerations, it is important that the category of the empirical be "deconstructed" or contested by exposing its socially conventional and hence political status. This is especially true in the context of a scientific culture which aims to control the conventions of "the empirical" and therefore to control what can count as knowledge and who has the authority to speak knowledgeably. Deconstructing "the empirical," or revealing it as a social artifice entangled in power, does not mean abandoning empirical analysis. We need empirical knowledges to get things done, to map social relations, to criticize social injustices, and to legislate policies, advocate social reforms, and so on. The question is the status of such empirical claims and the role of the empirical in authorizing knowledges. Deconstructing "the empirical" means that we recognize that discursive conflicts, even ones about the social, can never be resolved by appeals to the empirical alone and that such discourses should acknowledge their own entanglement in power and therefore, at times, when pragmatically useful, bring ethical reflection and political considerations into social discourse.

4 The refusal of sexual difference

1 Some twenty years after Bowman lamented the absence of a sociology of sexuality, Edward Sagarin (1971) reiterated this criticism. "Here and there an investigation, a minor paper, a little data, particularly in the literature of criminology . . . marked the totality of sex literature in sociology" (p. 384).
2 Placing all innovative homosexual studies in the 1970s and 1980s under the rubric of social constructionism and the project of minority theory admittedly simplifies matters. In particular, it marginalizes a powerful current of lesbian-feminist inspired theorizing (e.g., Rich [1980] 1983; MacKinnon 1989; Ferguson 1989). Much of this work was less concerned with issues of essentialism and constructionism or the rise of homosexual identities than analyzing the social forces creating, maintaining, and resisting the institution of heterosexuality. Departing from a tendency in constructionist studies to approach lesbian and gay theory as separate from feminism, this literature insists on tracing the link between a system of compulsive heterosexuality and patterns of male dominance.

8 Transfiguring sexual identity

1 The terms homosexual, lesbian and gay carry multiple meanings in US public culture and in this essay. Generally, I have used the term homosexual to refer both broadly to men who have sex with men and more specifically to men (men are the focus of this chapter) who have sex with men but who do not take this to be the basis of a social or subcultural identity. Gay refers, again broadly, to men who have sex with men and to the segments of that population who take this as a basis of a social or subcultural identity. Obviously, the terms homo-

sexual, gay, or lesbian in no way should suggest a distinctive human or personality type or an homogeneous social identity. As we say today, gay is more a subject position carrying multiple, fluctuating, and contestable meanings.

2 For examples of the public identification of AIDS as a homosexual disease, see "Gay Plague has Instituted Fear of the Unknown," *The Philadelphia Inquirer*, June 20, 1982; "New Homosexual Disorder Worries Health Officials," *New York Times*, May 11, 1982; "Killer Gay Disease Spreads to Kids," *New York Post*, Dec. 11, 1982; "Homosexual Plague Strikes New Victim," *Newsweek*, August 23, 1982.

3 CDC Task Force study, *Annals of Internal Medicine*, 99, August, 1983.

4 Richard Lyons, "Sex in America: Conservative Attitudes Prevail," *New York Times*, Oct. 4, 1983; "Homosexuals Find a Need to Reassess," *New York Times*, May 29, 1983; "Homosexuals Confronting a Time of Change," *New York Times*, June 16, 1983; "AIDS Education Takes on an Urgency Within the Homosexual Community," *New York Times*, Sept. 22, 1985.

11 The politics of sexual difference in late twentieth-century America

1 Nineteenth-century middle America did not proscribe all sexual-intimate differences. For example, youth dating and courting which involved sexual-affectional intimacy were legitimate (Rothman 1987; Lystra 1989) and same-sex intimacies, especially between women, acquired a degree of social acceptance (see note 2).

2 The extent to which nineteenth-century American culture was not organized around sexual identity categories is further suggested by the lack of a language of identity to describe same-sex intimacies (Faderman 1981; D'Emilio and Freedman 1988; Smith-Rosenberg 1975).

3 There is another aspect of the politics of sexual difference that should at least be mentioned. This relates to the formation of public sexual communities and the pressure they exert to have their differences publicly recognized and valued. To the extent that sexual communities such as the lesbian and gay community or the S/M community elaborate unique social perspectives (e.g., distinctive epistemological standpoints) and values (e.g., sexual-intimate values) or can be shown to exhibit distinctive modes of social oppression (e.g., the ability to "pass" suggests the need for unique strategies to address job or housing discrimination which typically takes the form less of direct discrimination than anticipatory discrimination), a case can be made that the state and social institutions should respect and respond to these social differences. In other words, the formation of public sexual cultures, like the formation of feminist or race-based or religious-based public cultures raises forcefully the question of "group or minority recognition or rights." Political philosophers (e.g., Dyke 1995; Kymlicka 1995b; Margalit and Raz 1995; Phillips 1995) have made the case that differences around say race, gender, or ableness in a society that discriminates along these dimensions makes them into sociocultural or collective differences. To the extent that such differences get elaborated into cultural communities and

to the extent that some of these differences "run deep" or extend into core values and beliefs and practices, doubts have been raised about a strictly individualistic-liberal model of a democratic polity (cf. Connolly 1991; Minow 1990; Taylor 1989; Young 1989).

12 Difference and democracy

1 In contrast to nations such as Israel which fuse religion and nationhood or Germany which has closely associated birth origin to citizenship, the United States attaches no substantive criterion to citizenship. In this nation, the separation of religion, ethnicity or national origin from citizenship or national identity shapes a public culture which encourages differences in private life and civil life but does not entail any recognition of these differences in the eyes of the law and public policy. It is indeed this lack of significance for citizenship or national inclusion of particularistic cultural ties and identities which is thought to make possible a socially diverse civil society without threatening nationhood or national unity. This view of citizenship in America received a powerful theoretical framing in Talcott Parsons' (1971) idea of a societal community.

2 Questions can, and should, be raised about the democratic implications of a position defending epistemological pluralism. This is especially the case in the context of strong traditions in the West which have favored the view that democracy is possible only if one can mark off knowledge from belief or truth from prejudice or ideology. While I cannot engage this issue in any detail, I can at least allude to the contours of what such an argument might look like.

My own "postmodern" position is defined in relation to the dominant cultural traditions of the Enlightenment. The latter has been defended on the grounds that it both respects difference and sustains a unifying and regulatory and therefore "rational" framework. "Modern" cultural traditions, whether liberal (e.g., Kant, Mill, Rawls) or left (e.g., Habermas) assert universal standards of truth, morality and beauty; aspire to articulate one metalanguage to resolve disputes over defining the social and natural orders, and other metalanguages to adjudicate value or normative conflicts. In the sphere of truth, the metalanguage has been, of course, science; in the sphere of morality it is ethics; in the sphere of beauty it is aesthetics. These metalanguages aim to regulate conflicts; they are supposed to serve as the court of last appeal when disagreement threatens to escalate into division and the recourse to manipulation or coercion. These metalanguages function at least as regulative ideals and promise to keep differences from bursting the bounds of a rational order. The appeal to metalanguages of truth, morality and beauty is said to make possible the consensual and civil negotiation of difference. Roughly speaking this is the promise of the culture of the Enlightenment and the basis for its claim to be on the side of civility and democracy.

The aim of elaborating metalanguages of cultural order, for example, to assert science as *the* language for understanding the natural and social worlds, has been criticized for perpetuating social hierarchies which privilege the west, men, the middle class, heterosexual, reproductive norms, and so on. Enlightenment universalism, for example, assumptions regarding the unity of humanity or the presumption of one standard of truth, have been contested by critics who maintain that humanity and knowledge are marked by differences of, say, gender, race, or nationality. The claims to the unity of the subject are, in some recent thinking, dissolved into the proliferation of differences as each axis of self and society e.g., gender, sexuality, or ethnicity, intersect in unique ways yielding a new infinite diversity of identities, selves or subjects. Efforts to impose intellectual or epistemic unity are seen as limiting difference and creating boundaries with the aim of imposing normalizing discursive and social norms.

The democratic implications of these critical or "deconstructive" gestures should be evident. The critique of Enlightenment foundationalism and universalism anticipates the public surfacing of hitherto submerged and subjugated voices and interests. In a "postmodern" culture, the existence of three metalanguages demarcating the boundaries of legitimate and illegitimate speech and deciding upon validity claims would pass into a plurality of heterogeneous metalanguages. For example, in the sphere of "the social" the privileging of social science would give way to the proliferation of languages of the social – scientific, religious, literary, poetic, and political. In place of a hierarchy of knowledges determined along the single axis of science/nonscience or truth/falsity, we would speak of different genres, vocabularies, conventions, and purposes of social talk. Again, the democratic implications should be obvious. A public sphere that legitimates multiple knowledges would recognize diverse cultural traditions and communities. A "postmodern" culture would, in principle, expand public debate over matters of social and political importance; it would allow hitherto excluded and subjugated voices to be heard and their interests and values to shape public life.

But surely, one might reasonably ask, there are anti-democratic implications to such a postmodern culture. If there are no agreed upon metalanguages to appeal to in the face of interpretive disputes, how would we avoid recourse to manipulation and coercion? Would not talk give way to force. If the public sphere is composed of a heterogeneity of cultural traditions and knowledges lacking a common language of truth and morality, would we not be endorsing a condition of social polarization and civil war? Would not a postmodern public sphere slide into a *Realpolitik* by denying the conditions of rational consensus?

Of course, I can only gesture towards a response. In a culture organized around the principle of difference, pragmatic justificatory strategies would replace the standard epistemological strategies of the Enlightenment which involve a standard of judgment anchored in a logic of the correspondence of word and world. The foundational and universalistic languages of Enlightenment culture would give way to a pragmatic culture whose justificatory rationales would feature a vocabulary of interest, situational advantage, consequentialist reasoning, local norms, and provisional agreements. In such a

culture, knowledges and norms would be provisionally and situationally negotiated with attention to the specificity of situation and consequence. In place of
metanarratives would be a multiplicity of cultural traditions and "local" narratives; rhetorics of persuasion would be multileveled, moving back and forth
between appeals to situational advantage and broader appeals to cultural traditions and ideals (see the epilogue).

3 The so-called new social movements (NSM) are unified neither in politics nor
social theory. It is perhaps useful to distinguish between at least certain strains
of identity politics and a more "postmodern" politic of difference. Although
identity-based political movements and theorizing has defended a version of the
politics of difference, it has often been figured in decidedly "modernistic" terms.
Identity politics has characteristically defended an epistemology and politics
grounded in an essentialist or unitary conception of the gendered, racial or
sexual self. For example, feminists have frequently invoked women's shared
experience, values or traits, for example, their "maternal thinking" or a relational self or an ethic of caring to justify a feminist concept of values, knowledge and politics. As important as identity politics has been it operates within a
decidedly modern framework.

A postmodern politic and theory appears sometime in the early 1980s in the
US, England, and Australia. In part, this development relates to the failure of
identity politics to press forward its progressive agenda in the face of a conservative backlash and in part due to the surfacing of differences within these
movements which sometimes criticized them for being "normalizing." I interpret at least some strains of a "postmodern" politics of difference as an effort to
rethink identity and politics for the purpose of reclaiming the oppositional force
of the NSM. In this regard, the postmodern decentering of the subject, the displacement of the science/ideology, knowledge/power, subject/object binaries,
the assertion of post-scientific knowledges, for example, deconstruction, Queer
Theory, and postmodern feminism, aims to reconfigure the dominant knowl-
edge/power regime *in order to imagine a radical pluralistic democratic politic.*
Such a politic would be organized around the value of social differences, the
intersection of body and institutional politics, multiple intersecting struggles,
coalitional agents, and a politics of anti-normalization. A postmodern politics
relocates identity from a language of the self and authenticity to the terrain of
discursive power and institutional practice; it abandons appeals to essentialist
ontologies of the self in favor of a vocabulary of multiple, composite subjects
or situational coalitional subjects, for example, Haraway's cyborgs or the
designation "people of color" or "Queer." A "postmodern" politics might
imagine collectivities as based on affinities related to social location, interest,
and situational advantage, rather than based on appeals to a unitary social identity; it would abandon the millenarianism of identity and class politics in favor
of a politics of permanent rebellion whose aim is to fashion a social space organized around the principle of difference, participatory democracy, and playful
innovation.

4 Until recently, the dominant strain of Dutch immigrant policy might be described as "integration with the preservation of identity." Ethnic minority "integration" meant learning the Dutch language and history as well as acquiring Dutch citizenship. The "preservation of identity" was to be accomplished through either creating ethnic schools (e.g., Muslim or Turkish schools) or instituting some form of bilingual schooling, providing cultural facilities and social services to the new ethnic immigrants, creating work and leisure associations, and establishing "participatory boards" (*inspraakorganen*) that allow each ethnic minority to participate in government policy (Prins 1995). In the last few years this quasi-pillarized view of immigrants, and the broad policy of "integration with the preservation of identity," has come under criticism by those who voice a stridently assimilationist, nationalist sentiment. As Prins makes clear these efforts to construct a national identity often have recourse to decidedly Western, liberal, Christian values which are exclusionary towards the growing population of Muslims, Turks, and Indian peoples in The Netherlands.

Epilogue

1 The pragmatic position that I outline here could be plausibly described as "postmodern," at least in certain understandings of the latter notion. To the extent that both perspectives, in some of their formations, assume a postfoundationalism and a "strong" version of the thesis of the interrelation of power/knowledge, there is an emphasis on a "pragmatics" in place of a "logic" of knowledge. However, I am not at all sure that others who articulate a postmodern perspective would subscribe to all or even most of the positions outlined here. If forced to distinguish between pragmatism and postmodernism, I would emphasize their broader views of self, modernity, history, and politics. For example, pragmatists, if we take say Dewey and Rorty as exemplars, being more friendly toward "liberal" versions of the Enlightenment tradition than postmodernists, if we take say mid-career Foucault or Lyotard as exemplars (see Rorty [1982] for one version of this argument).

References

Adam, Barry. 1987. *The Rise of a Gay and Lesbian Movement*. Boston: Twayne.

Adorno, Theodor and Max Horkheimer. 1972. *Dialectic of Enlightenment*. New York: Herder & Herder.

Agger, Ben. 1992. *Cultural Studies as Critical Theory*. Washington, DC: Falmer Press.

Ahmad, Aijaz. 1992. *In Theory*. London: Verso.

Alexander, Jeffrey. 1982. *Theoretical Logic in Sociology*. Vol. 1. Berkeley: University of California Press.

  1989. "Durkheimian Sociology and Cultural Studies Today," in Alexander, *Structure and Meaning*. New York: Columbia University Press.

  1991. "Sociological Theory and the Claim to Reason: Why the End is Not in Sight." *Sociological Theory* 9 (Fall):147–153.

  1995. *Fin de Siècle Social Theory*. New York: Verso.

Alexander, Jeffrey and Phillip Smith. 1993. "The Discourse of Civil Society: A New Proposal for Cultural Studies. *Theory and Society* 22: 151–207.

Allison, Dorothy. 1981. "Lesbian Politics in the 80s." *New York Native* December 7–20.

  1983. "Sexual Babel," *New York Native* 11–24 April 1983.

  1985. "Sex Talk," *New York Native* 29 July 11–Aug.

Almaguer, Tomas. 1991. "Chicano Men: A Cartography of Homosexual Identity and Behavior," *Differences* 3: 75–100.

Althusser, Louis. 1971. "On Ideology and Ideological State Apparatuses," in *Lenin and Philosophy and Other Essays*. New York: Monthly Review Press.

Altman, Dennis. 1971. *Homosexual Oppression and Liberation*. New York: Avon.

  1979. *Coming Out in the Seventies*. Sydney: Wild and Woolley.

  1982. *The Homosexualization of America*. Boston: Beacon Press.

  1984. "AIDS: The Politicization of an Epidemic," *Socialist Review*, 14: 95–115.

  1985. *AIDS and the Mind of America*. New York: Doubleday.

Ammerman, Nancy. 1991. "North American Protestant Fundamentalism," in *Fundamentalisms Observed*, ed. Martin Marty and R. Scott Appleby. Chicago: University of Chicago Press.

Andersen, Margaret. 1983. *Thinking about Women*. New York: Macmillan.

Anderson, R. D. 1975. *Education in France 1848–1870*. Oxford: Clarendon Press.

Antonio, Robert. 1989. "The Normative Foundations of Emancipatory Theory: Evolutionary versus Pragmatic Perspectives," *American Journal of Sociology* 94: 721–748.

    1991. "Postmodern Storytelling Versus Pragmatic Truth-Seeking: The Discursive Bases of Social Theory," *Sociological Theory* 9: 154–163.

Anzaldua, Gloria. 1987. *Borderlands/La Frontera*. San Francisco: Aunt Lute Foundation Books.

Anzaldua, Gloria and Cherrie Moraga, eds. 1983. *This Bridge Called My Back*. New York: Kitchen Table Press.

Appiah, Anthony K. 1994. "Identity, Authenticity, Survival: Multicultural Societies and Social Reproduction," in *Multiculturalism*, ed. Amy Gutmann. Princeton: Princeton University Press.

Aronowitz, Stanley. 1995. *Science as Power*. Minneapolis: University of Minnesota Press.

    1993. *Roll Over Beethoven*. Middletown: Wesleyan University Press.

Asad, Talal, ed. 1975. *Anthropology and the Colonial Encounter*. London: Ithaca Press. 1975.

Asante, Molefi Kete. 1987. *The Afrocentric Idea*. Philadelphia: Temple University Press.

Atkinson, Ti-Grace. 1974. *Amazon Odyssey*. New York: Links Books.

Ault, Amber. 1996. "The Dilemma of Identity: Bi Women's Negotiations," in *Queer Theory/Sociology*, ed. Steven Seidman. Cambridge: Blackwell.

Bad Object-Choices, ed. 1991. *How Do I Look? Queer Film and Video*. Seattle: Bay Press.

Baker, Houston, Jr. 1994. "Critical Memory and the Black Public Sphere," *Public Culture* 7: 3–34.

Balbus, Isaac. 1982. *Marxism and Domination*. Princeton: Princeton University Press.

Ball, Stephen. 1990. *Foucault and Education*. New York: Routledge.

Barber, Benjamin. 1992. *An Aristocracy of Everyone*. New York: Oxford University Press.

Barber, William. 1988. "Political Economy and the Academic Setting before 1900: An Introduction," in *Breaking the Academic Mould*, ed. William Barber. Middletown: Wesleyan University Press.

Barnard, H. C. 1969. *Education and The French Revolution*. Cambridge: Cambridge University Press.

Barry, Kathleen. 1984. *Female Sexual Slavery*. New York: New York University Press.

Baudrillard, Jean. 1975. *The Mirror of Production*. St. Louis: Telos.

    1981. *For a Critique of the Political Economy of the Sign*. St. Louis: Telos Press.

    1983. *In the Shadow of the Silent Majorities*. New York: Semiotext[e].

    1984. *Simulations*. New York: Semiotext[e].

Bauman, Zygmunt. 1988. "Is There a Postmodern Sociology?" *Theory, Culture & Society* 5: 217–238.

——— 1991. *Modernity and Ambivalence*. Ithaca: Cornell University Press.

Bayer, Ronald. 1981. *Homosexuality and American Psychiatry*. New York: Basic Books.

Beam, Joseph, ed. 1986. *In The Life*. Boston: Alyson.

Becker, Carl. 1932. *The Heavenly City of the Eighteenth Century Philosophers*. New Haven: Yale University Press.

Becker, Howard. 1963. *Outsiders*. New York: Free Press.

Bell, Allen and Martin Weinberg. 1978. *Homosexualities*. New York: Simon and Schuster.

Bell, Arthur. 1982. "Where Gays are Going," *The Village Voice*, June 29.

Bellah, Robert, et al. 1986. *Habits of the Heart*. New York: Harper & Row.

Bender, Thomas. 1984. "The Erosion of Public Culture: Citites, Discourses, and Professional Disciplines," in *The Authority of Experts*, ed. Thomas Haskell. Bloomington: Indiana University Press.

——— 1987. *New York Intellect*. New York: Alfred A. Knopf.

Benhabib, Seyla. 1992. *Situating the Self*. New York: Routledge.

Benhabib, Siyla, ed. *Democracy and Difference*. Princeton: Princeton University Press.

Berger, Peter and Thomas Luckmann. 1967. *The Social Construction of Reality*. New York: Anchor.

Bergler, Edmund. 1956. *Homosexuality: Disease or Way of Life?* New York: Hill & Wang.

Berlant, Lauren and Elizabeth Freeman. 1993. "Queer Nationality," in *Fear of a Queer Planet*, ed. Michael Warner. Minneapolis: University of Minnesota Press.

Berlin, Isaiah. 1980. "The Counter-Enlightenment," in *Against the Current*. New York: Viking Press.

Bhabha, Homi. 1992. "Postcolonial Authority and Postmodern Guilt," in *Cultural Studies*, ed. Lawrence Grossberg et al. New York: Routledge.

Bieber, Irving, et al., eds. 1962. *Homosexuality*. New York: Basic Books.

Birken, Lawrence. 1988. *Consuming Desire*. Ithaca: Cornell University Press.

Blau, Peter. 1975. *Inequality and Heterogeneity*. New York: Free Press.

Blumstein, Phillip and Pepper Schwartz. 1983. *American Couples*. New York: Morrow.

Bogard, William. 1995. *The Simulation of Surveillance*. Cambridge: Cambridge University Press.

Bologh, Roslyn. 1990. *Love or Greatness*. London: Unwin Hyman.

Boone, Joseph and Michael Cadden, eds. 1990. *Engendering Men*. New York: Routledge.

Bordo, Susan. 1990. "Feminism, Postmodernism, and Gender-Skepticism," in *Feminism/Postmodernism*, ed. Linda Nicholson. New York: Routledge.

Bornstein, Kate. 1994. *Gender Outlaw*. New York: Routledge.

Boswell, John. 1980. *Christianity, Social Tolerance, and Homosexuality*. Chicago: University of Chicago Press.

1994. *Same-Sex Unions in Premodern Europe*. New York: Villard Books.

Bowman, Claude. 1949. "Cultural Ideology and Heterosexual Reality: A Preface to Sociological Research," *American Sociological Review* 14: 624–633.

Brake, Mike. 1980. *The Sociology of Youth Culture and Youth Subcultures*. London: Routledge and Kegan Paul.

Bray, Alan. 1995. *Homosexuality in Renaissance England*. New York: Columbia University Press.

Bright, Susie. 1984. "The Year of the Lustful Lesbian," *New York Native* July 30–August 12.

Bronski, Michael. 1982. "Our Guilt and Fear," *Gay Community News* Oct. 7.

1984. *Cultural Clash*. Boston: South End Press.

Brown, Elsa Barkley. 1994. "Negotiating and Transforming the Public Sphere: African American Political Life in the Transition from Slavery to Freedom," *Public Culture* 7: 175–194.

Brown, Peter. 1988. *The Body and Society*. New York: Columbia University Press.

Brown, Richard. 1990a. "Narrative in Scientific Knowledge and Civic Discourse," *Current Perspectives in Social Theory* 11: 312–329.

1990b. "Rhetoric, Textuality, and the Postmodern Turn." *Sociological Theory* 8 (Fall): 188–198.

1993. "Modern Science: Institutionalization of Knowledge and Rationalization of Power," *The Sociological Quarterley* 34: 153–168.

Brown, Richard, ed. 1992. *Writing the Social Text*. New York: De Gruyter.

Brubaker, Rogers. 1992. *Citizenship and Nationhood in France and Germany*. Cambridge: Harvard University Press.

Buchanan, Patrick. 1983. "AIDS Disease: Is Nature Striking Back?" *New York Post* May 24.

Bunch, Charlotte. 1971. "Learning from Lesbian Separatism," *Ms.* November 1976.

1975. "Lesbians in Revolt," in *Lesbianism and the Women's Movement*, ed. Nancy Myron and Charlotte Bunch. Baltimore: Diana Press.

Burstyn, Varda. 1981. "Sex Issue." *Heresies* 12.

Burstyn, Varda, ed. 1985. *Women against Censorship*. Toronto: Douglas and McIntyre.

Bury, J. B. 1955. *The Idea of Progress*. New York: Dover.

Bush, Larry and Richard Goldstein. 1981. "The Anti-Gay Backlash," *The Village Voice* April 8–11.

Butler, Judith. 1990. *Gender Trouble*. New York: Routledge.

1991. "Imitation and Gender Insubordination," in Diana Fuss, ed. *Inside/Out: Lesbian Theories, Gay Theories*. New York: Routledge.

Butters, Ronald, et al., eds. 1989. *Displacing Homophobia*. Durham: Duke University Press.

Byars, J. 1991. *All That Hollywood Allows*. London: Routledge.

Calhoun, Craig. 1995. *Critical Social Theory*. Oxford: Blackwell.

Califia, Pat. 1979. "A Secret Side of Lesbian Sexuality," *The Advocate* Dec. 27.

    1980. *Sapphistry: The Book of Lesbian Sexuality*. Tallahassee: Naiad Press.

    1981. "What is Gay Liberation?" *Heresies* 3(12): 30–34.

    1982a. "A Personal View of the History of the Lesbian S/M Community and Movement in San Francisco," in *Coming to Power*, ed. Samois. Boston: Alyson.

    1982b. "The Issue of Public Sex: Pro," *The Advocate* Sept. 30.

Callen, Michael. 1983. Letter, *The Body Politic* April.

Callen, Michael, Richard Berkowitz with Richard Dworkin, 1982. "We Know Who We Are," *The New York Native* Nov. 8.

Caputo, John and Mark Yount. 1993. *Foucault and the Critique of Institutions*. University Park: Pennsylvania State University Press.

Castells, Manuel. 1983. *The City and the Grassroots*. Berkeley: University of California Press.

Castillo, Ana. 1991. "La Macha: Toward a Beautiful Whole Self," in *Chicana Lesbians*, ed. Carla Trujillo. Berkeley: Third Woman Press.

Chambers, Ian. 1985. *Urban Rhythms*. London: Macmillan.

    1986. *Popular Culture*. London: Methuen.

Chauncey, George Jr. 1985. "Christian Brotherhood or Sexual Perversion? Homosexual Identities and the Construction of Sexual Boundaries in the World War One Era," *Journal of Social History* 19: 189–212.

    1994. *Gay New York*. New York: Pantheon.

Chee, Alexander. 1991. "Queer Nationalism," *Out/Look* 11: 15–19.

Chodorow, Nancy. 1978. *The Reproduction of Mothering*. Berkeley: University of California Press.

Clark, Wendy. 1987. "The Dyke, The Feminist, and the Devil," in *Sexuality*, ed. Feminist Review. London: Virago.

Clausen, Jan. 1990. "My Interesting Condition," *Out/Look* 7: 13–21.

Clough, Patricia. 1994. *Feminist Social Thought*. Oxford: Blackwell.

Coats, A. W. 1988. "The Educational Revolution and the Professionalization of American Economics," in *Breaking the Academic Mould*, ed. William Barber. Middletown: Wesleyan University Press.

Cohen, Jean. 1985. "Strategy or Identity: New Theoretical Paradigms and Contemporary Social Movements," *Social Research*, 52: 663–716.

Cohen, Jean and Andrew Arato. 1992. *Civil Society and Political Theory*. Cambridge: MIT Press.

Cohen, P. 1972. "Subcultural Conflict and Working-Class Community," in *Culture, Media, Language*, ed. Stuart Hall et al. London: Hutchinson.

Collins, Patricia Hill. 1990. *Black Feminist Thought*. London: Harper Collins.

Collins, Randall. 1975. *Conflict Sociology*. New York: Academic Press.

Combahee River Collective. 1983. "A Black Feminist Statement," in *This Bridge Called My Back*, ed. Cherrie Moraga and Gloria Anzaldua. New York: Kitchen Table Press.

Connor, Steven. 1989. *Postmodernist Culture*. Oxford: Blackwell.

Coppola, Vincent. 1983. "The Change in Gay Life-style," *Newsweek* April 18.

Cornell, Drucilla. 1992. *Beyond Accommodation*. New York: Routledge.

Cory, Daniel Webster [pseudonym Edward Sagarin]. 1951. *The Homosexual in America*. New York: Peter Nevill.

Cott, Nancy. 1977. *The Bonds of Womanhood*. New Haven: Yale University Press.

Coward, Rosiland and John Ellis. 1977. *Language and Materialism*. London: Routledge and Kegan Paul.

Crighton, Elizabeth and David S. Mason. 1986. "Solidarity and the Green: The Rise of New Social Movements in East and West Europe," in *Research in Social Movements, Conflict and Change*, ed. Louis Kreisberg. Greenwich: JAI Press.

Crimp, Douglas, ed. 1987. "AIDS: Cultural Analysis/Cultural Politics." *October* 43 (Winter).

    1987. *AIDS: Cultural Analysis, Cultural Activism*. Cambridge: MIT Press.

Culler, Jonathan. 1982. *On Deconstruction*. Ithaca: Cornell University Press.

Curti, Linda. 1992. "What is Real and What is Not: Female Fabulations in Cultural Analysis," in *Cultural Studies*, ed. Lawrence Grossberg et al. New York: Routledge.

Daalder, Hans. 1971. "On Building Consociational Nations: The Case of the Netherlands and Switzerland," *International Social Science Journal* 23: 355–370.

    1981. "Consociationalism, Center and Periphery in The Netherlands," in *Mobilization, Center–Periphery Structures and Nation-Building*. Bergan: Universitets-forlaget.

Davidson-Messer, Ellen, David Shumway, and David Sylvan, eds. 1993. *Knowledges*. Charlottesville: University of Virginia Press.

Davidson, Donald. 1973. "On the Very Idea of a Conceptual Scheme," *Proceedings and Addresses of the American Philosophical Association*, 47: 5–20.

    1990. "A Coherence Theory of Truth and Knowledge," in *Reading Rorty*, ed. Alan Malachowski. Oxford: Blackwell.

Davis, Katherine Benet. 1929. *Factors in the Sex Life of Twenty-Two Hundred Women*. New York: Harper and Brothers.

Davis, Kingsley. 1937. "The Sociology of Prostitution," *American Sociological Review* 2: 744–755.

    1939. "Illegitimacy and the Social Structure," *American Journal of Sociology*. 45: 215–233.

Dawson, Michael. 1994. "A Black Counterpublic?: Economic Earthquakes, Racial Agenda(s), and Black Politics," *Public Culture* 7: 195–244.

Degler, Carl. 1980. *At Odds*. New York: Oxford University Press.

D'Emilio, John. 1983. *Sexual Politics, Sexual Communities*. Chicago: University of Chicago Press. *Matters*. New York: Harper & Row.

D'Emilio, John and Estelle Freedman. 1988. *Intimate Matters*. New York: Harper & Row.

de Lauretis, Teresa. 1987. *Technologies of Gender*. Bloomington: India University Press.

1991. "Queer Theory: Lesbian and Gay Sexualities," *Differences* 3: iii–xviii.

1994. *The Practice of Love*. Bloomington: Indiana University Press.

Delgado, Richard. 1990. "When a Story is Just a Story: Does Voice Really Matter?" *Virginia Law Review* 95: 108–145.

Denzin, Norman. 1991. *Images of Postmodern Society*. London: Sage.

Derrida, Jacques. 1976. *Of Grammatology*. Baltimore: Johns Hopkins University Press.

Dickinson, Robert and Laura Beam. 1932. *A Thousand Marriages*. Baltimore: The Williams and Wilkins Co.

Doty, Alexander. 1993. *Making Things Perfectly Queer*. Minneapolis: University of Minnesota.

Douglas, Mary. 1966. *Purity and Danger*. London: Penguin.

Duberman, Martin. 1986. *About Time*. New York: A Sea Horse Book.

Duggan, Lisa. 1992. "Making it Perfectly Queer." *Socialist Review* 22 (1): 11–31.

Dullea, Georgia. 1984. "Homosexual Couples Find a Quiet Pride," *New York Times*, Dec. 10.

Durkheim, Emile, 1977. *The Evolution of Educational Thought*. London: Routledge and Kegan Paul.

Duyvendak, Jan Willem. 1996. "The Depoliticization of the Dutch Gay Identity or Why Dutch Gays Aren't Queer," in *Queer Theory/Sociology*, ed. Steven Seidman. Oxford: Blackwell.

Dyer, Richard. 1982. *Stars*. London: BFI.

Dyke, Vernon Van. 1995. "The Individual, the State, and Ethnic Communities in Political Theory," in *The Rights of Minority Cultures*, ed. Will Kymlicka. New York: Oxford University Press.

Dyson, Michael. 1995. *Making Malcolm*. New York: Oxford University Press.

Eagleton, Terry. 1986. *Against the Grain*. London: Verso.

Edelman, Lee. 1994. *Homographesis*. New York: Routledge.

Eder, Klaus. 1985. "The New Social Movements: Moral Crusades, Political Pressure Groups or Social Movements?" *Social Research* 52(4): 28–42.

E'Eramo, James. 1984. "The New Medical Journal Homophobia," *The New York Native*, May 21.

Ehrenreich, Barbara and Deidre English. 1979. *For Her Own Good*. New York: Doubleday.

Elbaz, Gilbert. 1993. "New York ACT-UP," Ph.D. dissertation, City University of New York.

English, Deirdre, Amber Hollibaugh and Gayle Rubin. 1987. "Talking Sex: A Conversation on Sexuality and Feminism," in *Sexuality*, ed. Feminist Review. London: Virago.

Epstein, Steven. 1987. "Gay Politics, Ethnic Identity: The Limits of Social Constructionism," *Socialist Review*, 17: 9–54.

1995. "Impure Science: AIDS, Activism, and the Politics of Knowledge," Ph.D. University of California at Berkeley.

1996. "A Queer Encounter: Sociology and the Studies of Sexuality," in *Queer Theory/Sociology*, ed. Steven Seidman. Oxford: Blackwell.

Escoffier, Jeffrey. 1992. "Generations and Paradigms: Mainstreams in Lesbian and Gay Studies," *Out/Look* 24: 7–22.

Esterberg, Kristin. 1996. "A Certain Swagger When I Walk: Performing Lesbian Identity," in *Queer Theory/Sociology*, ed. Steven Seidman. Oxford: Blackwell.

Fabian, Johannes. 1983. *Time and the Other*. Chicago: University of Chicago Press.

Faderman, Lillian. 1981. *Surpassing the Love of Men*. New York: Morrow.

    1991. *Odd Girls and Twilight Lovers*. New York: Columbia University Press.

Feinberg, Leslie. 1993. *Stone Butch Blues*. Ithaca, New York: Firebrand Books.

Feminist Anti-Censorship Task Force, eds. 1986. *Caught Looking*. Seattle: Real Comet Press.

Ferguson, Ann. 1989. *Blood at the Root*. Boston: Pandora Press.

Fernandez, Charles. 1991. "Undocumented Aliens in the Queer Nation: Reflections on Race and Ethnicity in the Lesbian and Gay Movement," *Democratic Left* (May/June 1991).

Fernbach, David. 1981. *The Spiral Path*. London: Gay Men's Press.

Feyerabend, Paul. 1975. *Against Method*. London: New Left Books.

Fiske, John. 1982. *Introduction to Communication Studies*. London: Methuen.

    1987. *Television Culture*. London: Methuen.

Flax, Jane. 1981. "Do Feminists Need Marxism?" *In Building Feminist Theory*, eds. The Quest Staff. New York: Longman Quest Staff.

Foucault, Michel. 1978. *The History of Sexuality: An Introduction*. New York: Pantheon.

    1979. *Discipline and Punish*. New York: Vintage.

    1980. *Power/Knowledge*. New York: Pantheon.

    1985. *The History of Sexuality* Vol. II: *The Use of Pleasure*. New York: Vintage.

Fox, Robert. 1980. "Learning, Politics and Polite Culture in Provincial France: The Societies Savantes in the Nineteenth Century," in *The Making of Frenchmen*, ed. D. Baker and P. Harrigan. Waterloo: Historical Reflections Press.

Fraser, Nancy. 1992. "Rethinking the Public Sphere: A Contribution to the Critique of Actually Existing Democracy," in *Habermas and the Public Sphere*, ed. Craig Calhoun. Cambridge: MIT Press.

Fraser, Nancy and Linda Nicholson. 1990. "Social Criticism without Philosophy: An Encounter Between Feminism and Philosophy," in *Feminism/ Postmodernism*, ed. Linda Nicholson. New York: Routledge.

Frommer, Margot Joan. 1983. "Coping," *The Washington Blade*, Jan. 21.

Fuller, John. 1983. "AIDS: Legacy of the 60s?" *Science Digest*, Dec.

Fuss, Diana. 1989. *Essentially Speaking*. New York: Routledge.

Fuss, Diana, ed. 1991. *Inside/Out*. New York: Routledge.

Gagnon, John and William Simon. 1967a. "Homosexuality: The Formulation of a Sociological Perspective," *Journal of Health and Social Behavior* 8: 177–185.

    1967b. "The Lesbians: A Preliminary Overview," in *Sexual Deviance*, ed. John Gagnon and William Simon. New York: Harper and Row.

    1973. *Sexual Conduct*. Chicago: Aldine.

Gamson, Joshua. 1989. "Silence, Death an the Invisible Enemy: AIDS, Activism and Social Movement 'Newness.'" *Social Problems* 36: 351–67.

1996. "Must Identity Movements Self-Destruct?: A Queer Dilemma," in *Queer Theory/Sociology*, ed. Steven Seidman. Oxford: Blackwell.

Gane, Mike and Terry Johnson. 1993. *Foucault's New Domains*. New York: Routledge.

Gay Left Collective. 1980. "Homosexuality: Power and Politics." London: Allen and Busby.

Gay, Peter. 1966. *The Enlightenment: The Rise of Modern Paganism*. New York: Alfred A. Knopf.

1986. *The Bourgeois Experience*. Vol. 2, *The Tender Passion*. New York: Oxford University Press.

Geertz, Clifford. 1983. *Local Knowledge*. New York: Basic Books.

Giddens, Anthony. 1984. *The Constitution of Society*. Berkeley: University of California Press.

Gilligan, Carol. 1982. *In a Different Voice*. Cambridge, MA: Harvard University Press.

Glazer, Nathan. 1984. "The Emergence of an American Ethnic Pattern," in *From Difference Shores*, ed. Ronald Takaki. New York: Oxford University Press.

Goffman, Erving. 1963. *Stigma*. Englewood Cliffs, NJ: Prentice-Hall.

Goldberg, Jonathan. 1992. *Sodometries*. Stanford: Stanford University Press.

Goldsby, Jackie. 1990. "What It Means to Be Colored Me," *Out/Look*, 9: 8–17.

Goldstein, Richard. 1984. "The Other AIDS Story: Quarantine," *The Village Voice* May 1.

1989. "AIDS and the Social Contract," in *Taking Liberties*, ed. Erica Carter and Simon Watney. London: Serpent's Tail.

1985. "The Uses of Aids," *The Village Voice*, Nov. 5.

Goodstein, David. 1985. "Editorial," *The Advocate* August 6.

Gordon, Linda. 1977. *Woman's Body, Woman's Right*. New York: Penguin.

Gotanda, Neil. 1991. "A Critique of 'Our Constitution is Color-Blind,'" *Stanford Law Review* 44: 1–68.

Gottdiener, Mark. 1985. "Hegemony and Mass Culture: A Semiotic Approach," *American Journal of Sociology* 90: 979–1,001.

Goudsblom, Johan. 1967. *Dutch Society*. New York: Random House.

Gouldner, Alvin. 1971. *The Coming Crisis of Western Sociology*. New York. Basic.

Graff, Gerald. 1987. *Professing Literature*. Chicago: University of Chicago Press.

Gramsci, Antonio. 1971. *Selections from the Prison Notebooks*. London: Lawrence and Wishart.

Grant, Edward. 1984. "Science and the Medieval University," in *Rebirth, Reform and Resilience: Universities in Transition 1300–1700*. Columbus: Ohio State University Press.

Greenberg, Jay and Stephen Mitchell. 1983. *Object Relations in Psychoanalytic Theory*. Cambridge, MA: Harvard University Press.

Greene, John. 1976. "Science, Learning, and Utility: Patterns of Organization in the

Early American Republic," in *The Pursuit of Knowledge in the Early American Republic*, ed. Sanborn Brown. Baltimore: Johns Hopkins University Press.

Greer, William. 1986. "Violence Against Homosexuals Rising, Groups Seeking Wider Protection Say," *New York Times* Nov. 23.

Griffin, Susan. 1978. *Woman and Nature*. New York: Harper & Row.

Grimal, Henri. 1978. *Decolonization*. New York: Routledge and Kegan Paul.

Gross, Larry. 1993. *Contested Closets*. Minneapolis: University of Minnesota Press.

Grossberg, Lawrence, Cary Nelson, and Paula Treichler, eds. 1992. *Cultural Studies*. New York: Routledge.

Grosz, Elizabeth. 1990. *Jacques Lacan*. New York: Routledge.

Gunnell, John. 1993. *The Descent of Political Theory*. Chicago: University of Chicago Press.

Gusfield, Joseph. 1981. *The Culture of Public Problems*. Chicago; University of Chicago Press.

Habermas, Jurgen. 1971. *Knowledge and Human Interests*. Boston: Beacon.

   1977. *Communication and the Evolution of Society*. Boston: Beacon.

   1981. "New Social Movements," *Telos*, 49: 33–37.

   1984. *The Theory of Communicative Action*. Vol. 1. Boston: Beacon.

   1987. *The Theory of Communicative Action*. Vol. 2. Boston: Beacon.

Hall, Stuart. 1974. "Deviancy, Politics and the Media," in *Deviance and Social Control*, ed. Paul Rock and Mary McIntosh. London: Tavistock.

   1980a. "Cultural Studies and the Centre: Some Problematics and Problems," in *Culture, Media, Language*, ed. Stuart Hall et al. London: Hutchinson.

   1980b. "Encoding/Decoding," in *Culture, Media, Language*, ed. Stuart Hall et al. London: Hutchinson.

   1988. *The Hard Road to Renewal*. London: Verso.

   1990. "The Emergence of Cultural Studies and the Crisis of the Humanities." *October* 53: 11–90.

   1992. "Cultural Studies and its Theoretical Legacies," in *Cultural Studies*, ed. Lawrence Grossberg et al. New York: Routledge.

Hall, Stuart, Chas Critcher, Tony Jefferson, John Clarke, and Brian Roberts. 1978. *Policing the Crisis*. London: Macmillan.

Halley, Janet. 1993. "The Construction of Heterosexuality," in *Fear of a Queer Planet*, ed. Michael Warner. Minneapolis: University of Minnesota Press.

Halperin, David. 1990. *One Hundred Years of Homosexuality*. New York: Routledge.

Haraway, Donna. 1985a. "A Manifesto for Cyborgs: Science, Technology, and Feminism in the 1980s," *Socialist Review* 15 (March-April): 65–107.

   1985b. "Situated Knowledges." *Feminist Studies* 14 (3): 575–99.

   1989. *Primate Visions*. New York: Routledge.

   1991. *Symians, Cyborgs, and Women*. New York: Routledge.

Harding, Sandra. 1986. *The Science Question in Feminism*. Ithaca, NY: Cornell University Press.

Harding, Sandra and Merrill Hintikka, eds. 1983. *Discovering Reality*. London: D. Reidel.

Harry, Joseph and William Duvall. 1978. *The Social Organization of Gay Males*. New York: Praeger.

Harry, Joseph and Robert Lovely. 1979. "Gay Marriages and Communities of Sexual Orientation." *Alternative Lifestyles* 2 (May).

Hartley, John. 1982. *Understanding News*. London: Methuen.

Harvey, David. 1990. *The Condition of Postmodernity*. Oxford: Blackwell.

Harvey, Stephen. 1982. "Defenseless: Learning to Live with AIDS," *The Village Voice*, Dec. 21.

Haskell, Thomas. 1977. *The Emergence of Professional Social Science*. Urbana: University of Illinois Press.

Hebdige, Dick. 1979. *Subculture*. London: Methuen.

Hemphill, Essex, ed. 1991. *Brother to Brother*. Boston: Alyson.

Hennessy, Rosemary. 1993. "Queer Theory: A Review of the *Differences* Special Issue and Wittig's *The Straight Mind*," *Signs* 18: 964–973.

Henslin, James. 1971. *Studies in the Sociology of Sex*. New York: Appleton-Century-Crofts.

Hinkle, Roscoe. 1980. *Founding Theory of American Sociology 1881–1915*. Boston: Routledge and Kegan Paul.

Hobson, Dorothy. 1980. "Housewives and the Mass Media," in *Culture, Media, Language*, ed. Stuart Hall et al. London: Hutchinson.

Hodgen, Margaret. 1964. *Early Anthropology in the Sixteenth and Seventeenth Centuries*. Philadelphia: University of Pennsylvania Press.

Hoffman, Martin. 1968. *The Gay World*. New York: Basic Books.

Hoggart, Richard. 1957. *The Uses of Literacy*. London: Penguin.

Hohendahl, Peter Uwe. 1982. *The Institution of Criticism*. Ithaca: Cornell University Press.

Holland, R. F. 1985. *European Decolonization, 1918–1981*. London: Macmillan.

Hollibaugh, Amber. 1983. "The Erotophobic Voice of Women," *New York Native*, 26 Sept. – 9 Oct. 1983.

   1984. "Desire for the Future: Radical Hope in Passion and Pleasure," in *Pleasure and Danger*, ed. Carole S. Vance. Boston: Routledge and Kegan Paul.

Hooker, Evelyn. 1965. "Male Homosexuals and Their Worlds," in *Sexual Inversion*, ed. Judd Marmor. New York: Basic Books.

Hovenkamp, Herbert. 1978. *Science and Religion in America, 1800–1860*. Philadelphia: University of Pennsylvania Press.

Huggett, Frank. 1971. *The Modern Netherlands*. New York: Praeger.

Humphreys, Laud. 1970. *Tearoom Trade*. Chicago: Aldine.

   1979. "Exodus and Identity: The Emerging Gay Culture," in *Gay Men*, ed. Martin Levine. New York: Harper and Row.

Hutchins, Loraine and Lani Kaahumanu. 1991. "Bicoastal Introduction," in *Bi Any Other Name*, ed. Loraine Hutchins and Lani Kaahumanu. Boston: Alyson.

Huyssen, Andreas. 1986. *After the Great Divide*. Bloomington: Indiana University Press.

Ingraham, Chrys. 1996. "The Heterosexual Imaginary: Feminist Sociology and

Theories of Gender," in *Queer Theory/Sociology*, ed. Steven Seidman. Oxford: Blackwell.

Irvine, Janice. 1990. *Disorders of Desire*. Philadelphia: Temple University Press.

1996. "A Place in the Rainbow: Theorizing Lesbian and Gay Culture," in *Queer Theory/Sociology*, ed. Steven Seidman. Oxford: Blackwell.

Jacob, Margaret. 1981. *The Radical Enlightenment*. London: George Allen & Unwin.

1988. *The Cultural Meaning of the Scientific Revolution*. Philadelphia: Temple University Press.

Jacoby, Russell. 1987. *The Last Intellectuals*. New York: Basic Books.

Jagger, Alison and Susan Bordo, eds. 1989. *Gender/Body/Knowledge*. New Brunswick: Rutgers University Press.

Jameson, Fredric. 1981. *The Political Unconscious*. Ithaca: Cornell University Press.

1984. "Postmodernism, or the Cultural Logic of Late Capitalism," *New Left Review*, 146: 53–92.

1992. *Postmodernism, or The Cultural Logic of Late Capitalism*. Durham: Duke University Press.

Jardine, Alice. 1985. *Gynesis*. Ithaca: Cornell University Press.

Jay, Eric. 1982. "The Issue of Public Sex: Con," *The Advocate* Sept. 30.

Jay, Karla and Allen Young, eds. 1972. *Out of the Closets*. New York: Douglas/Links.

1977. *The Gay Report*. New York: Summit Books.

Joas, Hans. 1993. *Pragmatism and Social Theory*. Chicago: University of Chicago Press.

Johnson, Craig. 1985. "S/M and the Myth of Mutual Consent," *New York Native* May 29–June 11.

Johnston, Jill. 1973. *Lesbian Nation*. New York: Harper & Row.

Kantrowitz, Arnie. 1983. "Till Death Us Do Part," *The Advocate*.

Katz, Jonathan Ned. 1976. *Gay American History*. New York: Thomas Y. Crowell.

1983. *Gay/Lesbian Almanac*. New York: Harper & Row.

1990. "The Invention of Heterosexuality," *Socialist Review* 21: 7–34.

1995. *The Invention of Heterosexuality*. New York: Penguin.

Keller, Evelyn Fox. 1985. *Science and Gender*. New Haven. Yale University Press.

Kellner, Douglas. 1988. "Postmodernism as Social Theory. Some Challenges and Problems," *Theory, Culture & Society* 5: 239–269.

Kinsey, Alfred et al. 1948. *Sexual Behavior in the Human Male*. Philadelphia, PN: W. B. Saunders.

1953. *Sexual Behavior in the Human Female*. Philadelphia, PN: W. B. Saunders.

Kirkham, George. 1971. "Homosexuality in Prison," in *Studies in the Sociology of Sex,* ed. James Henslin. New York: Appleton-Century-Crofts.

Kleinberg, Seymour. 1982. *Alienated Affections*. New York: St. Martin's Press.

Kohlstedt, Sally Gregory. 1976. *The Formation of the American Scientific Community*. Urbana: University of Illinois Press.

Kramer, Larry. 1983. "1,112 and Counting," *The New York Native*, March 14.

Krauthammner, Charles. 1983. "The Politics of a Plague," *The New Republic* August 1.

Kreiger, Susan. 1983. *The Mirror Dance*. Philadelphia: Temple University Press.

Kriesi, Hanspeter. 1988. *Political Mobilization and Social Change*. Aldershot: Avebury.

1990. "Federalism and Pillarization: The Netherlands and Switzerland Compared." *Acta Politica* 4: 16–29.

Kroker, Arthur and David Cook. 1986. *The Postmodern Scene*. New York: St. Martin's.

Kumar, Krishan. 1995. *From Post-Industrial to Post-Modern Society*. Oxford: Blackwell.

Kymlicka, Will. 1989. *Liberalism, Community and Culture*. Oxford: Oxford University Press.

1995a. *Multicultural Citizenship*. New York: Oxford University Press.

Kymlicka, Will, ed. 1995b. *The Rights of Minority Cultures*. New York: Oxford University Press.

Laclau, Ernest and Chantal Mouffe. 1985. *Hegemony and Socialist Strategy*. London: Verso, 1985.

Lacquer, Thomas. 1990. *Making Sex*. Cambridge: Harvard University Press.

Lamont, Michele and Robert Wuthnow. 1990. "Betwixt and Between: Recent Cultural Sociology in Europe and the United States," in *Frontiers of Social Theory*, ed. George Ritzer. New York. Columbia University Press.

Larson, Magali Sarfatti. 1984. "The Production of Expertise and the Constitution of Expert Power," in *The Authority of Experts*, ed. Thomas Haskell. Bloomington: University of Indiana Press.

Lash, Scott. 1985. "Postmodernity and Desire," *Theory & Society* 14: 1–33.

1988. "Discourse or Figure? Postmodernism as a Regime of Signification," *Theory, Culture & Society* 5: 311–336.

Lash, Scott and John Urry. 1987. *The End of Organized Capitalism*. Cambridge: Polity Press.

1994. *Economies of Signs and Space*. London: Sage.

Latour, Bruno. 1986. *Science in Action*. Cambridge: Harvard University Press.

Lederer, Laura, ed. 1980. *Take Back the Night*. New York: William Morrow.

Lee, John. 1979. "The Gay Connection," *Urban Issues* 8: 175–198.

Lemert, Charles. 1991. "The End of Ideology, Really," *Sociological Theory* 9 (Fall): 164–172.

1992. "General Social Theory, Irony, Postmodernism," in *Postmodernism and Social Theory*, ed. Steven Seidman and David Wagner. Cambridge: Blackwell.

1995. *Sociology After the Crisis*. Boulder, CO Westview.

Lepenies, Wolf. 1988. *Between Literature and Science*. Cambridge: Cambridge University Press.

Levine, Martin. 1979. "Gay Ghetto," *Journal of Homosexuality* 4: 363–377.

Levine, Martin, ed. 1979. *The Sociology of Male Homosexuality*. New York: Harper & Row.

Lijphart, Arendt. 1969. "Consociational Democracy," *World Politics*: 207–225.

1975. *The Politics of Accommodation*. Berkeley: University of California Press.

1984. *Democracies*. New Haven: Yale University Press.

Loader, Colin. 1976. "German Historicism and Its Crisis," *Journal of Modern History* 48: 85–99.

Lorde, Audre. 1984. *Sister Outsider*. Freedom, CA: The Crossing Press.

Lukes, Steven. 1973. *Emile Durkheim*. London: Allen Lane.

Lyon, David. 1994. *The Electronic Eye*. Minneapolis: University of Minnesota Press.

Lyotard, Jean-François. 1984. *The Postmodern Condition*. Minneapolis: University of Minnesota Press.

Lystra, Karen. 1989. *Searching the Heart*. New York: Oxford University Press.

McIntosh, Mary. 1968. "The Homosexual Role," *Social Problems* 16: 182–192.

MacKinnon, Catherine. 1989. *Toward a Feminist Theory of the State*. Cambridge, MA: Harvard University Press.

Mains, Geoffrey. 1984. *Urban Aboriginals*. San Francisco: Gay Sunshine Press.

Margalit, Avishai and Joseph Rz. 1995. "National Self-Determination," in *The Rights of Minority Cultures*, ed. Will Kymlicka. New York: Oxford University Press.

Marriner, Gerald. 1972. "The Estrangement of the Intellectuals in America: The Search for New Life Styles in the Early Twentieth Century," Ph.D. Diss., University of Colorado.

Marotta, Toby. 1981. *The Politics of Homosexuality*. Boston: Houghton Mifflin.

Marsden, George. 1994. *The Soul of the American University*. New York: Oxford University Press.

Martin, Del and Phyllis Lyon. 1972. *Lesbian/Woman*. New York: Bantam.

Martin, John. 1986. "AIDS Risk Reduction Recommendations and Sexual Behavior Patterns Among Gay Men: A Multifactorial Categorical Approach to Assessing Change." *Health Education Quarterly* 13 (Winter).

Martin, John and Carole Vance. 1984. "Behavioral and Psychological Factors in AIDS," *American Psychologist*, 13: 3–17.

Martz, Steve, 1983. "A Quick Look Back and Some Thoughts On The Year Ahead," *The Washington Blade*, Jan. 7.

Mass, Lawrence, ed. 1990. *Homosexuality as Behavior and Identity, Vol. 2: Dialogues of the Sexual Revolution*. New York: Harrington Park Press.

McConnell, Michael. 1993a. "'God is Dead and We Have Killed Him!': Freedom of Religion in the Post-Modern Age." *Brigham Young University Law Review*: 163–188.

1993b. "Academic Freedom in Religious Colleges and Universities," in *Freedom and Tenure in the Academy*, ed. William W. Van Alstyne. Durham: Duke University Press.

McRobbie, Angela. 1992. "Post-Marxism and Cultural Studies: A Post-script," in *Cultural Studies*, ed. Lawrence Grossberg et al. New York: Routledge.

McRobbie, Angela and Jenny Gardner. 1976. "Girls and Subcultures: An

Exploration," in *Resistance Through Rituals*, ed. Stuart Hall and Tony Jefferson. London: Hutchinson.

Meek, Ronald. 1976. *Social Science and the Ignoble Savage*. Cambridge: Cambridge University Press.

Melucci, Alberto. 1980. "The New Social Movements," *Social Science Information*, 19: 199–226.

Messer-Davidow et al. eds. 1993. *Knowledges*. Charlottesville, VA: University of Virginia Press.

Meyer, Richard. 1991. "Rock Hudson's Body," in *Inside/Out*, ed. Diana Fuss. New York: Routledge.

Miller, D. A. 1991. "Anal *Rope*," in *Inside/Out*, ed. Diana Fuss. New York: Routledge.

Millet, Kate. 1969. *Sexual Politics*. New York: Ballantine.

Millman, Marcia and Rosabeth Moss Kanter, eds. 1975. *Another Voice*. New York: Anchor.

Minow, Martha. 1990. *Making all the Difference*. Ithaca: Cornell University Press.

Mitchell, Juliet. 1974. *Psychoanalysis and Feminism*. London: Allen Lane.

Moon, Michael. 1990. *Disseminating Whitman*. Cambridge, MA: Harvard University Press.

Moraga, Cherrie. 1983. *Loving in the War Years*. Boston: South End Press.

Morganthau, Tom. 1983. "Gay America in Transition," *Newsweek* August 8.

Morley, David. 1980. *The "Nationwide" Audience*. London: BFI.

1992. *Television, Audiences and Cultural Studies*. New York: Routledge.

Morton, Donald, ed. 1996. *The Material Queer*. Boulder, CO: Westview.

Murdock, George. 1989. "Cultural Studies: Missing Links," *Critical Studies in Mass Communications* 6: 436–440.

Murray, Stephen. 1979. "The Institutional Elaboration of a Quasi-Ethnic Community," *International Review of Modern Sociology* 9: 165–178.

Myron, Nancy and Charlotte Bunch, eds. 1975. *Lesbianism and the Woman's Movement*. Baltimore: Diana Press.

Namaste, Ki. 1996. "The Politics of Inside/Out: Queer Theory, Poststructuralism, and a Sociological Approach to Sexuality," in *Queer Theory/Sociology*, ed. Steven Seidman. Oxford: Blackwell.

Nestle, Joan. 1981. "Butch-Fem Relationships," *Heresies*, 12: 21–24.

1984. "The Fem Question," in *Pleasure and Danger*. Boston: Routledge and Kegan Paul.

Nicholson, Linda. 1986. *Gender and History*. New York: Columbia University Press.

1992. "On the Postmodern Barricades: Feminism, Politics and Theory," in *Postmodernism and Social Theory*, ed. Steven Seidman and David Wagner. Oxford: Blackwell.

1996. "To Be or Not To Be: Charles Taylor and the Politics of Recognition," *Constellations* 3: 1–16.

Nicholson, Linda, ed. 1989. *Feminism/Postmodernism*. New York: Routledge.

Nicholson, Linda and Steven Seidman, eds. 1995. *Social Postmodernism*. Cambridge: Cambridge University Press.

Nisbet, Robert. 1970. *Social Change and History*. New York: Oxford University Press.

O'Connor, Alan. 1989. "The Problem of American Cultural Studies," *Critical Studies in Mass Communications* 6: 405–413.

Offe, Clau. 1985. *Disorganized Capitalism*. Cambridge: Polity Press.

Ortner, Sherry and Harriet Whitehead, eds. 1981. *Sexual Meanings*. Cambridge: Cambridge University Press.

Parker, Andrew et al. eds. 1992. *Nationalisms and Sexualities*. New York: Routledge.

Parsons, Talcott. 1971. *The System of Modern Societies*. Englewood Cliffs, NJ: Prentice-Hall.

Patemen, Carole. 1988. *The Sexual Contract*. Stanford: Stanford University Press.

Patton, Cindy. 1985. *Sex and Germs*. Boston: South End Press.

1990. *Inventing AIDS*. New York: Routledge.

1995. "Refiguring Social Space," in *Social Postmodernism*, ed. Linda Nicholson and Steven Seidman. Cambridge: Cambridge University Press.

Paul, Harry. 1985. *From Knowledge to Power*. New York: Cambridge University Press.

Peiss, Kathy. 1986. *Cheap Amusements*. Philadelphia: Temple University Press.

Peller, Gary. 1990. "Race Consciousness," *Duke Law Journal* 4: 758–847.

Penley, Constance. 1992. "Feminism, Psychoanalysis, and the Study of Popular Culture," in *Cultural Studies*, ed. Lawrence Grossberg et al. New York: Routledge.

Peplau, Letitia Anne and Steven Gordon. 1983. "The Intimate Relationships of Lesbians and Gay Men," in *Gender Roles and Sexual Behavior*, ed. E. Allgeier and N. McCormick. Palo Alto, CA: Mayfield.

Persons, Stow. 1987. *Ethnic Studies at Chicago, 1905–45*. Urbana: University of Illinois Press.

Phelan, Shane. 1989. *Identity Politics*. Philadelphia: Temple University Press.

Phillips, Ann. 1995. *The Politics of Presence*. Oxford: Oxford University Press.

Pitts, Jesse. 1963. "Continuity and Change in Bourgeois France," in *In Search of France*, ed. Stanley Hoffman et al. New York: Harper & Row.

Plummer, Ken. 1975. *Stigma*. London: Routledge.

Plummer, Ken, ed. 1981. *The Making of the Modern Homosexual*. London: Hutchinson.

Plummer, Ken and Arlene Stein. 1996. "I Can't Even Think Straight: Queer Theory and the Missing Sexual Revolution in Sociology," in *Queer Theory/Sociology*, ed. Steven Seidman. Oxford: Blackwell.

Popert, Ken. 1982. "Public Sexuality and Social Space," *The Body Politic* July/August.

Popper, Karl. 1957. *The Poverty of Historicism*. Boston: Beacon Press.

Portoghesi, Paoli. 1992. "What is the Post-Modern?" in *The Post-Modern Reader*, ed. C. Jencks. London: Academy Editions.

Poster, Mark. 1990. *The Mode of Information*. Chicago: University of Chicago Press.

Prins, Baukje. 1995. "The Dutch Minorities Discourse," unpublished manuscript.

Radicalesbians. 1973. "The Woman-Identified-Woman," in *Radical Feminism*, ed. Anne Koedt et al. New York: Quadrangle.

Radway, Janice. 1984. *Reading the Romance*. Chapel Hill: University of North Carolina Press.

    1992. "Mail-Order Culture and its Critics: The Book-of-the-Month Club, Commodification and Consumption, and the Problem of Cultural Authority," in *Cultural Studies*, ed. Lawrence Grossberg et al. New York: Routledge.

Reiss, Albert. 1961. "The Social Origins of Peers and Queers." *Social Problems* 9: 102–130.

Reiss, Jr. Albert. 1964. "The Social Integration of Queers and Peers," *Social Problems* 9: 102–120.

Reiss, Ira. 1967. *The Social Context of Premarital Sexual Permissiveness*. New York: Holt, Rinehart and Winston.

Rich, Adrienne. 1976. *Of Woman Born*. New York: W. W. Norton.

    1980. "Compulsory Heterosexuality and Lesbian Existence." *Signs* 5 (Summer): 631–660.

Richardson, Laurel. 1991. "Postmodern Social Theory: Representational Practices," *Sociological Theory* 9: 173–179.

Riley, Denise. 1988. "Am I That Name?" *Feminism and the Category of Women in History*. New York: Macmillan.

Rochberg-Halton, Eugene. 1986. *Meaning and Modernity*. Chicago: University of Chicago Press.

Rorty, Richard. 1979. *Philosophy and the Mirror of Nature*. Princeton: Princeton University Press.

    1982a. *Consequences of Pragmatism*. Minneapolis: University of Minnesota Press.

    1982b. "Method, Social Science, and Social Hope," in *Consequences of Pragmatism*. Minncapolis: University of Minnesota Press.

    1991. *Objectivity, Relativism, and Truth*. Cambridge: Cambridge University Press.

Rosaldo, Michelle and Louise Lamphere, eds. 1974. *Woman, Culture and Society*. Stanford: Stanford University Press.

Rose, Jacqueline. 1986. *Sexuality in the Field of Vision*. London: Verso.

Rose, Susan. 1993. "Christian Fundamentalism and Education in the United States," in *Fundamentalisms and Society*, ed. Martin Marty and R. Scott Appleby. Chicago: University of Chicago Press.

Rothman, Ellen. 1987. *Hands and Hearts*. Cambridge, MA: Harvard University Press.

Rotundo, Anthony. 1989. "Romantic Friendship: Male Intimacy and Middle-Class Youth in the Northern United States, 1800–1930," *Journal of Social History* 23.

Rouse, Joseph. 1987. *Knowledge and Power*. Ithaca: Cornell University Press.

Rozwadowski, Franck. 1988. "From Recitation Room to Research Seminar: Political Economy at Columbia University," in *Breaking the Academic Mould*, ed. William Barber. Middletown: Wesleyan University Press.

Rubin, Gayle. 1975. "The Traffic in Women," in *Towards an Anthropology of Women*, ed. Rayna Reiter. New York: Monthly Review.

Rubin, Gayle. 1982. "Thinking Sex," in *Pleasure and Danger*, ed. C. Vance. New York: Routledge.

Ryan, Mary. 1979. *Womanhood in America*. 2nd ed. New York: New Viewpoints.

1992. "Gender and Public Access: Women's Politics in Nineteenth-Century America," in *Habermas and the Public Sphere*, ed. Craig Calhoun. Cambridge: MIT Press.

Sagarin, Edward. 1969. *Odd Man In*. Chicago: Quadrangle Books.

1971. "Sex Research and Sociology: Retrospective and Prospective," in *Studies in the Sociology of Sex*, ed. James Henslin. New York: Appleton-Century-Crofts.

Sahlins, Marshall. 1976. *Culture and Practical Reason*. Chicago: University of Chicago Press.

Said, Edward. 1979. *Orientalism*. New York: Random House.

1985. "Orientalism Reconsidered," *Race and Class* 27 (Autumn).

1993. *Culture and Imperialism*. New York: Vintage.

Samois, ed. 1982. *Coming to Power*. Boston: Alyson.

Schlesinger, Arthur Jr. 1992. *The Disuniting of America*. New York: W. W. Norton & Co.

Scott, Joan. 1988. *Gender and the Politics of History*. New York: Columbia University Press.

Schwartz, Stuart, ed. *Implicit Understandings*. Cambridge: Cambridge University Press.

Sedgwick, Eve. 1990. *Epistemology of the Closet*. Berkeley: University of California Press.

Seidman, Steven. 1983. *Liberalism and the Origins of European Social Theory*. Berkeley: University of California Press.

1991. *Romantic Longings*. New York: Routledge.

1992a. *Embattled Eros*. New York: Routledge.

1992b. "Theory as Narrative with a Moral Intent: A Postmodern Intervention," in *Postmodernism & Social Theory*, ed. Steven Seidman and David Wagner. Oxford: Blackwell.

1994b. *Contested Knowledge*. Oxford: Blackwell.

Seidman, Steven, ed. 1994a. *The Postmodern Turn*. Cambridge: Cambridge University Press.

Seidman, Steven and David Wagner, eds. 1992. *Postmodernism and Social Theory*. Oxford: Blackwell.

Seligman, Adam. 1992. *The Idea of Civil Society*. Princeton: Princeton University Press.

Shalin, Dmitri. 1992. "Critical Theory and the Pragmatist Challenge," *American Journal of Sociology* 98: 237–279.

Shapin, Steven. 1994. *A Social History of Truth*. Chicago: University of Chicago Press.

Sherwood, Steven, Phillip Smith and Jeffrey Alexander. 1993. "The British are Coming . . . Again! The Hidden Agenda of 'Cultural Studies.'" *Contemporary Sociology* 22: 370–375.

Shilts, Randy. 1987. *And the Band Played On*. New York: St Martin's Press.

Shumway, David. 1994. *Creating American Civilization*. Minneapolis: University of Minnesota Press.

Sica, Alan. 1989. "Social Theory's Constituents," *The American Sociologist* 20: 227–241.

Signorile, Michelangelo. 1995. *Queer in America*. New York: Random House.

Simmel, Georg. 1984. "The Relative and the Absolute Problem of the Sexes," in *Georg Simmel*, ed. Guy Oakes. New Haven: Yale University Press.

Simmons, Christina. 1982. "Marriage in the Modern Manner: Sexual Radicalism and Reform in America, 1914–1941," Ph.D. diss., Brown University.

Skocpol, Theda. 1986. "The Dead End of Metatheory," *Contemporary Sociology* 16: 10–12.

Skrentny, John. 1994. "Politics and Possibility: The Legitimation of Affirmative Action, Ph.D. diss., Harvard University.

Smith, Barbara and Beverly Smith. 1984. "Across the Kitchen Table: A Sister-to-Sister Dialogue," in *This Bridge Called My Back*, ed. Cherrie Moraga and Gloria Anzaldúa. Latham, NY: Kitchen Table.

Smith, Dorothy. 1979. "A Sociology for Women," in *The Prism of Sex*, ed. by Julia Sherman and Evelyn Torton. Madison: University of Wisconsin.

    1989. "Sociological Theory: Methods of Writing Patriarchy," in *Feminism and Sociological Theory*, ed. Ruth Wallace. Newbury Park: Sage.

Smith-Rosenberg, Carroll. 1975. "The Female World of Love and Ritual: Relations Between Women in Nineteenth-Century America," *Signs* 9: 1–29.

    1985. *Disorderly Conduct*. New York: Alfred A. Knopf.

    1990. "Discourses of Sexuality and Subjectivity: The New Woman, 1870–1936," in *Hidden from History*, ed. Martin Duberman et al. New York: Penguin.

Socarides, Charles. 1968. *The Overt Homosexual*. New York: Grune and Stratton.

Sontag, Susan. 1988. *AIDS and Its Metaphors*. New York: Farrar, Strauss, and Giroux.

Special Issue. 1994. The Black Public Sphere. *Public Culture*. 7 (Fall): 994.

Spelman, Elizabeth. 1988. *Inessential Woman*. Boston: Beacon.

Stambolian, George. 1982. "The Sex," *New York Native* Feb. 15–28.

Steffen, Monika. 1992. "France: Social Solidarity and Scientific Expertise," in *AIDS in the Industrialized Democracies*, ed. David Kirp and Ronald Bayers. New Brunswick: Rutgers University Press.

Stein, Arlene and Ken Plummer. 1996. "I Can't Even Think Straight: Queer Theory and the Missing Sexual Revolution in Sociology," in *Queer Theory/Sociology*, ed. Steven Seidman. Oxford: Blackwell.

Stein, Edward, ed. 1992. *Forms of Desire*. New York: Routledge.

Stocking, George W. Jr. 1982. *Race, Culture, and Evolution*. Chicago: University of Chicago Press.

1987. *Victorian Anthropology*. New York: Free Press.

Symposium on Critical Theory. 1996. *Constellations* 3 (April).

Tanner, Leslie, ed. 1971. *Voices from Women's Liberation*. New York: North American Library.

Tash, Robert. 1991. *Dutch Pluralism*. New York: Peter Lang.

Taylor, Charles. 1989. *Sources of the Self*. Cambridge: Harvard University Press.

1994. "The Politics of Recognition," in *Multiculturalism*, ed. Amy Gutmann. Princeton: Princeton University Press.

Thompson, E. P. 1963. *The Making of the Working Class*. New York: Pantheon.

Tocqueville, Alexis de. 1970. *Democracy in America*. 2 vols. New York: Schocken.

Touraine, Alain. 1981. *The Voice and the Eye*. Cambridge: Cambridge University Press.

Trimberger, Ellen Kay. 1983. "Feminism, Men, and Modern Love: Greenwich Village, 1900–1925," in *Powers of Desire*, ed. Ann Snitow et al. New York: Monthly Review Press.

Troiden, Richard. 1988. *Gay and Lesbian Identity*. New York: General Hall.

Trujillo, Carla, ed. 1991. *Chicana Lesbians*. Berkeley: Third Woman Press.

Trumbach, Randolph. 1977. "London's Sodomites: Homosexual Behavior and Western Culture in the Eighteenth Century," *Journal of Social History* 11: 1–33.

Tucker, Scott. 1981. "The Counterrevolution," *Gay Community News*, February 21.

1982. "Our Right to the World," *The Body Politic* July/August.

Turner, Bryan. 1978. *Marx and the End of Orientalism*. London: Allen and Unwin.

Turner, Charles, et al. eds. 1989. *AIDS*. Washington, DC: National Academy Press.

Turner, Graeme. 1992. *British Cultural Studies*. New York: Routledge.

Turner, Stephen. 1992. "The Strange Life and Hard Times of the Concept of General Theory in Sociology," in *Postmodernism and Social Theory*, ed. Steven Seidman and David Wagner. Oxford: Blackwell.

Turner, Stephen and Jonathan Turner. 1990. *The Impossible Science*. Newbury Park: Sage.

Turner, Stephen and Mark Wardell, eds. 1986. *The Transition in Sociological Theory*. Boston: Allen and Unwin.

Turner, Victor. 1967. *The Ritual Process*. Ithaca, NY: Cornell University Press.

Vance, Carole, ed. 1984. *Pleasure and Danger*. Boston: Routledge and Kegan Paul.

Van Mierlo, Hans J. G. A. 1986. "Depillarization and the Decline of Consociationalism in The Netherlands: 1970–85," *West European Politics* 9: 97–119.

Van Schendelen, M. P. C. M., ed. 1984. Consociationism, Pillarization and Conflict-Management in the Low Countries. Special Issue. *Acta Politica* 19.

1984. "The Views of Arendt Lijphart and Collected Criticisms. *Acta Politica* 19: 9.

Van Wijngaarden, Jan K. 1992. "The Netherlands: AIDS in a Consensual Society," in *AIDS in the Industrialized Democracies*, ed. David Kirp and Ronald Bayer. New Brunswick: Rutgers University Press.

Vaughan, Michalina and Margaret Archer. 1971. *Social Conflict and Educational Change in England and France, 1789–1848*. Cambridge: Cambridge University Press.

Velde, Theordore Van de. [1930] 1950. *Ideal Marriage*. Westport, CN: Greenwood.

Veysey, Lawrence. 1965. *The Emergence of the American University*. Chicago: University of Chicago Press.

Vollmer, Tim. 1985. "Another Stonewall," *The New York Native* Oct. 28–Nov. 3.

Wacker, R. Fred. 1983. *Ethnicity, Pluralism, and Race*. Westport, CN: Greenwood Press.

Warner, Michael, ed. 1994. *Fear of a Queer Planet*. Minneapolis: University of Minnesota Press.

Warren, Carol. 1974. *Identity and Community in the Gay World*. New York: Wiley.

Watney, Simon. 1987. *Policing Desire*. Minneapolis: University of Minnesota Press.

Weber, Max. 1958. "Author's Introduction," in *The Protestant Ethic and the Spirit of Capitalism*. New York: Free Press.

Weeks, Jeffrey. 1977. *Coming Out!* London: Quartet.

1985. *Sexuality and Its Discontents*. London: Routledge.

1995. *Invented Moralities*. New York: Columbia University Press.

Weinberg, Martin and Colin Williams. 1975. "Gay Baths and the Social Organization of Impersonal Sex," *Social Problems* 23: 124–136.

Weisstein, Naomi. 1973. "Psychology Constructs the Female," in *Radical Feminism*, ed. Anne Koedt et al. New York: Quadrangle.

West, Cornel.1994. "The New Cultural Politics of Difference," in *The Postmodern Turn*, ed. Steven Seidman. Cambridge: Cambridge University Press.

Westfall, Richard. 1986. "The Rise of Science and the Decline of Orthodox Christianity: A Study of Kepler, Descartes, and Newton," in *God and Nature*, ed. David Lindberg and Ronald Numbers. Berkeley: University of California Press.

White, Edmund. 1980. *States of Desire*. New York: E. P. Dutton.

White, Patricia. 1991. "Female Spectator, Lesbian Specter: The Haunting," in *Inside/Out*, ed. Diana Fuss. New York: Routledge.

Willenbecher, Thom. 1980. "Quick Encounters of the Closest Kind: The Rites and Rituals of Shadow Sex," *The Advocate* Sept. 30.

Williams, Bernard. 1985. *Ethics and the Limits of Philosophy*. Cambridge: Harvard University Press.

Williams, Raymond. 1958. *Culture and Society 1780–1950*. London: Penguin.

1961. *The Long Revolution*. New York: Columbia University Press.

1962. *Communications*. London: Penguin.

Williams, Walter. 1986. *The Spirit and the Flesh*. Boston: Beacon.

Williamson, Judith. 1978. *Decoding Advertisements*. London: Marion Boyars.

Willis, Paul. 1978. *Learning to Labor*. London: Saxon House.

1980. "Notes on Method," in *Culture, Media, Language*, eds. Stuart hall et al. London: Hutchinson.

Winch, Peter. 1963. *The Idea of Social Science and its Relation to Philosophy*. London: Routledge and Kegan Paul.

Wittgenstein, Ludwig. 1958. *Philosophical Investigations*. New York: Macmillan.

Wittman, Carl. 1972. "A Gay Manifesto," in *Out of the Closets*, ed. Karla Jay and Allen Young. New York: Douglas/Links.

Wolf, Deborah. 1980. *The Lesbian Community*. Berkeley: University of California Press.

Yingling, Thomas. 1990. *Hart Crane and the Homosexual Text*. Chicago: University of Chicago Press.

Young, Allen. 1972. "Out of the Closets, into the Streets," in *Out of the Closets*, ed. Karla Jay and Allen Young. New York: A Douglas Book.

Young, Iris. 1982. "Beyond the Unhappy Marriage: A Critique of Dual Systems Theory," in *Women and Revolution*, ed. Lydia Sargent. Boston: South End Press.

1990. *Justice and the Politics of Difference*. Princeton: Princeton University Press.

1995. "Gender as Seriality: Thinking About Women as a Social Collective," in *Social Postmodernism*, ed. Linda Nicholson and Steven Seidman. Cambridge: Cambridge University Press.

Young, Robert. 1990. *White Mythologies*. New York: Routledge.

1995. *Colonial Desire*. New York: Routledge.

Zeldin, Theodor. 1967. "Higher Education in France, 1848–1940," in *Education and Social Structure in the Twentieth Century*, ed. Walter Lacquer and George Mosse. New York: Harper & Row.

Zerubavel, Eviatar. 1981. *Hidden Rhythms*. Chicago: University of Chicago Press.

Index